ENRON
THE RISE AND FALL

LOREN FOX

JOHN WILEY & SONS, INC.

Published by John Wiley & Sons, Inc., Hoboken, New Jersey.
Published simultaneously in Canada.

For general information on our other products and services, or technical support, please contact our Customer Care Department within the United States at 800-762-2974, outside the United States at 317-572-3993 or fax 317-572-4002.

Wiley also publishes its books in a variety of electronic formats. Some content that appears in print may not be available in electronic books.

ISBN 0-471-23760-4

Printed in the United States of America.

10 9 8 7 6 5 4 3 2 1

CONTENTS

PREFACE

When Enron conducted a name-recognition survey in 1996, it found that ordinary people were guessing that "Enron" was a politician or a science-fiction weapon. It's now 2002, and "Enron" needs no introduction. Like Watergate, it has entered the collective vocabulary as a one-word symbol of an entire regime. Enron now represents greed and hubris, deceitful accounting and Wall Street favors, and, in short, everything that's wrong with corporate America.

As familiar as the word has become, the actual story of Enron's decline from business superstar to embarrassing bankruptcy is still not well understood. How did a $100 billion company collapse in a matter of weeks? What were the partnerships that shocked Wall Street and damaged some of its venerable reputations? Who were the people behind this complex enterprise? This book is one journalist's attempt to explain what happened from beginning to end.

Other accounts of the Enron scandal have concentrated on the company's decline, but the story really begins with the creation of the company in 1985. The fall of Enron would not be possible were it not for the preceding rise, and the company's missteps—both intentional and unintentional—were not possible had it not enjoyed successes early on. Those successes were what drew me to the story originally, and then my interest rose as this flourishing company began to encounter great difficulties. When I proposed a book about Enron in the fall of 2001, I knew it would make a fascinating topic. The drama then intensified at an amazing pace. In quick succession, Enron's weakened stock went into freefall, it struck a deal to be acquired, that deal then fell through, and Enron filed for bankruptcy. The story leapt from the business pages to the front pages, and then to everyday conversation.

My research uncovered details of the intense corporate culture and the recklessness with which the company pursued strategies. I found an organization that, in the spirit of the last decade, over-reached; Chairman Kenneth Lay, Jeffrey Skilling, and company believed they could transform a pipeline operator into a virtual corporation that traded a dizzying array of commodities. To support the financial underpinnings of that mission, Enron eventually cooked its books. While telling that story, my book highlights the system that allowed such rule breaking. Nearly everyone shares some blame, from Republicans to Democrats, from accountants to lawyers, and from Wall Street to Main Street.

This striving corporation sat at the epicenter of the most significant trends in finance, energy, and online commerce. As a result, the story continues even as I write this. The dimensions of business have been changed forever. Politicians are debating the regulations of energy trading. Enron's bankruptcy continues to frustrate the creditors fighting over the scraps. Meanwhile, one ex-employee has pleaded guilty to two felonies arising from his actions at Enron, and the public awaits criminal charges against other former Enron officials. We haven't heard the last of Enron, as either icon or business saga. With that in mind, the following pages explain the story behind the symbol.

Loren Fox
August 2002

TIME LINE

July 1985: Houston Natural Gas, run by Kenneth L. Lay, merges with InterNorth, a natural gas company based in Omaha, Nebraska, to form an interstate and intrastate natural gas pipeline company with approximately 37,000 miles of pipe.

November 1985: Ken Lay is appointed chairman and chief executive of the combined company. Later, the company chooses the name "Enron" after rejecting "Enteron."

October 1987: Enron discovers that oil traders in New York have overextended the company's accounts, costing the company $142 million.

1988: The company's major strategy shift—to pursue unregulated markets in addition to its regulated pipeline business—is decided in a gathering that became known as the "Come to Jesus" meeting.

1989: Enron launches Gas Bank, which allows gas producers and wholesale buyers to purchase firm gas supplies and hedge the price risk at the same time.

October 1989: Enron's Transwestern Pipeline is the first merchant pipeline in the United States to stop selling gas and become a transportation-only pipeline. Also, Enron sells 16 percent of Enron Oil & Gas to the public.

June 1990: Jeff Skilling joins Enron after leading McKinsey & Co.'s energy consulting business. He will lead the nascent trading and finance operation.

April 1993: Enron's Teesside power plant in England begins operation, one of the first big successes for the company's international strategy.

December 1993: Enron and Maharashtra reach agreement to build the massive Dabhol power plant. The $2 billion Indian project would be a continual headache for the company.

June 1994: Enron conducts its first electricity trade.

November 1996: Chief Operating Officer Richard Kinder announces that he'll leave the company. In December, Skilling becomes Enron's president and chief operating officer, beating out rival executive Rebecca Mark.

June 1997: Looking to expand in electricity, Enron closes its acquisition of electric utility Portland General Corp. in a $2.1 billion stock swap.

August 1997: Enron trades its first weather derivative. Enron goes on to trade coal, pulp, paper, plastics, metals, and bandwidth.

November 1997: Enron forms Chewco Investments, managed by Enron employee Michael Kopper, to buy out CalPERS' stake in a joint venture. This is the first "independent" partnership run by an Enron employee.

March 1998: Enron promotes Andrew Fastow to chief financial officer.

April 1998: In a dramatic change in strategy, Enron pulls out of California's residential electricity sector, citing problems with the state's deregulated market.

July 1998: Enron agrees to buy Wessex Water, a British water utility, for $2.2 billion. Wessex becomes the core of Enron's new water unit, Azurix, run by Rebecca Mark.

March 1999: Enron's giant Dabhol plant in India opens.

April 1999: Enron agrees to pay $100 million over 30 years for the naming rights to Houston's new ballpark, Enron Field. Also, Enron begins commercial operation of its nationwide fiber network for high-bandwidth uses.

June 1999: Azurix goes public with a $700 million initial public offering. Also, Enron creates the first LJM partnership in order to hedge its investment in an Internet company. Fastow gets a waiver of the code of conduct to manage LJM.

August 1999: Enron withdraws from oil and gas production by divesting its remaining stake in subsidiary Enron Oil & Gas.

October 1999: Enron announces the launch of EnronOnline, its Internet-based system for wholesale commodity trading. Also, Enron forms the LJM2 partnership.

December 1999: Enron conducts its first bandwidth trade.

February 2000: Enron launches EnronCredit.com, which buys and sells credit risk to help companies manage the risk incurred in trading transactions.

May 2000: Enron creates the first Raptor special purpose entity. Modeled after LJM, the Raptors would be used to hedge Enron investments. But, mostly backed by Enron stock, they are risky vehicles.

July 2000: Enron and Blockbuster announce a 20-year deal to provide video-on-demand service to consumers over high-speed Internet lines. Eight months later, the companies would terminate the deal.

August 2000: Enron's stock hits an all-time high of $90.56. However, Azurix chairman Rebecca Mark resigns as the water company's prospects and stock price tank.

February 2001: Skilling becomes chief executive of Enron (Lay remains chairman). Also, a group of Andersen partners meet to discuss Enron's accounting and disclosures, but decide to retain the company as a client.

March 2001: Azurix public shareholders approve a buyout of the company by Enron. Also, Enron buys out the Chewco partnership, netting Michael Kopper $10 million.

April 2001: Lay meets with U.S. Vice President Dick Cheney to discuss energy policy. Cheney's energy task force releases its report on May 17, and the report includes some recommendations favorable to Enron.

May 2001: Enron attorney Jordan Mintz retains Fried Frank Harris Shriver & Jacobson to review Enron's LJM dealings; the law firm advises Enron to stop the LJM transactions. Also, Maharashtra, the Dabhol power plant's sole customer, says it will cancel its contract.

June 2001: During a public appearance in California, Skilling is hit in the face with a cream pie as Enron comes under fire for "profiteering" from the state's electricity crisis, which had begun in May 2000.

August 14, 2001: Skilling resigns as Enron president and chief executive officer, citing personal reasons. Ken Lay returns to position of CEO.

August 15, 2001: Enron accountant Sherron Watkins sends Ken Lay a letter detailing her concerns about the LJM and Raptor entities, and admits, "I am incredibly nervous that we will implode in a wave of accounting scandals."

September 21, 2001: After a "preliminary" investigation to follow up on Watkins' worries, Vinson & Elkins tells Ken Lay there is no cause for alarm.

October 16, 2001: Enron takes $1.01 billion charge related to write-downs of investments, including the buyout of the Raptors. Enron also discloses that shareholder equity shrank by $1.2 billion as a result of transactions including ones undertaken with Fastow's investment vehicle.

October 19, 2001: The *Wall Street Journal* reveals that Fastow made at least $7 million from running the LJM partnerships, raising eyebrows on Wall Street.

October 22, 2001: Enron announces that the SEC will begin a probe of the company's "related party transactions."

October 23, 2001: Arthur Andersen employees begin shredding Enron-related documents, despite knowing of the SEC inquiry.

October 24, 2001: Enron replaces Fastow as CFO with Jeffrey McMahon, the 40-year-old head of the company's industrial markets division.

October 31, 2001: The SEC elevates to a formal investigation its inquiry into Enron's financial dealings. Enron forms a special committee of the board, headed by new director William Powers, to investigate the partnerships.

November 8, 2001: Deciding it should have consolidated Chewco and a related partnerhip into its financial results, Enron restates its earnings for 1997 to 2001. This reduces net income over that time by $586 million and boosts debt by $2.6 billion.

November 9, 2001: Dynegy announces a deal to buy Enron for about $9 billion in stock. ChevronTexaco will inject $1.5 billion into the deal immediately, and an additional $1 billion upon closing.

November 20, 2001: Enron warns that credit worries, asset value declines, and reduced trading could hurt its fourth-quarter earnings. And, in a disclosure that surprises Dynegy, it reveals that lowered credit ratings will trigger another $690 million obligation.

November 28, 2001: Major credit rating agencies downgrade Enron's bonds to "junk" status. As a result, Dynegy terminates its agreement to buy Enron. Enron stock ends the day at 61 cents per share.

December 2, 2001: Enron files for Chapter 11 bankruptcy protection in a New York bankruptcy court. With $62 billion in assets, this is the biggest such filing in U.S. history up to that time. Simultaneously, Enron sues Dynegy for terminating their merger.

December 3, 2001: Enron secures almost $1.5 billion in debtor-in-possession financing, and lays off roughly 4,000 employees in the United States.

December 12, 2001: Ken Lay presents the first reorganization plan for Enron, which envisions emerging from bankruptcy within a year as a smaller energy company.

January 18, 2002: The U.S. Bankruptcy Court approves the sale of Enron's trading business to UBS Warburg. Enron gets no cash, but the promise of one-third of future profits. Enron's board fires longtime auditor Arthur Andersen, but Andersen says the relationship ended when Enron's business failed and it went into bankruptcy.

January 23, 2002: Lay resigns as chairman and chief executive of Enron less than 24 hours after the court-appointed creditors committee requested his removal.

January 29, 2002: Enron names Stephen Cooper, a principal at New York restructuring firm Zolfo Cooper, as acting CEO.

February 2, 2002: Enron's special board committee probing the partnerships releases the Powers Report. The report spreads the blame for Enron's woes among Lay, Skilling, Fastow, Arthur Andersen, and others.

February 12, 2002: Lay tells a congressional committee he feels "profound sadness" at Enron's collapse, but declines to testify by taking the Fifth.

May 3, 2002: Stephen Cooper unveils the latest reorganization plan for Enron to creditors. It envisions a $10 billion company focused on pipelines and power plants.

June 15, 2002: A jury finds Arthur Andersen guilty of obstruction of justice in the investigation of Enron, probably dooming the firm.

August 21, 2002: Michael Kopper pleads guilty to two felonies arising from his dealings with Enron partnerships, marking the first criminal charges against an Enron insider.

1

PIPELINE TO PROFIT

Politicians, journalists, laid-off workers, and curious onlookers milled about Washington, D.C.'s Russell Senate Office Building. Traditionally this dignified, marble-laden building is the scene of budget conferences, discussions of international treaties, and historic hearings such as those on Watergate. But on the morning of February 12, 2002, the building was abuzz with a different kind of subject: the fall of Enron Corp.

The columned, high-ceilinged hearing room grew quiet at the appearance of Kenneth Lay, Enron's former chief. Lay, in a gray suit, sat calmly in the front row while members of the Senate Committee on Commerce, Science and Transportation—Democrats and Republicans alike—glowered down from the raised dais and disparaged him with zeal. "The anger here is palpable," explained Senator John Kerry (D-Massachusetts). "Lives have been ruined."

"The bankruptcy of this corporation is not a garden-variety business failure," said Senator Byron Dorgan (D-North Dakota).

Indeed, Enron's failure was anything but typical; it was one of the most thrilling rise-and-fall sagas of recent years. Staring in 1985, Enron grew in a decade and a half from a large natural-gas pipeline company to an energy-trading firm that bought and sold gas as well as electricity. In the late 1990s, Enron had even evolved beyond energy trading, trafficking in metals, paper, financial contracts, and other commodities. By that time, so much of its business came from trading that Enron had essentially stopped being an energy company and functioned as a kind of bank. That transformation spurred massive expansion, so that from revenue of $4.6 billion in 1990, Enron grew to $101 billion in revenue in 2000. That made Enron the seventh-largest company in the United States, bigger than IBM or Sony. Lay and other top executives landed on the covers of business magazines, and the company was hailed as a model for innovation.

Ken Lay was at the Senate hearing, however, not because of Enron's rise but because of its downfall. To help sustain its rapid growth, the company played fast and loose with its accounting, hiding debt and inflating profits. The previous October, the company revealed that its use of semi-independent investment partnerships, some of which were run by Enron's own chief financial officer, reduced shareholder value by $1.2 billion, and that sparked an accounting scandal that spiraled out of the company's control. On closer examination, these partnerships appeared to do nothing more than shuffle debt and hide losses. The Securities and Exchange Commission, which oversees the stock markets, launched an inquiry that caused trading partners to back away from Enron. Enron's stock price tumbled from a high of $90 to a piddling 36 cents, wiping out more than $60 billion of shareholder value—even as Lay and other top officers sold much of their own stock for millions of dollars. After the market lost confidence in Enron and a last-minute merger attempt fell through, Enron's descent came to a thundering crescendo on December 2, 2001, when it filed for bankruptcy; with assets of roughly $62 billion, it was at the time the largest bankruptcy in U.S. history. Enron was facing hundreds of creditors, more than four thousand angry ex-employees—some of whom had lost all their retirement savings—and a criminal probe by the U.S. Justice Department.

In that hearing room, senators took the opportunity to lecture Lay because, as Senator Conrad Burns (R-Montana) put it, "it was on his watch that the wreck occurred."

Senator Peter Fitzgerald (R-Illinois) called Lay an "accomplished confidence man," and went on to lambaste him: "I'd say you were a carnival barker, except that wouldn't be fair to carnival barkers. A carnie will at least tell you up front that he's running a shell game. You, Mr. Lay, were running what purported to be the seventh largest corporation in America."

The senators also seized on Lay's well-known political connections, which included strong ties to the Republican Party. He had been a top contributor to George W. Bush long before Bush rose to the presidency, earning the affectionate nickname "Kenny Boy" from the Texas politician. Enron had also enjoyed a swaggering reputation as a powerful lobbying force in Washington, arguing for the deregulation of energy markets that created the opportunities for Enron's trading business. Senator Ernest "Fritz" Hollings (D-South Carolina) said, "There's no better example than 'Kenny Boy' for cash-and-carry government," and said he hoped this would lead to campaign finance reform.

And Enron, which once championed the liberation of energy markets from government oversight, was accused of tainting free-market economics. "This is not capitalism," said Senator Gordon Smith (R-Oregon). "This is a conspiracy that may be a crime."

Lay did not respond to the hail of criticism, and everyone knew he would stay silent. He'd twice backed out of previously scheduled appearances before the committee, and Congress went so far as to issue subpoenas to compel his testimony. A few weeks before appearing in front of the committee, Lay's attorney had written to Congress to explain that the 59-year-old executive felt he wouldn't get a fair hearing. "Judgments have been reached and the tenor of the hearing will be prosecutorial," the attorney wrote. So Lay took the Fifth Amendment—his constitutional right to remain silent rather than say something that might incriminate himself.

Instead of answering the senators, Lay waited until every member of the committee had spoken. Then he read a brief statement. "I come here today with a profound sadness about what has happened to Enron, its current and former employees, retirees, shareholders, and other stakeholders," he said.

He explained feeling torn about taking the Fifth. "I am deeply troubled about asserting these rights, because it may be perceived by some that I have something to hide. But after agonizing consideration, I cannot disregard my counsel's instruction. Therefore, I must respectfully decline to answer, on Fifth Amendment grounds, all the questions of this committee and subcommittee and those of any other Congressional committee and subcommittee."

Meanwhile, in League City, Texas, Robert Smoot was watching the hearing on television with mixed feelings. Smoot, married with an 11-year-old daughter, had been laid off from Enron that December. As he watched Lay get humiliated by Congress, part of Smoot felt sorry for the former CEO, but part of him felt Lay had it coming. "Someone had to say that," he said. "He should've known what was going on. He's the captain of the ship."

An electrical engineer, Smoot was out of work and hadn't had a job interview since January. In addition, he and the others laid off in December had received just $4,500 of severance pay, rather than the sort of severance to which they would normally be entitled, larger sums based on how long they had worked at Enron. For him, that would be worth several months' salary—if the bankrupt company ever paid it. Instead, Smoot was spending down his savings. "We're doing okay right now, but that money's going to run out," he said. "I'm angry at what happened—treating the people who were laid off like trash."

The dramatic collapse of Enron took people like Robert Smoot completely by surprise. But most people were surprised. There were innocent victims like Smoot, who lost not only his job but also thousands of dollars in worthless stock options and in the Enron stock he'd bought with his 401(k) retirement savings plan. There were public pension funds, which had seen their Enron investments plunge to minuscule value. There were small investors who'd had their faith in the market shaken. There were the banks that had lent Enron billions and could expect to get just a small portion of the loans back. There were the politicians scrambling to distance themselves from this omnipresent campaign contributor. And there was the U.S. stock market, which was convulsing with fears that more accounting implosions lay hidden in any number of large corporations.

The senators disapproving of "Kenny Boy" were frustrated because they'd wanted to grill him for answers that might explain what happened to Enron. But even if Lay had testified that day, he could have given only part of the explanation. Because the Enron story was much larger than just Lay.

The heart of the story, of course, is Enron. The company, which at its height had more than 20,000 employees and operations in 40 countries, pioneered real innovations, many of which are still in use; rather than just sell energy to a factory, Enron could package that energy in an array of customized contracts, delivering more energy in December than in November, or making sure that contract provisions guaranteed certain prices. It created or entered new markets—allowing financial calculations on even the weather itself—and eventually built an Internet trading system that handled billions of dollars in commerce. But the early successes fueled an ever-larger ambition, causing the company to overreach. As its markets matured and became less profitable, Enron was forced to continually enter new fields to keep up its rapid growth. Fixated on its stock price, Enron pursued a strategy of growth and more growth, often at the expense of profits.

A big part of the story was that energy trading operation—a Byzantine market that exists behind the gas and electricity business and is every bit as large and sophisticated as the stock market. Enron handled roughly one-quarter of all trading in electricity and natural gas in the United States, a dominance that would be unheard-of in the world of stocks. As that market developed over the course of the 1990s, it became so complex that even after Enron's collapse it was difficult to tell whether some of Enron's maneuvers to hide loans as trades and to bury debt in special partnerships had violated any rules.

The stars of the story were Enron's top executives, including Lay and the man who became his trusted lieutenant, Jeffrey Skilling. Enron's leaders had been held up as a creative force that had injected "New Economy" spark into an old-economy, industrial company by emphasizing intellectual prowess over pipelines and power plants. But somewhere along the line, either at the behest of Lay and Skilling or under their noses, Enron executives in the late 1990s began to fool around with the books in order to support the huge growth engine. They created special partnerships that weren't reported on Enron's books, which were able to make its earnings and debt levels look better than they really were. As Enron grew as a financial firm, it increasingly relied on such accounting trickery to keep its credit rating high, making it seem a solid and reliable trading partner.

The story cannot be told without describing Enron's corporate culture of innovation and competitiveness, where employees enjoyed autonomy if they produced quarterly results. That culture fed its appetite for new ideas and for creative, hardworking people. But the drive and independence also helped enable financial deception, because the company encouraged experimentation but discouraged anything other than success. In its effort to create new markets, Enron inevitably had some misses along with its hits; for instance, it had an energy outsourcing business whose profits were questionable, and a business trading telecommunications network capacity, known as bandwidth, which lost hundreds of millions of dollars. Reluctant to acknowledge stumbles, the company relied even more on accounting trickery to paper over the losses.

The story included Enron's accounting firm, Arthur Andersen. Andersen, which, like other big accounting firms, also did consulting work for Enron, signed off on the company's questionable accounting practices. Frankly, the accounting rules were vague enough and the company's deals complex enough that it was often difficult to tell when Enron violated rules. But Andersen downplayed questions about the accounting. It was only in October 2001 that Andersen reined in some of the more creative accounting moves, and that began Enron's downward spiral. Andersen then compounded its errors by shredding Enron-related documents when it knew the company was being probed.

Wall Street also had a big part in the story, because it wanted so much to believe in Enron's wondrous story and it helped keep the stock inflated. Analysts touted Enron's stock, even as the investment banks that employed them tried to get business with Enron. Although Enron's financial statements were opaque, that didn't bother the Wall Street machine so long as Enron's stock continued rising throughout the jubilant stock market of the mid and late 1990s. They were held in thrall with the Enron story, even if the company wasn't really quite as successful as it portrayed itself. That's why Wall Street and the business community so easily felt betrayed by Enron when Andersen revealed one accounting mishap. When the world got a peek at its rickety financial underpinnings, the market lost confidence in the company. Without confidence, hence without trading partners, Enron's core business withered quickly. The cash stopped coming in, the debt grew, and the company came crashing down. The result was the bankruptcy, thousands of layoffs, several congressional investigations, and the potential for criminal charges.

The Enron story, with all its moving parts, is a tale of genuine achievement, but also of arrogance, ambition, and deceit. It's the story of how so many people and agencies missed the cracks in Enron's facade, in part because the system was set up that way. In short, it's the story of how American capitalism worked at the close of the twentieth century.

■ ■ ■

Many businesspeople like to portray themselves as rags-to-riches successes, in accordance with the American love of individualism and self-reinvention. Although he didn't start in rags, Kenneth Lee Lay really did rise from modest circumstances. He was born to a rural family on April 15, 1942, in Tyrone, a medium-sized town in Missouri.

His father, Omer, was a Southern Baptist minister who usually held down a couple of other jobs to support the family, such as selling farm equipment and working at a feed store. Omer married Ruth Rees in 1937, and they had three children: Bonnie the oldest, Ken in the middle, and Sharon the youngest.

When Ken was six, the family moved to Rush Hill, a tiny town in the center of the state, a little more than 100 miles northwest of St. Louis. Omer became the minister of the nondenominational Rush Hill Community Church, but still had to work other jobs. Although they pinched pennies, the Lay children never went without food or clothes. And though Omer and Ruth had never gone to college, they wanted their children to go. Omer was an optimist, someone who believed that even if circumstances were difficult or complicated, things would work out later. It was a trait that influenced his son.

By the time he was nine, Ken was helping bring in money with part-time work, such as driving tractors on neighboring farms and delivering papers. Working on tractors gave young Ken Lay time to think, and his thoughts sometimes turned to the business world, a world that seemed very far away from the small towns and farms he knew.

Omer and Ruth Lay realized they wouldn't be able to give their children college educations if they stayed in Rush Hill. So the summer after Lay's sophomore year in high school, the family moved to Columbia, Missouri, so Ken and his sisters might be able to live at home and attend the University of Missouri (eventually, all three obtained degrees from the university). In Columbia, Lay wound up at Hickman High School, where he worked hard and got good grades. He played slide trombone in the school marching band, sang in a choir, and was elected to the National Honor Society. In 1960, he graduated 10th out of the class of 276 students.

With the help of scholarship money, loans, and various jobs, Lay put himself through the University of Missouri at the Columbia campus. He joined the Theta Beta Pi fraternity, and, in an early testament to his political skills, he became president of the frat in his junior year. It was also in college that he seriously studied economics, learning the value of free markets, imbued with competition and unhampered by massive regulations. In college, he also learned the basics of accounting by taking 12 hours' worth of classes to help prepare him for business; ironically, his understanding of accounting would years later prove a major issue in Enron's collapse. Lay graduated Phi Beta Kappa with honors in 1964, and then, at the urging of an economics professor, he stayed one more year to collect a master's degree in economics.

Finally leaving Missouri, Lay moved to Houston to work as a corporate economist at Humble Oil, a large and well-known oil company that eventually became part of energy giant Exxon. Energy wasn't an industry he'd thought about much growing up in Missouri, but he was attracted to its importance in national affairs. "I was very impressed with the capital-intensive nature of it, which, with my economics background, I found very interesting versus a more labor-intensive type of industry," he told one writer. "It required a lot of long-range planning and interface with government and regulatory bodies, which also tended to fit into my economics training." While working for Humble, he earned a doctorate in economics from the University of Houston in night school. And in 1966, Ken married Judie Ayers, whom he'd met in French class at the University of Missouri.

In 1968, as America's war in Vietnam escalated, Lay chose to leave Humble Oil for Naval Officer Candidate School in Rhode Island. He was soon at the Pentagon, where he spent his three-year tour working for the Assistant Secretary of the Navy for Financial Management. The Pentagon was a prestigious climb from little Rush Hill, and he took advantage of the opportunity by leading a study of defense spending that earned him plaudits; the study was later credited with saving the Pentagon billions of dollars. Lay also used the findings from this study—notably, the impact of defense spending on the economy—for the basis of his Ph.D. dissertation at the University of Houston. After his 1971 discharge, he stayed in Washington, D.C., working for two years at the Federal Power Commission, the precursor to the Federal Energy Regulatory Commission (FERC).

At the Power Commission, he was an assistant to Pinkney Walker, the economist who had urged Lay to get a master's degree and was then a commissioner. (Years later, Lay would donate money and help raise funds for a Pinkney Walker Endowment at the University of Missouri.) Lay spent less than two years at the Power Commission, which helped oversee the natural gas and electricity industries, but the time was crucial. It gave him insights into regulation of energy, and, of course, the often mysterious workings of government. During that time he was promoted to deputy undersecretary for energy of the U.S. Department of the Interior. While in Washington, Lay was also an assistant professor at George Washington University, teaching graduate courses in micro- and macro-economic theory and government-business relations.

In 1973, Lay joined natural-gas utility Florida Gas as vice president for corporate development, and moved his family to Winter Park, in central Florida. He rose through the ranks. He became an active member of the community, serving on various boards and raising money for the arts and education. Lay also started to develop his management style of surrounding himself with smart people and making sure they were included in decision making. But although he had attained some measure of the business success he'd longed for back on the tractor in Missouri, there were problems. In 1979, Florida Gas was purchased by Continental Group, a diversified industrial company that started off making cans. After a couple of years, Lay didn't like management changes. Also, he and Judie grew apart, not helped by Ken's long hours at work. In 1981 they divorced amicably (although Judie stayed behind in Winter Park when he returned to Houston, and she remained friendly with the Lay family). Ken Lay had always been the sort of hard worker who seemed married to his job. Shortly after his divorce he married Linda Phillips, who was his secretary.

Jack Bowen, who had been Lay's boss at Florida Gas, had by now moved on to a natural gas pipeline company based in Houston called Transco, which supplied a majority of the gas to the New York–New Jersey area. Bowen brought Lay to Transco in 1981 as his right hand, and Lay rose to president and chief operating officer.

Unlike Florida Gas, which distributed natural gas directly to homes and businesses, Transco operated interstate gas pipelines. Some of these went to utilities like Florida Gas, but some went to large businesses; it's interesting to note that home use is not the major end point of gas— more than 60 percent of gas is used for other purposes: as fuel for factories; as a raw material for chemicals (processing gas will extract from it such chemicals as butane and propane, known as "natural gas liquids"); and as a fuel for electricity-producing power plants. The vast majority of U.S. natural gas wells are drilled in five regions: the Texas/Louisiana Gulf Coast; West Texas; New Mexico; a large swathe of land stretching from Kansas to Oklahoma; and the Rocky Mountains. There's also Canada's gas industry, which is centered in Alberta (roughly north of Montana). More than 280,000 miles of gas pipelines sprawl across North America to transport natural gas from processing plants in those producing regions to the various customers around the continent, whether those customers are local gas utilities or paper mills.

In later years, Enron presented itself as having evolved from just a sleepy, simple gas pipeline company. But running a pipeline system is not easy. Because it's a gas, transportation is more difficult than it is for oil, which can be stored in barrels and moved by ship, train, or truck. Gas pipelines use compressors to push gas across states, operating at high pressures that must be closely monitored. The industry was tightly regulated. For decades, gas producers explored for gas and pumped it out of fields, selling the gas to pipelines at prices set by the federal government. The pipelines, in turn, sold their gas to local gas utilities, also at government-set rates; the government allowed the pipeline operators to earn what it considered a fair profit. With these strict controls in place, there was no competition and no "market" setting the prices.

By the time Lay was at Transco, this setup had begun to change. The strict regulation of the gas industry provided little incentive to increase gas production, and that led to gas shortages in the 1970s. In 1978, the government began to lift its control of gas prices at the wellhead—in other words, the prices that natural gas producing companies could fetch for their gas. Also, to avoid similar shortages in the future, many pipeline companies signed long-term "take-or-pay" contracts with gas producers, guaranteeing a minimum amount of gas would be purchased and thus creating a reliable demand for gas. The take-or-pay contracts typically called for a pipeline company to buy 70 percent of the gas that a field (a collection of wells) could deliver, and the pipeline could either "take" ownership of the gas or else "pay" the producer for it and pay a penalty. Either way, the producers got their money. It was then up to the pipeline company to sell this gas to local utilities or anyone else.

If Ken Lay the economist had wanted an illustration of how badly the government could screw up a market, he picked the right time to join Transco. The 1978 change worked well, and gas production soared. But shortly afterward, an economic slowdown hurt the nation's appetite for gas. This larger supply and smaller demand pushed prices down; gas that had cost as much as $6 per thousand cubic feet dropped to $3. By the early 1980s, there was actually a glut of gas. Unfortunately for the pipeline companies, they were saddled with take-or-pay contracts that they'd signed when gas was scarce and prices were high—which meant that pipeline companies had expensive gas they were trying to sell at above-market rates. Sometimes the pipeline company could come to terms with producers; in 1984, for instance, Transco reduced the terms of one take-or-pay contract from $380 million to $240 million.

Making matters worse, some industrial customers were switching from gas to oil, which fell in price in the early 1980s. Transco and other pipeline companies developed business units that "marketed" gas, selling excess gas outside of long-term contracts, but often at discount rates.

Having learned the pipeline industry, in June 1984 Lay jumped to Houston Natural Gas, another pipeline company, where he finally had the top job of chairman and chief executive. When Lay joined, HNG was trying to surf the waves of change buffeting its industry, and it had survived a takeover attempt a few months earlier by fellow pipeline operator Coastal Corp. In addition to giving Ken Lay his first job as CEO, Houston Natural Gas was crucial because it would later help form the company that became known as Enron.

■ ■ ■

It's possible to say that Enron was a child of deregulation. Although Enron's domain would later expand to include electricity and electric deregulation, in the early years deregulation concerned natural gas. For gas, deregulation—in essence, allowing some free-market competition into an industry that had been strictly regulated by the government—didn't happen in one dramatic stroke of a pen, but in a series of steps.

The first step had been the 1978 deregulation of gas prices. In the early 1980s, gas producers were selling much of their gas at market prices, although there was an oversupply of gas. Transco's response was to foster sales of excess gas through a "spot" market for gas, a move Lay helped lead. As opposed to long-term contracts, this allowed monthly allotments of gas to be bought and sold literally on the spot, during the same week each month (known as "bid week"). At Transco, Ken Lay guided the effort to gain federal regulatory approval for gas producers and pipelines to sell natural gas directly to large wholesale buyers on a spot basis. The spot market was also completely guided by market prices, rather than long-term contracts. This spot market involved traders haggling over the phone for gas that would be transferred between pipelines at interconnect points known as "hubs."

At HNG, Lay continued to push the spot market of natural gas. He teamed up in late 1984 with Transco and four other pipeline companies, investment bank Morgan Stanley, and law firm Akin, Gump, Strauss, Hauer & Feld to create Natural Gas Clearinghouse—a gas sales consortium aimed at supporting a national spot market for gas. The Clearinghouse proved successful enough that in late 1985 Morgan Stanley took majority control of it and turned it into a semi-independent gas marketing firm.

At the same time, the hard times for gas pipeline operators had been sparking an urge to merge companies, a result of both a shakeout of smaller players and an effort to spread their high costs over larger operations. Feeding the merger trend was the stock market: Some smaller pipeline companies' stock prices fell to cheap levels. Lay decided that if HNG, fresh from rejecting the overtures of Coastal, were to remain independent, it would have to be bigger. And so Lay proceeded with his first reinvention of a major corporation.

HNG's pipeline system was mostly within the borders of Texas, but it needed to go national. Late in 1984, Lay paid a total of $1.2 billion to buy two pipeline systems—Transwestern Pipeline, running from Oklahoma and West Texas to California, and Florida Gas Transmission, the sole supplier of gas to Florida—more than doubling the size of HNG's pipeline network and stretching it from California to Florida. (The

Florida pipeline had once belonged to Lay's old employer, Florida Gas.) Lay also focused the company on natural gas, selling off a coal mining business, a barge and tugboat outfit, and other interests. Now HNG was one of the largest pipeline companies in the United States, with a diversified customer base of local utilities, refineries, and chemical companies. The big acquisitions increased HNG's debt, but that also made the company less attractive as a takeover candidate.

Then in 1985, a second step was taken in gas deregulation. As in 1978, the order (officially known as Order 436) came from the Federal Energy Regulatory Commission (FERC), a little-known U.S. agency that regulates the country's natural gas industry, hydroelectric projects, oil pipelines, and wholesale rates for electricity. This order essentially encouraged pipeline companies to voluntarily make their lines available to all gas utilities, which meant that local utilities could buy gas from the producers and then pay the pipeline just for transporting the gas. It meant pipeline companies had to separate their businesses of gas transportation and gas sales.

Against this backdrop, pipeline companies continued to merge. Early in 1985, the rebuffed suitor Coastal Corp. bought another pipeline company, American Natural Resources, for $2.5 billion. Finally, the pressure to consolidate was too much. Over a period of roughly two weeks, HNG executives negotiated a deal with InterNorth, a much larger pipeline company based in Omaha, Nebraska. On May 3, the two companies unveiled the news: InterNorth agreed to buy Houston Natural Gas for $2.3 billion in cash, or $70 per share of stock—a nice premium over the $46.88 price that HNG's stock was at just two days earlier. The deal would join InterNorth's pipelines in Western Canada, the American Southwest, and the Rocky Mountains with HNG's network. The deal also called for Samuel Segnar, the chairman and CEO of InterNorth, to head the combined company until 1987, when he would be succeeded as top dog by Lay.

The merger wasn't without obstacles. InterNorth was paying a high price for Lay's company. And one large InterNorth shareholder, Irwin Jacobs, opposed the deal. Jacobs, a Minneapolis-based financier known as "Irv the Liquidator," made a name taking on such well-known companies as ITT and Walt Disney. But the merger deal allowed InterNorth to begin buying HNG's stock, so Jacobs couldn't stop the deal. Shareholders of the two companies approved the deal in July. A new company was born, HNG/InterNorth, with $12.1 billion worth of assets, 15,000 employees, and the nation's second-largest pipeline network (after Tenneco).

Over the next few months, the companies went about integrating their operations, with the headquarters technically in Omaha but many corporate offices in Houston. There were suspicions, though, that HNG and InterNorth executives were jockeying for position. In November, Segnar surprised the industry by stepping down early, elevating Lay to CEO. In a statement, Segnar explained that the restructuring of the gas industry was happening so quickly that he wanted the new management team in place right away. Others wondered if Lay, the consummate politician, had outmaneuvered Segnar. The following February, Lay completed his ascension when the acting chairman of HNG/InterNorth stepped down and Lay was named company chairman. But the company continued to grapple with a difficult business environment—for 1985 it reported a loss of $14 million.

A new year, however, brought a new challenge. To come up with a better name than simply HNG/InterNorth, the company hired the consultants Lippincott & Margulies, who suggested "Enteron." Of Greek origin, Enteron suggested energy and sounded futuristic, and had the sort of vague dynamism that's popular in corporate names. In addition, "enteron" had an industrial meaning of "a pipeline system transmitting nourishment."

However, less than two days before the new name was to be unveiled, company employees learned that "enteron" also has the medical meaning of "alimentary canal, intestines, guts." Not pleased that their new corporation's name referred to the bowels, the company demanded a new name. The board told Lippincott & Margulies that it had 24 hours to come up with a new moniker, and the firm quickly shortened the name to Enron.

■ ■ ■

The newly christened Enron began confronting challenges. First, the company consolidated control over the combined HNG and InterNorth organizations. When the Enron name was adopted in April, the company had already cut 1,000 jobs from the combined companies. Lay promised that another 500 jobs would be cut by the end of 1986. This was typical. Any merger is predicated in part on the ability to lay off redundant staff, and the elimination of 1,500 jobs was expected to save Enron $70 million a year.

Although Enron originally kept its main office in Omaha, where the larger InterNorth had been headquartered, Enron's headquarters officially moved to Houston as of July 1, 1986. The company gave strategic reasons for the move, saying that Houston was an acknowledged center for the energy industry, and that situating its corporate offices with the offices running its pipelines, gas processing, and other major operating groups would improve overall coordination. But the fact also remained that Lay was in Houston and had become the company's head honcho.

Another obstacle was the lingering presence of Irwin Jacobs, whose reputation at the time put him in the company of such financiers as Carl Icahn and T. Boone Pickens. Earlier in the decade, Pickens and other corporate raiders had helped ignite a wave of mergers in the oil industry that resulted in big names such as Getty Oil and Gulf Oil being devoured by other oil giants. It was Pickens who famously said he could make more money drilling on the floor of the New York Stock Exchange than drilling in Texas. While this was going on, the pipeline mating game that produced Enron had yet to run out of gas.

In this environment, Jacobs had held onto his InterNorth stock, which was converted into Enron shares. By July 1986, Jacobs had increased his ownership in Enron shares to an 11.4 percent stake. This sparked speculation that he'd try to take over Enron. But the speculation turned more to the thought that Jacobs would try to "greenmail" the company. Greenmail, which rose to prominence in the 1980s, worked like this: a financier bought a major stake in a company, threatening a takeover attempt, then backed off after the company agreed to buy back the financier's stock at a premium. This had worked before at larger companies. At the same time, an insurance and finance company called Leucadia National bought a 5.1 percent stake in Enron and disclosed that it might try to take over the company.

Faced with these not entirely covert challenges, Enron decided in the fall of 1986 to shake Jacobs and Leucadia once and for all. After consulting with two investment banks, Lazard Freres and Drexel Burnham Lambert, Enron bought Jacobs' and Leucadia's shares for a total of $348 million. Enron paid $47 per share for 7.4 million shares of stock. In line with greenmail maneuvers of the time, the $47 price was a slight premium: Enron's stock had closed at $44.38 the day before. Reportedly, Jacobs made an estimated $14 million profit on the deal.

The stock purchase was funded in a slightly complex manner. Enron's employee retirement plan had done well enough that by mid-1986 it had $230 million in excess funds. Enron created a new employee stock ownership plan (ESOP) by rolling over the $230 million and adding $105 million it borrowed from a bank. That $335 million ESOP acquired the Jacobs and Leucadia stock. The company also took a charge to earnings for the remaining cost of the stock purchase.

This wasn't the most popular move that Enron could have made. The stock dropped nearly 9 percent on the day it was announced. None other than T. Boone Pickens, who had made greenmail raids on Phillips Petroleum, among other companies, criticized Enron. "Enron's executives have folded in a big way," he said. Lay later explained to employees that the buyback "defused a potentially disruptive situation," and putting 16 percent of the company's stock in the ESOP made the company less vulnerable to raiders. But for all of Pickens' bluster, he did make one interesting point: Enron had earlier planned to use the $230 million in retirement plan overfunding to reduce company debt.

Debt was a real concern at Enron. Combining the debt of HNG and InterNorth, especially after Lay's HNG had bought two big pipeline systems, had the left the company owing a lot of money. Adding the millions it cost to buy back stock from Jacobs and Leucadia didn't help matters. In addition, the energy business was going through rough times due to low oil and gas prices. To cut costs, Lay froze salaries of the 60 top-paid employees at Enron, and the company sold some real estate, including an apartment in New York and a ranch in Colorado. Enron also formed a cost reduction committee at the end of 1986 headed by an executive named Richard Kinder.

Enron sold off businesses and other assets through 1987, but it was still highly "leveraged," which meant that it was carrying a lot of debt compared to its assets. Starting 1987 off on a sour note, Moody's Investors Service, a leading agency that reviews the credit of corporations, downgraded Enron's debt rating in January. Moody's lowered Enron's main credit rating from a low investment grade to a high speculative grade. This meant that many of Enron's bonds could be bought only by investment funds that dealt in junk bonds. For that reason, issuing any more bonds would require paying a very high interest rate on them. Moody's explained that it expected "neither cash flow nor capital structure will show substantial improvement in the near term," and "debt leverage has not improved."

Enron refinanced some of its debt in 1987 with a sale of 12-year instruments known as debentures. The company raised $585 million in February selling this debt, underwritten by Drexel Burnham Lambert. But at the end of the year, Enron had $3.43 billion in long-term debt, and that didn't count short-term obligations, such as loans that were due within six months. Wall Street often measures the debt load of a company by comparing how much debt it has to its total capitalization—capitalization being the company's stock market value (the stock price times its total shares of stock) minus its debt. At the end of 1987, Enron's debt equaled a whopping 75.6 percent of its total capitalization. A debt-to-capital ratio above 50 percent is often considered high, so Enron's was towering.

The company did make some progress. In the first quarter of 1988, Enron lowered its debt-to-capital ratio to roughly 67 percent. Moody's raised Enron's debt rating back up to investment grade, although the rating was "Baa," the firm's lowest investment-grade rating. But the campaign against debt wasn't over. At the April 1988 annual shareholder's meeting, Lay said: "One major 1988 objective is to reduce Enron's debt." By the end of the year, debt-to-capital slipped to 65.7 percent. But debt would remain a constant issue for Enron for the rest of its existence.

While grappling with its debt, Enron was also wrestling with its take-or-pay contracts. At one point these totaled more than $1 billion in high-priced commitments. But the FERC encouraged gas producers to renegotiate these pacts with pipeline companies, and over the course of the late 1980s Enron resolved thousands of take-or-pay deals.

Renegotiating these contracts didn't help endear Enron to the small and medium-sized natural gas producers, who were also hurt by low gas prices. Enron and other pipeline companies often agreed to buy additional gas beyond that covered in the take-or-pay contracts if the producer agreed to lower the take-or-pay prices. "Small producers sometimes felt Enron was taking advantage of them in price negotiations," and thought the company arrogant, according to Raymond Plank, chairman and CEO of oil and gas producer Apache Corp. It wouldn't be the last time that Enron was accused of arrogance.

■ ■ ■

Enron had its share of tussles, but it was surviving and making money. In 1987, it generated $5.9 billion in revenue, and it earned $53.7 million from its "ongoing" operations, which were those that it didn't sell or shut down.

The company was already conducting some energy trading, because it had a small oil-trading operation based in New York. Oil trading had grown in the 1980s, and by 1987 companies bought and sold not only barrels of oil in spot markets but also financial contracts for oil. Enron Oil, as the business was known, reported a nice little profit in 1985 and 1986. Two senior traders at the subsidiary felt confident enough from their prior success to try to make some big bets. But their big bets ran into trouble. They invested a lot in bets that oil prices would rise, only to see oil prices fall. Then they switched tactics and bet that oil prices would keep falling. But oil prices rose instead. The result was losses on both ends.

But the two traders not only were making unauthorized trades, they went 10 to 20 times past the company's internal limits on trade sizes and losses. Worse, they weren't reporting these trades to Houston. Instead, the traders kept the actual trades on a second set of books, and sent false records to headquarters. They evidently hoped to trade their way out of the losses before their deceit was uncovered. But Enron investigated and uncovered the fraud. The result was a loss to Enron of $142 million, including an $85 million charge to its 1987 earnings. Enron Oil was shut down entirely.

Enron fired the two traders, Louis Borget and Thomas Mastroeni, and sued them in civil court—partly because they'd constructed bogus trades before 1987 that led Enron to pay them sizable bonuses. In 1988, the U.S. Attorney's office investigated their secret trading as well. Federal investigators found that the traders created a shell company with which they conducted dozens of fake trades. In 1990, the two pleaded guilty to conspiracy to defraud and to filing false tax returns.

The trading scandal took Enron out of the oil-trading business, but it did raise an interesting question. Would energy trading have any place at the company? After all, Enron was "trading" gas contracts in the spot market, although gas wasn't being bought and sold like stocks. Perhaps it was time to look at other opportunities.

By selling off ranches and other peripheral businesses, Enron had trimmed down to a company that was mostly a pipeline operator. It owned 37,000 miles of pipelines all over the country. Thanks to changes in regulations, the pipelines were shifting toward a model whereby they transported the gas for government-approved fees, while Enron had a separate, unregulated unit that sold the gas to utilities and other users. Enron also owned gas processing plants, which extracted ethane, propane, and other chemicals out of the raw gas, and Enron sold those chemicals on the market as well. The company also owned some interests in power plants.

Enron also had an oil and gas producing business, aptly named Enron Oil & Gas, which explored for and produced a good amount of natural gas. It sold a lot of its production to Enron, assuring Enron of gas supplies and giving Enron a way to benefit just in case gas prices rose. In the late 1980s, most of its reserves were in the United States and Canada, although it had interests in a few international areas, including Ecuador, Syria, Egypt, and Malaysia.

The businesses had their share of excitement, what with trading scandals and gas wells in exotic lands, but they had a cozy side, too. There could be a small-town feel to the Texas oil business, embodied by an Enron project in Martin County, Texas. There, in October 1986, Enron Oil & Gas cooperated on a well in which a 10 percent stakeholder was Spectrum 7, an oil and gas company run by George W. Bush—the same Bush who would become U.S. president in 2001. Spectrum 7, which soon was acquired by Harken Energy, took minority interests in lots of wells, and there's no evidence that Bush at that time had any special relationship with Enron or Ken Lay—this was probably coincidence. Still, if Bush had any particular sympathy for Enron and the energy business in later years, part of the reason was certainly his time in "the oil bidness" in West Texas.

But was this business of running regulated pipelines, selling some gas, and doing some drilling really what Enron wanted? Deregulation had already roiled the gas business, and more convulsions were sure to come. After conferring with consultants from McKinsey & Co., Lay wanted change. One executive who agreed with him was Richard Kinder, the man who had headed the company's cost reduction committee in late 1986.

Kinder, two years younger than Lay, was also a graduate of the University of Missouri. Armed with a law degree, Kinder entered the business world and worked as an executive at Continental when it owned Florida Gas. He moved over to Houston Natural Gas in early 1985, and rose to become Lay's chief of staff in 1987.

In late 1988, Kinder became vice chairman of Enron, and he was the de facto second in command. By then, he was more involved in running the day-to-day operations of the company, while Lay focused on the bigger picture. They were a team, with Lay schmoozing politicians and other company executives, while Kinder oversaw Enron's various operations and drove employees to meet quarterly performance targets. Not that Lay was in the dark—instead, this was part of Lay's practice of arm's-length management at Enron. Just as in the past, he found executives he could trust to run their businesses, and he let them run things. Kinder's job was making sure Enron worked, and he was good at it.

And so Team Enron was set—at least for the moment. Kinder developed a reputation as a hard-ass. But that was somewhat misleading. Like Lay, Kinder was open and approachable. On the other hand, he could also be "very tough" in demanding a lot from employees, and kept people on their toes, recalled one former executive.

One of Kinder's biggest roles was in 1988, when he and Lay held the landmark meeting that set Enron's future direction. Kinder actually led the meeting, which included some 70 top executives of the company. Rather than fight deregulation, he and Lay told the executives, Enron was going to embrace it. Deregulation had opened up an unregulated part of the gas business, which then consisted of just selling natural gas. The company was going to focus on this unregulated business and look for more opportunities in it. And the company was going to move quickly.

Although Lay was anything but flashy, he had absorbed a few lessons from his minister father, and he made it clear that the unregulated market was the new religion at Enron. The executive confab was like a management revival meeting, and executives later dubbed it the "Come to Jesus" meeting. But the path was clear. Enron was going to move into uncharted waters that would eventually change the company and the gas industry.

2

WHERE THE MONEY IS

Ken Lay had thrown down the gauntlet for Enron: deregulation was splitting the gas industry into a regulated business and an unregulated business, and the growth opportunity would be in the unregulated side. Just as for other pipeline companies, the late 1980s was a time for Enron to explore the separation of transporting gas and selling gas. The matter of gas transportation was the simpler business, because the pipelines charged government-approved rates for sending gas through the lines. Gradually, Enron's pipelines began specializing their function, focusing on transportation only; the gas sales business was moved to another Enron division. For example, in October 1989, Enron's Transwestern Pipeline, stretching from Texas into southern California, became the first merchant pipeline in the United States to stop selling gas and become a transportation-only pipeline.

It was the gas sales business, which was not regulated by the Federal Energy Regulatory Commission (FERC), that held interesting wrinkles. In the beginning, the business consisted of buying and selling supplies of natural gas, including spot market deals: As explained in Chapter 1, the spot market emerged outside of regulated gas contracts, allowing wholesale buyers to purchase a month's worth of gas based on true market prices that responded to supply and demand. Because much of this business was catch-as-catch-can and Enron was able to sell to any available buyers, it was known as "merchant" sales, as Enron was truly acting as a free-agent merchant of gas.

In doing so, Enron was at the leading edge in energy markets. While gold and other commodities had long been freely traded in the United States, energy markets were traditionally regulated with a heavy hand. In 1989, electricity was almost entirely regulated by a mix of federal and state governments. And natural gas was still at the early stages of deregulating in the wholesale market, while the home market for gas was regulated by the states. Even oil prices were subject to some management by federal and state governments until the early 1980s.

Enron's gas sales businesses gave birth to its gas trading business. Enron bought and sold standard amounts of natural gas—the way stock trading might involve buying 100 shares of stock in the morning and then selling those shares at a small profit that afternoon. But in addition to buying gas in the morning and selling it in the afternoon, Enron's gas trades also followed a longer timetable. By the late 1980s, Enron was making deals for a month's supply of gas or several months' supply.

The company was intent on finding voids in the gas market and then filling them with new services. The spot market for 30-day gas supply contracts that arose in the late 1980s offered one such void. By 1990, the spot market accounted for more than 75 percent of gas sales, which increased gas price volatility. Spying that there might be demand for longer-term deals, Enron offered a range of two-to-10-year contracts with fixed pricing. By offering customers greater reliability, Enron could also charge a premium for its services; profit margins were higher on long-term deals than on spot-market deals.

There was some worry that wholesale customers wouldn't want to sign long-term gas supply contracts while gas prices were volatile. Enron promoted the idea over a three-week time period in 1989, and to its pleasant surprise, it received indications of interest in more than 600 billion cubic feet of gas. Enron Oil & Gas was able to agree to supply most of this long-term gas. In 1990 alone, Enron contracted to sell 190 billion cubic feet of gas in new, long-term deals. In that way, Enron was offering services to help provide greater security, in terms of both price and supply, to the gas market.

The "physical" trading moved gas around the country's pipeline system in both short-term and long-term contracts. This only became possible because a growing part of the gas market was not tied to long-term contracts, allowing Enron the freedom to shop some of its gas around to get the best price. The goal was to send gas to the best place in order to make the most money—in other words, to optimize the transportation of gas. So if Enron had some gas in the Permian Basin of West Texas, the company had to decide whether it made sense to pipe it up to Chicago or to send it to the Appalachia hub in Sabine, West Virginia. Enron might buy gas in the Permian Basin and sell it in West Virginia. Or it might re-deploy the gas to Chicago if that area's weather cooled and gas prices rose; in that case, Enron might fulfill its obligation in West Virginia by purchasing gas from the Appalachia market, possibly with no profit, in order to make money on its sales in Chicago.

In addition, buying and selling gas at the right time was crucial. In 1990 and 1991, Enron and other gas traders were doing basic deals that relied on betting whether gas prices would rise or fall in the following month or following several months. Enron and others engaged in "for-ward" sales, which were contracts to deliver gas at specified prices at fu-ture dates. These forwards could only be resolved with the delivery of gas. Making these trades required data. Gas traders spent lots of time talking to people at gas production, pipeline, and gas-consuming compa-nies, finding out what the sentiment was in a certain regional market, how much gas was in storage, and what the weather was expected to be. "It was all driven by having an information advantage," recalled John Sherriff, who worked as a gas trader at American Hunter Energy before joining Enron as a senior trader in 1994.

Enron also worked to standardize gas delivery contracts. Because many of these delivery contracts were interruptible, when gas prices surged com-panies would default on their supplies, either because it was too expensive to buy the gas they were reselling or because they wanted to sell the gas elsewhere for more money. This would send customers scrambling to other suppliers or to spot markets to buy replacement gas at what were then much higher prices. Obviously, this didn't create the most trusting atmosphere for gas customers. To engender trust and thereby help the gas market develop, Enron insisted that its contracts were "firm," which meant that gas supplies couldn't be interrupted except for a "force ma-jeure"—i.e., an act of God such as a major hurricane. Under a firm con-tract, if the supplier interrupted delivery, it would have to refund to the purchaser whatever extra costs that customer had paid to replace gas.

Sticking to firm contracts wasn't always easy. For example, Enron might have had a firm contract to supply gas to an electric utility, and an interruptible contract to buy gas from a major oil company. If the oil company interrupted its deliveries to Enron, Enron had to go into the spot market and buy gas at higher prices so it could fulfill its firm contract to the utility. But Enron knew that firm contracts would be needed to create a truly viable gas trading market; otherwise many customers wouldn't trade. Over time, other market players came around to Enron's thinking (partly because Enron was the biggest trader of gas and often insisted on firm contracts), and the majority of gas contracts became firm, according to Sherriff. There were still interruptible contracts, and contracts known as "semi-firm" (which gave greater leeway for interruptions to a seller's gas production system), but because these were less reliable, these contracts were priced at a discount to firm contracts. In that sense, Enron's emphasis on firm contracts also helped it charge more for its gas.

Size was key to Enron's strategy. Enron didn't buy and sell gas just in Texas and Louisiana. Over time, Enron was all over the country, at every hub. More than just a broker, Enron became a "market maker" for gas: a trading firm that stood ready to make deals in order keep the flow of trades going. Although investment bank Goldman Sachs had acted as a market maker in oil trading, Enron adapted that strategy to the relatively closed market of U.S. gas.

Buying and selling gas was just one piece of the puzzle. Enron also wanted to trade financial contracts based on the price of gas—in a word, "derivatives." Derivatives are financial instruments—often akin to contracts—that derive their value from some underlying asset. Although derivatives can be mind-bogglingly complex, millions of ordinary Americans are familiar with one of the most fundamental derivatives: options. Thanks to the growth of employee stock options over the past decade, many people know that stock options give the right, but not the obligation, to buy or sell a stock at a predetermined price on or before a given date. An employee of Enron might have options to buy 100 shares of Enron stock for $20 per share, and those options might expire in three years; if Enron's stock is trading at $30 per share within those three years, the employee would do well to choose to cash in the options (known in the lingo as "exercising" the options), but if the stock is trading at $10 per share, the employee could choose to let the options expire unused rather than overpay for the stock.

Any basic option, whether on stock or on natural gas, works that same way, giving the owner the choice (hence the name "option") of whether to go through with the transaction. Although options are believed to date back to ancient Greece, the use of options in the modern business world exploded in the 1970s when economists came up with ways to calculate how much options should cost given the many uncertainties they involve. This innovation, which began with something known as the Black-Scholes formula (and would, decades later, warrant a few Nobel Prizes for Economics), used advanced mathematics and a dollop of physics to calculate an option's price based on the expected price volatility of the underlying asset. The complexity of the calculations demanded that options traders use computers or advanced calculators; fortunately, the desktop computer came along soon after Black-Scholes. With this combination of mathematical formulas and technology, Wall Street finance was able to evolve throughout the 1970s and 1980s into something more closely resembling rocket science. The result was the creation of new markets, slicing such products as home mortgages and junk bonds into bite-size portions that could be traded easily.

Options are a perfect example of derivatives, because they illustrate the ideal use of any derivative—to provide a way of reducing future risks. Stock options, then, give an employee the potential to secure cheap stock in the future if the stock becomes very expensive. Similarly, Enron used derivatives to reduce risks associated with future gas prices. Enron was in many ways latching onto a derivatives revolution that had already begun in the finance area, including bonds and interest rates. But it was new to the natural-gas industry. Over the years, trading derivatives would become one of Enron's hallmark talents. While some derivatives, including some options and futures, are standardized contracts that trade on exchanges, most derivatives are not. So most of Enron's trading involved customized contracts used outside of exchanges, which meant that there was no exchange regulating these deals. These customized derivatives, which were the bulk of Enron's trading, are a booming business. Nowadays, people in the business world use the term "derivative" to refer not to options but to the more complex custom derivatives, which carry exotic terms such as "swaps" and "collars" and "swaptions."

So Enron wanted to get into financial trading to complement its physical trading. To do so, the company partnered with Bankers Trust, a well-known New York bank with derivatives expertise. Under a joint venture, BT sent some traders to Houston to set up a financial trading desk. The goal was to use options and other derivatives to allow gas producers and gas consumers to hedge their bets on prices using purely financial means. This meant that aside from securing a supply of gas, Enron would be using derivatives to lock in prices, or at least lock in maximum and minimum prices.

One signature hedging deal involved a Louisiana aluminum producer that wanted to buy gas at a fixed price. Transporting gas to the company wasn't profitable for Enron. So in 1989, Enron wrote a financial contract under which the aluminum company bought its gas locally at the fluctuating market prices, but paid Enron a fixed price. Enron paid the ever-changing market prices that the aluminum maker would ordinarily have had to pay. Only money, not gas, changed hands. And it was up to Enron to figure out how to make money between the fixed price it was receiving and the floating prices it was paying. Enron and the customer had essentially swapped floating prices for a fixed price, a basic version of a derivative known as a "swap." The first energy swap had occurred in 1986 in the oil market, and with the aluminum deal Enron had just done the first big gas swap.

This financial trading wasn't fast-paced back in 1990. To sell a contract using derivatives to lock in one year's supply of gas at a fixed price might take six weeks to negotiate. But BT helped make the operation more efficient. For one thing, its people centralized all prices at one source, instead of allowing individual traders to quote different prices, recalled a former Bankers Trust employee. This helped impose discipline on the new trading operation, often by pulling aside an Enron trader after a mistake had already been made and giving him a talk. As one BT trader explained his mission at the time: "My job is being a lifeguard at a pool in the summertime, and trying to figure out which kid pissed in the pool."

BT also helped Enron wring more money out of its financial trading business. They identified options that were embedded in Enron contracts. For example, say Enron had a purchase contract that guaranteed it a supply of 20,000 cubic feet per day of gas, but the contract also allowed Enron to vary the daily volumes between 15,000 and 25,000 cubic feet.

This flexibility increased the value of the contract. Enron could, for instance, sell this flexibility in the form of a "call" option (an option that enables the holder to buy an asset). The call option would cover the extra 5,000 cubic feet of gas per day. Enron could use the money from the option sale to help pay for the gas purchase contract.

Tensions arose between Enron and BT. Given Enron's ambition, it may have been inevitable that sharing the trading operation could not last. Enron had the physical assets and the customers, making it difficult to value the bank's contribution. In 1991, BT and Enron dissolved the joint venture, and Enron decided to go it alone. The company brought in Joseph Pokalsky, an experienced interest-rate trader at Chemical Bank, to run the financial trading desk. Bankers Trust went on to remain a rival to Enron in the gas derivatives market, competing as well with the likes of Morgan Stanley and AIG Financial. (Interestingly, in a development unrelated to Enron, Bankers Trust ran into trouble with its large derivatives operation in 1994, both losing money on it and incurring the wrath of clients who claimed the bank misrepresented the derivatives it sold them. Bankers Trust was never the same after the derivatives scandal; it stumbled along for a few years, and in 1999, Germany's Deutsche Bank acquired a weakened BT.)

■ ■ ■

Enron dived into gas hedging, but the market wasn't balanced between producers and consumers. Gas production companies looking to assure their future cash flows were willing to try gas hedging, in part because many were familiar with oil trading, which had been around for a few years. Gas users, mostly industrial users, were not so willing to hedge their bets on gas prices. As a result, traders had to be good at hedging their own risk, too. Traditionally, a trader would hedge risk by offsetting one trade with a similar trade on the other side—offsetting a deal to buy 100 million cubic feet of gas for $25,000 with another deal to sell 100 million cubic feet of gas for $25,000 (or, ideally, for $26,000). With more gas producers than gas users willing to hedge at the time, traders had to be careful or be willing to take risks where they couldn't find offsetting trades.

Help arrived in 1990. In April, natural gas trading developed so much that the New York Mercantile Exchange (NYMEX) introduced a gas futures contract to trade on its exchange. A future is the most straightforward derivative, even simpler than an option: it's a contract to buy or sell something at a specified price at a predetermined future date. Futures developed in the 1800s as a vehicle for commodity producers such as farmers to guarantee the prices they'd be getting in six or nine months, and for buyers to hedge their bets on a possible rise in prices in the future. A futures contract on natural gas meant that industry players could easily buy or sell contracts for 10,000 cubic feet of gas, delivered at the Henry Hub in Louisiana, as soon as one month in the future or as far off as 12 months hence (later expanded to 18 months). The NYMEX chose Henry Hub because it was a processing plant that interconnected with 12 different pipeline systems, and so was already one of the more popular spot markets.

By the time it introduced a gas contract, the NYMEX had a lot of experience in trading energy. Founded in 1872 as the Butter and Cheese Exchange (its name changed 10 years later), the NYMEX was fading into irrelevance by the late 1970s. But in 1978, the exchange saved itself and revolutionized the energy markets when it introduced a futures contract for heating oil. Its biggest success was a futures contract for crude oil (the oil that comes up from the ground, before being refined into gasoline or chemicals or heating oil), launched in 1983. Its crude oil futures soon became the benchmark for world oil prices, and surpassed gold as the most active commodity futures contract in the world.

One of the advantages to a gas futures contract was that the ease of trading also allowed for buyers and sellers who didn't actually own or want gas. These financial traders, once known as speculators, hopped in and out of the contracts just to profit on the contract price's ups and downs. This was aided by the fact that futures don't have to result in the delivery of gas or other commodities—they can be settled in cash, and most are. By jumping in and out of the market, financial traders fulfilled a legitimate purpose of broadening the market for the contract and thus helping to determine prices. The theory is that the more participants in a market, the easier it is to determine a fair price; and in practice that's the way it works almost all the time. After April 1990, traders constructing deals that happened off the exchange—the customized trades worked out directly between traders and known as "over-the-counter trading"—

could conceivably hedge some of their risk by buying and selling gas futures; for example, if a trader agreed to a deal supplying 100,000 cubic feet of gas, but had no complementary deal to buy 100,000 cubic feet of gas, the trader could buy gas futures.

There was some resistance to the NYMEX gas futures, however. In the early years, Texas traders willfully ignored it. "New Yorkers shouldn't set the price of gas," traders would say. Other indexes were used, drawn from trade publications such as McGraw-Hill's "Inside FERC Gas Market Report," or *Gas Daily*. But by mid-1991, more than one-quarter of futures trading consisted of hedges of deals that occurred over the counter.

Over time, the futures contract became a briskly traded standard that changed throughout the day and was visible to everyone. So what the NYMEX natural gas contract did was create a benchmark price for natural gas in the United States: a reliable index, not unlike the way the Dow Jones Industrial Average provides a highly visible index of how the U.S. stock market is doing at any given moment. True, the NYMEX contract didn't reflect all gas prices in every region of the country, just the prices at the Henry Hub delivery point in Louisiana; but the other parts of the country could at least refer to the NYMEX prices. Trades that would happen off the NYMEX were easier to price, and therefore easier to negotiate, thus helping the over-the-counter market grow.

As useful as it was, the NYMEX futures market was incomplete because the Henry Hub price didn't take into account regional pricing differences and didn't offer much flexibility in making or receiving deliveries of gas. Henry Hub gas prices were often different from prices in New Mexico or Chicago, because gas markets are regional. Similarly, the exchange's futures contracts called for gas to be delivered at the Henry Hub, so if you wanted gas delivered in Texas or Oklahoma you were out of luck. To address this lack of flexibility, Enron in 1990 started a "Hub Pricing Program" that offered prices and delivery points beyond Henry Hub—at four points, or hubs, along its pipeline system. The goal was to offer more customized pricing and delivery alternatives. The program instantly gained some traction: In its first year, Enron executed 85 customer contracts and priced 80 billion cubic feet of natural gas through the Hub Pricing Program.

■ ■ ■

Expanding its use of gas supply deals, Enron had to ensure it had access to firm supplies of gas. So Enron's gas sales arm began a program called Gas Bank in 1989 to acquire supplies for serving long-term markets. Gas Bank pooled various gas supplies for Enron. The company then had a separate business that could dip into this pool of gas supply for sales deals; it worked similarly to how a bank pools customer deposits and uses them to make loans. Enron signed pacts for gas that included the traditional long-term gas purchase contracts, but also included the acquisition of working interests in producing properties, and prepaying for secured long-term supplies. By using Gas Bank, Enron aimed to enable gas producers and wholesale buyers to purchase firm gas supplies and hedge the price risk of the new spot market at the same time.

A crucial function at Enron was the financing of gas exploration and production. In the late 1980s and early 1990s, small oil and gas companies often found it difficult to get bank loans for drilling wells; energy prices had been extremely volatile, and the banking industry was recovering from the Savings and Loan crisis that saw many big banks collapse. The Enron Finance subsidiary stepped into the void and agreed to grant loans to these small producing companies so they could afford to develop fields where reserves of oil and gas had been proven to exist, and begin pumping out oil and gas. Enron hired top engineering consultants to review the projects and help estimate how much oil and gas could be recovered from each one. Unlike a bank, Enron asked for the loans to be repaid with gas instead of cash. Although Enron was taking a risk, this was smart because if these projects succeeded, then voilà!—Enron had guaranteed supplies of gas.

One of Enron's innovations along this line was to structure these financing arrangements known as Volumetric Production Payments with oil and gas producers. The VPP gave cash up front to the producer in exchange for set amounts of oil and gas production, but the financing was secured only by the production fields, not by the producing company or any other of its assets (so a problem wouldn't result in the producer going bankrupt). The VPP was the first kind of Special Purpose Entity in which Enron would dabble. Although Enron's Special Purpose Entities—in the form of partnerships—later become notorious for their misuse in hiding debts and losses, these VPPs were perfectly legal and useful financial deals.

The first VPP, in 1990, was with Forest Oil, a struggling gas producer. Enron paid $44.8 million in exchange for 32 billion cubic feet of gas over five years. Another typical deal was a 1991 VPP with Zilkha Energy, in which Enron provided $24 million so that the independent production company could develop some properties in the Gulf of Mexico, a project that carried a large amount of up-front costs. Enron then hedged its own risks from VPPs with transactions to hedge oil and gas prices and interest rates.

One thing to keep in mind is that various partnerships and entities have long been a part of the energy business, because exploring for oil and gas and then producing it—which can include setting up pipeline and gathering systems—is often an expensive undertaking. A few other trading companies followed Enron in putting together VPPs, including investment banks, but Enron was far and away the preeminent provider of this financing, said Shannon Burchett, who worked at Salomon Brothers' Phibro energy division, an Enron rival, in the early 1990s.

At the same time, federal electricity regulations allowed for the construction of independent power plants that were not owned by electric utilities. These independent plants could sell their power to local electric utilities at "avoided cost," which was the price equivalent to the costs the utility avoided by not having to build more power-generating capacity. For many of these new power plants, this promised to be a very profitable arrangement. The problem was that power plants cost money to build, and banks were not eager to finance them because the plants' single biggest operating expense—fuel—was such a volatile cost. Again Enron stepped in, this time by offering long-term gas contracts for gas-fueled plants, thereby stabilizing the cost structure for these power plants. Thus, Enron was building up a new base of gas customers.

Enron was a leader in putting together these long-term gas supply deals. The company achieved a milestone deal with its 20-year gas supply contract for Sithe Energies, an operator of independent power plants. In January 1992, Enron signed a contract to provide all the natural gas for a 1,000-megawatt plant that Sithe was developing in Oswego, New York. Requiring 195 million cubic feet of gas per day, it was an unprecedented deal in its scale, estimated at $3.5 billion to $4 billion of gas over the 20-year period. The gas prices would be fixed for the first five years, then fluctuate with market prices for the next 15; this deal had convinced

Sithe to use gas as the fuel instead of coal. The power plant, called Independence, was the largest such independent power project at the time. It started operation in January 1995, with much of its electricity sold to Consolidated Edison, New York City's electric utility.

The massive Sithe deal was the showcase for Enron's business of supplying gas to power plants. To make the deal work, Enron had to combine gas supply commitments stretching from the Gulf of Mexico to Canada, and use derivatives to hedge its price risks. It was an aggressive and creative use of its financial capabilities. Enron was the first to line up long-term gas pacts behind the independent power plant industry, but in coming years others would again follow Enron's lead. And while another company might have brought in partners to spread the risk, Enron was daring enough to handle the entire gas supply contract. At a wine and cheese celebration of the deal's signing, Enron executives crowed that they had the only company that could pull together all the moving parts.

■ ■ ■

During the early 1990s, Enron was turning into a pipeline-and-finance company, and Ken Lay wanted help with that transformation. He got help, and a jolt of new energy, on June 26, 1990, when Enron hired itself a new chief executive for its Enron Finance unit. That man's name was Jeffrey K. Skilling.

Born in Pittsburgh in 1954, Jeff was one of four children of Betty and Tom Skilling, who was a mechanical engineer. During his childhood, the family moved to New Jersey and then to Illinois. More than the moves, Jeff's childhood was notable for his taste for slightly dangerous activities, which sometimes caused mishaps like crashing down dunes or falling out of a tree house. This trait would later show itself at Enron, too, where he had a penchant for adventuring, taking customers and associates on safari in Africa, surfing in the Caribbean, and to the Australian outback.

In high school he enjoyed working at what was then Aurora, Illinois', new community-access cable-television station, WXLT Channel 61. Skilling liked to work the controls for ad-hoc shows that resembled the "Wayne's World" skits that would be featured on *Saturday Night Live* decades later.

Enron colleagues would later describe Skilling as whip smart and able to grasp concepts instantly. By high school he showed signs of being an intellectual force; in 1971 he went to Southern Methodist University in Dallas on a full scholarship. There he became known as someone who was politically conservative and ambitious. He married classmate Susan Long shortly after their 1975 graduation, and Jeff went to work at First City National Bank. Then he went to the two-year master's degree program at Harvard Business School, where he finally showed himself to be outstanding by graduating in the top 5 percent of the class.

Skilling joined the well-known consulting firm McKinsey & Co. out of Harvard and went to work in the Houston office. There he rose to become the head of McKinsey's energy consulting practice. In the late 1980s he did some consulting work for Enron, and in 1987 he helped Lay develop the first forward sales contract for natural gas. Skilling agreed with Lay's focus on the unregulated side of the pipeline business, and Lay tried to recruit him to Enron in 1988 and 1989.

When Lay finally lured Skilling to the company full-time, Skilling came with some ideas that were prevalent at McKinsey, such as flattening the management organization so decisions could be made faster and knocking down walls so workers could communicate better. He also came with an idea about Enron. He wanted the company to develop its intangible assets, meaning trading and financial prowess, and put less emphasis on its so-called hard assets, such as pipelines and gas-processing plants. His "asset-light" strategy was in many ways opposed to Enron's brief tradition of doing things—building trading businesses around existing hard assets. Asset-light also served as a vision that could help distinguish Skilling within Enron's hierarchy.

Enron's trading, its creation of the Gas Bank, and even its introduction of Volumetric Production Payments and long-term gas contracts for power plants all grew up around its core natural gas business. These newer businesses either built financial contracts around supplying gas or erected financial mechanisms for securing more gas. One view held that trading and finance existed to complement the gas supply and transportation business. But Skilling believed that the natural gas business may have led Enron into trading and finance, but those latter operations had become an Enron skill that existed apart from gas. In other words, Skilling saw the future in focusing on the trading and finance functions. But Skilling's group was still new, and Ken Lay, Richard Kinder, and Enron weren't ready to choose trading and finance over the known quantity of pipes, pumps, and processors. Enron was still expanding its base of hard assets. In 1991, for example, Enron plotted a $424 million extension of its Midwestern pipeline, Northern Border; bought a gas processing business from rival Tenneco for more than $500 million; and helped arrange $1.3 billion in financing to build a huge power plant in Teesside, England. Still, the debate between asset-light and asset-heavy started in 1990 and would frame Enron's big picture for years to come.

When he arrived at Enron, Skilling was bright, confident, and driven. But he wasn't yet the charismatic leader who would rise to be CEO of Enron in 2001. Lay described him as a strategic thinker who always came up with new ideas. But the patriarch of Enron also admitted that Skilling wasn't able to relate well to most other employees. Even Lay could tell some staffers felt Skilling talked down to them.

In the early 1990s, Skilling worked to remake Enron into a new entity that was ready for the energy industry of the 1990s. He wasn't without his softer side. He routinely left work early so that he could spend time with his children. But his ambition was also very clear. "I had the impression that Jeff wanted to see himself recognized by his peers as someone . . . who had changed the world," said Pokalsky, who worked for Skilling in the early 1990s. "Jeff was really interested in changing the world."

■ ■ ■

Before Jeff Skilling could change the world, he had to make some changes to Enron's finance arm, including Gas Bank. Gas Bank was in essence a bank that included the deposits from gas producers and the loans to power plants and other customers. But by another definition, it was a trading book—the ledger of buy and sell orders in any trading business—made up of long-term "trades." So Enron hired more people to manage this trading book, a task that included making more trades.

In order to manage the risk of price changes and their effects on these long-term deals, the financial trading desk bought and sold financial contracts that were tied to gas prices, such as options and swaps. Although it was called the financial trading desk, most of the initial contracts were for physical delivery and resulted in gas being sent somewhere. This required joint pricing between the financial desk and the physical trading desk. The physical trading desk also provided the "spread," or the difference between buy and sell orders, that the financial desk used to settle firm contracts.

Eventually, the financial desk was trading more derivatives, such as swaps. In a swap, ever-changing prices are swapped for a fixed price; gas producers often like to lock in a fixed price so they can ignore price fluctuations and concern themselves with drilling and delivering gas from the field. For example, a swap might call for Enron to guarantee that a gas production company gets $2 per 10,000 cubic feet for its gas over the course of a year, but without actually buying the gas at that price. How? The swap would require that if the market's going rate—as measured by the Henry Hub spot market price—fell below $2, Enron would pay the producer the difference between $2 and the spot market price. Conversely, if the spot price went above $2, the producer would pay the difference between $2 and the spot price to Enron. It would be up to the gas producer to sell its gas, and then the terms of the swap would, via cash payments, even out the price to $2. In this example, the gas producer protects itself from gas falling below $2 by giving up the potential profits from gas above $2.

Although the financial trading group arose to manage the risk coming out of Gas Bank, it outgrew Gas Bank and started to do its own deals as well. One type of transaction that Enron did in these early days was constructing swaps of oil for natural gas. Because large exploration and production companies often produce both oil and gas, Enron seized the opportunity to secure more gas supplies by swapping oil for these companies' gas. The production companies were willing to do this because they were more optimistic about oil prices, but Enron, based on its internal price forecasts, was more optimistic about gas prices. So to figure out these swaps, Enron converted oil to gas based on the equivalence of the energy they would produce—measured in British thermal units, or BTUs. Then Enron took delivery of gas, while settling the difference between oil prices and gas prices (using NYMEX prices) in cash each month. Enron would then hedge these prices by trading oil and gas futures.

Another type of trade that Enron employed in the early days involved natural gas options and geography. One of the differences between oil and gas is the ease of transporting oil, which makes it possible to sell oil at fairly uniform prices all around the United States. Not only is gas demand highly regionalized (because it may be cold in Vermont but warm in Arizona), but the difficulty in piping it over thousands of miles means that its price can vary even from Texas to New Mexico. The risk involved in trading between different locations that may have different prices is known as "basis" risk. This was a new dimension to energy trading, and Enron purposely hired traders like Pokalsky who had no experience with energy but did have experience with basis risk in finance (such as the different interest rates in different countries). In using options to hedge basis risk between gas prices at Louisiana's Henry Hub and gas prices at Houston's Ship Channel, some firms priced their options wrong. Using the Black-Scholes formula, they didn't take into account the fact that sometimes the basis would actually flip; in other words, the vagaries of supply and demand were such that gas would sometimes cost more in Houston, but sometimes it would cost more at the Henry Hub. That subtle distinction distorted the complicated way the options prices were calculated. This enabled traders like Pokalsky to buy Henry Hub–Ship Channel basis options at a cheap price, then sell them for handsome profits.

If these deals sound complex, it's because they were. And this kind of financial trading was new even to Enron, and so it was kept separate from the physical trading operation. At first, physical trading was even on another floor, and the two operations rarely communicated. Skilling spent a great deal of time explaining what the financial trading desk did, because even the physical traders didn't understand at first. Over time that would change, but it was a gradual process. Skilling's number two at what was then known as Enron Gas Services, John Esslinger, also helped by eventually merging the physical and financial trading desks. It was all part of Enron's slow evolution into a trading company from a pipeline company. Pokalsky credited Skilling with helping open up the trading culture: "He turned everybody's office wall into glass walls, he knocked down the cubicles and built a trading floor, and relaxed the dress code."

Echoing Wall Street firms even further, Enron hired an internal research team in 1992 to help calculate the mathematical models for the derivatives. To head this team, the company hired Vincent Kaminski, who had a Ph.D. in mathematical economics as well as an MBA, from the bond research group at investment bank Salomon Brothers. "We were the group developing the tools, but we didn't price the deals," Kaminski explained. Instead, his group, like similar groups at investment banks all over the financial world, created the framework for complex deals using options, collars, swaps, and such. While traders could calculate many deals right there at their desks, Kaminski's group handled anything that required advanced mathematics, and often worked as internal consultants on specific deals. For instance, if a contract gave a customer an option to buy an option, the volatility equations in that kind of deal (volatility on volatility) could be complicated and would require the help of the research team.

Enron made it look easy. What looked to a customer like a simple contract might for Enron require a set of three, four, or more contracts in order to make the "simple" contract economically viable. In adapting options, swaps, and other investment tools, Enron stood on the shoulders of the financial community to build its trading business. But "Enron was the first to bring that skill set and those ideas into the energy market," said Edward Krapels, a director at consultant Energy Security Analysis. These were real innovations—so real that by the mid-1990s it became possible to talk about an energy industry "before Enron."

Adapting to this Wall Street-ish financial trading culture caused some ripples at Enron. Other Enron employees were suspicious of the financial traders, and some complained about the way their work area had more computers and televisions, and the fact that they were paid so well. The financial trading operation, the financing group (formerly known as Gas Bank), and the gas marketing operation had a thorny relationship. And their interests sometimes clashed: The financing group did better if gas prices were high, but the marketing group, which sold gas to local utilities, did better if gas prices were low. Because they were all originating gas deals based on their own analyses, the three groups had some heated discussions about where gas prices were headed.

More than just price strategy was at work, however. As early as 1991 and 1992, Skilling encouraged the three groups to view each other as competition, because he liked to have the competitive juices flowing in the company. Some speculated that Skilling also wanted to see which department head had more drive and ambition. According to a former Enron trader, the competition spilled over into which group got credit for deals—after all, it was an intertwining enterprise in which the gas from a VPP might be traded on the physical desk with some of the price risk hedged on the financial desk. Partly as a result, the heads of financial trading, gas marketing, and financing really didn't get along.

And the competition filtered down into the trenches, so that the workaday traders and even fresh recruits out of business school felt derision toward their counterparts at the other divisions. One result, according to the former trader, was that employees at one of the three groups weren't always open and honest with employees at the other groups. That made it difficult to function as a team. Traders sometimes changed price assumptions to benefit their trading books; occasionally, these changes were made just before the signing of long-term contracts, thus changing the economics of highly complex deals and sapping profits from another group. Despite the internal competition, there were also times when different units were able to work together. The infighting, though, was a constant bit of sand in the gears.

Even with that friction, Enron's trading prospered. By being the most prominent trader of gas and broker of gas deals, Enron had its hands in every part of the market. It also created "liquidity," which is the steady flow of buying and selling needed to maintain an orderly market. (A market like the New York Stock Exchange, for instance, is considered liquid because 99.9 percent of orders can be carried out without drastically changing the price of what's being traded.) Liquidity is a critical concept in trading. Having so much liquidity in gas gave Enron another informational advantage over other traders. "You could see when everyone was buying and selling," explained Sherriff. For example, if Enron saw that production companies were actually buying gas, it was a sign these firms believed that gas prices were cheap and would rise. Liquidity fed liquidity. By 1992, Enron was the largest marketer of gas in North America, selling nearly 5.6 billion cubic feet daily.

The trading and financial businesses became an ever-larger part of the company, as the number of employees in the trading and finance operations grew from 144 in 1990 to 548 in 1992. In 1990, Enron's gas sales and trading business accounted for $29 million of earnings before interest and taxes, or 3.7 percent of the company's total. In 1992, the sales and trading business generated $122 million of earnings before interest and taxes, or 12.4 percent of the company's total. Skilling's unit was still second in size to the regulated, steady pipeline operations, but it was the driving force for growth in the corporation.

■ ■ ■

At this point in the early development of the trading business, accounting entered the picture as a critical cog in the Enron machine. In January 1991, Enron began using an accounting method known as "mark-to-market" for booking the value of its trades. This was done because Enron believed this flavor of accounting more fairly presented the results of managing its portfolio of trades and contracts.

Mark-to-market accounting takes all the trades and contracts extending out into the future and figures out what their values would be based on current market prices; in other words, the trade is "marked to market." So if Enron held futures contracts to sell 100 million cubic feet of gas in one year's time, and the NYMEX futures market showed that gas futures in a year were trading at $2.50 per 10,000 cubic feet, Enron would value the contracts at $25,000. If Enron had bought those futures contracts for a total of $23,000, Enron could book $2,000 as its profit, even though it had yet to sell the futures.

In this way, mark-to-market accounting isn't so different from figuring out the value of one's portfolio of investments. Many people look at their mix of stocks, bonds, and mutual funds to see how their investments change in value from month to month or day to day. If an investor bought 100 shares of IBM stock at $30 per share and now it's trading at $50, the investor thinks of those 100 shares of IBM as giving a profit of $2,000, even though the stock hasn't been sold, so it's just a profit on paper. The brokerage firm would look at the IBM stock the same way, because it may charge a fee if the account's total value falls below a certain level, or it may have loaned the investor money to buy the IBM stock and is estimating whether the account has sufficient collateral.

Enron entered its paper profits into its books as profits, which made a lot of sense given that Enron had lots of long-term trades and contracts and needed some way to assign a value to them. Then in each subsequent quarter, it was up to Enron to double-check these valuations, and amend them if the market had changed; in other words, if the IBM stock in the example falls over the course of 90 days from $50 to $40, the paper profit has to be marked down to $1,000. Banks had been using mark-to-market accounting for years, but in 1991 it was still rare for a nonfinancial firm to use mark-to-market. Before 1991 Enron had valued contracts based on their historical cost; using the IBM example, that means the 100 shares would remain valued at $30 each until the stock was sold.

Of course, Enron's use of mark-to-market wasn't quite as simple as the IBM example: Enron also discounted future income to account for inflation, and often set aside reserves to protect against changes in the market value of its positions. Mark-to-market accounting is straightforward when the market value of the holdings can be easily calculated. It's easy to find the price of a publicly traded stock, or a price for some exchange-traded futures contract. But this accounting becomes more complicated when applied to over-the-counter trades and sophisticated long-term contracts—which were the majority of Enron's trades. How would Enron value a contract to supply gas four or five years in the future, when the NYMEX futures contract, for instance, stretched forward only 18 months? In those cases, it was up to Enron to make its best calculation of the mark-to-market value of its trades.

This relied on Enron's views of where gas prices were headed, which often involved calculating probable gas production, transportation capacity, future gas demand (which in turn involved forecasting economic growth and the growth of gas-consuming facilities such as power plants and refineries), and U.S. interest rates. It may not be too difficult to use these factors to make an estimated guess on natural gas prices 12 or 18 months down the line, but the further into the future Enron projected, the more those calculations rested on judgment calls. And traders' judgments can vary.

So it was often up to the traders to decide what sort of assumptions to plug into their mark-to-market valuation models. As a result, Enron traders sometimes used mark-to-market accounting to massage their results. They could be optimistic with their forecasts, boosting their immediate mark-to-market profits. Or if they'd had an especially good fiscal quarter, they could be conservative with their assumptions in the short term, so that they could adjust them upward the following quarter and boost the mark-to-market income then. "Unless you had a really good accountant, they couldn't catch it. The trader could defend it," said a former Enron gas trader.

The problem with mark-to-market accounting is that this sort of manipulation is not out-and-out illegal. So it's common to see some goosing of the results here and there, without any dramatic lies. "Derivatives are so flexible, and the participants in this market are very good financial engineers," said Randall Dodd, director of the Derivatives Study Center.

There's no evidence that Enron engaged in egregious fabrication of trading profits with its mark-to-market accounting. But this practice planted a seed in Enron's thinking that it was possible to manage earnings a bit within the accounting rules.

Using this accounting on its trading positions added to Enron's risk. Until long-term positions are closed out (i.e., the trade ends and is settled), there's the risk that the market may change and prices could move against the trader, hurting the positions' value.

The other result of mark-to-market accounting was more insidious. It emphasized short-term thinking, in that even 20-year deals were essentially just good for a profit in the quarter they were signed. Because Enron booked the profits from long-term deals immediately, its trading business wasn't building up any backlog of future income. It wasn't like signing deals for its pipelines, where the company could often count on several years of steady income from transporting gas for a specific project. Each quarter, Enron's traders had to start again with a blank page. To continue growing, more and more deals were needed. "You put yourself in a position where you had to kill to eat," is the way one former Enron executive put it.

The trading business fueled Enron's growth. By the start of 1990, Enron had a market capitalization—the value of the company based on its stock price—of $2.65 billion. That rose to a market value of $8.26 billion at the start of 1994. As a public company, Enron felt a responsibility to maintain a healthy rate of growth. But because of mark-to-market accounting, a sizable portion of Enron's growth depended on a rising volume of deals. Enron's growth was slowly turning into a momentum monster that needed constant feeding.

MAJOR AMBITION

As the middle of the 1990s approached, Enron had turned itself into the biggest trader of natural gas in America. But the trading business didn't dominate the corporation. The company simultaneously concerned itself with expanding its "hard" assets, like pipelines, oil and gas fields, and natural gas–fueled power plants. At the time, these were not contradictory goals. Enron was trying to become an integrated gas company, with operations in producing gas, delivering and selling gas, and trading gas.

One aspect was its Enron Oil & Gas (EOG) subsidiary, which was one of the largest of the class of independent "exploration and production" companies in the United States that operated at a scale below that of the major oil companies such as Exxon. It wasn't unusual for a gas pipeline company to also have an exploration and production arm, as Coastal Corp. and other large pipeline operators had them. Enron Oil & Gas enjoyed rising production and sales: It sold an average of 564 million cubic feet per day of gas in 1992, up from 491 million per day in 1991. Ken Lay's training to keep a sharp eye on federal regulations helped, as Enron Oil & Gas took advantage of one regulation in particular: Since 1980, an era of natural gas scarcity, the federal government had been offering tax credits to companies that drilled for gas in unconventional sources. In the early 1990s, Enron Oil & Gas generated a good portion of its production from "tight sands," a type of extra-dense rock formation that qualified for these federal tax credits. So, for example, Enron received $16.9 million from tight sands tax credits in 1991, and $42.5 million from the credits in 1992. When Congress considered eliminating these tax credits in 1992, the Senate, led by Enron ally and Minority Leader Robert Dole (R-Kansas), voted to extend the tax credits.

Enron wanted to highlight this unit, relatively buried within the larger Enron Corp. So in October 1989, the company sold stock worth 16 percent of Enron Oil & Gas to the public, for $18.75 per share. This initial public offering raised $202 million for the company after fees, and left Enron owning 84 percent of the business. With Enron Oil & Gas having its own stock, the corporation hoped it would be easier for Wall Street to value it. Of course, a higher value for that unit would boost the overall value of parent Enron Corp. as well. It wasn't clear that this happened, however, as there were many other factors affecting Enron's stock, especially the ever-changing price of natural gas. Nevertheless, by the end of October 1989, EOG was trading at $20 per share; it reached $30.50 three years later, which was not a bad rate of growth. In addition to stock performance, the semi-independence resulting from the initial public offering suited EOG, whose head, an experienced oil hand named Forrest Hoglund, received a lot of autonomy from Lay.

Beyond being viewed as a multifaceted company within the United States, Enron wanted to also be an international presence. This wasn't just a matter of pride. American energy companies had always taken an interest in foreign properties, whether in drilling for oil or in helping to build pipelines and power projects. So Enron always had an eye on overseas business opportunities.

Far more than Enron Oil & Gas, Enron's international businesses came to embody the hard-asset side of the company, and therefore the opposite of its trading operation. Enron's highest-profile foray in the international arena in its early years was not all that successful, to say the least. The company had a unit called Belco Petroleum Corp. of Peru that explored for and produced oil and gas in that country. But in late 1985, Peru's populist government seized U.S. oil holdings in the country and nationalized them, including Belco. Enron suffered a $218 million loss as a result of the nationalization of its Peruvian unit. The company collected about $162 million of insurance in 1989 to cover the incident, then in 1993 reached a deal with the Peruvian government and insurer AIG to receive another $33 million.

Enron was not discouraged by the Peruvian experience. Large gas companies besides Enron were looking to internationalize. In some ways, London's British Gas had sparked the competition at the end of 1990 when it acquired a local gas utility in Ontario, Canada, and then began touting itself as "the first global gas company."

Across the Atlantic, Margaret Thatcher's government had been pushing privatization, and the United Kingdom started deregulating its energy industry in 1988. This entailed separating power generation from power distribution, and privatizing these various businesses. One of the private power generation companies, National Power, teamed with Enron and with another British company, ICI Chemicals and Polymers Ltd., to look for power-related opportunities. In 1989, the three companies began studying the possibility of building a large gas-fired power plant at ICI's Wilton site on Teesside, in northeast England, for roughly $1 billion. Enron would design, construct, and run the power plant. ICI would buy electricity and steam from the proposed power station for its chemicals manufacturing business, and any surplus electricity would be sold on the open market (at that point, the United Kingdom had begun planning wholesale electricity markets). Where would the gas come from? From the North Sea, which had become a tremendous source of oil and gas over the course of the 1970s and 1980s.

It would be a huge, prestigious project, which at the time was estimated as the world's largest "cogeneration" plant (generating both steam and electricity). Enron estimated the 1,875-megawatt Teesside plant would add 4 percent to the power generating capacity of the United Kingdom. And in January 1990, Enron and ICI took the first step for the Teesside plant when they signed a deal for gas supplies. The supplier would be a group led by U.S. oil giant Amoco, and also included Amerada Hess and an affiliate of British Gas. The deal would provide for up to 300 million cubic feet of gas per day from two new fields sitting under the North Sea. Later that year, Enron signed 15-year deals to sell the electricity generated from the Teesside plant to ICI and to four local British electric utilities; these four utilities would also together own 50 percent of the plant, with Enron owning the remaining half. The contracts assumed that less than 10 percent of the electricity would be sold on the U.K. wholesale market.

Enron soon added a separate plant at Teesside to process the incoming gas, extracting natural gas liquids such as propane and butane. The company also negotiated a loan of £795 million to help finance the project. And as the construction of the Teesside power plant continued, Enron considered building another cogeneration plant on the site. That would require more gas supplies, but that fit with Enron's idea of being a player in British exploration and production. Specifically, it wanted a piece of the so-called J-Block in the North Sea, which contained prospects named "Judy" and "Joanne," two big sources of natural gas and oil that were expected to be ready for production in 1996. In August 1992, the company agreed to buy a 25 percent stake in the J-Block, a stake owned by U.S. oil major Chevron. But a month later, the deal was scotched by the other partners in the J-Block—British Gas, Phillips Petroleum of the United States, and Italy's Agip—who had the right to buy out Chevron's stake.

Instead, Enron agreed to buy natural gas from the J-Block under a long-term contract. The J-Block partners, led by Phillips, agreed to supply Enron with 260 million cubic feet of gas per day, which was a majority of the fields' expected output. What's more, the contract was take-or-pay, guaranteeing the J-Block partners a market for their gas but giving Enron a familiar risk. That contract would later come back to haunt Enron, but not for a few years.

Enron was not worrying about the J-Block issue in April 1993, when the Teesside cogeneration plant opened on the 23-acre site owned by ICI. The construction took 29 months for the crew of 3,000 (employed by Enron Power Construction Ltd.), at a cost of $1.2 billion. It would operate at a normal capacity of 1,725 megawatts per day, but could increase that to 1,875 at peak demand times. The connected processing plant would produce up to 7,500 barrels a day of natural gas liquids, which Enron would sell in the United Kingdom.

The Teesside plant was a showcase. At 23 acres in size, it was a fraction of the size of an analagous coal-powered plant. It also was estimated to produce half the carbon dioxide emissions that a 1,875-megawatt coal plant would. Teesside was relatively high-tech, with a computerized power station that needed only 65 people to operate.

For Enron, it was a triumph of the corporation's multitasking capabilities—a sort of hard-asset version of its Sithe gas-supply contract, in that Enron was able to pull together many facets of a complicated project. As with Sithe, the company felt it was exceptional in its ability to manage an undertaking of this scale. "We believe Enron is uniquely qualified to develop all aspects of a large integrated natural gas project such as the one at Teesside," said Lay.

■ ■ ■

Teesside was just part of a growing international business for Enron. By the time the Teesside plant flipped the "on" switch, an Enron-led consortium had also paid $561 million to own and operate a 3,800-mile gas pipeline system in southern Argentina; Enron had commissioned a $92 million, 110-megawatt power plant in Puerto Qetzal, Guatemala, which was its first power generation project in Latin America; Enron had two power plants under construction in Batangas and Subic Bay in the Philippines; and the company was trying to win approval to build a power plant in India.

Global breadth played a key role in Enron's ambition. Just as Exxon or Chevron were classified was oil majors, Ken Lay wanted to turn Enron into the world's first "gas major." Enron was already a huge pipelines operator. By 1993, it had earned additional respect for its project financing and for structuring long-term supply contracts for power plants. And now Enron was also the company that had built Teesside. Lay's profile continued to rise, and within the gas industry he was already being connected to the term "visionary." Enron was seen as big, but also daring and motivated. The company was a leader in taking advantage of deregulation, and it didn't miss the opportunity to brag about it. "Rather than resisting change, we're trying to lead it and prosper from it," said Lay. Enron's stock rose 75 percent from the start of 1991 to the start of 1993. When, in early 1993, the stock topped $50 per share, Lay handed out $50 bills to all employees.

Outside the gas industry, Lay's profile also rose. The early 1990s saw him make a splash as a contributor to various political campaigns, although with a mostly Republican bent. In July 1991, he was named to a 25-member panel set up to advise President George H. W. Bush on how to balance environmental protection with business needs—a panel, it must be said, that was mostly packed with industry executives. And in August 1992, the Republican Party was holding its national convention in Houston, where President Bush would be nominated for reelection; Lay served as the chairman of the Houston host committee for the convention. Enron also donated $250,000 toward the convention's costs.

With 50,000 convention-related visitors, the convention (like the Democratic Party's convention) proved to be a big tourist event that poured tens of millions of dollars into the local economy.

Lay worked the corridors of power, whether they were in Washington, D.C., in foreign capitals, or in other CEOs' offices. In early 1993, not long after Bush left office, Enron hired former Secretary of State James Baker and former Secretary of Commerce Robert Mosbacher, both Bush cabinet veterans, as consultants. The two put their impressive contacts to work, visiting foreign nations on behalf of Enron's ambition to develop more overseas energy projects. Baker and Mosbacher, Lay said, "will greatly enhance Enron's goal of becoming the world's first natural gas major."

A few months later, Enron named Wendy Gramm as the newest member of its board of directors. This was interesting because Gramm not only was the wife of GOP heavyweight Senator Phil Gramm (R-Texas), but she also until recently had been chairman of the Commodity Futures Trading Commission (CFTC), the leading federal regulator of energy commodities. Gramm believed in free markets, and under her leadership the CFTC decided not to regulate the over-the-counter energy derivatives contracts that had become such a big part of Enron's business. Not surprisingly, Enron had lobbied hard for that decision, because having the CFTC oversee its energy derivatives would have slowed down the company enormously. So in a few months Gramm had gone from overseeing Enron to being an Enron director, a part-time position that paid $22,000 per year. Following the hiring of Baker and Mosbacher as consultants, this kind of move fed Enron's reputation for being extremely well connected.

Enron's big picture and myriad associations were shaped by Lay, as Richard Kinder oversaw day-to-day operations. Lay was frequently a hands-off manager. John Sherriff remembered him as a "relationship guy," who focused on the big picture. "You could always count on Ken if you had to get in to see an executive of another company or see a regulator," he said.

While Lay cultivated his persona as Enron's most public face, new faces were rising within the hierarchy of Enron. The spotlight began to shine on the company's international division, which evolved from its power business. In the late 1980s and early 1990s, the leader of Enron Power was John Wing, a West Point graduate who got the Teesside project off the ground. But in late 1991, Wing left Enron to cofound his own firm. Taking over for him was Rebecca Mark, a sharp executive who was something of Wing's protégé. Mark became the CEO of Enron Development Corp., a unit created to develop power projects overseas. And so Mark took her place as one of Enron's big guns.

Rebecca Mark was not a typical Enron executive, if there even was such a thing. For one thing, she was a woman, and while Enron didn't discriminate against women, it was still unusual for a woman to rise to high levels in the energy business. She grew up on a farm in Missouri, not unlike Lay, and got her master's degree from Baylor University in Texas. She eventually landed at Continental Resources, which was acquired by Houston Natural Gas in 1985. After that company evolved into Enron, Mark wound up analyzing possible power-plant deals.

Mark liked sports cars and didn't mind the long days and traveling, and she fit into the corporate culture. She also made a bold move in leaving Enron while still rising up the corporate ladder, and getting an MBA from Harvard Business School in 1990 (working part-time for Enron). She returned to Enron full-time and resumed working under Wing, and soon she was involved with the Teesside project. She was not shy about her ambition, and earned the nickname "Mark the Shark." "She was very sophisticated and likable," said Diana Peters, a former Enron employee. "She was sort of larger than life, but she wasn't arrogant."

Mark also insisted on being feminine. The mother of twin boys, she wore short skirts and high heels, and liked to flirt. As she told one magazine, "I don't mind being remembered as, 'Oh, that's that beautiful woman I talked to.' " Unfortunately for her, Enron, filled with young, energetic people, was a hotbed of sexual innuendo and rumors. Although it was never confirmed, company gossip had it that Mark and Wing were engaged in an affair, and this was later published in business magazines. Although rumors followed and she sometimes raised eyebrows, Mark was highly regarded at Enron. And it didn't hurt that, like Jeffrey Skilling, she had the sort of charm and charisma that appealed to Lay.

Under Mark, Enron Development Corp. fashioned itself as a group of capitalist cowboys who were spreading the gospel of privatization and free markets to developing nations. "We are a very eclectic bunch with some ex-military people and some ex-entrepreneurs. We are brought together with a certain amount of missionary zeal which I think you have to have in this business," Mark said. She concluded, "We like to be pioneers."

By 1993, Rebecca Mark and Jeff Skilling were rivals of a kind. Although they were colleagues, both were jockeying for Lay's approval. They also represented different sides of Enron. Skilling oversaw "asset-light" businesses, such as trading and finance. Mark's job was to literally build more hard assets that Enron would own or co-own. At this stage, while both of these competing visions were growing, the rivalry was subdued. But it would get hotter.

■ ■ ■

Mark's biggest test came in India, where Enron pursued its biggest and most controversial foreign project. India's State Electricity Boards had been losing money on their poorly managed power systems, which were also plagued by shortages, and the thinking was that one solution was to privatize the electricity sector. As a result, India was opening its electricity market to foreign investors, and Enron, in the middle of building its Teesside plant, had proposed building a large power plant in Dabhol, about 100 miles south of Bombay.

The project was conceived in 1992, and it all came together in December 1993. Enron, the U.S. conglomerate General Electric, and Bechtel Enterprises, an engineering and construction firm, signed a contract to build a power plant and sell the electricity to the Maharashtra State Electricity Board. The deal called for building a 2,015-megawatt plant, big enough to meet the electricity needs of a U.S. city of two million people. Enron, which was taking an 80 percent stake in the project, would develop and run the plant; Bechtel, taking a 10 percent stake, would design and construct the plant; and GE, taking a 10 percent stake, would provide the turbines and other equipment. Maharashtra, India's third largest state, agreed to buy all the plant's power for 20 years.

As a "combined-cycle" plant, the Dabhol facility would produce power and steam, with the steam being used to fuel other turbines to produce more power. The first phase, providing 695 megawatts of generation capacity, would run on fuel oil and would begin construction in 1994. The second phase, providing 1,320 megawatts of capacity, would run on liquefied natural gas (LNG) and would begin construction in

1995. Dabhol, costing around $2.9 billion, would be the first private power project in India—and the largest foreign investment in India, too, aimed at showing the world that the new India was ready to join the global capitalism game. In other words, Dabhol was another showcase, but this time for India as well as for Enron. In a statement, Mark said, "I look forward to rapid progress."

Rapid progress did not materialize. India's notoriously fractious politics made sure of that. Maharashtra's agreement to buy power from the Dabhol plant had been negotiated by the state's ruling party, the long-entrenched Congress Party. Two opposition parties, Shiv Sena and the Hindu nationalist Bharatiya Janata Party (BJP), immediately criticized the deal. They alleged that corruption was involved in the Congress Party's acquiescing to the deal, and they made the Dabhol project a campaign issue. Opponents attacked the large contract as providing windfall profits for Enron—a powerful argument in a poor country where, despite badly needing more power plants, the majority of the population lacked electricity. In addition, the Congress Party was accused of taking a $13 million bribe from Enron, which Enron vehemently denies. Although the allegations were never proved, it put Enron in a strange position; the company was very visible in Maharashtra, spending a lot of time educating Indian politicians about capitalism and promoting the Dabhol project.

There were other challenges. Enron began the search for financing, including looking at agencies that lent money for projects in developing nations. In 1993, the World Bank, at India's urging, looked at the proposed project. But it concluded that Dabhol "was not economically viable, and thus could not be financed by the Bank." The World Bank felt the project was too big, and the electricity generated would cost too much money. The World Bank also criticized the plan to fuel the second phase with liquefied natural gas, which, as the name implies, involves supercooling the gas to the point where it becomes liquid. Besides pipelines, LNG was the only alternative for transporting natural gas in any form. Enron was simultaneously negotiating with Qatar for an LNG project there, which could conceivably ship LNG to Dabhol. But, as the World Bank pointed out, LNG cost a lot of money.

In Maharashtra, critics abounded. Various Indian groups sued. Many questioned the fact that the various contracts called for the Dabhol

Power Co. to earn a 25.22 percent return on its investment (before U.S. taxes). Skeptics also claimed that the government had used a closed, uncompetitive process to award the contract to Enron; they protested that the Congress Party had ignored some standard environmental approvals to get the project done quickly; and they objected to a provision in the contracts that required Maharashtra to buy power from Dabhol even if it wasn't needed, and a provision requiring India's federal government to take over payments for the electricity if the Maharashtra Electricity Board defaulted.

Despite the World Bank's doubts, Enron managed to line up $643 million in project financing to build the first phase of Dabhol. U.S. Secretary of Commerce Ron Brown, accompanied by Ken Lay, visited India to oversee the signing of some loan agreements for the project. By March 1, 1995, the U.S. Export-Import Bank, which helps finance the sale of U.S. goods and services overseas, provided a $298 million loan; the Overseas Private Investment Corp., which helps finance U.S. business in less developed nations, provided a $100 million loan; a syndicate of Indian banks loaned $95 million; and Bank of America and ABN Amro together loaned $150 million. Enron also cut its stake in Dabhol to 60 percent by selling a 20 percent share to Entergy, a large U.S. utility. Workers cleared a site overlooking the Arabian Sea to make ready for construction.

Enron's international operations were on an upswing. In late 1994, the company had bundled together its gas pipelines and power plants in "developing" nations into a partnership called Enron Global Power & Pipelines (EGPP), and sold shares in the partnership (known as limited partnership units) to the public. The offering raised about $200 million for Enron, leaving the corporation with 52 percent ownership of the business. Technically, the partnership bought the foreign businesses from Enron Corp. and operated them; the partnership also had the right of first refusal to buy other projects developed by Enron. This innovative structure allowed Wall Street to precisely value Enron's ventures in developing countries, provided some tax benefits to Enron, and took some of those operations' risks off Enron's books. The EGPP partnership initially consisted of its two power plants in the Philippines, the power plant in Guatemala, and the pipeline system it managed in Argentina. By 1995, Enron added a natural gas pipeline in Colombia and half of a power plant in the Dominican Republic, and the company was developing a $150 million power plant in China.

But the good vibes didn't last long. Following 1994's signing of the international trade liberalization pact that led to the creation of the World Trade Organization, protests broke out in several Indian cities, boosting opposition to foreign corporations. Maharashtra held state elections in March 1995, and an alliance of the BJP and Shiv Sena won, based largely on an anti-Enron campaign (they promised to "throw Enron into the sea"). The new government decided to review the first phase of the project amid complaints that it planned to charge too much for the electricity—the contract called for Maharashtra to buy Dabhol's power for roughly 8 cents per kilowatt-hour, compared with the 5.6 cents the state was paying at the time from existing sources, and the Dabhol rate would gradually increase until 2016.

On May 12, a crowd of several hundred villagers protested the project at the site, which was conveniently clear; at the protest, the villagers and the Dabhol workers tossed rocks at each other. "What we are experiencing here is every investor's nightmare," said Mark, who noted that about $300 million had already been spent on phase one. Washington, D.C., warned that scrapping the deal would be a blow to future business investment in India.

But in August, Maharashtra decided to suspend phase one and cancel phase two. Given the heated rhetoric, the decision didn't shock anyone. Enron didn't stand still. It threatened to pursue its claims in court, but added, "The company remains available for discussions with the government."

Enron filed a complaint with arbitrators in London seeking as much as $300 million, and Maharashtra filed suit to void the original agreement, and the clock was ticking. Interest payments and other project delays were costing the Dabhol Power Co. some $250,000 a day. Of course, if the Maharashtra government lost the arbitration, it would be liable for those costs. Enron had built a large plastic bubble at the work site to protect the construction from monsoons, and now, in an unusually apt play of imagery, the bubble was deflated. Dabhol looked dead.

But Enron tried to resuscitate the project; as Rebecca Mark wittily explained, "Indians believe in reincarnation." U.S. Ambassador to India Frank Wisner, a strong backer of Dabhol, appealed to Indian politicians to demonstrate that the nation really wanted foreign investment. Seeing

Enron's problems, other foreign companies put their Indian projects on hold. Mark, who'd already made more than 30 trips to India while putting Dabhol together, had dinner with Bal Thackeray, the national leader of the Shiv Sena party. Enron officials including Ken Lay flew to Bombay and held talks with Maharashtra state officials, then traveled to New Delhi to talk with Indian federal politicians.

In September 1995, formal talks began to revive the project. Maharashtra created a new six-member panel to review it, and this time the panel included economics and energy experts, not just politicians. The goal was to lower the project's costs, with Teesside as a useful benchmark. The panel, after four weeks of deliberations that included meetings both with Enron and with project critics, made its recommendations on November 19.

Under the new proposal, worked out with Enron, Dabhol's total cost would come down to $2.5 billion from $2.9 billion, yet the total capacity would rise to 2,450 megawatts. Three factors enabled Enron to do this: India agreed to an accelerated construction of the second phase of the project; the latest models of power turbines were more efficient; and power-generating equipment costs had fallen in the marketplace. The original pact had made completion of phase one of the project mandatory and the larger second phase optional, but now phase two was also mandatory. The price charged for electricity from phase one would sink to roughly 6 cents per kilowatt-hour. Phase one would also be fueled by naphtha, a liquid derived from refining crude oil, rather than by fuel oil. Further cutting expenses, the facility to turn LNG back to gas, estimated to cost more than $300 million, would be treated as a separate project that would likely take on outside partners. The Maharashtra Electricity Board would buy 30 percent of the Dabhol Power Co., making it a much larger partner in the project (Enron would own 50 percent), and Enron and Dabhol Power would pay for monthly air and water surveys and take other measures to minimize environmental damage. As Mark concluded in a column she penned, "In our business, you have to be willing to adjust and be flexible."

In January 1996, the state announced it would accept a revised agreement, and the details were agreed upon the following month. But national elections in India that spring caused more delays in restarting the project. Enron finally resumed construction of Dabhol in December.

The controversy didn't end there. Many skeptics in India were still unhappy with the new agreement. The sheer size of it made it a target for charges of foreign profiteering. By one estimate, the revised deal required Maharashtra to pay a total of $30 billion over the life of the pact—by far the largest contract in India's history. Dabhol's return on investment was still much higher than the 16 percent allowed by Indian law. Also, some local inhabitants were being displaced by the project because their land was seized for building. Opposition groups filed new lawsuits.

Local organizations, made up of villagers, lawyers, and activists, emerged to oppose the project with marches and hunger strikes. Opponents held a large rally with about 3,000 protesters on January 30, 1997. But Dabhol Power Co.'s response inspired charges of human rights violations. According to human rights organizations, Dabhol Power Co. subcontracted its own security guards and gave money to Maharashtra specifically to provide heavier police protection. These forces, according to rights organizations, harassed the protesters. At the January 30 protest and in a series of instances throughout 1997, Indian police arrested protesters (some of whom were minors) and kept them in jail for periods of four or five days. There were reports that a few of the protesters were even beaten by police in the course of arrest. Amnesty International claimed the arrests were used "to suppress peaceful protests." Human Rights Watch accused Dabhol security forces of teargassing demonstrators and, in general, employing "security forces who routinely beat and harass people demonstrating peacefully against the power plant."

Enron denied any role in the arrests or beatings. But the company's image was hurt by the fact that it led a project that was linked, even indirectly, to the forceful suppression of protests. Enron was far from alone in being involved in an energy project that stirred controversy among local communities in poor countries: for example, Shell Oil faced heavy criticism for its involvement in Nigeria; and Occidental Petroleum faced criticism for its work in Colombia. Still, the storm surrounding Enron's Dabhol project carried an unpleasant taint, even when the first phase of the power plant finally went into operation in 1999. Unlike Teesside, the Indian project would not be known as Enron's "showcase" Dabhol plant, but as Enron's "controversial" Dabhol plant.

■ ■ ■

With interests in England, India, Latin America, and Asia, Enron had become the global player that Ken Lay wanted. One consequence was that Lay, despite a balding, mild appearance that suggested an accountant, turned into an international statesman for natural gas, spending one-quarter of his time traveling overseas. At one luncheon, he even expressed to Daniel Yergin, the author of the award-winning oil history, *The Prize*, his view that the oil era was giving way to the gas era. Enron (and to a lesser extent its nearest rival, British Gas) was pioneering a new model for a gas company: global empire. That was a far cry from the localized, heavily regulated industry that had characterized gas a decade earlier. Experts were predicting that the international development of gas-fired power plants would amount to $500 billion worth of projects over the following decade.

But the company's global objectives kept facing obstacles. While Enron was still wrangling with opposition to Dabhol, problems began to arise with the take-or-pay contract it had signed for natural gas from the J-Block in the North Sea. When Enron struck the deal in 1992, it had effectively made a long-term bet that the appetite for natural gas would continue growing in the United Kingdom, partly as a result of construction of more gas-fired power plants. That may well have occurred at some point in the distant future, but in the ensuing three years it looked very much like a wrong-way bet; gas supplies had grown and demand had fallen, and companies hadn't jumped into the business of building gas-fired power plants all over Britain. The contract turned out to have been negotiated when North Sea gas prices were at a high point, and by 1995 Enron's contracted prices were almost double the prevailing market rates. The deal had yet to cost Enron money, as the J-Block wasn't expected to go into production until early 1996. If the original agreement were honored, though, Enron would be locked into buying expensive gas that it couldn't possibly hope to resell at such high prices; the result could have been hundreds of millions of dollars in losses. Enron made no plans to accept any of the gas, and said it wanted to renegotiate the contract.

Phillips Petroleum delayed the start of J-Block production, as it now had lost its sole customer. Negotiations followed, but to little avail. Eventually, Phillips decided to begin producing oil from the J-Block, and to reinject any natural gas that came up back into the well; reinjecting gas was a common practice used to maintain pressure inside a well. In April 1996, Enron sued Phillips and its partners, claiming that the reinjection plan violated operational and technical specifications that could affect the quality of the gas, thus nullifying the contract. Enron also claimed that Phillips' partners hadn't completed a pipeline system to deliver the gas in time. Enron was in effect trying to void the contract on a technicality. And thus began a long legal fracas between Enron and Phillips, which was becoming a minor black eye for Enron's international operations.

Enron also unsuccessfully tried to move the venue of the litigation from London to Houston. Enron then wanted to delay delivery of the gas until October 1997. Phillips argued that the contract called for Enron to begin receiving the gas in October 1996. In October 1996, the English Court of Appeals ruled that the start date was indeed October 1997, which meant that Enron didn't have to start making payments (under the take-or-pay provision) until late 1997. This back-and-forth continued through 1996. On Wall Street, where nothing is as despised as doubt, brokerage analysts following Enron's stock began to view the J-Block as an ominous cloud hanging over the company, and therefore a drag on its stock.

In April 1997, Phillips began pumping oil from the J-Block. This also produced some gas, but that gas was reinjected into the field to boost oil production and to save the gas for Enron, which was now claiming that it wouldn't take any gas until 1999.

The J-Block had been viewed as a serious issue within Enron for some time, and was originally the responsibility of Enron's international business, which had led the Teesside development. By 1996, however, the company decided to hand it over to Skilling's division, now called Enron Capital & Trade Resources (ECT). The trading and finance group now had the mandate to resolve the J-Block issue. Calling in Skilling's people was a big blow to the internal standing of Enron's international arm, and by proxy a blow to Rebecca Mark. ECT didn't mind, because it saw itself in competition with what was then called Enron International. At stake was which division would be preeminent within Enron Corp., and therefore which strategy would dominate—asset-heavy or asset-light.

Some ECT staff moved to London to take over negotiations. But ECT dragged its feet on resolving the issue, all the while pointing out what a big mess Enron International had created. Negotiations were very complex, involving many companies. But in June 1997, the two sides finally came to an agreement. Enron made a one-time cash payment of $440 million to Phillips and its partners, which resulted in a $675 million pre-tax expense for Enron and a reported loss in its second-quarter results. Enron also agreed to accept delivery of the gas at a new, lower price that wasn't disclosed. "Enron is pleased to remove this item of uncertainty for our company and our shareholders," Lay said in a statement.

The issue may have been resolved, but the J-Block problem and the Dabhol controversy had reflected poorly on Enron International. Every stumble by Enron International made it look a little worse, and, in contrast, made Skilling's ECT look a little better. ECT also had the advantage of being able to book its trades and long-term deals right away. Enron International often took years to negotiate a big project, and even then it could fall through. For example, Enron signed a letter of intent with Qatar in January 1995 to build a $4 billion plant for making LNG from gas in a humongous field in the Persian Gulf; it seemed a coup for the era of gas, because big LNG projects had previously been handled by major oil companies. But in 1999 Enron and Qatar dropped the project, without ever advancing beyond the letter of intent.

When Dabhol was renegotiated in 1996, Rebecca Mark was still a powerful figure within Enron. But Mark (perhaps unfairly) had become the personification of the asset-heavy philosophy, juxtaposed against Skilling's asset-light philosophy. In a way, the two divisions were competing for the soul of Enron. Enron International was rapidly expanding its footprint. Meanwhile, Skilling's group was gaining on Mark's. In 1995, ECT generated earnings before interest, taxes, and one-time charges of $232.5 million, while Enron International generated earnings before interest and taxes of $142 million. At one time, Mark and Skilling were running neck-and-neck for Lay's approval. But Skilling was about to leap ahead, as the trading operation readied for a huge expansion in the mid-1990s with a plan that would elevate Enron's aspirations to a whole new level.

4

ELECTRIFYING OPPORTUNITY

While Enron busily planted its flag in various foreign locales, the company continued to grow in North America and as a whole. In 1993, the company reported net income of $386.5 million, excluding a one-time charge related to taxes, which was up 26 percent from 1992's earnings. Revenue for 1993 totaled $10.1 billion.

Earnings before interest and taxes rose 37 percent to $167.4 million at Enron Gas Services, the division housing its trading and finance operations. Long-term contracts such as those supplying gas to power plants, and structured finance arrangements such as Volumetric Production Payments, drove this earnings growth. On average, Enron traded the equivalent of 11.4 billion cubic feet of gas per day in 1993, a figure 75 percent higher than its average trading volume the year before.

At the end of 1993, Enron's debt situation also looked better. The company's debt-to-total capitalization ratio, which had been 75.6 percent at the end of 1987, stood at 46.7 percent on December 31, 1993. As it had in years past, Enron continued to keep close watch of its "balance sheet," the financial report listing its assets and liabilities. Wall Street liked to see what it called a "strong" or "healthy" balance sheet, which meant that debt didn't threaten to overwhelm assets.

Enron's stock was also doing well. As a result of all this accomplishment, Enron started to grab headlines outside of the energy industry. Flattering profiles appeared *The Economist*, *Business Week*, and other publications. In 1995, Enron Europe established a trading center in London, marking the company's entry into European wholesale markets. As a spokesman for natural gas, Ken Lay speechified on the benefits of "open access," the deregulation that turned pipelines into neutral transporters of gas and allowed gas users to buy their gas from anyone in a competitive market. According to Lay, the first decade of competition and open access resulted in a 20 percent increase in gas usage and a one-third drop in gas prices adjusted for inflation.

This success wasn't lost on the rest of the business world. Competitors followed Enron's lead into gas trading and finance. Some of these rivals were gas pipeline companies such as Williams Cos. and Coastal Corp., and some were gas producers, such as Atlantic Richfield Co. and Mobil Corp. A few were financial firms, such as Bankers Trust, Morgan Stanley, and insurance giant AIG. Natural Gas Clearinghouse, which Transco had helped form during Lay's tenure to create spot markets for natural gas, had become an independent gas-marketing company and competitor to Enron. Gas trading grew so quickly that spot trades evolved from a hub for monthly contracts to one for daily contracts.

Many within Enron argued that it had an edge over the banking and trading firms such as Bankers Trust, because Enron also had a physical presence in the gas business. With pipelines, gas storage facilities, and gas-processing plants, Enron felt it had a better feel for supply and demand, and for the differences in markets between regions. Even if this wasn't entirely true, it did give Enron more confidence to become larger, as it had physical supplies to back up its trading operation. And customers on the physical side—those actually delivering or receiving gas—also provided more business on the purely financial side.

In essence, it exemplified Enron's philosophy at the time, of leveraging physical assets like pipelines to build up a complementary financial business. This proved one way to reconcile Skilling's vision of an asset-light company built on trading and finance with the traditional model of building up assets such as pipelines and power plants. On the traditional side of the ledger, Enron had been taking interests in independent power plants in the United States. Well before Teesside began operating, Enron already controlled and operated a 450-megawatt power plant and a 340-megawatt plant in the Houston area, and had acquired 90.5 percent of a 237-megawatt power plant in Richmond,

Virginia. It also built a 149-megawatt independent power plant at Milford, Massachusetts. Gas-fired power plants were a natural extension of Enron's business of supplying gas for power generation, just as long-term gas contracts were a natural extension of the company's business of transporting and selling gas.

Enron wasn't the only company interested in independent power plants. The 1978 federal legislation that gave rise to such projects as the big Sithe plant in New York was proving that it was possible for power plants to be built and operated by companies other than utilities. In addition, gas-fired plants emitted less pollution than those burning coal or oil, and this became a more important feature after 1990's Clean Air Act tightened regulations on industrial pollution. By the end of 1992, independent producers accounted for at least 5 percent of the nation's electric-generation capacity, or about 39,000 megawatts. Besides Enron, the big players in this industry included the utilities Southern California Edison and Virginia's Dominion Resources, and the chemical manufacturing giant Dow Chemical.

The Federal Energy Regulatory Commission (FERC) in Washington, D.C., played a role in overseeing the growth of independent power plants, but the retail side of the electricity industry, delivering power to homes and businesses, was (and still is) regulated by 50 separate state agencies. Like the gas industry, power was dominated by local electric utilities that were privately owned geographic monopolies. But unlike the gas industry, where most natural gas production was produced in a few regions and then piped all over the country, electricity was generated in every state, almost entirely by utilities' own power plants. The utilities were closely regulated by state agencies, which determined what sort of returns these companies were allowed to earn. In the nation's capital, lawmakers and President Bush's policy advisers decided to introduce more competition into the business.

In October 1992, as the presidential campaign wound down, Bush signed into law the Energy Policy Act, an attempt at a comprehensive energy strategy for the nation. The legislation addressed not only electricity, but also oil, nuclear waste, energy conservation, alternative fuels, and other issues. Two facets of the law were supremely important to the power industry. First, it completely opened up wholesale electricity production by creating a new class of independent power generators known as "exempt wholesale" generators. Unlike the first generation of independent power producers, this new class had no guaranteed market of utilities required to buy electricity at "avoided cost" prices—but the new power producers were free to sell energy to anyone.

Second, the law required that utilities open up their power transmission systems and give equal access to any electricity producer or merchant, the same way pipelines had to be neutral transporters of gas. This meant that a power plant in Connecticut wanting to sell electricity to a utility in New Jersey had the right to send its power (known in the industry as "wheeling" its power) over the high-voltage lines of the New York utilities in between. Those New York utilities could charge a small fee, or toll, for the service, of course. A new class of power plants with access to transmission lines promised a new era of competition in power generation.

These two provisions started to set up the power industry more along the lines of the natural gas business. But the gas business already had a vibrant wholesale market for gas, with prices readily available on NYMEX or at other sources. Wholesale electricity trading had been mostly limited to the occasional sale of power from one utility to an adjacent utility during unusual shortages. The new law ordered FERC to begin developing a true wholesale market for power. However, the law specifically forbade FERC from demanding competition on the retail side, which would theoretically have allowed residents to buy electricity from a number of providers the way they chose long-distance phone service. Retail competition was left to the individual states. But even without a retail component, wholesale power seemed promising enough. Enron estimated the wholesale electricity market at some $90 billion a year, or roughly three times the size of the wholesale gas market.

A rough form of electronic trading of power emerged quickly. In 1992, the Western Systems Power Pool in the western United States allowed member utilities to electronically post daily bids to buy electricity and offers to sell electricity on the Telerate system, a computer network best known for distributing bond prices. This was more of an experiment, and would eventually evolve into a more sophisticated trading system. But the groundwork was gradually being laid for a competitive wholesale market in power. Electricity was becoming a much more interesting industry.

■ ■ ■

As the gas trading operation grew, Enron began its first extensive use of Special Purpose Entities. An SPE is simply a trust created by a company to hold some of the company's assets; typically, the SPE would then either borrow against those assets or conduct more complex financing arrangements backed by those assets. Because the SPE contains some assets but none of the company's existing debt, it's a less risky borrower and can therefore borrow money at lower rates. In general an SPE is a legitimate way of segregating a special risk from a company's core operations and help it pay less to borrow money.

Enron had begun dabbling in SPEs as far back as 1991, when it created its first Volumetric Production Payments to loan money to oil and gas production companies, asking to be repaid in oil and gas. While the VPP could be considered a kind of special purpose entity, Enron took the idea a step further. The reason? The VPP strategy created a major difficulty in the lag time between lending the money to produce gas and then getting the money from selling the gas that was later produced. Enron wasn't in a financial position to just hand out tens of millions of dollars to oil and gas producers and then wait a couple of years for the gas sales. So the company set about to create financing vehicles to raise the money for the VPPs. These vehicles, which were perfectly legal, laid the groundwork for the more complicated entities Enron created in the late 1990s that eventually led the company's demise.

Enron pooled the VPP contracts in limited partnerships that Enron named the Cactus Funds; this pool produced a stream of gas supplies that could be sold at spot prices. Enron then used natural-gas swaps to stabilize the prices Cactus could get for the gas, lowering the risk. With this, a Cactus Fund produced a known series of cash payments almost like a bond. Enron could then divvy up the Cactus payments as securities and sell them to banks the way an investment firm might sell a corporate bond to big investors. Selling a kind of massaged pool of VPP contracts this way raised the cash Enron needed to make the VPP loans. Enron didn't hide its use of the Cactus Funds, instead pointing to them as creative solutions to the problem of raising funds inexpensively. By mid-1993, Enron had used Cactus partnerships to raise some $900 million.

Enron's first Cactus partnership was formed in 1991, raising $340

million from a group of 15 banks to support VPP contracts. The key to
the Cactus deals is a process called "securitization." A security is essentially anything representing ownership or debt that can be traded, such as
a stock or bond—which is why the U.S. agency overseeing stocks is
called the Securities and Exchange Commission. Securitization takes a
cluster of assets and turns them into tradable securities that are backed by
assets that, directly or indirectly, represent future streams of income. For
instance, a large number of home mortgages can be bundled together
and a bunch of securities issued against that mortgage pool, known as
mortgage-backed securities; these securities are backed by the mortgage
payments that will be coming in. In Enron's case, the VPP-backed securities were based on the value of the future oil and gas production Enron
would get from the VPPs.

That signature Cactus partnership created two classes of investments. The Class A securities were bought by an SPE using money borrowed from the banks. The securities paid interest (based on the
hedged income from oil and gas production) to the SPE that was used
to repay the banks. That way, the banks didn't directly own pieces of
the Cactus partnership. The Class B securities were sold to General
Electric Credit. An overt goal of the Cactus partnerships was to enhance Enron's credit by moving these financing deals off its balance
sheet. The intricate structure was fashioned by Enron with the help of
its longtime accounting firm, Arthur Andersen. In Cactus, Enron had
also created a vehicle with which the company could do more business.
For instance, in 1992 Enron Oil & Gas sold an interest in 124 billion
cubic feet worth of gas and other fuels to Cactus for $327 million; this
guaranteed production sales for four years from some Enron properties
in Wyoming.

The Cactus transactions were a legal and innovative way to transfer
the risks and the debt associated with the VPP contracts off Enron's corporate balance sheet. True, the Cactus Funds moved some profits off
Enron's books, too—but the company was willing to record just a portion of the profits in its financials if that income came without adding to
the company's debt. And the financial wiz behind the Cactus vehicles
was a young employee who joined Enron in 1991 from the Continental
Bank in Chicago named Andrew S. Fastow. Clever and ambitious, but
with a reputation for being temperamental, Fastow devoted much en-

ergy to financing strategies, as he had his eye on becoming chief financial officer one day.

In addition to Cactus, Enron had a partnership known as Joint Energy Development Investors, or JEDI, purposely named after the characters in the *Star Wars* movies. It was a 50–50 partnership between Enron and the public pension system of California, known as CalPERS, or the California Public Employees' Retirement System. Starting in 1993, Enron and CalPERS each committed $250 million over three years (CalPERS in cash, Enron in stock) to JEDI to invest in natural gas projects; also, one-half of the money was designated to buy Enron stock. JEDI was believed to be the first partnership of its kind, in that a pension fund initiated and helped structure it. CalPERS, the nation's largest pension fund, had a tradition of innovative and proactive investing.

One of JEDI's ambitious early campaigns ended in failure: an attempt to buy an Australian oil and gas production company called Bridge Oil. JEDI bid against Texas energy company Parker & Parsley Petroleum for Bridge, and the two companies battled for a while. But the rival obtained a court order blocking the JEDI offer, and finally JEDI dropped out in mid-1994, allowing Parker & Parsley to buy the company for $278 million.

But JEDI pursued other deals with success. Among them: It loaned $62 million to Forest Oil, the company that negotiated the first VPP with Enron, and later restructured the loan to include an investment in Forest Oil; it loaned $60 million to Flores & Rucks, an oil and gas production company that borrowed heavily to buy production properties and was also a VPP customer of Enron; in 1995, JEDI acquired Coda Energy, a Dallas-based oil and gas production company, for $161 million; and in 1996, JEDI spent over $37 million buying Clinton Gas Systems, an Ohio oil and gas producer.

The acquisition of Coda Energy was particularly instructive. Enron identified Coda as an intriguing opportunity; the company specialized in buying proven oil and gas properties in Texas, Oklahoma, and Kansas, and maximizing production out of them by flushing wells with water and other means. JEDI acquired Coda's stock for $161.3 million, repaid Coda's existing $93.5 million of bank loans, and paid $6 million in various transaction fees, which included a $4.4 million fee to an Enron division for structuring the deal. JEDI financed all this with a combination of stock, 10-year notes (which are short-term versions of bonds), bank loans, and a VPP. Buying Coda created numerous business opportunities for Enron, from transporting and selling its oil and gas to hedging prices for its production to providing hedges for interest on the debt. The VPP, possible because Coda's assets were known to produce oil and gas, provided cash for near-term costs. And Enron kept Coda's management in place by allowing it to buy 5 percent of the company and by allowing it to earn additional stock if the rates of return on the original investment met certain benchmarks. According to Enron, it was a very successful investment: The value of the Coda properties grew by 36.4 percent per year over the next three years.

The use of the Cactus and JEDI partnerships merely extended Enron's history of innovative financial practices. Enron was blazing new financial trails as early as 1989, when it became the first company to issue a new kind of debt known as "credit sensitive notes." Enron's unique notes paid interest rates that varied based on Enron's credit rating. Enron's credit rating, as determined by rating agencies Moody's and Standard & Poor's, had already displayed the ability to move up and down quickly—as illustrated by the 1987 downgrade to junk status and then the rebound to investment grade level described in Chapter 1.

In June 1989, Enron issued $100 million worth of 12-year notes paying 9.5 percent interest. At the time, Moody's rated Enron's debt at Baa3, which meant it was a medium-grade investment, in between blue-chip and junk. But according to this new credit-sensitive offering, if Moody's raised Enron's rating to Aaa, the notes' interest rate would drop to 9.2 percent. Conversely, if Moody's lowered Enron's rating to Ba1, the interest rate would jump to 12 percent. This rewarded investors for taking the risk of investing in Enron's medium-grade notes. Enron's innovation was successful enough that within a year of its first credit-sensitive note offering, five other companies offered credit-sensitive notes, including computer company Unisys and paper giant Georgia Pacific. Enron's credit-sensitive notes were early stabs at innovation that the company would build on throughout the 1990s.

■ ■ ■

Natural gas trading was obviously a success, and Enron was looking for another energy commodity to which it could apply the same system. Although Enron traded crude oil, that commodity didn't fit the bill the way gas did. For one thing, Enron was not one of the first companies to move into the oil market, so it had no "early-mover" advantage. Also, John Sherriff recalled, "The market was incredibly liquid before we got into it. Oil companies were dominant." This meant that one of Enron's key innovations in gas—becoming a market maker by providing liquidity, and thus garnering an informational edge on rivals—didn't work in oil.

But electricity was another matter. The FERC was trying to foster a wholesale market in power, and this new business seemed a ripe opportunity for Enron. The company studied the issue, and at the very end of 1993 it obtained from FERC one of the early "power marketer" licenses the agency was giving out. The company set up a separate team of power traders, and in June 1994 Enron North America traded its first electron.

Enron wasn't the very first company to trade electricity, but the company recognized that it could serve as a middleman in this business. It already knew a lot about power, both from supplying power plants with gas and from operating a few of its own plants. Also, its natural gas experience gave it an edge, because unlike other commodities, both gas and electricity trading involve basis risk, or the fluctuating difference between energy prices in different parts of the country due to weather and supply patterns. That's an added risk not present in trading gold or yen, for example.

By October 1994, Enron was, on an average day, selling nearly 500 megawatts of electricity per hour. Again, others jumped into the business. The 1992 energy law allowed utilities more freedom to set up subsidiaries for engaging in unregulated businesses, and so many utilities formed power-marketing units. And among the early entrants were power plant developer AES, Natural Gas Clearinghouse, and Morgan Stanley.

Electricity wasn't just a larger wholesale market than gas. It was potentially more lucrative because it was more volatile. Thanks to fluctuating demand and a greater difficulty in transporting power, electricity prices were roughly twice as volatile as gas prices—and gas prices could swing by 40 percent in a year. The key to Enron's trading was volatility. The more volatile the energy prices, the more opportunities for Enron to make money. The company made money two ways—similar to Wall Street firms—in trading: by collecting a tiny cut of thousands of individual trades between buyers and sellers other than Enron, and by taking the other sides of trades—in other words, selling energy that someone else is buying, and vice versa. Either way involves arbitrage, which is profiting from pricing disparities in different markets. If the wholesale energy market were a casino, Enron would be the house.

Another reason that electricity prices were (and are) more volatile than gas prices is that there is no way to store electricity. Once generated, the power has to be sent somewhere. Natural gas, however, can be stored underground, which means that extra gas can be used to cover contract needs and some excess gas can be put away if not sold. While a lot of gas is stored in salt caverns and in aquifers (water-bearing rock formations), the most prevalent storage facilities are, ironically, depleted oil and gas fields. Storage facilities in the United States can hold more than 3 trillion cubic feet of gas, or enough gas to supply the country for at least 40 winter days.

Gas traders can take storage into account, as well. Let's say a trader finds nearby storage that will cost 40 cents per thousand cubic feet to store gas from May to October. And suppose October gas futures are selling for $2.50 per thousand cubic feet, while May futures are selling for $2. The trader can buy May futures and sell October futures for a 50-cent difference, then subtract the 40-cent cost of storing the gas from May to October, leaving a profit of 10 cents per thousand cubic feet.

All this meant that power trading (a.k.a. electricity trading) was more complicated than gas trading. It involved bigger risks and more factors to calculate. But Enron went for it, and soon climbed to the top of the power marketing heap. By early 1995, Enron was boasting in typical fashion that it could grab 20 percent of the wholesale power market. In 1995, Enron sold 7.8 million megawatt-hours of electricity—about the amount of electricity used in a city the size of Portland, Oregon, for one year. By comparison, the number-two electricity marketer in the United States in 1995 was Louis Dreyfus Electric Power, which sold 4.3 million megawatt-hours.

Enron's methods required knowledge and size. Trades in this market couldn't be made without an intimate knowledge of the various energy markets in the United States, which can be quite localized. For example, cheap electricity can be purchased in Oregon to sell at a high price in Northern California. And, as for size, Enron was large enough to be able to funnel electricity all around the country, or at least negotiate with other energy traders to do so. This demanded an ability Enron had in spades to navigate various electrical grids, regional power markets, and the orders being handled by other traders. As it had done in gas, Enron locked up some guaranteed electricity supplies that it could later resell; for example, at the start of 1996 the company signed a deal with Oglethorpe Power Corp., an electricity cooperative in Georgia, to both supply it with energy and buy some of the cheap power it produced for later resale; while strategically sound, Enron later lost millions on this deal.

Experience also counted. Enron and other companies with trading expertise leapfrogged electric utilities in the new wholesale power markets because utilities were struggling with a new set of skills. Some utilities tried to fashion traders out of employees who had been doing other things, such as scheduling power delivery. One veteran energy trader recalled the time he watched a utility's power trader get phone call after phone call asking for price quotes on electricity, only to see the trader continue quoting the same price (which modestly covered the costs) to every interested buyer instead of raising the price based on the obvious demand. Utility companies, which were conservative and didn't pay big bonuses to employees, didn't have staffs of traders they could unleash on wholesale electricity.

"When electricity trading started, utilities that got into it were novices," explained Shannon Burchett, who headed up trading at Duke–Louis Dreyfus at the time. "Utilities were used to a cost-based, regulated system. They had to enter a market-based system looking for profits." Those with gas-trading experience already had both the trading mentality and the mathematical skills that could be transferred to electricity, he said. A learning curve did exist, but that involved learning the physical side of electricity, such as the cost of generating power, the location of major trading hubs, how quickly different power plants could be switched on, and where transmission bottlenecks were likely to occur.

In 1995, the Enron Capital & Trade division generated $232 million of income before interest and taxes, excluding a one-time charge, which was up from $202 million in 1994. With the addition of electricity trading, Enron's vision also changed. Whereas it had once wanted to be the first natural-gas major in the world, it now wanted to be the leading energy company in the world. Enron wanted corporate customers to be able to come to it to buy both gas and electricity, and to trade or hedge prices on either commodity. Enron's bigger rivals pursued similar ambitions, as Natural Gas Clearinghouse changed its name to NGC so it would no longer be associated with just natural gas.

Enron also began arguing for competition on the retail side of electricity. What the company really wanted was to be able to market power directly to homeowners and businesses. It leaned on the analogy to long-distance phone service, picturing a near future where Enron employees would call someone at home and ask if the customer would like to switch electricity supply from Consolidated Edison to Enron. "The retail side will be telemarketing," Jeffrey Skilling told a newspaper. "It will be 800 numbers and sophisticated billing and huge paper-processing and metering capabilities." By the time Skilling made this prediction, Enron employed 200 power marketers in two trading rooms in Houston.

So Ken Lay was soon giving speeches about the benefits of deregulating the retail power market. He audaciously testified to Congress that retail competition in electricity would save homes and businesses a total of $60 billion to $80 billion (an estimate that was unrealistically gigantic), which would be "equivalent to one of the largest tax cuts in U.S. history." Large industrial consumers of electricity were also lobbying for deregulation, hoping that competition among power suppliers would lead to lower costs.

Lay's vision had some resonance. The political environment favored deregulation. Although the Republican administrations of Reagan and Bush had given way to the Democratic White House of Bill Clinton in 1993, Clinton favored a light touch when it came to business regulation. After all, this was the Democrat who declared, "The era of big government is over." He paid attention to the bond markets, and he took advice from Wall Street veterans. Stricter monitoring of the financial markets was not a priority, and in many ways Clinton took an approach of benign neglect to the energy industry.

But Congress left electricity deregulation as it was—in other words, there was no retail deregulation at the federal level. Deregulation would have to occur on a state-by-state basis.

■ ■ ■

Enron was so committed to the vision of gas and electricity under one roof that it decided to take its biggest gamble. On July 22, 1996, the Houston company announced that it had agreed to purchase its own electric utility, Portland General, for $2.1 billion and the assumption of $1.1 billion of the utility's debt. It was an unprecedented deal, in that never before had a gas pipeline company acquired an electric utility. Portland General, based in Portland, Oregon, was a utility known for being efficiently run and providing relatively low-cost power to about 650,000 customers; in 1995, the utility had earned a profit of $131 million on $984 million in revenue. Portland General's 2,600 employees would join Enron Corp.'s 7,000, and the combined company would rank as the seventh-largest seller of electricity in the United States, ahead of such utilities as Houston Lighting & Power and Southern California Edison.

The companies' boards of directors approved the proposed deal, but it still needed the approval of shareholders and of various federal and state regulators, so it would be months before the merger could actually be completed. The deal was expected to be a tax-free exchange of one share of Enron stock for each share of Portland General stock. Enron expected the deal to begin adding to its profits in the first year after the merger was completed. Ken Harrison, the chairman and CEO of Portland General, would remain in charge of the utility and also would become a vice chairman of Enron. The low-key Harrison seemed like a good fit for Enron, with a belief in deregulation that meshed with Ken Lay.

In one stroke, Enron announced that its vision of gas and electricity under one roof was more than just talk. Suddenly, Enron was poised to combine its gas, trading and risk management, and logistics expertise with Portland General's expertise in operating power generation, transmission, and distribution. Enron also claimed it would build on Portland General's experience in automated metering, billing, and other customer-service activities as it tried to expand in the retail power market, which it estimated to be worth $200 billion a year. "Every CEO, as well as customers and regulators, will start thinking about their strategy a little differently," Lay said.

Wall Street was impressed. While there were local utilities that provided both gas and electricity to their customers, the Enron–Portland General merger seemed to herald an imminent convergence of gas and electricity. "I think that we are going to see the conversion of the two industries into one quite rapidly," PaineWebber Inc. analyst Ronald Barone said the day of the merger.

Enron was an intriguing choice for Portland General. The utility had negotiated with PacifiCorp, a larger electric utility in Oregon that surrounded it, but those talks fell apart due to clashes of the respective managers' personalities. For Enron, Portland General provided a perfect opportunity to deepen its knowledge of the electricity industry it wanted to dominate. It fit well with Enron's power trading and selling business, as Portland General bought a lot of its electricity from the nascent wholesale market. Also, the New York Mercantile Exchange had introduced its first two electricity futures contracts that April, and one of the contracts was based on delivery at the California/Oregon border; Portland General gave Enron a huge asset with delivery capability right near this key trading point. Portland General's proximity to California gave Enron another geographical advantage by providing a cheap source of electricity with which to sell power to Californians; the previous December, California became the first state to pass legislation to deregulate its electric industry, and Enron wanted to become a competitive power supplier in the nation's most populous state.

And there was another potential rationale for Enron to do the deal. The company had been lobbying for electricity deregulation, a vision in which utilities would be split up into three businesses: power plants generating electricity; distribution wires that provided electricity directly to homes and businesses; and transmission lines sending power over long distances, sort of like highways that led to the local streets of distribution wires. Here was a chance for Enron to acquire a utility and split it up along those three lines. It could be an example for how the larger industry should restructure.

The Enron–Portland General merger occurred in an era of consolidation in the electric and gas industries. Chevron agreed to acquire a 25 percent stake in NGC, shuffling that company's ownership so that British Gas and Canadian gas company Nova Corp. would also each own 25 percent stakes. El Paso Energy agreed to acquire Tenneco. Dallas-based Texas Utilities Co., one of the largest U.S. electric utilities, agreed to buy Enserch Corp., Texas' largest gas utility.

And the merger bandwagon rolled on after Enron unveiled its deal. In

August, electric utility Houston Industries agreed to buy gas utility Nor-Am Energy Services for $3.8 billion. In the biggest of the post-Enron deals, electric utility Duke Power agreed in November to acquire gas pipeline company PanEnergy for $7.4 billion; the new company, Duke Energy, eventually was able to transport gas through its pipelines to fuel gas-fired power plants around the nation.

Meanwhile, Enron pressed onward with its Portland General purchase. In September, the company filed with the Oregon Public Utilities Commission (OPUC) for approval of the merger, then filed with the FERC for merger approval. Some utilities on the West Coast, however, started to voice concerns about the merger giving the new Enron so much market power. Northwest Natural Gas, PacifiCorp, Southern California Edison, and others wanted regulators to be sure that competition would be fair, and some critics called for Portland General to quickly open its territory to competition from other power providers.

Southern California Edison, for example, told regulators it was concerned that Enron would split Portland General into its underlying components of generation, transmission, and distribution, then use those parts to boost its core businesses. Some experts believed that if a local distribution-only utility sold off its power plants, it could then buy its electricity from the wholesale market for less money. Enron replied that it had no immediate plans to sell any of Portland General's assets, but couldn't guarantee that it would never do so.

In November, shareholders of the two companies approved the merger in a vote: 75 percent of Enron shares and 77 percent of Portland General shares were voted in favor. A few days later, Portland General reached agreement with the Oregon Public Utilities Commission on a 7 percent rate cut for 1997, which would lower the average residential electric bill by $4.50 per month; the utility said the cut was made possible in part by the merger with Enron.

Enron and Portland General did agree later in the month that within 60 days of the close of the merger they would send a plan to Oregon regulators for the opening of Portland General's service territory to competition. Such a plan would separate Portland General's power plants from its transmission and distribution system, and would allow customers to choose their energy provider; that energy would then be transmitted over the neutral distribution system.

Enron, always attentive to politicking, lobbied Oregon groups to support the merger. It succeeded in winning the backing of the Seattle-based Northwest Conservation Act Coalition, an alliance of 80 different groups. But local opposition held firm. Eight organizations, including the Industrial Customers of Northwest Utilities, filed their objections with state regulators in December. They argued that state law required a utility merger be in the "public interest," and the Enron–Portland General deal hadn't demonstrated any positive public benefits. Enron countered that the law required that the merger simply do no harm, and that in the long run the merger would prove beneficial. It became clear that this was a contentious issue, and it would drag on well into 1997.

■ ■ ■

Although the proposed acquisition of Portland General was a nod toward acquiring hard assets, it was hardly a repudiation of Skilling's vision. The merger was being pursued precisely because the utility would enhance Enron's trading and finance capabilities. Portland General would also boost the amount of electricity that Skilling's people could access for trading purposes, and thus indirectly boost Skilling's Enron Capital & Trade Resources division.

If Enron were assembling a passel of gas and electric assets in the United States, Skilling's trading and finance division would clearly be called upon to tie it together in a coherent strategy. That operation, known as ECT, was becoming the biggest single force inside Enron. And ECT wasn't just about trading. The division was also increasingly an all-around energy finance business, and sometimes acted as a bank. One example of this occurred in January 1996, when ECT invested in Hanover Compressor, a private company that rented natural gas compressors, which move gas from the well through the processing plants and to the interstate pipelines.

The gas compressor industry was consolidating. But that process was slowed by the reluctance of traditional banks to lend money for expansion, fearing a downturn in the up-and-down industry. So Enron stepped in with financing, just as it did in the late 1980s and early 1990s with its willingness to lend to gas production companies when banks wouldn't.

Enron bought $20 million of common stock in Hanover, bought $10 million of preferred stock (which gets preferential treatment over common stock in case of a bankruptcy), and agreed to provide a $100 million line of credit to Hanover. Enron also took a $450,000 fee from Hanover for arranging the entire deal.

Enron felt Hanover was a good bet because of its track record: Its revenue had grown from $33 million in 1992 to $100 million in 1995. Also, Enron had its own fleet of gas compressors, but Hanover's were smaller than Enron's and so served a different segment of the industry. Beyond Hanover's innate business prospects, one key to the deal was synergy. Enron could refer some of its pipeline clients to Hanover for compression business, and Hanover could refer some of its compressor clients to Enron for gas sales and trading business.

What happened? Hanover Compressor went public in 1997. Over time, Enron earned a return of close to 20 percent on its $30 million investment in Hanover. The Hanover deal was just one more example of how ECT was growing: in scope, with its ability to make merchant investments and loans; and in size, able to afford betting $30 million on an outside company. Although Enron's gas pipeline network was still its single biggest business, ECT was consistently growing faster and was the second-biggest business at the corporation. In 1996, ECT generated income before interest and taxes of $280 million, which amounted to 22.6 percent of the total for the company—up from 13.5 percent of the company's income in 1995.

Indeed, ECT was on its way to becoming the largest unit of Enron by 1998. Skilling's division, more than any other, led to Enron being named the "most admired company in America" in a 1996 poll by *Fortune* magazine.

Skilling, meanwhile, increasingly became the public face of Enron's conquest of energy markets. At a 1995 oil and gas symposium sponsored by accounting firm Arthur Andersen, Skilling gave the crowd of energy executives the Enron spiel on how the industry was changing. "I don't know who is going to win," he said. "They'll have to be very fast-moving; this market is moving at just unbelievable breakneck speed. . . . They are going to have to be creative; we don't know what the products and services are going to look like five to 10 years from now, so you will have to have people creatively designing those. I think their competitive advantage won't be based on assets any longer. It won't be based on pipes and wires and generating facilities; it will be based on intellectual capital."

Not by coincidence, Skilling outlined a vision of the industry that echoed the traits of the division he'd built up. ECT's success gradually proved to Ken Lay that his protégé's strategy was the right way to address the energy business. Skilling's importance within Enron continued to expand, and it would soon grow further.

5

CULTURE OF CREATIVITY?

In a football-field-sized office in Houston, dozens of men and women vigorously worked their computers and phones. A few miles away, one could see the extensive railroad yards and oil derricks that made Houston a center of the industrial economy. But this office's products were information and money, giving it a look like a brokerage office or computer services firm. Yelling and gesturing with the cockiness most associated with traders of stocks and bonds, the employees were constantly working computers and phones. Television sets blared out weather news and forecasts. The office, of course, was one of the trading floors at Enron.

Although Jeff Skilling didn't single-handedly create it, that Wall Street–type scene was unthinkable at Enron (or any pipeline company) before Skilling came to Enron. He had a large impact on Enron's business strategy, but his impact on the corporate culture was also significant. Throughout the 1990s, the company increasingly developed a name as a center for smart, ambitious, young professionals. The gleaming, 50-story office tower in downtown Houston buzzed with activity from early in the morning until late at night. It was more than just an office. It was *the* place to be. For those interested in the latest trends in the energy business—or in business, period—Enron was the place either to learn the ropes or to land when a worker was ready to step up.

The company deserved some of its luster, because with its Gas Bank, its Volumetric Production Payments, and its product lines such as "EnFolio GasCap" (a gas supply contract that capped the maximum gas price), the company had figured out how to add value to basic energy commodities. As Skilling said in early 1996, "Selling natural gas is getting to be a real business, like selling washing machines. We're taking the simplest commodity there is, a methane molecule, and we're packaging and delivering it under a brand name, the way General Electric does."

This approach worked very well in transforming the pipeline operator. Enron's return on equity, a measure of performance calculated by dividing shareholder equity into net income, surged from 6 percent in 1985 to nearly 17 percent in 1995. For a company whose purported function was to move gas along its pipelines, Enron added a heck of a lot of other businesses, from sales of gas to trading, finance, and development of overseas projects. The basic business of gas transportation accounted for 51 percent of Enron's revenue in 1985; by the end of 1996, gas transportation generated just 8 percent of Enron's revenue. That year, Enron hired top advertising agency Ogilvy & Mather to craft the biggest ad campaign in its history, designed to boost its name recognition and spread the Enron brand to new customers.

Even before Enron plunged into trading, Ken Lay had sought to shake up the company's stodgy, hierarchical culture. "It was a regulated utility," recalled Kenneth Rice, a longtime employee whose many positions included running Enron Capital & Trade North America. "We really didn't run economic models. We ran cost estimates, and then we spent all of our time analyzing whether we could convince regulators that it was a just and reasonable investment." Because Enron relied on regulators to set its rates, Rice explained that in the 1980s Enron didn't even refer to "customers" but rather to "ratepayers." That subtle difference in semantics meant a difference in thinking about the business.

To change all that meant bringing in new blood from outside the pipeline industry—the sort of new blood exemplified by Skilling and Mark. Inevitably, this also meant that new people displaced veteran employees. Ken Lay said, "That's got to help shake the whole culture. In some ways, when you go through a profound restructuring, long years of experience in your industry really turn out to be a detriment, not an asset."

As the evolution of Enron continued, Skilling became the single biggest factor in a determined effort to reshape Enron's culture, starting in the early 1990s. The company had to have a group of careful engineers who were concerned with delivering gas on time, but Skilling also wanted a workforce concerned with taking risks and pursuing new opportunities. The company wanted to create an organization that resembled more of a Wall Street firm or consulting practice. Hence the alliance with Bankers Trust, and the hiring of people from Salomon Brothers and other investment banks. By the mid-1990s, the company had become one of the top recruiters of MBA grads among nonfinancial companies.

It wasn't just about money and a fast pace. Enron stressed what it called its four "core values," defined as respect ("We treat others as we would like to be treated ourselves"), integrity ("We work with customers and prospects openly, honestly and sincerely"), communication ("We have an obligation to communicate"), and excellence ("We are satisfied with nothing less than the best in everything we do"). Although Enron managers talked up these core values, in truth Enron employees often displayed arrogance and ruthlessness that went against the "respect" value, and communication was sometimes a problem in such a pressure-cooker atmosphere.

Still, those with experience working at Enron became highly sought after by other energy companies. Enron employees went on to jobs at such energy companies as Houston Industries' NorAm Energy Services, Pacific Gas & Electric (PG&E), and Southern Co.

Lay not only supported Skilling's efforts, but he firmly believed in paying top dollar for top minds. It was an outgrowth of his hands-off management style, in which he found a good person to run a division and then let that individual run it. "My goal when I came into this business was to try to get a superstar in every key position," Lay said. In the same way, Skilling and his lieutenants picked good traders to manage a book of trades, and then let those traders go their own way. By 1996, Enron's best traders could earn $125,000 to $200,000 a year, not including stock options.

"An important part of our corporate culture is individualized compensation in each of our business activities," explained Lay. "There are big payouts. Forrest Hoglund, chairman, president and CEO of Enron Oil & Gas, topped a local list of the most highly compensated executives in 1994, with a remuneration of around $19 million, primarily through stock option exercises. There's not a CEO of any major oil company in the country that made nearly that much. But that compensation was based almost entirely on the performance of EOG. He has quadrupled the market value of that company in about six or seven years in a very tough market, and he is presiding over a company making 15 percent to 16 percent return on equity. That's very good in the oil and gas business today, when the best independents are making closer to a 5 percent return. He obviously created a lot of wealth for himself, but he has also created a lot more wealth for his shareholders, including Enron Corp."

To hire and train a swarm of bright young workers plucked from top schools, in the early 1990s Enron developed two programs for the two entry-level routes into the corporation: the analyst program, for college graduates; and the associate program, for those with an MBA. The analyst program put college grads through a two-year curriculum consisting of one-year rotations in different business areas, including acquisitions, risk management, trading, logistics, sales, and technology. At the end of the two years, some of the best analysts were given the chance to go to graduate school with an Enron-sponsored loan for tuition, having attained the two years' experience required by many top business schools; having gotten an MBA, they were then required to return to Enron for at least three years' work.

Enron determined an analyst's first-year assignment based on the company's needs and the analyst's background and interests. Often, the company's needs outweighed the analyst's desired assignment and analysts were sent to where more hands were needed, just as Enron moved natural gas to where demand was strongest. Year two required the analyst to essentially apply for the desired rotation, and the first year's performance was a big factor in determining where he or she landed. Based on the analysts' performances, a few were chosen to stay on at Enron, and some were chosen to be third-year analysts (the best of whom could graduate to the associate program).

Because they were hiring college graduates, company executives focused on those with raw skills, and the trading operations were loaded with math and economics majors. "When I graduated from college I had a high GPA. And when I got to Enron, I felt stupid," said Beau Ratliff, a veteran of the analyst program.

Enron's reputation alone attracted new recruits. Whether they were analysts or associates, at Enron these newbies would get more responsibility than they'd get at comparable companies, from making trades to helping structure complex deals. The company also paid college graduates more than other energy companies did. Even by the late 1990s, when rivals had caught up to Enron's methods, a top college graduate could still get a $50,000 salary at Enron plus a $10,000 signing bonus, compared with a $40,000 salary at a rival energy concern. But the money only partly made up for the insecurity. Analysts were told that after the two-year program, only the top 10 percent would be kept on at the company. "It was cutthroat and very fast-paced—not just on the trading floor but everywhere. But it was exciting," Ratliff said.

Among analysts, one important competition was who got to trade; often this involved office politics as much as talent. This set up situations where there might be 15 standout analysts competing for five spots on the trading desk. Those who lost this competition might wait in less desirable jobs for another opening at that trading desk (in 6 or 12 months), or they might try another trading desk, or even leave Enron for another company.

Associates had a similar program, although with more responsibility and a better chance of advancement, as they had more experience. Armed with MBA degrees from top schools such as Harvard, Stanford, Wharton, and Rice University, associates typically had two years of experience or more on Wall Street or at a big financial firm. When an associate became a trader, he or she had the financial and mathematical skills, but had to learn the physical side of the gas or electricity market from the ground up. Enron liked that system, as it brought in fresh perspectives, even if it didn't respect the idea of seniority. Within Enron, employees who had been there for 10 or 15 years felt a little animosity toward the young associates who came in and became top traders.

Almost all associates had to spend a short rotation in a deal-structuring group, where they could sink their teeth into complicated commercial deals. These often provided a trial by fire with sophisticated risk management calculations or a complex derivative transaction. Some Enron employees described their time in the associate program as akin to being at a top law firm and struggling to make partner.

If analysts and associates felt they were fighting over a limited number of long-term opportunities at Enron, they were right. The company preferred to overhire analysts and associates, because they were a cheap source of smart, hard workers. Associates who were not promoted after their two-year program usually left Enron.

The associate program was eventually bringing in more than 100 MBA-toting employees each year. This created a huge reservoir of talent to feed into the Enron system; in a sense, it served as a "call" option on human capital. Because they were handed real duties that mattered, the fresh recruits were tested early on and the best ones learned to trust their skills. As Lay said (in a grandfatherly way), "The area I'm proudest of is seeing so many, many bright people realize their dreams and their potential."

To change the culture of Enron required more than just hiring some investment bankers and some smart, young graduates. Skilling and others changed the organizational structure, flattening what had been a rigid hierarchy. As Skilling said, "To get good people and motivate them and give them the ability to exercise initiative, they need to have control." So he eradicated layers of management. In the old Enron of the 1980s, there had been 13 levels in the management hierarchy between the lowest-level employee and the business unit head responsible for profits and losses. Skilling flattened that structure in the nonregulated businesses to just four layers of management. "It empowers people," he said. "You have to empower them because suddenly they have no one to tell them what to do."

This flatter hierarchy also enhanced Enron's increased emphasis on new ideas. With fewer layers of management to navigate, an employee with a new idea tended to meet with fewer barriers to the idea. In Skilling's opinion, most companies set up a new idea review process that simulated running a gauntlet. This created little chance that a new idea remained intact when it got to the top. To encourage new ideas, he believed, Enron had to reduce the barriers for them.

Skilling also made organizational changes to foster the development of new businesses. New businesses were removed from the core businesses. "Because what happens if it's embedded in the existing organization, there's always some firefight going on in an existing organization and you tend to put your best people on the firefight. [But] you want your best people focusing on new business development," Skilling said. "And you want them focusing on that 100 percent and they can't get pulled back. They have to wake up at three o'clock in the morning in a cold sweat." In addition, separating new businesses made it easier to hold that new business accountable—so that it would be clear whether the new business was succeeding and what needed to be fixed if it wasn't succeeding.

■ ■ ■

One of the most important and controversial aspects of Enron's organization was its system for assessing employees' bonuses and promotions. Starting in 1990, Enron managers formed committees to review employees' performances. What came to be known as the Performance Review Committee (PRC) process was a twice-yearly exercise, in which managers would gather at a hotel and spend a week or two just on PRC assessments. A number of set categories were used in the evaluation depending on the job, and they could include comfort with numbers, product knowledge, intellectual curiosity, innovation, dependability, teamwork, effective communication, and client relationship skills. Managers' feedback was obviously a crucial part of the data used for PRC evaluations, but assessments from colleagues and from customers were also important.

The evaluation was done in a committee process because Enron didn't just compare a worker against his or her job expectations—the worker was compared against all the other employees in the same business unit. Thus, employees were evaluated on a bell curve. This played a large role in determining year-end bonuses—a crucial factor in that, depending on the division, the bonus could account for 10 percent to as much as 26 percent of total compensation. The key to getting a large bonus? Perform well within a business group that performed well.

The employee's supervisor always had a seat on the review committee, and was the employee's chief representative arguing on his or her behalf. Some employees complained that the PRC process was overly political. But "it wasn't enough to just kiss up to your supervisor," said Sherriff.

In the early 1990s, this bell-curve approach had a harsh Darwinian twist that resulted in performance rankings determining who would stay at Enron and who would be fired. This system became known informally among the employees as "rank-and-yank," because the employees who wound up being ranked in the bottom 10 to 20 percent were yanked off the Enron payroll. The institution of the rank-and-yank system at the start of the 1990s made a humongous difference on Enron's culture by instilling a competitive streak in every employee. "That was probably the most unsettling thing from a cultural standpoint that the company went through," said Gene Humphrey, the former chairman and CEO of Enron Investment Partners. "Initially because of the people that we had, we started with a forced ranking. We put people in different categories. And the bottom 10 percent were eventually to be let go."

Executives explained that Enron needed the rank-and-yank system to eliminate the deadwood in an organization growing so quickly. Employees who ranked in the bottom decile were not immediately discarded in the first go-around—they were given six months to improve their performances and raise their rankings at the next PRC review. But during the six-month probation period, these employees had to spend about an hour each day documenting their daily activities and how they helped Enron.

The PRC process remained unique within the energy industry. General Electric was the only other big corporation where such a system was used and well known. Rival energy trading firms were aware of Enron's rank-and-yank system but didn't copy it, because they felt it wouldn't inspire teamwork.

Inevitably, because of the bell-curve aspect of PRC reviews, internal competition became a part of life at Enron. "The people you were competing against for a bonus were sitting next to you," explained one ex-Enron employee. "It could get hairy, especially at year-end as bonuses were on everyone's minds."

Sometimes workers even sabotaged each other. Occasionally, when one trader got up to go to the bathroom, another trader would go over to his computer screen and either steal his trade or change his position on a trade. This happened mostly in a fraternity-house style of prankishness. "It was kind of like a game—screw the next guy over and see if he could get out of it," recalled Ratliff. The internal competition could be harsh at times, but employees were not beset by unrelenting paranoia. The trading desk also featured collegiality. "Mostly there was lots of cheering for one another's deals," said Ratliff.

More insidious was the competition between different groups within the same business division. Originators—Enron's term for those who structured and negotiated long-term deals—sometimes had friction-filled interactions with traders, who executed the buy and sell orders that made those long term deals work. So, for example, if originators in the gas group negotiated a volumetric production payment contract guaranteeing steady supplies of gas for seven years, those gas volumes would go into the trading desk's book so that gas could be turned into profits through savvy trades. This sort of intertwined dealing raised tough questions, though: How much credit should each side get when it came time for the PRC process and the awarding of bonuses?

Adding to the tension, traders were in charge of calculating forward price curves. So if an originator wanted to put together a big contract to sell power over an eight-year period, he or she would have to rely on traders' estimates for what electricity will sell for in year five, as well as in years six, seven, and eight. Originators often complained that traders were changing the price projections just before long-term contracts were signed, or the traders were adjusting their projections so that the pricing would favor their trades at the cost of the long-term deals. Attempts to get the PRC to award a larger portion of the bonuses sometimes created a focus on grabbing a larger share of the corporation's profits, and this made it more difficult for originators to sign long-term contracts. As a consequence, less business came from long-term contracts and the company had to rely even more on the shorter-term trading operation for profits.

Sometimes, the PRC culture set different business groups competing against each other as though they were different companies. Skilling subtly encouraged such competition, the way he encouraged the early-1990s competition between different groups in the trading operation, because he felt it would bring out the best in people and lead to the best solutions. In practice, though, this competition often solidified a compartmentalization of the company into contending fiefdoms.

Beyond bonuses, rankings also helped determine where an employee would be deployed. The more senior the employee, the less tolerance there was for subpar performance. The lower-ranked analysts and originators were often rotated to other business units. Frequently they were shunted off to less important areas of the company, a de facto punishment because PRC bonuses were based in part on how the entire business group performed. But an underperforming worker with a title such as vice president or managing director was usually asked to leave the company.

"You had to run very fast to keep up," recalled ex-Enron employee Diana Peters. She noted that the PRC process could reward those who were perceived as adding value, but that same process could discard them once that value was seen as used up. The competitive nature of the PRC tradition fed off the tendency to hire lots of young, ambitious people fresh from school. Peters described the thinking as: "Bring them in young, bring them in smart, drain them, and drop them." Job burnout was sometimes a problem.

Beyond a culture of traders, Skilling had also brought much of the McKinsey culture with him. His tenure at McKinsey & Co., one of the most prestigious consulting firms in the world (ex-McKinsey men had gone on to run huge corporations such as IBM and American Express), had given Skilling a taste of a meritocracy. McKinsey was open to younger employees' ideas, less hierarchical than typical companies, aggressively competitive, and very focused on intellectual talent. Notably, McKinsey also had a tradition of grueling performance reviews for its employees.

Skilling and the rest of Enron's management made no apologies for the competition resulting from the PRC tradition. Said Skilling, "Our culture is a tough culture. It is a very aggressive, very urgent organization."

One of the prime rationales behind the PRC process was the high value Enron placed on intellectual capital. This meant that it was worth Enron's time to identify top intellects among employees, the way the company might identify the top sites for a new power plant. Then Enron could identify which employees were worth an investment of its time and resources, and which were not. It was a corollary of the asset-light strategy—viewing the employees as assets or as projects to be pursued or not pursued. Skilling felt that in the 1990s, traditional capital investments (such as those in factories and pipelines) could not make a good return anymore. As he put it, "You need to add intellectual value-added to make a buck anymore." And to get the most out of the company's intellectual capital, "you have to weed out the dead weight."

The goal was, according to Skilling, "extraordinary performance," not unlike extraordinary investment returns. "In new businesses where capital is not an issue, the difference between someone that's good and someone that's mediocre is not a factor of 50 percent—it's a factor of 200 or 300 times," Skilling said. "Really good people that can figure things out and make things happen can make 200 times as much happen as someone who can't do that. There are huge differences in performance capability." No wonder the company put such an emphasis on ranking the employees.

The recruitment programs created a skilled workforce. In 1990, 12 percent of Enron employees had college degrees and 4 percent had advanced degrees; in 1995, 27 percent had college degrees and 14 percent had advanced degrees. This trend continued, so that in 1999, 40 percent of Enron employees had college degrees and 20 percent had advanced degrees. Enron was usually happy to pay for additional training for its employees, particularly in finance, risk management, and technology, and an Enron staffer often underwent 10 to 20 hours of training per year.

The combination of recruitment goals and the PRC process shaped Enron into a young, well-compensated culture. By 1999, the average age of an Enron employee was 40 years old, with 7.6 years of service at the company. But this "average" reflected wide divergences in tenure, as the average gas pipeline employee had been at Enron for 16 years, while the average ECT employee had been there for three or four years. The company did strive for diversity. By 1999, 78 percent of its staff was Caucasian, but only 71 percent of new hires were Caucasian. In addition, 35 percent of the workforce was female, but 38 percent of new hires were women. The diversity was also a product of the emphasis on results. Enron cared only about performance, so it didn't matter if an employee was Caucasian, just as it didn't matter if an employee had a nose ring or green hair, or was homosexual.

By 1999, the average salary at Enron was $71,455 a year, and the average bonus was over $16,000. Not surprisingly, these numbers varied measurably depending on the business unit. Total compensation, including salary and bonus, ranged from an average of over $120,000 in Enron International to less than $70,000 at the more stuffy, less entrepreneurial gas pipeline business.

Global Change Associates, a consulting firm that studied Enron, concluded: "The Enron corporate culture clearly places profits first." The company hired smart, ambitious people, granted them autonomy and responsibility, set them loose in a competitive environment, and then ranked their performances. Employees who didn't add to profits or at least provide a strategic function were deemed expendable, like a power plant that was no longer economic to keep in operation. But this created a stressful workplace where some employees wanted to make their mark and then move on to another company before it was too late. This only accentuated Enron's tendency to focus on the short term.

■ ■ ■

Despite the increasing reliance on intellectual assets, hard assets had their place. Even Skilling favored investing in those hard assets that seemed like good strategic opportunities. The idea was to get a physical presence in a business to learn the ins and outs of that market, then build trading and finance businesses around that. That method began in the late 1980s, when Enron realized it could develop trading and finance activities around its gas pipelines. In addition, Enron had experience in developing trading skills and computer systems and software for finance, risk management, and trading. For example, Enron was ready to apply this knowledge and experience to power, but wanted the institutional knowledge of how the electricity grid worked. So the company decided to buy a utility, and that set in motion the Portland General deal.

Enron was continually redefining its core competency. The company's core competency was, arguably, natural gas transmission. But the company's gas trading arm, an outgrowth of its gas transmission business, was very successful. Enron realized that its *true* core competency was trading, logistics, and risk management. This was a more flexible core competency, which could be applied to other commodities, such as electricity.

Corporate skills weren't the only things considered transferable. Employees were often transferred from one division to another. In many of Enron's divisions, different projects were almost like self-contained jobs: Once a project was over, it was up to the employee to find work elsewhere within the company. So employees who were willing to be flexible and move around could lengthen their tenure at Enron. Diana Peters, for example, started in 1993 at Enron Oil & Gas, then went on to such jobs as working for ECT, dabbling in marketing for Enron International, and helping with information technology work for the corporate staff (which consisted of Lay and the other top officers).

The company prized flexibility and adaptability. Employees could count on being redeployed at Enron, as the company itself liked to restructure its divisions every once in a while. That's why Enron Gas Services became Enron Capital & Trade Resources, Enron Development evolved into Enron International, and other units were shuffled around. "If you weren't being reorganized, your seats were being moved to another floor," said John Spitz. In many parts of the company, managers told employees it would hurt their chances of advancement if they stayed too long on one project.

Because the PRC process was standard across nearly the entire corporation, it made this kind of employee movement much easier. With this single compensation system in place, the employee's performance evaluation and compensation didn't change if the employee changed jobs or moved to a different business unit. Enron went even further than that, decreeing that the job title moved with the person, and was not attached to the specific position.

Skilling explained that this system encouraged people to gravitate to promising new business ideas. "So the whole organization is like a free market of people," he said.

There were many drawbacks to this philosophy, however. For one thing, employees stuck in a poorly performing group spent a lot of time trying to transfer into a better performing group, in hopes of moving up the PRC bonus ladder. This encouraged, to some extent, a mercenary and selfish attitude. In addition, it meant that only a few people at the top of the corporation had a handle on the overall picture of Enron and what was going on at the company.

Also, the tendency to reorganize its different business groups and divisions added to whatever confusion was innate in such a sprawling company. "The joke was that if there wasn't a fundamental reorganization in three months, then something was drastically wrong," recalled one former executive. With people moving from one business to another, there was little institutional memory in each business area. This also added to the focus on short-term results. Deal originators and traders looked to maximize their mark-to-market profits on a deal (booking all the profits from the life of the deal up front) before they moved on to another business unit. They didn't worry too much about whether the mark-to-market value of their deals would change three or four years down the line, because by then they'd be in a different business group, and any erosion in the value of the old deal wouldn't affect their current PRC evaluations.

This short-timer mentality filtered through the organization, creating a lack of long-term strategic planning.

Instead, the focus was on the here and now, and this was only accentuated by the fast pace of the trading operation. Enron's every-minute-counts business sense emerged fully grown in the mid-1990s, at a time when the Internet was threading its way through American business. By the end of the decade, large sectors of the business world were consumed with the notion of making things happen on "Internet time," which assumed that corporations had to accelerate to keep up with the speed of, say, sending an e-mail. In a sense, Enron prefigured this emphasis on speed because its traders were making and reshaping deals with one eye on the changing prices of gas and electricity. Energy prices could change by 1 or 2 percent in a matter of three minutes, and Enron traders had to react. Except for the fact that at the time Enron wasn't using the Internet for much, the trading operation really was operating on Internet time.

To help support the high-speed pace of its energy business, Enron spent loads of money on technology. For example, it wired its electricity control system so that it could send power to a grid, or take it away from the grid, in just 20 seconds. If gas or electricity prices moved enough, Enron could flip a switch to respond, sending the right kind of energy toward the place with more demand (and therefore, higher prices). Skilling boasted that a delay of even one minute in responding to the shifting markets could cost Enron millions of dollars.

Few areas of the company embodied this fast pace as much as the trading desks. A natural gas trader would typically arrive at work at 7 A.M., and start studying what happened overnight—what were the weather patterns, which pipelines had operations changes (such as maintenance work), and how much gas was transported. At about 7:30, a staff meteorologist would give the traders a report on weather forecasts for that trading desk's market; Enron was the first gas trading company to hire meteorologists, to give it yet another edge in information.

Before 8 A.M., there'd be a "morning meeting" among the heads of the different trading desks within a region. Gas and other products were separated into regions, so at one time there was a Texas trading desk, a West desk, an East desk, and a Mid-Continent desk. The morning meeting included each region's desks for different kinds of trading, such as the spot-market trading desk, the desk trading gas forwards, and the "financial" desk trading options and more complex derivatives. Individual traders tended to specialize in trading on a handful of pipelines.

By 8 A.M., it was off to the races: traders, surrounded by computer screens displaying various prices and news alerts, were let loose to buy and sell. "There wasn't a lot of guidance as to what to do," recalled a former trader. "One of the beauties of Enron was that they really gave you a lot of rein." As long as a trader made money, he or she wasn't bothered by managers.

Trading lasted all day. Just as at a Wall Street firm, there was no break for lunch. Instead, Enron catered lunches for the traders, and many ate at their desks. Most of the trades were shorter-term: Roughly 70 percent of them involved buying or selling gas within the next 12 months. As much as 60 percent of the trades were settled with cash, and perhaps 40 percent resulted in the actual delivery of gas. Although NYMEX had launched gas futures contracts, the majority of the trades were over-the-counter. Helping each trader was the fact that at his or her desk was more than $30,000 in computer and phone equipment.

Trading at this frenzied pace lasted until 5 or 6 P.M. In a very hectic day, there might even be a traders meeting, similar to the morning meeting, at 5 P.M. After trading was done, each trader had to go over the books and mark the trades to market.

In assessing this trading paradigm, the obvious comparison was to Wall Street, but this was only partly apt, because the potential profits at Enron were bigger. A trader of stocks at an investment bank might have been generating profits of $30,000 per day. But that was chicken feed at Enron, where on any given day the top six or seven traders booked a daily profit (or loss) of $2 million or $3 million. One ex-Enron trader said, "My best day I made $26 million. The next day I lost $13 million."

With so much money riding on traders' jobs, they felt pressure to perform. The fast pace and the big risks involved led some traders to leave Enron. Some even left for more lucrative trading positions where they thought they'd be better compensated for their stress. A few traders were upset that they were making $50 million a year or more for the company, taking bets that were so big that they sometimes lost sleep, and in return these traders got bonuses of only $1 million or $2 million—and much of that in Enron stock, to boot.

The trading operation, as it got better and better, developed a certain swagger. And this seeped into the overall corporation. Enron's swagger meshed well with the culture of Houston, which retained some of the snazzy excess and cowboy mentality of the last oil boom—which, ironically, was depicted so well in the television series *Dallas*. Top traders could earn $1 million a year, thanks to the hefty bonuses, but many Enron employees were well paid. At Enron headquarters, the company parking lot was filled with expensive sports cars such as Porsches and BMWs.

Enron fit its hometown, a sprawling, decentralized city that often seems like a collection of separate hamlets. Houston prides itself on its Texan roots, but it's a place where the new often sweeps away the old, the way the old stone-and-brick buildings in the small downtown area have been overtaken by lustrous modern skyscrapers built in the 1980s and 1990s—including the Enron building, a curved slab of glass and aluminum. Houston likes things big, from the Astrodome to risky oil wells. And Enron lived big. Its top executives bought million-dollar homes and condominiums in the best neighborhoods, and Lay and other Enron officials sat on civic boards and handed out prizes at the local university to Colin Powell and Mikhail Gorbachev. Enron's self-assurance fed Houston's ego as well as its own.

Enron hyped itself to Wall Street, to customers, and to investors. Inevitably, the company hyped itself to its own employees. Enron's zeal to change markets soon had a sister zeal: to believe that Enron was great. Although dissent was supposedly encouraged within the company, employees who did dissent were too often dismissed as people who "just didn't *get* it." Skilling was the epicenter of the hype, with his consultant's knack for spinning Enron's story. The slight arrogance that had long been a part of his personality started to become part of Enron's personality.

As part of the internal corporate hype, the company liked to show how well it was doing. During a dinner to celebrate the revival of Enron's Dabhol power project, the company hired acrobats to perform for employees at Houston's Ariel Theatre. At another party for Enron International in 1996 (and again in 1997), the company brought in a live elephant. At one Christmas party for Enron's engineering and construction division, the company booked rooms at the posh Houstonian hotel so that every attendee could sleep over.

Employees' long hours, which usually involved late nights, enhanced Enron's sense of self-absorption. Office romances, such as the rumored affair between Rebecca Mark and John Wing, were the talk of the hallways. One illicit affair between top executives was reportedly visible through their offices' windows. There was even a rumor that top Enron executives belonged to an exclusive Houston sex club where price of entry was $50,000. Many of the rumored sexual exploits may well have been just that—rumors. However, it was indicative of Enron's freewheeling culture that these rumors spread so rapidly. It didn't help matters when employees looked around the company only to see that a good number of Enron executives had gotten divorces. This included Skilling, who began dating Enron employee Rebecca Carter in the late 1990s. Carter would later become corporate secretary, reporting to Lay, and so the high-profile relationship between her and Skilling may have broadcast the notion that Enron employees could mix business and personal relationships.

Despite the company's attempts to hire a mix of men and women, Enron had within it a boys' club typical of trading rooms that reveled in rowdy times involving members of the opposite sex and strippers. Not surprisingly, sexual hi-jinks resulted in rumored sexual harassment complaints from some female employees. Even married traders and executives boasted of womanizing. In one infamous incident at a 1992 bachelor party at Lipsticks, a Houston strip club, up-and-coming executive Lou Pai bragged to traders that he avoided his wife's detection of strippers' perfume on his clothes and alcohol on his breath by splashing himself with gasoline at a nearby service station before heading home. According to a former employee who attended the party, one of the traders hearing this couldn't resist quipping, "Hey Lou, maybe your wife thinks you're fucking the gasoline attendant!" Everyone there roared at Pai's expense, including Pai himself. But Pai ultimately had the last laugh. "The guy who cracked that joke ended up getting transferred out to Calgary," recalled the former employee.

Another key element of the trader culture became part of the company's overall culture. The mark-to-market emphasis on the short term crystallized in an obsession with Enron's stock price. Lay and other top executives encouraged this, putting a big electronic board at the entrance to the headquarters at 1400 Smith Street that displayed Enron's stock price in real time (along with the latest NYMEX prices for oil and gas). The elevators in the buildings had television screens showing CNBC, the financial news channel, so riding from one floor to another was also an opportunity to see how the Dow Jones Industrial Average was doing.

Why did the employees buy into this stock-price mania? Because Enron tied compensation to the stock price by increasingly rewarding performance with stock options. Although the bonuses awarded by the PRC were cash, the company encouraged its workers to take those bonuses in the form of Enron stock and stock options instead. In this way, Enron was an example of the 1990s trend of corporations loading up their top people with stock options; the dot-com boom would later perfect this strategy, so that executives at Internet companies wound up getting the majority of their pay in stock options. In keeping with the internal hype, the company encouraged workers to invest at least some of their 401(k) retirement plans in Enron stock, which was touted to employees as vigorously as it was to Wall Street. So even secretaries watched the day-to-day fluctuations in the stock price. On a daily basis, the staff was more aware of the stock price than of performance measures such as the debt-to-capital ratio.

More and more employees depended on Enron's stock going higher. And because Wall Street gradually put more and more weight on meeting quarterly expectations, the need for stock-price performance became wedded to the need to gear everything to making that quarter's numbers. Employees were pulled into this quarter-to-quarter myopia, and concerns about long-term performance took a backseat. Unlike banks, Enron didn't build long-term financial relationships with customers, relying instead on the profits from daily and monthly trades. The resulting pace could be exhausting. As one former executive put it, "You can't keep running faster and faster." Some charged that certain Enron executives even orchestrated bogus deals just before the end of the quarter to meet performance targets and trigger the payments of bonuses and restricted stock.

■ ■ ■

Part of Enron's swagger came from its willingness to take on big risks. Enron Gas Services, and then later ECT, often constructed its trading strategy around its internal forecasts for energy prices. This meant that while most of the operation sought to balance sell orders with buy orders; for instance, if Enron believed that Permian Basin gas prices would soar over the next 12 months, the trading unit might put together some trades that were direct bets on Permian Basin gas going higher. The decisions on big bets like that were made by the entire trading staff, not individual traders. But in addition to having confidence in its own ability to calculate forward price curves, this also allowed the traders more freedom in taking risks overall.

Even in the early 1990s, the trading operation had a reputation for making occasional big bets, or as some in the trading community put it, "swinging a big bat." Enron did have risk controls in place, so there were limits to how much of the company's money a trader was allowed to play with. Like many companies, Enron used a variety of risk-measuring calculations, the most popular of which was Value at Risk (VAR). The VAR was essentially a measurement of how much money was at risk of being lost in one day 95 percent of the time. This was often expressed as either a percentage (as in Enron could lose 2 percent of its capital 95 percent of the time) or a dollar amount.

Compiling the VAR number was a complex affair that worked from the bottom up. Enron simulated spot prices and forward price curves for various commodities, while keeping track of relationships between prices in different markets. All the different risks that were calculated from these price simulations were added together, and the different clusters of risks, and the relationships to each other, were then compiled. These portfolios of risks were totaled until there was a single number for the entire company.

Individual traders had limits that were defined by the VAR numbers, but they were loosely enforced. If a trader had a position that, at the end of the day, worked out to a mark-to-market loss of $250,000 and the limit was $200,000, a manager might direct the position to be partly unwound so that the potential loss was closer to $200,000. Even as late as 1996, though, a good trader at Enron who was making money could violate the VAR rules without consequences more serious than a winking reminder of the VAR limits. "If you went over the VAR limit and made money, they wouldn't ask you questions. As you got cold, they asked you questions," explained one former trader. The risk limits for traders grew in dollar size as the trading business grew. As a result, it was possible that a trader could make $26 million one day and lose $13 million the next.

Trading was something Enron considered within its control, and so it was willing to load itself with risks because they were risks the company felt it could manage. As Skilling said, "We like risk because you make money by taking risk. The key is to take on risks that you manage better than your competitor."

As the 1990s wore on, Enron's board grew increasingly worried about the risks of trading. Trading derivatives was exotic and dangerous, like handling nitroglycerin but more complicated. It watched former ally Bankers Trust get hammered by devastating lawsuits over its sale of derivatives to Procter & Gamble and other corporations. It also watched in horror as the oil market was roiled by the derivatives blowup at Metallgesellschaft, the German industrial conglomerate.

The company, known as MG, had sold long-term oil supply contracts to U.S. gasoline stations and heating-oil suppliers. Because MG was committed to providing oil, it needed some way to hedge the price risk on its purchases of oil. MG's answer was to buy short-term oil futures on the NYMEX. MG and others believed that the natural state of the oil futures market was a downward slope, so that prices would decline the farther out the delivery date: February futures would sell for $18.00 per barrel, March futures for $17.50, April futures for $17.00, and so on. But in 1993, the oil futures market was often in the reverse situation. MG kept rolling its futures positions over into the following month, waiting to recoup its losses. But the losses grew. The company had also become the single largest player in NYMEX oil futures, aggravating its situation as other firms were able to trade against MG's positions and its reliable strategy. In early 1994, MG finally terminated its futures hedging, taking a loss of roughly $1 billion and nearly sinking the company. As one consulting firm put it, "No case [had] done more to sully the name of derivatives in the energy industry."

Inside Enron, the company felt one of its core skills was risk management, and this included figuring out how to put a price on risk so that it became a business prospect. Although Enron's culture equated risk with opportunity, the MG debacle seemed like proof to the rest of the world that risk usually meant danger. On December 21, 1995, rumors spread through the market that Enron had sustained heavy trading losses on soaring natural gas prices, and its stock fell nearly 8 percent that day. There was even a rumor that Skilling had been led out of the trading room in handcuffs, when in truth Skilling was skiing in Colorado. The next day, Lay defused the rumor and announced that Enron would start buying back its stock. Crisis averted.

Although the rumor was wrong, the incident revealed investors' unease about Enron's reliance on its risky ECT division. Wall Street was ready to believe that Enron's huge trading business could cause massive losses just as easily as it had been a source of profits for years. After all, ECT was large enough that at any moment it had open agreements to buy and sell $12 billion worth of gas. But Enron executives countered that the division was never exposed to more than $25 million of losses on a given day, thanks to internal risk controls and Enron's insistence on hedging its bets. Still, the fact that ECT dealt with such large numbers kept the investment community uncomfortable. The market typically penalized the stocks of companies whose profits depended on trading, because those profits were seen as unpredictable. "The market will doubt one company's ability to be perfectly hedged at all times under all circumstances," said one analyst.

Could an MG-type debacle happen at Enron? By the mid-1990s, Enron employees regularly joked that the company was a "house of cards," because the trading operation was just so large that it seemed like a disaster waiting to happen. The staff seemed to expect a trading blowup that would send the stock price reeling, while also knowing that the risks that could lead to such a blowup were an integral part of the trading business.

Concerned, the company's board started pushing for tighter controls. And, gradually, risk controls on Enron's traders grew tighter in the mid and late 1990s. This dovetailed with the development of more sophisticated risk-management systems and software. As the decade edged toward its close, going over internal risk limits slowly became a more serious offense. Going over the VAR limit meant a fine of $100,000, and some offenders were even fired.

But even these more serious limits on risk were the cost of doing business, and did nothing to tame the brash culture at Enron. As Skilling's stock was rising within the company, Enron took on more of the entrepreneurial and extremely competitive personality that he had hoped to fashion. Unfortunately, it could also be a greedy, self-involved, overconfident personality—and those characteristics sowed the seeds of hubris.

6

THE ENERGY BUFFET

In November 1996, Richard Kinder jolted Enron with a decision that was far more significant than a $3 billion acquisition. Kinder had decided to leave Enron.

Ken Lay had just extended his employment contact with Enron for five more years, meaning Kinder would have to wait at least that long to get the top job. So the 52-year-old, who wanted to be a CEO, chose to strike out on his own. "They offered me the chance to stay on but it was sort of like 'been there, done that.' I want to go somewhere where I can run my own show," he said.

Kinder left Enron on good terms. He had done well at Enron: For 1996, he was estimated to have earned $2.3 million in salary and bonus, and $30 million from cashing in his stock options. But his departure was a turning point for the company. As president and chief operating officer, he had been the one making sure that Enron functioned well and met its quarterly targets. While Lay handled the vision, Kinder, with his good head for numbers, was in charge of the efficiency. Enron staffers felt that Kinder was more naturally comfortable with the part of the business that dealt in pipelines and power plants, but he appreciated the innovation and profitability of Enron Capital & Trade. Like Lay, he hadn't favored one strategy over another, preferring the cooperation of hard assets, with their dependable stream of revenues and profits, along with trading savvy.

Kinder's natural inclination toward hard assets asserted itself in January 1997, when he decided what he would do after Enron: He and a business partner, Bill Morgan, formed a company called Kinder Morgan, which spent $40 million to buy Enron Liquids Pipeline Co. To some, this looked like either a kind of golden parachute for Kinder or proof that Kinder had a superior grasp of asset values. After all, Enron Liquids Pipeline operated and owned 15 percent of Enron Liquids Pipeline L.P., a limited partnership owning two natural-gas liquids pipelines and one carbon dioxide pipeline—assets worth more than $300 million. The strategy would be to expand the pipeline systems, and, with Kinder's help, squeeze more profits out of them. And Kinder had the title of chairman and CEO of Kinder Morgan.

Gruff and hardheaded, Kinder wasn't going to vault into the CEO superstar category like Disney's Michael Eisner or GE's Jack Welch. But he commanded respect in the industry and on Wall Street, and everyone knew his leaving would be a loss to Enron. At the time, no one knew just how big a loss it would be.

Before Enron cut the deal to help form Kinder Morgan, there was the matter of who would succeed Kinder at Enron. The two top candidates were Skilling, 43 years old, and Rebecca Mark, 42. Both had put their stamps on Enron. And both of them could spin Wall Street, charm executives, and negotiate big deals—their flash complementing Lay's soft-spoken courtliness. But neither of them had demonstrated the operations expertise that Kinder had, the ability to make the trains run on time.

While Mark traveled the globe, Skilling remained mostly in Houston, pushing his vision of an asset-light company. In a speech at the University of Virginia's business school, he noted approvingly that Standard Oil Company, once the largest corporation in America, had a policy of not owning oil-production assets under founder John D. Rockefeller. Instead, Rockefeller stressed the lighter assets of distributing and marketing—which were a large part of what Skilling saw as Enron's core strengths. "[Standard] focused strictly on logistics and marketing. That was what they controlled," he said. "Because that was the only place that there was a bottleneck in the system, and by owning the network they would maintain the economics."

Under Skilling, ECT had blossomed into the company's nexus of innovation and growth. But it was a sprawling and complicated business, what with the trading and finance operations, and also Enron's natural gas storage facilities, and two intrastate pipelines (one that was entirely in Texas and one entirely in Louisiana).

Enron already had rather a complicated structure that reflected the company's preference to be decentralized and to separate the results of different businesses. For example, the company had partly spun off its crude oil marketing business in 1994 as EOTT Energy Partners, a partnership whose shares traded on the New York Stock Exchange; in 1993, it had combined its stake in the Northern Border pipeline system with two other companies to form Northern Border Partners L.P. (also traded on the NYSE); it owned 50 percent of a Texas-to-Florida gas pipeline called Florida Gas Transmission; Enron was majority owner of Enron Oil & Gas (similarly on the NYSE); it owned 52 percent of Enron Global Power & Pipelines (also on the NYSE); and the company had huge stakes in Teesside and Dabhol Power, and in the JEDI partnership.

So ECT's complex structure was very much in keeping with the corporation's personality. According to Enron, ECT had three businesses: cash and physical, risk management, and finance. The cash and physical operations included earnings from physical contracts (meaning contracts that resulted in delivery) of one year or less involving natural gas, liquids, electricity and other commodities; earnings from the management of ECT's contract portfolio; and earnings related to the physical assets of ECT. Although the cash and physical business handled the one-year-or-less contracts, also included were the effects of actual settlements of some long-term contracts. ECT's risk management operations consisted of the long-term energy commodity contracts (transactions greater than one year). ECT's finance operations provided such financing arrangements as Volumetric Production Payments, loans, and equity investments; these were offered through ECT directly or through ventures such as JEDI.

As dense as ECT's structure was, the division was clearly making money. In 1996, ECT generated income before interest and taxes of $280 million, which was topped only by the $570 million produced by the steady interstate pipeline business. By contrast, Enron International generated income of $152 million that year.

On top of that, Skilling had an ability to articulate Enron's ambition in a way that made audacious visions seem like reasonable three-year plans. He talked the talk. Skilling had a slight build and his dark hair was thinning, but he had well-groomed good looks that complemented his energetic charm. Ken Lay was a warm and cordial figure at the company, with a studied intelligence that was different from quick wit. Skilling was cool and yet one of the boys. He was clever and quickly grasped new concepts. Skilling could be impatient with those who weren't shrewd, so he wasn't above the occasional sarcastic retort, or staring down an employee and grimacing, "You have *got* to be kidding me." If someone suggested entering the business of trading wood pulp, Skilling could sketch out on the back of an envelope the size of the market and potential revenues Enron could generate by grabbing a chunk of the pulp market. Granted, that wasn't the same thing as executing the plan and actually capturing market share, but it was a valued skill inside Enron and on Wall Street. As long as Enron had the vision and the drive, he made it seem as though the rest was purely a matter of will. "I have never met anybody who had as much raw intellect and drive as Jeff Skilling," recalled former Enron executive Joseph Pokalsky.

Skilling was spreading his trader's culture throughout more and more of the company. But Rebecca Mark was far from forgotten within Enron. Lay liked her for a number of reasons, including her tendency to be charming. Mark the Shark was good at schmoozing, and building Enron International (EI) into a unique division within Enron. It was her domain. The rank-and-yank employee evaluation tradition was far less pervasive at EI than at ECT. The employees at EI thought of themselves as jet-setting merchant bankers. With expensive wood furniture and rugs, EI's offices projected a more old-fashioned sense of luxury and corporate power than ECT's more modern, Spartan furnishings.

At the end of 1996, Mark was riding high as the force behind Enron's global expansion. She had entered the realm of Enron legend several times, most recently by motoring into an EI meeting-cum-pep rally on a motorcycle and clad in leather. By then, Mark was credited with saving the Dabhol project. "I think what worked was that we never stopped talking," she explained of the Indian situation. "I think most people thought [our project] was too grandiose. . . . The problem is, not enough people in India and the world look forward."

In the previous few years, Mark's global empire had expanded considerably. In January 1996, Enron had completed construction of a 154-megawatt power plant on Hainan Island, an economic free-trade zone off the southeastern coast of China, marking the first such power project developed by a U.S. company in China. In September 1996, Enron began building a 478-megawatt gas-fired power plant at Marmara, Turkey, and already had a 20-year contract to sell power to the state. Enron was leading the development of a 1,875-mile gas pipeline from Bolivia to Brazil, a project whose total cost was estimated at over $1 billion. Enron was set to begin building a 551-megawatt power plant in Sardinia, Italy, in which it held a 45 percent stake. And Enron was scouting out projects in Indonesia, Poland, and other places.

But Skilling subtly tried to erode EI's standing within the company. There were small things, like the way his group rubbed EI's face in the fact that ECT negotiated the settlement of the J-Block dispute. He also slowly moved a few of his own people into EI with the argument that Mark's division needed better financial controls. This was actually true. EI kept making far-flung overseas investments and the division was producing profits, but there were concerns about whether it was getting good returns on its investments. Dabhol was turning out to be expensive, given all the delays. What would the eventual returns be on the projects in China and Turkey and elsewhere?

Enron International developed the idea that it had an unlimited budget for projects. So long as a power plant or pipeline seemed worthwhile, Enron would pursue it. Skilling recognized the power of controlling the purse strings. So he set up a policy whereby ECT, which was the financial engine of the company, was the division that arranged financing for other parts of Enron. That meant Mark's group had to go to ECT first to get the initial financing for a project. And ECT often rejected EI's requests for funding, so Mark frequently went outside Enron and got the financing from a third party who charged higher interest rates. "It was an attempt to strangle EI through attrition," recalled one insider.

Skilling's strategy didn't stop EI in its tracks so much as slow it down with extra hurdles and make it look even more profligate than it was. Mark wasn't without resourcefulness, though. She sometimes bypassed ECT and appealed directly to Lay that a project deserved funding because it was "strategic" even if the return on investment seemed dicey—the argument was that Enron needed to have a foothold in China, or in Brazil, or elsewhere, because that was the next big market. (Despite his purported dislike of hard assets, Skilling actually supported Enron's moves into Latin America, sensing that would be a big growth opportunity.)

Skilling didn't acknowledge that Mark was a direct rival, but his actions implied otherwise. Meanwhile, Mark realized too late that Skilling was trying to outmaneuver her. She'd made the mistake of underestimating him as a flashy consultant.

Skilling won. He was named president and chief operating officer of Enron in December, and he kept his duties overseeing ECT. "As chairman and CEO of ECT, Jeff has been instrumental in helping put Enron at the forefront of the natural gas and electricity industry. . . . Since he joined the company in 1990, ECT's earnings before interest and taxes have increased nearly tenfold," Lay said in a statement. "I am pleased that Jeff will assume a larger role in our very strong management team."

The company's statement didn't mention Rebecca Mark. And to the outside world, she still looked like Skilling's only real rival to succeed Lay. For the time being, she continued as the head of EI. But within the company, it was understood that Skilling had been anointed by being given Kinder's former titles.

The elevation of Skilling was a crucial moment for Enron. It represented the triumph of his trader's mentality. While some described Skilling as smart or visionary, others used words such as "cunning." And although Kinder was known to be tough as a boss, Skilling had flashes of meanness that came out when he sometimes disparaged a competitor or an underling. Unlike Lay, Skilling was much more hands-on, happy to throw himself into Enron's latest venture. Although he worked at it, he was not the politician that Lay was. Skilling often didn't remember employee's names. To some it seemed he never bothered to learn them in the first place.

Skilling was a quick study, but he could also be impulsive. For example, there was the time Skilling was impressed by an article in *Forbes* magazine touting the success of MBIA, a company that insured municipal bonds. The next day, he asked Enron's research department to look into whether the company should buy MBIA, even though Enron had no experience in municipal bonds or insurance. The researchers spent a few days looking into it, and came back with a reasoned argument, backed by numbers, for why Enron should not buy the insurance company. But their work was moot. By then Skilling had dropped the let's-buy-MBIA concept and had moved on to other ideas. To some, Skilling's emphasis on moving quickly seemed like he was all surface, not interested in digging deep to understand the fundamentals of a business such as insurance.

Skilling's victory also meant that Enron was essentially choosing to pursue his asset-light strategy. Skilling was now free to pursue his idea of turning Enron into more of a "virtual" company, whose assets are increasingly "intellectual"—even if that also meant turning Enron into more of a financial company. With Skilling winning out over the asset builder Mark, it seemed Lay had finally decided that the asset-light strategy was the key to the company's aspirations. But without Kinder, Lay and Skilling had no foil to ensure their visionary ambitions would remain grounded.

■ ■ ■

Meanwhile, Enron struggled to complete the $3.2 billion purchase of Portland General. The Oregon Public Utilities Commission (OPUC) had planned to issue a final decision in February, but a judge pushed the date back to March. Portland General's stock started to slip. Even so, Enron began setting the stage for its move into the California power markets just south of Oregon. In January 1997, it allied with the Northern California Power Agency to sell power to the state agency's 700,000 customers in 11 cities and four utility districts; the nonexclusive agreement was the first of its kind in California, and paved the way for allowing residents served by the agency to choose their electricity provider.

Enron talked up consumer choice. The company imagined a near future where power plants were owned separately from power distribution lines, and those lines would provide transport services to any number of competing power marketers. In this vision, consumers could choose their electricity supplier the way they chose a long-distance phone company, with the assurance that the power they ordered would be sent down the wires of the local utility. Destroying the traditional monopolies and forcing electricity suppliers to compete for business would, theoretically, force down power costs the way long-distance phone costs went down. But even more than residential consumers, who may or may not be inspired at the thought of saving $5 on monthly electric bills, choice would appeal to businesses, where saving money on energy could be a very visible change. Businesses were the logical first segment of customers that Enron would go after, then residents. Ultimately, all would gain from this deregulation.

But there were those in Oregon who wanted the Portland General merger to accelerate the benefits of the deregulation that Enron was touting. They feared that the Pacific Northwest, which had relatively low electricity prices thanks in part to abundant hydroelectric power, would have to stand by and watch Enron simply send that cheap power to California where it would be sold for large profits. Then prices in Oregon would rise. Would Portland General customers subsidize Enron's lucrative vision of deregulation? "There will be some leveling of electricity costs," said Congressman Peter DeFazio (D-Oregon). "And you know who the losers are going to be? The Pacific Northwest."

In late January, the OPUC staff recommended that the commissioners approve the merger if it met 23 conditions, the key provision being an electricity rate cut of $47.4 million per year for four years, a figure that Enron felt was high. Taking into account Portland General's recent independent rate cut, Enron offered rate reductions of $3 million per year for four years. Enron and Portland General staffers sat down with state officials to negotiate compromises, but after a while the talks hit a wall over the rate cut. In a meeting with the OPUC in early February, commissioners criticized Enron and Portland General for failing to demonstrate a public benefit from the merger. One commissioner actually called some of Enron's tactics "bush league." Given the impasse over the rate cut, one commission staff member said that the merger should be rejected. This was starting to look as difficult as Maharashtra.

By mid-March, Enron had sweetened its offer to an electricity rate cut totaling $61 million over four years. The OPUC agreed not to include Enron's unregulated business profits when calculating rate-cut recommendations, lowering its demand from $189.6 million over four years to roughly $141 million. With the two sides deadlocked, they postponed the OPUC's vote all the way to June 4. Wall Street began to wonder if the deal might really fall apart.

Then in May, Enron relented and agreed to $141 million in power rate cuts. The deal with the OPUC also included commitments to renewable energy and $20 million in contributions to Portland General's charitable foundation. Enron's chief negotiator said the merger would benefit consumers, but one critic said Enron was obviously concerned with money above all else. On June 4, the OPUC approved the merger. To help pay for the increased rate cuts, Portland General agreed to trim its purchase price, so Enron would exchange 0.9825 shares of its stock for each share of Portland General rather than the original one-for-one swap.

The merger closed on July 1. Enron exchanged roughly $40.10 worth of its stock for each share of Portland General's stock. The Oregon company's stock price had been $28.13 before the merger, so Enron wound up paying a hefty 42 percent premium for the utility. If the price seemed high, it was because Enron saw Portland General as a "strategic" acquisition, where the larger strategy enhanced the financial benefits of the deal. It just happened to be one of the biggest examples of Enron's willingness to pay a premium for a deal it considered to be strategic. It was a trend that Enron would continue to follow.

But company officials were not worrying about price. They were excited to get their hands on the utility. At the time, executives were thinking that electricity would overtake Enron's gas-trading business in a matter of years. This was a big change to the thinking at a company that had, just a few years before, wanted to be the first natural gas major.

Instead, Enron wanted to be a one-stop shop for energy needs. While Lay and others highlighted the benefits to homeowners, the real target was business and industry, because they spent enough on energy to actually switch between natural gas, oil, and electricity if the prices made sense.

Enron started to engage in some trades based on the "spark spread," which was the spread between gas and electricity prices. The idea was that a power plant could use a spark spread to hedge the difference in price between the gas it would use to fuel its generators and the electricity it would produce and sell. Because the only way to compare gas and electricity prices was to break both commodities down to the basic measure of energy known as the British thermal unit, or BTU, this spread was also known as a BTU spread. Whatever the name, the spark spread remained a small market because not enough companies demanded it. It was also held back by the need to coordinate such trades between electricity traders and gas traders, and Enron's infamously competitive culture meant that the electricity trading desks and the gas trading desks were reluctant to cooperate.

Other companies were trying to offer a buffet of energy for business customers. Rival NGC, headquartered nearby in Houston, started referring to itself as an "energy store" as it offered gas, electricity, oil, and coal. Aquila Energy, Duke Energy, and other gas traders built up their electricity businesses. The ability to deal in both gas and electricity seemed like a very attractive flexibility, especially given the fluctuations of prices for both.

Flexibility played a key role in Enron's thinking. The company also referred to it as "optionality," a common concept in finance that basically means flexibility in a business can be thought of as having option contracts built into that business. This makes sense because options are derivative contracts meant to provide alternatives, and they have an inherent value based on the probability that the alternative provided will be chosen; for example, the price of an option to buy gas is based on the price at which the option would be exercised, the volatility of gas prices, and certain basic assumptions about the general economy.

In a simple sense, optionality in a contract means that flexible terms in a contract can be expressed in terms of options. Back in Chapter 2, Bankers Trust helped Enron identify options that were embedded in contracts, and the example given is a good illustration: If Enron had a contract that guaranteed it a supply of at least 20,000 cubic feet per day of gas, but the contract also allowed Enron to vary the daily volumes between 15,000 and 25,000 cubic feet, that contract could be thought of as one contract for 20,000 cubic feet per day plus two options on 5,000 cubic feet per day. More than just a fancy term for flexibility, optionality referred to the fact that some financial value could be placed on the flexibility in the business.

"The entire purpose of the business is to gain alternatives," Skilling said of Enron's overall strategy. "You might even do things as a business just to help you identify options that you might want for the future." In this way, Enron's ability to move gas and electricity all around North America, using both transportation and trades, offered many alternatives for fulfilling contracts. Skilling gave an example of an electric utility in California wanting to buy electricity and willing to pay $29 per megawatt-hour. One tactic for Enron was to find someone in the same region to sell it power at $28.50 per megawatt-hour, so that Enron could sell it for $29 and make 50 cents per megawatt-hour. But another tactic, Skilling supposed, would be to look at Enron's entire network of alternatives: If it's hot in New York City, Enron might buy excess gas cheaply there, send that gas to a power plant in upstate New York as a substitute for Canadian gas, use freed-up capacity on a Canadian pipeline to send gas to Kansas, then send cheap Midwestern gas to California where that gas can be traded for electricity costing $20 per megawatt-hour. This tactic, although more complex and based on more variables, can yield a fatter profit. As Skilling said, "Now, I'm not going to do that every time, but I just need to do it enough to make a lot of money in this system."

To Enron, being a major player in both natural gas and electricity was a way of giving the company many more options. At the corporation, "optionality and flexibility are important drivers as a result of the common theme of innovation and risk taking," said Mark Tawney, director of Enron's North America's Weather Risk Management business. "Enron acquires a portfolio of options that it has a sense of the value of, but it does not know what the ultimate outcome will be. . . . But that portfolio exposes Enron to opportunities."

■ ■ ■

The latest opportunity to grab Enron's attention was retail electricity—selling power not just to utilities and other traders, but directly to small businesses and residents. To do so, Enron envisioned lofting its name into the brand stratosphere alongside Coke and AT&T. It faced a problem in that outside of industry most people didn't know what Enron was. The company asked people on the street "Who is Enron?" and received such guesses as a senator, a fruit importer, a cosmetics company, and a weapon used by Klingons on *Star Trek*.

With help from its ad agency, Ogilvy & Mather, Enron launched its first national television ad campaign in January 1997 with a commercial that aired before and after America's biggest annual television spectacle, the Super Bowl. On January 26, the millions of people who watched the Green Bay Packers defeat the New England Patriots also got to see a 30-second commercial for Enron, featuring people testifying that Enron had given them cheaper, more reliable energy. The TV spot closed with an announcer saying, "You can choose your neighbors, and soon you may choose your energy company: Enron."

Enron ran the commercials in several major markets, including New York, Houston, and Washington, D.C. It also featured Enron's new logo, the letter "E" tilted at an angle. Newspaper spreads followed the next day, with advertisements in business magazines and on cable television. The goal was to spread the name of Enron, but also to spread the idea of electricity deregulation.

Enron pounded the table on consumer choice in power supply, but also did more than that. The first states had already begun pilot projects allowing residents to choose their power suppliers, and Enron participated. In 1996, New Hampshire (the state whose motto is "Live Free or Die") allowed about 3 percent of its population to choose their electricity supplier. Two dozen companies, including Enron, descended on the state to try to lure some 17,000 customers to sign up with them. Participants were given just under one month to pick a supplier, so the companies aggressively marketed their strengths—Green Mountain Energy Partners, which promised environmentally friendly power, flew a hot-air balloon sporting its logo, while Freedom Energy used direct mail and phone calls stressing its local roots in Concord, New Hampshire, and Working Assets gave away free pints of ice cream. The deals offered to residents were often confusing for people who had never shopped around for electricity before: Was it better to get a $25 rebate check and buy electricity at 3.3 cents per kilowatt-hour or to pay a 2.75-cent rate with the first 500 kilowatt-hours free?

Enron landed a small number of customers. But its biggest coup in the state was in Peterborough, a town where a large number of residents agreed to let their board of selectmen negotiate for them. In June 1996, Enron won the endorsement of Peterborough's selectmen to provide power for the town's roughly 1,400 homes and businesses, and then Enron signed up most of the residents. Enron pursued Peterborough forcefully, knowing that winning the small town at the early stages of deregulation would be more symbolic than profitable; months later, Enron's TV commercials included one about Peterborough.

Enron won Peterborough on price and reliability, but also because of the company's plunge into civic spirit: It donated $25,000 to a downtown revitalization program, hosted a picnic for residents, helped pay for chamber of commerce functions, and sponsored a local high school's solar-powered car project. The company opened an office in town, and flew in 22 salespeople, housing them temporarily at a local motel. All told, Enron spent $100,000 on the Peterborough campaign. And Peterborough residents wound up paying Enron roughly 2.3 cents per kilowatt-hour, less than the 3.5-cent rate they had been charged by the incumbent utility.

Other states also launched pilot programs, including Massachusetts and New York. Meanwhile, the company readied an effort to sell electricity the way other companies sold cornflakes, hoping that people would prefer to buy Enron electricity rather than, say, Southern Co. electricity, or Con Edison electricity. And the company continued to tell lawmakers and regulators that this kind of freedom to choose energy suppliers would benefit everyone in the long run.

■ ■ ■

Enron proselytized loudly about the gospel of free markets, and this stance played well in an era when the laissez-faire economics of Milton Friedman had overshadowed the regulation-friendly thinking of John Maynard Keynes. Such ideological messages provided an intriguing intellectual underpinning for the energy deregulation that Enron wanted. But in the end, Enron was a corporation, not a think tank. So, like any good company, it welcomed the occasional government intervention when it benefited Enron.

Take, for example, Enron's embrace of anti-emissions treaties. The energy industry wasn't happy with the 150-nation agreement to combat global warming that was reached at an environmental summit in Rio de Janeiro in 1992. This treaty, which eventually led to 1997's so-called Kyoto Protocol, targeted industrial emissions as a prime cause of global warming. But Enron supported the Rio pact, and later urged the United States to sign onto the Kyoto treaty (although the United States never did). Did Enron worry so much about global warming that it felt the invisible hand of the market would not be enough to address it? Well, Enron did make some noises about protecting the environment throughout its history. But what the company really liked in the Kyoto treaty was the provision for global trading of permits allowing the emission of so-called greenhouse gases. Enron anticipated a market for trading pollution allowances, the way it already traded electricity futures or gas options.

Frankly, the electricity industry had not been efficient, and so was ripe for some regulatory changes. Utilities had to provide power under all circumstances, which meant that most had power plants, or parts of power plants, that were used only to meet peak demand—say, when every air conditioner in New York City was running on a hot August afternoon. But the majority of the time, these so-called "peaking plants" remained idle. Enron estimated that half of the money invested in the U.S. electricity industry was put to work just three days per year. Because utilities had had to answer only to state regulators, there had been little incentive to cut costs. And customers had to foot the bill to pay for this setup. At last change had crept into this world so that utilities, for instance, could buy extra power from the wholesale market. But, because it was happening on a state-by-state basis, it was changing too slowly for Enron's tastes.

In the mid-1990s, Enron worked its political ties to push for a nationwide plan for electricity deregulation. Enron flaunted its large lobbying force in Washington, as well as the upper-level connections that got it the backing of Commerce Secretary Ron Brown and Ambassador Frank Wisner for its Dabhol project. Although connected to the Bush family and the Republican Party, Enron's access in Washington remained strong under the Democrats. And no wonder. Besides President Clinton's efforts to steer a business-friendly path, Enron was very active in Washington, with a lobbying staff of more than 20. Between 1988 and 1996, Enron and its officers donated $1.9 million to congressional and presidential candidates and to political parties, including $527,000 in "soft money" (loosely regulated donations made directly to a party) to the Republican and Democratic parties.

Enron would go on contributing to political parties, especially the GOP—not surprising, given that party's greater inclination toward deregulation and free markets. From January 1991 through June 1999, Enron donated a total of $1,463,200 in soft money to the Republican Party. To be fair, this was all perfectly legal and Enron was one of many large corporations that put a priority on political contributions. During that 1991–1999 period, Enron was outspent in GOP soft money contributions by such campaign stalwarts as Philip Morris ($6.21 million), AT&T ($2.91 million), and Pfizer ($1.55 million). And the Republicans had competition in the soft money race: At the same time, the Democrats took in millions from such corporations as Seagram ($2.67 million) and Disney ($1.88 million). However, Enron's very visible role as a player in politics still rankled its opponents and its competitors. Having political influence was an important part of the company's image, even if it sometimes seemed to conflict with its message of free markets and less government intervention.

Several bills were proposed in Congress to mandate power deregulation on the national level. Various interest groups, including electric utilities, independent power generators, and rural electric cooperatives, fought over the bills and lobbied lawmakers. The battle was so fierce that energy groups spent $37 million on lobbying in the first six months of 1996 alone. Enron's phalanx of lobbyists marched through Washington's corridors so often that critics started calling the company "Darth Vader."

One bill picked up special support from Enron—a bill sponsored by Representative Tom DeLay (R-Texas). DeLay's bill carried extra significance because DeLay was the House majority whip, which made him the third most powerful member of the House of Representatives. DeLay was also a friend of Enron; in the late 1980s and early 1990s, no campaign contributor had been more generous to him than Enron, according to the Center for Public Integrity.

The DeLay bill would have deregulated the industry within just two years, a timetable that played into the hands of the ready-to-compete Enron but would have rushed many utilities that were still just preparing for competition. The bill would also provide no relief to utilities for the debt they incurred building inefficient power plants, many of which were demanded by state regulators. And while few people had much sympathy for the utilities that had to pay off these white elephants, the bill would have provided Enron another advantage in that it could charge lower prices for electricity than utilities that needed to collect a little extra to pay off their debts. Lay talked to the congressman personally about deregulation. DeLay's bill became known as the "Enron bill" on Capitol Hill, although DeLay's office said many energy companies were consulted on the bill and not just Enron.

When DeLay proposed his bill in late 1996, he set a goal of starting national deregulation by 1998. "This is an ambitious time line, I know, but the time to act is now," he said then. But 20 House oversight hearings later, DeLay's bill was no closer to passage. Other powerful legislators wanted to slow down the deregulation timetable. Representative Dan Schaefer (R-Colorado) proposed a bill that would give states until the end of 2000 to pass deregulation plans. What happened? Congress ended its session in 1997 without taking any action on electricity. The issue got tied up again in 1998 without any resolution—and indeed, a national law on retail deregulation of electricity never passed.

Enron was not completely discouraged. Ken Lay had to know, after all, of former House Speaker Tip O'Neill's famous dictum that "All politics is local." So Enron also attacked deregulation on the state level. By the time of Enron's July 1996 proposal to acquire Portland General, California, New Hampshire, and Rhode Island all had passed power deregulation laws.

In Enron's home state of Texas, the company lobbied hard for a state deregulation plan. Efforts to open the power market to competition met with opposition and conflicting agendas, even though Enron liked to boast that it had a lot of influence in Austin, the state capital. After all, George W. Bush, son of the former president, was elected governor of Texas in 1994, and Enron had strong connections to the Bushes. For Governor Bush's $1.5 million inauguration, Enron had been one of several corporations that donated $50,000, and the guest list had included Richard Kinder and a few other top Enron executives.

Enron's association with the Bush family orbit went further back than 1994. According to a 1993 report in the *New Yorker*, James Baker, the close friend of the first President Bush who served as both his secretary of state and later his chief of staff, lobbied Kuwait to try to get Enron a deal to develop a $600 million power plant project—an effort that looked like an attempt to exploit Kuwait's gratitude to the Bush administration after the Gulf War. Baker, who was working as a paid consultant for Enron, told the magazine he was just trying to direct some business to U.S. companies. Ken Lay defended the actions, telling a newspaper that just because the Gulf War wasn't fought to help American companies, it didn't mean Enron couldn't try to land some business after the war. "Is there any reason American companies shouldn't profit from the war in Kuwait?" he said. Enron may not have been a war profiteer, but critics saw such behavior as an unseemly example of the company's naked opportunism.

Enron was also criticized for its heavy-handed lobbying efforts in Texas. In 1997, for example, Ken Lay presented a Texas deregulation plan at a meeting of business executives at the governor's mansion. Deregulation proponents conflicted, however, with the state electric utilities, which wanted to slow deregulation. Bush even tried to intervene in the deregulation debate, proposing a plan that would open up power markets, would allow utilities to recover all their stranded costs (investments made uneconomical under deregulation), and would cut residential electric rates by 10 percent right away. But all the jockeying ran into too much static, coupled with the state's system that has the legislature meeting only every other year. The year passed without a deregulation law, with the issue to be taken up again in 1999.

■ ■ ■

To serve the slowly growing deregulated market for retail electricity and gas, Enron created a new business unit called Enron Energy Services (EES). Underscoring how important this new business was, the company moved Lou Pai, the president and chief operating officer of ECT, to the new post of chairman and CEO of Enron Energy Services. EES was Skilling's baby, and not only did he closely oversee the unit, but in early 1997 he was even granted a 5 percent stake in it. No other executive had such an arrangement. Skilling didn't appoint Pai so much as deploy him, calling the quietly brainy executive "his ICBM," a strategizing missile. One former executive said Pai was "extremely clever" although he wasn't good with finances. Skilling's backing enabled Pai to overcome his utter lack of presence and charisma to become one of Enron's top executives.

One of the first big projects for the new unit was entering a gas-deregulation pilot program in Toledo, Ohio. In the largest such pilot at the time, the "Clean Start" program allowed residential customers in Toledo to choose their own natural gas supplier, with the promise that the gas would be delivered to them by their traditional gas utility, Columbia Gas. Enron Energy Services offered them gas at a 15 percent discount to the average of the previous 12 months' costs.

Enron launched radio, print, and direct-mail advertising. But, as in many other pilot programs, Toledo residents were not especially eager to try a new supplier for something as crucial as energy. In the end, however, more than half of the program's 25,000 participants chose to stay with the gas-marketing arm of Columbia Gas, even though Enron picked up a few customers. The experience bolstered the argument of those who compared gas and electricity deregulation to the deregulation of the long-distance phone business: After about 10 years of that market being open to newcomers such as MCI and Sprint, AT&T retained some 60 percent of the long-distance market. The lesson was that incumbents have strong advantages, and capturing retail customers would be an uphill battle.

Enron Energy Services started off its life losing $14 million in the first quarter of 1997, a loss that Enron attributed to its "systems, regulatory, and branding costs" needed to ready Enron to sell power and gas at the retail level. The company was willing to lose money on EES, betting that the eventual gains would be substantial. Wall Street waited as well. Enron had long been a favorite of many brokerages' research analysts, whose job it was to analyze stocks and issue recommendations such as "sell" or "buy" to investors (mostly institutional investors, such as pensions and mutual funds). They continued to attach positive ratings to Enron's shares.

But by July 1997, Enron's stock was suffering from its expensive ambition. While the broad stock market had risen in 1997, Enron's shares had slipped. The stock price had been $42.625 on January 2, and it slid to $39 on July 15, when Enron released second-quarter results. With those results, the company lowered its estimates for profits in 1997 and 1998. Enron explained that it lost $25 million in the second quarter from its investment in Enron Energy Services, and planned to lose a total of $90 million that year on the business. EES would post more losses in 1998. Responding to the news, PaineWebber Inc. lowered its rating on the stock to "neutral" from "attractive," and Merrill Lynch cut its opinion to "near-term neutral" from "near-term accumulate."

"The company is clearly struggling with the enormous investment in wholesale electric marketing and the investments in retail electricity," Steven Parla, an analyst at Credit Suisse First Boston, said that afternoon. "These are two businesses which investors have heard about for two years, and they're losing some patience." But Parla counseled continued patience, because he believed the retail market was two years away from busting wide open. Meanwhile, Enron executives suggested they might sell a piece of EES to an outside partner to share its costs.

The unit forged ahead. It struck an agreement with SMC Business Councils, an organization of 5,400 small businesses in western Pennsylvania, to provide its members with natural gas and related services. Healthcare Services of New England, which conducted group purchasing for several hundred health-care facilities in order to lower their costs, signed a pact with EES for "energy solutions." EES agreed to provide seminars on lowering energy costs, then to provide site-specific programs on each customer's energy needs, including energy purchasing and conservation.

But California, the golden goose that planned to open its electricity markets at the start of 1998, began to look like a disappointment. California's deregulation law separated power generation from power distribution so that the local utilities would carry energy provided by any company, including Enron. But the state included a surcharge to all electricity rates to pay off bonds that California would sell to help the utilities pay off their stranded costs—the debt they still had tied up in uneconomic power plants. This would inflate all electricity rates, blunting the impact of savings, and leading Enron to question how big an effort it wanted to make in California. Some consumer groups also opposed the stranded-costs bond plan. "The competitive veil has not been lifted," Lou Pai said.

In the fall of 1997, Enron already had 400 employees in California, but Pai backed away from promising that Enron would pour more resources into the state. "We cannot justify the millions of dollars we were originally committed to spending in this state the way the current regulations read," he explained.

Still, Enron couldn't ignore California, by far the most populous state in the United States, with an economy that would outrank most nations'. In the Olympics of deregulation, California was the gold medal. In October EES launched its first competitive electricity offer to California residents: two weeks of free electricity and a guarantee of at least 10 percent off 1997's electric bills if they signed up with Enron. The company kicked off the campaign with 60-second TV spots and other advertising.

Enron also bought a California firm called the Bentley Company, which provided energy services, energy management, and engineering. The purchase, Enron explained, would help it provide energy-efficiency services, electricity metering (to measure power usage), financing, and other services. In many ways, this move represented a fundamental change in strategy. At the same time that selling to retail customers was proving difficult, EES was adding facilities management to its business strategy.

The aggressiveness with which EES went after retail customers became the talk of the industry. One of the most heated of these battles took place in Pennsylvania, and could have been called "The Philadelphia Story." In the summer of 1997, local utility Peco Energy Corp. reached agreement with state regulators on a plan to slowly ease into competitive

power markets, allowing Peco to remain the default electricity provider
to Philadelphia residents (so if someone didn't choose a new power sup
plier, he or she would automatically become a Peco customer). In return,
Peco promised an immediate 10 percent cut in electric rates. But in October, days before the two sides were to sign the deal, Ken Lay launched a
surprise attack. He proposed cutting electric rates by 20 percent if Enron
were given the opportunity of being the default electricity provider. That
day, an Enron-sponsored plane flew above the skyscrapers of Philly drag-
ging a banner that read: "Enron Choice Plan Saves 20%."

As usual, Enron had grabbed the spotlight, in the process agitating the
system so that deregulation would have to be addressed more quickly.
The company had struck boldly, especially in an industry that was still
used to cordial cooperation between regulated monopolies. It chose Peco
as an opponent partly because of its vulnerability: Although one of the
largest U.S. utilities, it charged some of the highest electric rates in the
country, in part because more than half of its power came from costly
nuclear-power plants that would prove unprofitable in a completely
competitive market. As in many situations, Peco wanted state help in
paying these stranded costs.

Enron and Peco engaged in a public-relations blitz for several months.
Lay appeared on Philadelphia radio shows, and Enron ran TV commercials. Lay compared the process to a political campaign, as he lobbied officials in Harrisburg, the state capital. Peco ran its own commercials,
including one that featured actor David Leisure (best known for playing
a sleazy, lying salesman in a series of memorable Isuzu commercials) pre-
tending to be a sleazy Texan electricity seller who made big promises
along with his offer of cheap power, adding, "I'll even throw in the
Brooklyn Bridge."

Peco's first agreement allowed the utility to pay off, using electric rate
surcharges, about $5.4 billion of its estimated $7 billion of stranded
costs. Enron's pitch of a 20 percent rate cut also proposed paying off $5.4
billion in stranded costs, but the company argued that it could finance
the repayment of those costs more cheaply, allowing for larger customer
savings. There was no free lunch here, however. To achieve that savings,
Enron angled for the state to guarantee some of its debt financing so it
could borrow more cheaply, which the state didn't agree to. Peco portrayed Enron as an out-of-state profiteer, claiming, "Enron's goal is to

cripple Peco Energy financially without exposing itself to any risk. . . . Enron's plan will not work."

In early December, the state's Public Utilities Commission voted three to two to approve its own deregulation plan, which differed from the plans put forth by Peco and Enron. The commission plan called for 15 percent cuts in electric rates, a shopping credit for customers to apply to whomever they chose as their electricity supplier, and allowing Peco to recover $5 billion in stranded costs. Enron did not win. But its interference caused a different outcome for Peco. Enron called it "a win for consumers."

While EES tried to grab residential customers, it was slowly shifting its focus to large businesses and institutions—as seen in its pacts with Healthcare Services of New England. The unit's more promising business was managing a customer's complete energy needs on an outsourced basis. If a company hired Enron to manage its energy needs, Enron would supply all the gas and electricity, manage energy-related equipment such as heaters and boilers, and even install energy-saving devices. Sometimes, Enron would even buy the small power plant that a factory had on its site (large factories such as paper mills often had such plants) and manage it, selling the power back to the customer. In exchange, Enron's compensation would be a cut of the savings it produced for the client.

This fit into Skilling's vision of turning energy into more than a commodity—it was a commodity around which Enron could provide services, including trading, financing, risk management, and, now, the management of facilities' energy. If successful, Enron would make the running of a customer's energy needs seem invisible.

The company's ability to deliver both gas and electricity, and to switch fuels if prices warranted it, aided this energy-management effort. Enron could supply any dish from its energy buffet. As Skilling explained, "Customers don't care if they're buying natural gas or electricity. Customers want some function—they want light, they want air conditioning, they want motor power. And they don't care if it comes from natural gas or electricity or petroleum."

The newer EES mission started reaping immediate deals and seemed to be working. In January 1998, the unit struck a large pact with Pacific Telesis, California's local phone company, to supply energy and run energy management projects for that company's 8,000 facilities. The deal included buying electricity from Enron for four years, the company's first huge win in California's new deregulated market. At the start of 1998, EES had long-term contracts in place worth over $1 billion in revenue, estimated by Enron to be worth $50 million to $60 million in eventual profits.

Enron Energy Services kept signing up more large customers for energy outsourcing contracts. An example was Owens Corning, the large maker of construction products best known for its glass fiber insulation. Enron first contacted the company in February 1999 about the outsourcing of its energy supplies, which ran to more than $100 million per year. Enron looked smart; months later, Owens Corning was hit with a summer heat wave that caused tremendous price spikes at several factories. The company signed a 10-year, $1.1 billion contract with Enron Energy Services in September. Enron guaranteed that it would provide Owens Corning with at least $60 million in savings over the 10 years, and that didn't even include additional cost savings from falling rates in states with deregulated markets. Enron agreed to manage energy needs at 20 Owens Corning manufacturing facilities across the United States, stretching from California to New York; this would include supplying and managing all purchases of energy, as well as the hedging of price volatility. As with all its EES contracts, Enron would get a share of the savings.

In addition, Enron Energy Services would design, build, and finance some "energy infrastructure projects" the manufacturer needed, involving boilers, process chillers, backup generators (for handling price spikes), and energy efficiency upgrades. But that wasn't all. EES and Owens Corning created a 50–50 joint venture for buying some of this energy equipment from Owens Corning and leasing it back to the company, and for buying new equipment and leasing it to the company. Enron provided $24 million to buy this equipment, and the structure of the joint venture allowed EES to record $10.3 million in projected earnings from the deal in 1999's fourth quarter—which wouldn't have been possible without the arrangement. Also, by putting the sale/leaseback deal into a joint venture, which was technically a separate entity from Enron, EES was also able to get it off Enron's balance sheet.

The Owens Corning deal was not unique. In addition to managing electricity, gas, and other energy supplies, EES sought to use its financial muscle to finance the equipment used in its outsourcing pacts. There wasn't anything wrong or illegal about this; rather, it was Enron being resourceful. In some ways, this strategy of helping to finance a project so that Enron could generate business from that project was Gas Bank all over again, but on a smaller scale. Enron would often seek to buy the necessary energy-management equipment and lease it back to the customer in a contract that's similar to the typical car lease.

But in many cases, Enron sought to lease the equipment back to the client company in leases that were more complex than car leases. The most sophisticated of these deals were known as "synthetic leases," which allowed the company to essentially acquire assets using off-balance sheet debt. This provided additional flexibility for negotiating the outsourcing agreements by sweetening the deal for the prospective client. In some cases, the client corporation would benefit because the deal would make the client's net worth and borrowing base look better. At the same time, the client would get certain tax benefits associated with owning the equipment outright. The synthetic lease is part of the long tradition of hybrid deals that combine debt and ownership to lessen taxes while making balance sheets look better. These activities also posed huge risks to Enron because it inherited the terminal value of the assets once the leases ran their course.

Although EES won a healthy volume of business, it was still losing money. In many ways, the low-profit-margin retail business was out of sync with Enron's high-margin culture. "It was hard to be the low-cost provider in facilities management when EES executives were compensated like investment bankers," says one Enron executive. So in January 1998, the company sold a 7 percent stake in EES to two pension funds for a total of $130 million. Enron didn't disclose the names of the two funds, but they were the Ontario Teachers' Pension Plan and CalPERS, the California pension fund that had teamed up with Enron in the JEDI investment partnership. The CalPERS investment actually came from a new, second investment partnership with Enron, also formed in January, into which CalPERS and Enron each contributed $500 million.

The sale of a piece of EES gave Enron a way to value the new business. If 7 percent was worth $130 million, it meant the whole business was worth roughly $1.85 billion (it also meant that Skilling's 5 percent piece was worth more than $90 million). That was a pretty penny for a unit that had yet to turn profitable. But that didn't stop Skilling from telling Wall Street analysts that EES's value suggested that Enron's stock, then trading at about $41 per share, should have a price of more than $50 (his assessment didn't raise the stock price, however). CalPERS took a risk, but it was investing in a business that seemed to have tremendous potential. Inside Enron, the sale looked like an admission of weakness in which CalPERS came to the rescue, putting a valuation on EES so that Enron could borrow money against it as the unit continued losing money.

In early 1998, Enron offered one-stop shopping for energy, from gas and electricity sales to pipelines and from a local electric utility to out-sourced energy management. It had positioned itself to become one of the premier energy companies in the world, and in so doing seemed to achieve its goal. But in the hypercompetitive world of business in the 1990s, when the Internet was trumping all traditional notions of stock price and corporate growth rates, achieving goals was not enough. Enron's success gave it the confidence to set new, higher goals. Conquering the world of energy would not be enough.

7

TAKING THE PLUNGE

Enron's sale of a stake in Enron Energy Services to CalPERS held significance beyond just setting a value on the new business and finding a partner to share some of the new business' costs. It sparked the first instance in which Enron used Special Purpose Entities (SPEs) run by company employees to engage in questionable accounting, starting the trend that eventually led to Enron's collapse.

In November 1997, Enron wanted to form a second investment partnership with CalPERS to succeed the JEDI partnership that they formed back in 1993. This second partnership would, a few months later, buy a piece of EES. Enron liked how the original JEDI partnership worked out: Enron estimated its piece of JEDI was worth $392 million at the end of 1997, up from $320 million a year earlier; also, Enron included $68 million from its share of JEDI's profits in its 1997 earnings. As for CalPERS, the pension fund had garnered a roughly 23 percent return on its investment in JEDI.

But in November, Enron figured that CalPERS wouldn't invest in both JEDI and the new partnership. And the company seemed to want to finalize the new partnership quickly so it could be used in deals before year-end. So Enron proposed buying out the pension fund's 50 percent stake in JEDI. Enron still wanted to avoid consolidating JEDI into its financial statements, however, for two reasons: Enron didn't want to add JEDI's debt to its own; and Enron wanted to maintain the ability to do the occasional business deal with JEDI and have it count as a transaction with another company. To keep JEDI as an independent partnership, the company sought a new limited partner so that Enron was still investing with an outside party—otherwise, JEDI would have been an all-Enron entity, and consolidated into the company.

Andrew Fastow, the financial expert who had pooled Volumetric Production Payments into the Cactus Funds in the early 1990s, had a solution. Fastow, the company's senior vice president of finance, proposed that Enron form another partnership named Chewco Investments—after the *Star Wars* movie character Chewbacca—to buy CalPERS' stake in JEDI. The key was to structure Chewco so that it qualified as an entity that was independent of Enron. Fastow initially suggested that he manage Chewco because he knew the underlying assets of JEDI. But Jeff Skilling wanted someone else as manager because Fastow was a senior officer of Enron and so his running the partnership would have to be disclosed in the company's proxy statement (the disclosure issued for the annual shareholders meeting). Instead, Michael Kopper, an Enron employee who reported to Fastow, became the proposed manager of Chewco.

Despite his role as Chewco's manager, Kopper was a quiet man who operated mostly in the background and didn't display the self-possessed brilliance that others at Enron tried to show off. He'd grown up on New York's Long Island as an unassuming kid who didn't particularly stand out at high school. After graduating from Duke University and studying at the London School of Economics, Kopper worked at two banks, and then joined Enron in 1994. He worked closely with Fastow and the two became friends. Among his greatest assets was his loyalty to Fastow.

In November 1997, Chewco was formed on very short notice, with Enron's outside counsel, Vinson & Elkins, preparing the necessary legal documents in just two days. Enron agreed that Chewco buy CalPERS' stake in JEDI for $383 million. Documents to get this deal through were faxed to members of the Enron board, giving them three short days to review. Time was clearly of the essence.

If Chewco were to be Enron's new partner in JEDI, Chewco needed outside investors to be considered an independent special purpose entity. According to the Securities and Exchange Commission (SEC), an SPE created by a company has to meet two requirements in order to be considered independent. First, it has to have at least 3 percent of its equity, or ownership, come from a third party not related to the company. That has to be a real investment, so that the outside investor risks losing that 3 percent stake (and the requirement that the equity is at risk would later prove significant for Enron). Second, a party other than the company must control the SPE. This is a tricky rule, because the SEC doesn't specify what "control" means. If these two rules aren't met, the SPE is essentially no different from a subsidiary of the company, and its finances must be combined into the financial statements of the company.

Fastow originally suggested that members of his wife's family be included in Chewco's outside investors, but Skilling rejected that idea. To quickly assemble the partnership, Enron actually proposed borrowing Chewco's entire $383 million from banks on a short-term basis, and then replacing 3 percent of those loans with equity before the end of the year. The proposal didn't specify where the 3 percent of equity (around $11 million) would come from.

On November 5, the executive committee of Enron's board of directors heard about the Chewco deal on a telephone conference call. Fastow described Chewco as "a special purpose vehicle not affiliated with the company or CalPERS," and described the transaction, including the short-term bank loan. Ken Lay joined the meeting during the presentation. Then the board's executive committee approved the whole deal. However, there was no evidence that Kopper received the approval of either the chairman or the CEO of Enron (at the time, Lay held both roles) to manage Chewco, which was required under the company's code of conduct.

Because Kopper controlled Chewco and was an Enron employee, it was possible to conclude that Enron controlled Chewco, disqualifying it as an independent SPE. To solve this problem, Enron converted Chewco to a limited partnership, which placed some restrictions on Kopper's power as manager, and added a new partner to Chewco. This new, "limited" partner was yet another partnership set up just for this deal. On December 18, Kopper transferred his stake in the limited partner to William D. Dodson, creating a partner in Chewco that was technically independent from Enron. Why Dodson? He was Kopper's domestic partner.

Involving family members and other loved ones in Enron's business was questionable, but not without precedent. Enron did business with one of Ken Lay's sisters and one of his sons. Sharon Lay, a sister of Ken Lay, owned half of Lay/Wittenberg Travel Agency, which had a contract to arrange travel for Enron employees. In 1996, Lay/Wittenberg earned commissions of roughly $1.6 million from Enron employee travel, and in 1997 the agency earned $2 million in commissions from Enron staff.

Lay's son, Mark K. Lay, had worked for Enron Gas Services in the early 1990s, but left in 1992 and worked for insurance giant AIG. He then went into business for himself, owning one-third of Bruin Interests, a natural gas company. In 1996, Enron Development Corp. hired Bruin as a consultant to study possible gas processing projects, and paid it $33,500. While still involved with Bruin, Mark Lay helped found Paper & Print Management, a company that wanted to trade contracts for paper and pulp, much the way Enron traded contracts for gas and electricity. Although Paper & Print had no customers, Enron bought the company in 1997. In place of a purchase price, Enron paid $1 million to buy out an investment in it by electric utility Southern Co., and hired Mark Lay and his partners to work inside Enron Capital & Trade to develop the trading of finished paper products. Mark Lay was named a vice president and given a three-year contract guaranteeing a salary of at least $150,000 per year, a signing bonus of $100,000, and minimum annual bonuses of $100,000.

The dealings with Lay's family members sparked questioning from an investor at Enron's 1997 annual meeting in Houston. Lay responded that the contracts were won through competitive bidding, and pointed out that the transactions were properly disclosed in the company's proxy statement.

Beyond the issue of William Dodson, the Chewco situation became murkier. Enron had patched together the partnership with only debt and still needed outside equity in it. By the end of the year, Enron and Kopper rejiggered Chewco so that it was funded by a $240 million loan from Barclays Bank (guaranteed by Enron), a $132 million loan from JEDI, and $11.5 million in equity from Chewco's partners that represented the magic 3 percent. Where to find that outside equity? Enron started with Kopper himself, who invested about $115,000 in Chewco's general partner and $10,000 in its limited partner before transferring his interests to Dodson. But Enron couldn't find any other companies to invest the outside equity. So Barclays loaned $11.4 million to Chewco's partners, which were essentially paper entities controlled by Kopper and Dodson. The loan was set up so that Enron and Chewco could portray it as equity; this wasn't unusual for SPE financing at the time, and there were a range of securities that functioned as hybrids of debt and equity.

The Barclays loan to Chewco's partners complicated things even further. Barclays required Chewco's partners to set aside cash reserves to back up the repayment of the $11.4 million loan. To fund the reserves, JEDI made a special distribution of $16.6 million to Chewco, taking the money from its share of selling its stake in Coda Energy and Coda's Taurus subsidiary. When this transaction occurred on December 30, 1997, Chewco suddenly had the reserves, including cash collateral of $6.6 million, securing the Barclays loan.

The cash collateral created a problem that wasn't rectified until years later. To explain the problem, it's necessary to leap ahead to 2002. In late 2001 and early 2002, a special committee of Enron's board of directors investigated Chewco and other Enron deals, in an attempt to understand Enron's financial troubles. The committee, chaired by then-director William C. Powers, issued a report in 2002 that became known as "The Powers Report," and that report criticized, among other things, the structure of the Chewco deal. Looking back on Chewco's formation, the report said, the board concluded that the $11.4 million from Barclays could barely count as equity—and even if it could, it couldn't count as the SPE's 3 percent outside equity because it wasn't *at risk*, seeing as how it was secured by a $6.6 million cash collateral. Furthermore, Barclays' contribution fell short of the 3 percent mark because the "equity" included Kopper's $125,000 investment, and Kopper was affiliated with Enron. This all meant that Chewco didn't count as an independent SPE and should have been consolidated into Enron's financial statements. And if Chewco wasn't an independent SPE, that meant JEDI wasn't, and it, too, should have been consolidated into Enron's financials.

Enron's accounting firm, Arthur Andersen, had reviewed the Chewco transaction and billed Enron $80,000 for the review. David Duncan, Andersen's lead auditor on the Enron account, would later testify that the accounting firm didn't know about the $11.4 million side agreement with Barclays; had it known, that would have changed the auditors' treatment of the partnership. When he later found out about the equity-like loan from Barclays, Duncan actually felt deceived by Enron.

But Kopper, who stood to gain from his investment and from fees for running Chewco, and a few other employees clearly knew about the Barclays deal. Indeed, from December 1997 through December 2000, Enron paid Kopper $2 million in "management fees" and other fees related to Chewco, even though the partnership required little management. It's also unclear how these fees, apparently negotiated by Kopper and his boss Fastow, were calculated.

In addition to holding debt, the Chewco-JEDI arrangement generated some income for Enron. For guaranteeing the $240 million loan from Barclays, Chewco paid Enron a fee of $10 million, plus $7.4 million in other fees. Chewco's existence allowed JEDI to remain a separate SPE, which resulted in other income. For one thing, JEDI paid Enron (as the managing partner) a management fee of at least $2 million per year, which it wouldn't have had to pay if it hadn't been an independent partnership. On March 31, 1998, Enron recognized a lump sum of $25.7 million in income from a portion of all the management fees that JEDI would be paying through June 2003, not unlike the up-front profits recorded in a mark-to-market transaction. Enron also recorded an undetermined amount of income from the appreciation of Enron stock held by JEDI, which wouldn't have been allowed if JEDI had been folded into Enron.

"Enron had every incentive to ensure that Chewco was properly capitalized," the Powers Report opined. It wasn't clear why Chewco was formed improperly—whether it was bad judgment, or carelessness, or the result of Enron employees putting their own interests ahead of Enron's. Whatever the case, Chewco was a Rube Goldberg contraption of a partnership just waiting to bite Enron. And the company appeared to tolerate it just to keep debt off its balance sheet and generate a little extra income.

■ ■ ■

Enron had a real need for a healthy balance sheet. The company's trading businesses and overseas developments required reams of cash, and Enron was a frequent borrower, issuing bonds or other debt securities. If the company's balance sheet started to look unhealthy—say, its debt load started to look too heavy compared with its assets—then credit rating agencies would lower their ratings on Enron's debt. Lower credit ratings would mean Enron had to pay higher interest rates on its debt, because it was a worse credit risk. Higher interest rates would cut into Enron's earnings. And it was all about earnings growth.

There are many ways to assess the financial condition of a company, such as the value of its assets, or how much cash it generates, or its return on equity. By the mid-1990s, earnings had become the premier measure of a company's health. While it might seem like common sense to gauge a company by its profits, earnings are in some ways a creation of accounting rules. Earnings, or "net income," includes taxes, interest, depreciation, and amortization of debt. This doesn't mean that net income is a bad measure. But earnings *can* be massaged using such tactics as aggressive use of mark-to-market accounting or choosing to book contracts just before a fiscal quarter ends. Unexpected costs, under certain circumstances, can be characterized as one-time expenses, and Wall Street analysts would often downplay these "extraordinary items" in the quarterly reports because they were focused on assessing a company's "core" business. Enron often reported one-time expenses in its earnings reports, and because the analysts saw these items as peripheral, it made the company's earnings look better.

An example was Enron's litigation over the J-Block contract to buy natural gas at above-market rates. When Enron settled the dispute with a lump-sum payment in June 1997, the company accounted for it as a one-time charge to its earnings totaling $675 million before taxes. This meant that for one fiscal quarter Enron's profits looked awful, and then the problem was gone. This was fair, because it was a legal settlement and not a cost associated with Enron's regular business. But seen another way, the settlement allowed Enron to renegotiate a contract that would have resulted in recurring losses on U.K. gas sales. Because selling gas was Enron's regular business, the original contract's losses might have been included in Enron's operating results, depressing them for years. Instead, the legal settlement resulted in one bad quarter, and then subsequent quarters looked much better.

As business became more of a spectator sport, with the rise of the CNBC business-news network and Internet chat rooms about investing, investors needed a handy way to track companies. Earnings became it. Analysts published estimates of what they expected a company to earn in a given quarter on a per-share basis, and then the actual results were compared. If a company exceeded analysts' expectations, this was viewed as confirmation of its robust growth and the stock often went up. When Enron released its third-quarter earnings in October 1997, it reported earnings of 42 cents a share; that far surpassed the 34 cents that was the consensus of analysts' estimates, and Enron's stock rose 1 percent. The goal of many companies became beating analysts' expectations.

Analysts, meanwhile, started to expect a lot. The economic expansion of the mid and late 1990s boosted corporate profits, and soon steady earnings growth became anticipated. It was no accident that in the mid 1990s Enron set a goal of 15 percent earnings growth every year. Of course, growth was always an important part of business and Wall Street. Capitalism is dynamic, always moving, like a cascade of stars or a school of sharks, depending on one's perspective: Companies were perceived as either moving forward or slipping behind. There was no standing still.

Two things had happened to accelerate the focus on growth in the late 1990s. First, shareholders had become more demanding. This had its roots in the 1980s, when corporate raiders such as Irwin Jacobs and Boone Pickens upended the rules in the nation's boardrooms. They demanded that CEOs put shareholder interests above all else, and often boosted shareholder returns by taking over and then selling companies. This helped lead to the idea that management had to have the same stake in the company as the shareholders. As a result, companies increasingly granted their executives employee stock options, which, after a few years, turned into substantial stakes in the companies. By the mid-1990s, executives had huge portions of their compensation riding on their companies' stocks. If the stocks were flat, the options were worthless, but if the stocks rose, the options could be worth millions of dollars for senior executives. So the executives also demanded growth, along with their investors.

Second, the Internet hit. Netscape, which pioneered the Web browser, went public in 1995 and its stock more than doubled in its first day of trading. Other Internet-related stocks followed, and many skyrocketed, doubling and tripling in no time. This was growth like Wall Street hadn't seen in a generation. Amazon.com, the online book retailer, reached a market capitalization greater than that of any bookstore chain. Priceline.com, which offered discount airline tickets, was eventually awarded a market value bigger than any airline. These companies were growing their revenues, not their profits (most had no profits), but that distinction was small. Even if it wasn't sustainable, Internet companies changed what investors thought was possible in terms of growth.

To help squeeze out an extra 1 or 2 percent of growth, and thus meet or beat analysts' estimates, more and more managements took advantage of accounting rules. So a company would classify costs as one-time expenses when it could, or start acquiring lots of other companies to boost its earnings. Or a bank might shift some reserves for bad credit into profits for one quarter just to meet analysts' estimates. Or a company might form an SPE to acquire customers, and then buy the customers from that SPE because purchased assets received better accounting treatment than customer acquisition costs. And the adjustments, stretches, and partnerships (such as Chewco, had it been structured properly) nearly always fell within the parameters of the traditionally vague accounting rules; companies' finance departments became expert at steering around bookkeeping regulations. Manufacturing quarterly earnings growth to increase the stock price became imperative, even if that "growth" came at the expense of the company's long-term health.

A training manual on derivatives that Enron used actually put it this way: "Reported earnings follow the rules and principles of accounting. The results do not always create measures consistent with underlying economics. However, corporate management's performance is generally measured by accounting income and not underlying economics."

These were the earnings-growth pressures facing Enron. But achieving consistent growth is difficult, for even the best companies. So it was also no surprise that in the late 1990s Enron changed its goal from 15 percent growth *every* year to an *average* of 15 percent growth over a number of years.

Still, Enron's managers did well under this growth-and-reward system. About three-quarters of compensation for Enron's senior executives was based on the company's performance. So Enron's continued growth created rising pay packages larded with stock options, most of which became exercisable over five-year periods. In 1997, Lay took home $1,675,000 in salary and bonus, and was awarded options to buy roughly 950,000 shares; if Enron's stock appreciated by 10 percent per year, those options would be worth $37.9 million. Jeff Skilling was paid $1.2 million in salary and bonus in 1997, and was awarded 1 million stock options that would be worth about $61 million if Enron's stock appreciated by 10 percent a year. Enron felt the 10 percent growth target was achievable: The company estimated that its stock more than doubled from 1992 through 1997, although it lagged a little behind its peer group of pipeline companies over that period.

This arrangement produced a tier of senior officers well paid in Enron options and stock. By February 15, 1997, Ken Lay owned 3 million shares of Enron, or 1.49 percent of the company, and Jeff Skilling owned nearly 619,000 shares. Top executives may seek to excel because of some innate competitive drive, but Lay, Skilling, and the rest of Enron's management had the added incentive of big paydays if they succeeded. So the race was on to generate more growth.

■ ■ ■

Growth meant new markets. When Enron entered a new market and turned the product there into a tradable commodity (say, electricity), it would reap fat profit margins. But as the market matured, the profit margins would slowly shrink. That this would happen makes intuitive sense, if profits are considered as inefficiencies in a market that are captured by a company. So as competition made the market more efficient, the profits would shrink—the way commissions on stock trading gradually declined from around $300 per trade to $50 per trade to $30 or less.

In the natural gas market, the average profit margin of five cents per trade in the early days turned into one cent per trade by the late 1990s. Partly offsetting this trend was a growth in the overall market, so Enron wound up making many more trades while each one yielded less profit on average. Skilling and the rest of Enron's brain trust understood this. Enron Energy Services, which was turning its focus to managing energy systems on an outsourced basis, was one attempt to address this phenomenon by adding what were considered "value-added" services (a popular business buzzword) to the commodities of gas and electricity.

The slowly shrinking profit margins of gas, and soon electricity, would send Enron on a search for fatter profit margins. This meant the company had to find fresh markets to Enronize.

One fresh market was renewable, or "green" energy: This comprised energy generated from renewable sources such as wind, water, and light, as opposed to fossil fuels. Enron dove into this business in January 1997 by acquiring Zond Corp., a California company that made and operated wind turbines. Zond completed its first wind farm (a collection of wind-powered turbines) in 1981 and since then had installed more than 2,400 wind turbines with a total capacity of 260 megawatts. Zond generated about 600 million kilowatt-hours of electricity in 1995, enough to supply the yearly residential needs of over 300,000 people. Zond became the centerpiece of a new Enron subsidiary, Enron Renewable Energy Corp.

Although it was providing only 2.5 percent to 4.5 percent of U.S. power, depending on estimates, renewable energy enjoyed rising popularity at the time. The Clinton administration promoted renewable energy, and the deregulation of electricity in a few states had opened the door for some customers to choose to use "green" power. In addition to buying Zond, Enron was also a partner with oil giant Amoco in Amoco/Enron Solar, the largest U.S.-owned producer of solar photovoltaic cells and the second largest worldwide.

Enron Renewable quickly won contracts to build two huge wind generation projects using its Z-750 kilowatt wind turbines—MidAmerican Energy's 112.5-megawatt project in Iowa, and Northern States Power's 100-megawatt project in Minnesota. The company followed its usual growth strategy with renewable energy, purchasing Tacke Windtechnik, a German company making 1.5-megawatt wind turbines in Europe, the world's largest wind power market. Enron tapped Thomas White, a former Army general, to run Enron Renewable Energy.

To take advantage of the demand among some for green power, Enron folded its renewable energy business into EES. Later in 1998, the unit won a contract to provide wind power to all 14 California facilities of Patagonia Inc., a manufacturer of outdoor clothing that decided to use only wind energy. In 1999, Enron opened a 22-turbine, 16.5-megawatt wind farm near Palm Springs to supply Patagonia and other customers; the company estimated that the project produced 88 million fewer pounds of carbon dioxide and 300,000 fewer pounds of smog emissions than a similar-sized fossil-fuel plant.

Enron focused mostly on wind power, as wind farms were able to generate energy on a large scale, while solar energy was used mostly on a small, retail scale for individual homes or buildings. One of the attractions of renewable energy was the fact that customers would sometimes pay more for it, just because it was green. Back in 1998, Enron thought this premium-priced renewable energy might develop into its own tradable commodity, distinct from other electricity.

To find even more new markets to conquer, Enron had to reach beyond energy. It did this, taking its first step with paper and pulpwood. A former employee in Enron's printing department named David Cox had cofounded a printing company that handled annual reports and other jobs for Enron and other Houston firms. Paper prices fluctuated based on demand and on the supply of pulpwood, and could be volatile. From January 1994 to mid-1995, paper prices more than doubled. Cox sought to stabilize his paper costs with a long-term fixed-price contract, similar to the ones Enron offered on gas and power. But such contracts didn't exist in the paper industry. Not yet.

He pitched the idea to two big newspaper publishers, and they agreed the concept was promising. Then he contacted Skilling, and discovered that Enron had been thinking about the paper and pulp business as well, as that industry was a large power customer of Enron's. After all, it was a large commodity business that might be able to use risk-management tools just as natural gas did. Soon Cox was back at Enron, but this time as a vice president developing paper and pulp derivatives. In 1997, Enron was handling forwards, swaps, and options for this business, performing just 17 deals; eventually, Enron's pulp and paper trading business grew to 432 deals worth $4 billion in 1999.

Paper was just the beginning. Next was weather. According to the old saying, everybody talks about the weather but nobody does anything about it. Enron decided to do something about it.

Just as paper derivatives were backed by David Cox, weather derivatives came to be championed by an employee working at the grassroots level and seeing customers' daily needs. John Sherriff, who at the time managed gas trading for the western United States, began looking at derivatives linked to the weather in late 1995, and Vincent Kaminski's research group worked on the idea in 1996. A gas trader named Lynda Clemmons was very interested in the idea, based on her conversations with executives at electric utilities that used coal-fired power plants. During heat waves when air-conditioner use spiked, these utilities had to either restart idled power plants at great cost or pay a lot to buy power on the wholesale market. The utility managers wished they had a product to provide a financial hedge against the weather. In 1997, Enron handed off its weather derivatives effort to Clemmons, who was only 27. She began a one-person weather-hedging department within ECT, although many others such as Sherriff had contributed to ECT's overall effort.

The idea was intriguing: Because warm weather and snowflakes can't be bought or sold, use financial instruments that would allow bets placed directly on temperature, rainfall, or snowfall, where cash would change hands based on the weather's outcomes. It seemed like a natural outgrowth of using financial instruments to hedge weather-sensitive commodity prices. Why use weather derivatives? Take the example of a seller of heating oil. A warm winter would mean lower product prices as well as less heating oil sold. Using existing derivatives such as heating oil futures, the company could hedge the drop in heating oil *prices*. But weather derivatives would offer the additional chance to hedge the drop in heating oil *sales volume*. Theoretically, the weather derivatives would entitle the heating oil company to receive set sums of money for each degree that the temperature rose above a predetermined level; that cash would then offset some of the losses from the warmer weather.

Enron figured that weather derivatives would be useful in covering lost revenue and unexpected costs, and back up planned expenses such as sales promotions. Because the concept was "very far out there," it took a while to get the first weather derivative deal, recalled Sherriff. Enron conducted the first weather derivative deal in August 1997 with an unnamed "eastern U.S. utility," linking the price for 50 megawatts of electricity to weather conditions in the utility's service area. Once again, the Houston giant had pioneered an area of trading. Insurance companies had long offered weather insurance, but here was weather insurance in the form of a tradable commodity.

Enron went on to do 24 more weather deals that year, constructing contracts with swaps and options. The business was helped in part by El Niño, the ocean-atmosphere phenomenon that was disrupting weather patterns around the globe. Aquila Energy, Koch Energy, and a few other energy-trading companies jumped into the weather derivatives market. Most of the weather derivatives centered on temperature, as Enron (which had already invested in meteorologists) and its rivals could sort through decades of temperature data from the National Weather Service in order to structure deals and make their own forecasts. Weather derivative contracts tended to be short-term, with an average length of five months, and Aquila even introduced five-day products.

Enron sold weather hedges to a fertilizer maker, a brewery, a sports-drink company, a movie studio, a golf resort, and others. As Enron's weather derivatives desk grew, Clemmons got employees reassigned from other areas to work for her. "You create your own network," she said, alluding to Enron's entrepreneurial culture. Perceived by her colleagues as smart and likable, Clemmons built up Enron's weather business so that it did 350 transactions (hedging up to $400 million in potential revenues) in 1998, turning its first profit that year.

Renewable energy, paper, and weather derivatives were beginnings. The company would go on to sell and trade coal, plastics, and other commodities. In one sense, Enron was taking the admirable strategy of trying a bunch of new things and seeing what would stick. Just as Enron executives back in 1986 probably never imagined themselves running a company that traded bets on the weather, the management in 1996 was not sure what Enron would look like in 10 years and didn't worry too much about it. The company was certain that its smart, talented staff would find ways to adapt to changes in the market and the emergence of new markets. Enron was developing the confidence that it could handle any new business, and this only enhanced its missionary zeal to trade everything.

■ ■ ■

Meanwhile, Rebecca Mark searched for a new role at Enron. She continued to oversee the company's expanding international power plant and pipeline division, as it busily developed such projects as the Bolivia-to-Brazil gas pipeline and power plants in Turkey, Poland, and Italy.

Enron even beefed up Enron International in 1997 by reacquiring Enron Global Power & Pipelines, the partnership it formed in 1994 to buy foreign projects from Enron Corp. and manage them. After some negotiations with Enron Global's independent directors, Enron bought the 48 percent stake it didn't own for more than $430 million in stock. This simplified Enron's corporate structure, putting Enron Global under EI's umbrella. The company didn't say so, but folding the partnership also eliminated criticism the company had endured that Enron was able to "manage" its earnings by selling projects to Enron Global at just the right time.

But even this larger EI was not enough in a company that prided itself on constantly taking on new challenges. In May 1998, Enron named Mark one of two vice chairmen, the other being Portland General CEO Ken Harrison. Mark gave up day-to-day responsibilities for EI to coordinate with other Enron businesses and focus on bigger-picture issues; she was already eyeing the water business, which she thought held great opportunities.

Although the promotion officially vaulted her into the top ranks of the company, in the new role she reported not only to Lay, but also to Skilling, her former rival.

Her curiosity about the water business was anything but offhand. Enron had been looking for more than a year to enter the water utility industry, but felt that it needed to buy or partner with a large, operating water company with experienced management. Like the acquisition of Portland General, the idea would be to buy a water utility and learn the water market from it; it was part of Enron's strategy of buying just enough hard assets to learn a new business, so it could then focus on asset-light operations such as sales and trading. Water was even more crucial than gas or electricity, so the demand was there. And around the world, the water business was slowly deregulating, as countries sold government-owned utilities to private companies. The private water industry was dominated by two French companies well versed in privatization, Suez Lyonnaise des Eaux and Vivendi, both of which owned water utilities and water projects in numerous countries. Perhaps there would also be room for Enron in what it estimated was a $300 billion-a-year global business. It seemed no more difficult a proposition than entering the paper or weather derivatives businesses.

In July 1998, Enron agreed to purchase England's Wessex Water, a water and sewage company serving some 1.1 million customers. The pact called for a price of $2.2 billion in cash (or £1.4 million), a 28 percent premium over Wessex's stock price. Wessex, with annual revenue of $434 million, was one of Britain's smaller water utilities, but it was well run and profitable. It would be the centerpiece of a new water business within Enron, headed by Rebecca Mark, which would own and operate water distribution and water treatment assets around the world. The new business also included Enron's stake in a privatized water and sewage company in Argentina, which it had purchased as part of a consortium the month before. Enron paid top dollar for these assets, but the standard logic of "Enronization" prevailed: Developing new, big markets would be good for the company in the long run.

Enron pitched the water idea as a logical extension of EI's business, and the next big market that it would make its own. Water could be as large as Enron's gas and electricity businesses in just a few years, Lay said. It was another daring gambit for two reasons: No energy company had expanded into water before; and U.K. regulators were soon due to review, and possibly reduce, the rates charged by Wessex and other water utilities.

Enron also promised that the water company would be self-funding, not drawing on Enron's financial resources; this implied a degree of autonomy for Mark and her new business (which had its own headquarters at a different address than Enron's). Skilling and other senior executives backed the water strategy. Within Enron, the news was also seen as a way for Mark to save face after having been trumped by Skilling.

Wall Street reacted calmly, and some company watchers were surprised. On the day Enron unveiled the acquisition, its stock fell $1.25 to $55.25. Investors were concerned that Enron might spread itself too thin by adding yet another core business to a corporation already focused on gas, electricity, energy outsourcing, and international energy projects. After all, ECT had just established itself as the growth engine of the company. And less than one month earlier, EI had won the bidding to acquire control of Elektro Eletricidade e Serviços S.A., a Brazilian electric utility, for $1.3 billion (another hard asset that Enron felt would help eventually build "asset-light" businesses in South America). Was Enron taking on too many major projects at once?

Analysts believed Enron's choicest growth opportunities lay in gas and electricity, both in North America and in Europe. They wondered if water would distract Enron from its extensive and already promising energy business. In addition, there was no clear synergy between the new water business and the gas and electricity businesses, which were slowly converging. Enron admitted that it would be much more difficult to build trading and derivatives businesses around water than it had been for energy.

Enron also pursued typically complicated means to finance the Wessex purchase. Water is a very expensive enterprise, the kind of business that executives describe as "capital-intensive," requiring costly projects similar to EI's power plants and pipelines. Enron knew that its water business would use debt to pay for projects, and wanted to keep that debt off its own balance sheet. First, Enron put its water business, which it named Azurix, in a holding company called Atlantic Water Trust. Then Enron created another SPE, named Marlin Water Trust, which bought a 50 percent voting interest in Atlantic. Marlin Water Trust issued $1.15 billion in notes and certificates (other short-term debt securities) to buy the 50 percent interest; Enron retained the other 50 percent interest. Five institutional investors bought the certificates, giving them the ability to appoint half of Marlin's board of directors. This influence helped allow

Marlin Water Trust to be considered an independent SPE for accounting purposes. By structuring the ownership of Azurix through two layers of trusts, its debts could be kept off Enron's books even though Enron essentially controlled Azurix.

The complicated deal took almost four months of work from bankers at Donaldson Lufkin & Jenrette and Bankers Trust. Azurix and Marlin received investment-grade credit ratings from the rating agencies, largely because Enron promised that stock would be issued to repay some of the debt. But even one of those agencies, Standard & Poor's, called the structure "highly complex."

Azurix also sought to follow the Enron model in hiring headline-worthy personalities who could grease the government wheels. In November 1998, Enron hired Claire Spottiswoode, the outgoing regulator for the U.K. natural gas industry, to join the senior management team at Azurix. Spottiswoode was to help develop the company's global water investment business, with particular emphasis on European water regulation. But Spottiswoode left Azurix just four months later to join a consulting firm.

While Skilling was busy developing his asset-light business, Mark worked quickly to build up Azurix into a successful asset-heavy corporation. In the first few months of 1999, Azurix acquired a 49.9 percent interest in the water and sewage concession for Cancún, Mexico, for $38.5 million, and bought Philip Utilities Management, a Canadian company that designed and built water and wastewater treatment plants, for $120 million.

Then Azurix struck its largest deal besides the Wessex purchase: It was the winning bidder to operate the water and sewage concessions for two regions of Argentina's Buenos Aires province. Azurix paid $439 million for the 30-year concessions, which served just under 2 million people. With operations in Argentina, England, and Mexico, Azurix was a globe-spanning company, just as Mark felt it had to be in order to succeed in the water business. She had also promised Wall Street to accumulate $10 billion of assets in Azurix in just a few years.

The Buenos Aires bid smacked of Mark's deal-making bravado, but perhaps it was too ambitious. The company overpaid, reportedly bidding over $100 million more than its own analysts had estimated the concessions were worth. Some Azurix employees felt that Mark was making deals quickly in order to prove that she could compete with Skilling. As a result, Mark may have felt pressure to make a big splash with something as large as the Buenos Aires concessions, rather than cautiously build up Azurix with smaller transactions first.

But the Buenos Aires deal also provided Azurix with a lot of press coverage just weeks before it sold stock to the public. In June, Azurix went public at $19 per share, valuing the company at nearly $2 billion and providing about $300 million for the water company's use (some of which helped pay for the Buenos Aires transaction). As promised to the debt buyers, Azurix had sold equity. After the initial public offering, Atlantic Water Trust owned roughly two-thirds of the company; Atlantic remained owned 50–50 by Enron and Marlin Water Trust. It was a pretty quick jaunt for the young company to go from formation to public offering in eight months, and in hindsight it may have seemed rushed. But there was debt to pay, projects to buy, and a high profile to be maintained. And Mark had promised 20 percent returns on Azurix's capital, which was double the water industry's average.

Meanwhile, the company found it difficult to compete against Suez Lyonnaise des Eaux and Vivendi, as the French companies were used to making large water investments that might not pay off for years, while Azurix was captive to Enron's focus on reporting growth in each quarter. Azurix's stock began to decline from its initial $19 level. And the Buenos Aires concessions turned out to be in worse shape than Azurix had expected; faulty billing systems meant that it couldn't collect money from a large segment of its customers.

The deal flow at Azurix was small, which wasn't what people expected from the Rebecca Mark who had negotiated Teesside and saved Dabhol. Privatization occurred, but much more slowly than Azurix and Enron had hoped, as political gridlock proved an enormous obstacle. In developing nations, privatization often meant higher water prices, as government subsidies disappeared and corporate owners spent money on improving the water systems. And in the United States, cities were often reluctant to turn their municipal water systems over to private companies for fear that they were selling an irreplaccable asset.

In October 1999, *Fortune* named Mark one of the 50 most powerful women in business; she was listed as 29th, just three spots below Oprah Winfrey. But Mark wasn't given much time to enjoy the laurels. The following month, Azurix warned that higher costs (stemming partly from the Buenos Aires problems) would result in fourth-quarter earnings of 10 or 11 cents per share, below the 17 cents a share that Wall Street analysts had been estimating. It also warned that 2000 profits would be below expectations. The day of the warning, Azurix shares fell 39 percent to $7.81. The company also unveiled a strategy shift away from auction-style public privatizations and more toward what it called "privately negotiated transactions."

To make matters worse, U.K. regulators ordered a 12 percent price cut for Wessex's water rates. A rate cut had been expected, as the quasi-governmental body overseeing water was reducing rates for most water utilities, but it seemed to be another piece of bad news. It also made that 28 percent premium paid for Wessex look even pricier. Azurix then cut 85 jobs, which amounted to almost one-third of its non-Wessex workforce, including positions in its Houston and London offices, sparking a one-time charge to earnings of more than $30 million.

Although Azurix was profitable, it wasn't living up to the majestic expectations that Mark—or Ken Lay—had touted. The company reported net income of $37.7 million in 1999, on revenues of $618 million. That wasn't an awful rate of profitability unless one considered that as an independent company, Wessex Water earned $153 million in 1997. At the start of 2000, the company had assets valued at $4.85 billion, a far cry from $10 billion, although Azurix wasn't earning a high rate of return on the assets it did have. Mark didn't receive a bonus for 1999, because Azurix fell below internal performance targets.

The company tried another strategy in February 2000. It would seek to trade water and water-related equipment on the Internet; perhaps trading would make Azurix more like Skilling's ECT. It partnered with software company Ariba to create a virtual marketplace called Water2Water.com for trading water itself, mostly in the western United States where water is scarce. Rather than have a team of water traders, the goal was to charge fees for accessing the service and also sell ads on the site. A subsidiary web site, WaterDesk.com, was developed to buy and sell equipment and chemicals for water.

The water trading strategy seemed promising given Azurix's pedigree as a stepchild of trading expert Enron. But water was different enough from energy that it made trading water much harder. For one thing, the laws around water in the United States are complex, and the emotions around water make it politically charged. And unlike gas, the system of pipes to move it around the western United States is not fully developed, and there was no federal order requiring water system owners to transport water owned by a third party. Finally, water comes in more varieties of quality than gas or electricity, making standardization difficult and treatment of the water expensive. There may have been people in and around Enron who believed that everything could be traded, but Water2Water.com never flourished.

Through Atlantic Water Trust, Enron continued to own a major stake in Azurix as well as control its board, and the company didn't perform as well as Enron's other businesses. It just couldn't generate the profits that ECT seemed to produce. For the first six months of 2000, Azurix reported net income, including charges, of only $14.4 million, down from $29.5 million a year earlier. On August 25, Mark resigned as chairman and CEO of Azurix, and also resigned from Enron's board. John Garrison, Azurix's new CEO, said, "We are going to conduct a thorough review of all of our businesses, our cost structure and our strategy." Azurix's stock closed that day at $4.94.

Mark's departure was another sign that Skilling had won, both personally and in terms of overall business strategy. Azurix was Enron's first big failure, but it failed on Enron's terms. A more patient steward than Enron might have allowed Azurix to slowly blossom. But the poor profit and stock showing seemed to confirm to Enron that hard-asset businesses were useful only if they supported asset-light businesses such as trading, financing, and services.

Enron was constantly shuffling its assets, and it would soon look for a buyer for Azurix. But it was clear even earlier that Enron was trying to unload a large portion of its hard assets. For example, in 1999 it started shopping around its wind business—wind-powered turbines, wind-power project development and financing, power plant design, and customer support. It tried again, unsuccessfully, in 2000—a year in which Enron's wind-power business generated revenue of $461 million and cash flow of $57 million. (It wouldn't be until 2002 that Enron finally reached a deal to sell the wind business to GE Power Systems, a unit of General Electric.)

The Azurix experience, from founding to Mark's exit, was emblematic of Enron in the late 1990s. The company believed it could do anything, jump into any market. Rebecca Mark may have taken the blame for Azurix's failures, but Lay, Skilling, and others at Enron allowed the company to speed ahead with little regard for investment returns or costs. The sort of attention to detail that Enron once displayed seemed to have faded with Richard Kinder's departure. Instead, Lay and Skilling's Enron was obsessed with innovation, dexterity, and new markets. Nothing would embody that trio of imperatives more than the Internet.

8

ENRON GETS WIRED

There was a time in the late 1990s when the Internet was such an all-consuming passion for Wall Street and the media that Netscape's initial public offering in 1995 almost seemed like an historic moment rivaling Neil Armstrong's first steps on the Moon. A few years later, people were listening to CEOs' conference calls over the Web, sending large documents or even short films over the Internet, and bypassing travel agents to search for airline tickets on the Web. The Internet inspired some genuine innovations, which in turn spurred a new cult of business innovation that was in many ways right up Enron's alley. Pundits spoke of a "new economy." Businesses thought outside the box. Challenging precepts was mandatory. Executives couldn't just manage and lead, they were required to i-manage and e-lead. Companies even had to be wary of their own success, lest that blind them to the stealthy innovations that might eventually wreck their business models.

But Enron stayed away from direct involvement in the Internet while Yahoo!, Amazon.com, and eBay were capturing the business world's heart. For instance, from the start of 1997 to the start of 1999, Yahoo! shares rose a staggering 4,200 percent in value. And companies from General Motors to Southwest Airlines boasted of how they'd cut costs, attracted customers, and streamlined procurement processes using the Internet.

Enron was busy, after all. It had many responsibilities in building up its retail energy business, its paper and other new commodities businesses, and further growing its wholesale energy business. The company also had its share of rivals who also had seemingly fast-growing trading businesses. By 1999, other companies with large gas-and-electricity trading operations were using mark-to-market accounting for booking their trading profits. These included UtiliCorp United's Aquila subsidiary; the power utility-and-pipeline combo Duke Energy; El Paso Energy, a pipeline company that expanded into energy trading; and NGC, which in mid-1998 changed its name to "Dynegy" (a mix of the words "dynamic" and "energy").

In addition, Enron was trying to maintain a good credit rating, which was needed both to keep its borrowing costs down and to continue as a derivatives dealer. Customers bought options, swaps, and more complex derivative instruments from Enron in part because the Houston company was creditworthy. At the same time, Enron was expanding in costly businesses that required big outlays of money for long-term paybacks, and it faced a challenge: Issuing more equity to pay for these investments would dilute the value of its stock, but issuing more debt would endanger its credit rating.

One strategy, of course, consisted of using Special Purpose Entities to keep debt off its balance sheet. In addition to Chewco and the trusts set up around Wessex Water, Enron pursued this course in late 1998 when it bought three gas-fired power plants in New Jersey from a company called Cogen Technologies. The deal was part of Enron's goal of owning or controlling power plants in various parts of the United States in order to help it trade and transmit electricity around the country. Enron paid $1.1 billion for the three plants and assumed $350 million more of the plants' debt. Enron made the purchase through an SPE called East Coast Power, into which Enron put $65 million. JEDI II, the second 50–50 investment partnership between Enron and CalPERS, bought East Coast Power with debt and a small amount of equity. East Coast Power then sold $850 million of notes (backed by the future income from the power plants' long-term electricity supply contracts) to refinance a large portion of the original debt, but that short-term debt stayed off Enron's books. In August 1999, JEDI II sold a 49 percent stake in East Coast Power to El Paso Energy. In the end, Enron had accessed $1.5 billion in capital to buy the power plants, but had added only $65 million of debt to its own balance sheet.

Another strategy was to tighten its controls over trading risk. Enron did this in the late 1990s, focusing more on Value at Risk and other risk metrics. But the risk controls only kept Enron from putting too much capital at stake in each deal it made. Capital investment decisions, not part of the trading book, also posed significant risk if Enron paid too much for its aggressive push into new markets. The risk controls didn't ensure Enron made good deals. For example, the company made one investment—a 50 percent stake in the water company Azurix—that was already turning sour.

Besides Azurix, Enron faced other difficulties and disappointments. Enron's July 1998 purchase of control of Elektro Eletricidade e Serviços S.A., a Brazilian electric utility serving São Paulo, was massively expensive. Enron bought its stake in Elektro for $1.3 billion, nearly twice the government's minimum asking price of $670 million. At that price, it would be challenging to make an attractive return on its investment, although Enron considered the deal part of its strategic buildup in Brazil, where it was developing a pipeline and a power plant. But in 1999, the exchange rate for the Brazilian real to the U.S. dollar declined, reducing the value of Enron's Brazilian assets and shareholder equity by $600 million.

Enron wasn't doing so well with its retail energy sales. Enron Energy Services, which was in investment mode and so expected to lose money, went on to lose $119 million before interest and taxes in 1998. The big blow came in April of that year, when Enron gave up on the golden goose of California. Explaining that the way the state deregulated energy didn't provide a truly competitive playing field, the company announced that it was pulling out of selling power to the state's residential market in order to focus on commercial and industrial customers.

Margins, as Enron discovered, were razor thin in retail power sales. Hampered by electricity surcharges, bad press, and glitches in California's system, Enron had signed up only 30,000 residential customers in a state populated by 30 million people. The company also indicated it wouldn't try to compete for residential customers in Massachusetts and Rhode Island for similar reasons. Enron hinted that it might try to enter the residential market again in several years, but for now selling "Enron" brand power to individual homes was not a viable business. The shift in strategy may have been inevitable, because serving large customers such as factories or colleges is much easier and potentially more profitable. But the move was still a disappointment to supporters of energy deregulation and a big blow to Enron's ambition. The company would not, it seemed, become the Coca-Cola of energy.

Once again, Enron was far from alone. The hopes surrounding consumer electricity choice just a year earlier had quickly faded. National brands of energy aimed at small customers, similar to MCI or Sprint in the telecommunications world, did not emerge. In May, an even more visible attempt at this was unplugged by its partners, UtiliCorp and Peco Energy. They had created EnergyOne, a brand of bundled energy services including electricity and natural gas, that they'd hoped to franchise to local utilities for a fee, much like the Visa credit card concept. But a year later, no other utilities had signed up. "We were ahead of the marketplace," explained a UtiliCorp spokesman.

Deregulation was too new to support the concept of selling electricity the way other companies sold cornflakes. The state-by-state pace of deregulation made it difficult to craft a national strategy, and building a brand name across the United States simply may not have been worth it. Enron was disappointed, but it was excited by its energy outsourcing businesses, and it relied much more heavily on wholesale energy businesses anyway.

Enron had other reasons to not mind its stumbles. The company happened upon a new business that would finally link Enron to the growing Internet phenomenon: bandwidth. Bandwidth is the capacity of telecommunications lines for carrying data, and the appetite for bandwidth grew as the Internet grew in use. The old copper phone lines providing the foundation of the U.S. telephone network for so long were no longer enough. Companies were building fiber-optic networks with high-tech switches designed to carry data at faster speeds.

When Enron acquired Portland General in 1997, it discovered that the utility had built a small fiber-optic network around its territory by installing fiber lines along its power lines' rights of way (the small areas around its power lines). Enron had originally thought it would simply sell the fiber network. But then Enron officials looked more closely at the business. It consisted of selling capacity on its fiber network under long-term contracts, much the way Enron sold capacity on its gas pipelines before deregulation. And, company executives thought, why couldn't bandwidth be managed with more flexibility, the way Enron managed gas and power?

"So we started digging into that," recalled Ken Rice, who later became the CEO of Enron Broadband Services. "The way we approached problems, we'd go, 'First of all, is it something we can make a market out of?' It's growing at 35 to 40 percent a year. There's a demand for more flexible types of contract structures. So let's figure out how we can jump in."

Managing data over networks was more difficult than managing electricity over networks. For example, it usually didn't matter if Enron substituted California electricity for Oregon electricity as long as the price was the same, but in data, one cannot substitute one e-mail for another e-mail just because it's closer. "So we tackled some big technical problems. And we came up with solutions to manage that effectively," Rice said.

Enron decided to bulk up its fiber network. In autumn 1997, Enron teamed with Williams Cos. and Montana Power (an electric utility) to build a 1,620-mile fiber network linking Los Angeles to Portland, Oregon. The new links would also serve Salt Lake City and Las Vegas.

The fiber strategy followed some proven footsteps. Just as Portland General had built fiber loops using its rights of way, Williams Cos. had, years earlier, built a fiber network alongside (and sometimes inside) its gas pipelines. In 1995, Williams sold that network for $2.5 billion to LDDS, which later became part of WorldCom. Williams, which had a small telecommunications business, kept a single strand of that fiber stretching 11,000 miles, and was building a new network around that. This put Williams in competition with IXC, Qwest, and other telecom companies building more bandwidth. And in August 1997, electric utility Texas Utilities bought a small phone company, Lufkin-Conroe, for $328 million. The thinking by Texas Utilities, Williams, and then Enron was that telecommunications was just another vast set of wires to manage, and they already had that expertise in managing electricity and gas infrastructures.

At the time, the hype surrounding electric deregulation led industry players to wonder if electric utilities would be offering phone service over their wires, and whether all phone, gas, and electric utilities would start to merge with one another to offer customers one place to buy all those services. Reality hit in 1998. Electric deregulation was a slow, cautious process, and electricity providers didn't become *über*-utilities. The hype started to fade. But Enron's fiber plans still made sense, and it pushed forward. In late 1997, Enron bought Optec, a data integration company, to help hook up corporate customers to its fiber network. A new business, Enron Communications, began planning two more fiber loops to add to its network, one from Salt Lake City to Miami, and one from Miami to Houston—both of which were largely built using Enron's pipeline rights of way.

In July 1998, Enron unveiled its bandwidth plans to Wall Street analysts. In addition to its three loops, it planned to swap fiber on its network with other networks so that Enron's fiber network would reach into the Upper Midwest and Northeast. That way, Enron expected to have a nationwide fiber network of more than 14,000 miles in place by the end of 2000, offering wholesale capacity to Internet service and phone providers. At the time, no one seemed to question a company with an "asset-light" philosophy that was once again looking asset-heavy in building out this fiber network. After all, Enron's stock price was on a roll.

The company's leap into bandwidth allowed it to rub shoulders with the hot technology companies of the day, including Cisco Systems and Sun Microsystems. After Enron inked a deal to buy computer equipment from Sun for its fiber network, and the two companies then agreed to cross-market each other's services, Skilling had Sun CEO Scott McNealy, one of Silicon Valley's true luminaries, appear with him at an analyst meeting. Although Enron's acquisition of computers from Sun was a straightforward purchase similar to the way Enron might buy compressors to build gas pipelines, and although the cross-marketing agreement was one of dozens that Sun signed with a wide range of companies, the meeting presented an image of Enron as a high-tech player allied with Sun and McNealy. Skilling had once again added the patina of spin to Enron's business.

By April 1999, the fiber network, though still being expanded, was open for business. Enron used Internet-protocol technology, which moved data around in efficient packets. Rather than have a central data storage facility, it deployed data-storing computer servers throughout the network to keep data closer to the end user. Although Enron didn't break out the investment costs or income from its new communications business in its financial reports (and this was no surprise), the company had embarked on another business with real prospects. And Enron had its first foothold in the Internet world; it wouldn't be the last.

■ ■ ■

Another way to play the Internet craze was to invest in Internet companies. Enron invested $10 million in Rhythms NetConnections, a private provider of high-speed Internet access using digital subscriber line (DSL) technology; DSL can enable high-speed data connections over traditional telephone lines. In March 1998, Enron bought 5.4 million shares of then-private Rhythms for $1.85 per share. In April of the following year, Rhythms sold stock to the public. It was still the dot-com boom; the stock went public at $21 a share, and zoomed to $69 by the close of its first day of trading. That meant Rhythms as a whole was worth more than $5 billion, which was a rich valuation for a company that was losing money and expected to continue losing money as it matured. In those days, as individual investors hoped to nab the next Netscape, Yahoo!, or eBay, it was not unheard-of for an initial public offering (IPO) to triple in its debut. By May 1999 Enron's investment in Rhythms was worth $300 million.

An interesting feature of the IPO is that nearly all the shareholders who put in money beforehand are barred from selling shares for the first six months after the IPO date; this lockup prevents many—but not all—of the early investors from suddenly bailing on the stock in the first-day euphoria. So Enron was sitting on this huge gain in the value of Rhythms stock and had no way to immediately turn it into cash. If the stock couldn't be sold, Skilling wanted to at least hedge the company's position in Rhythms against future volatility, so that any Enron gains would be protected from a drop in Rhythms' stock price. But hedging the stock in a traditional manner was virtually impossible: The stock was too illiquid to support options trading, and there really were no comparable stocks to either short or hedge with options. Skilling also was concerned that Wall Street wouldn't give Enron any credit for its one-time investment gain on Rhythms. He wanted Enron to be viewed as a savvy investor beyond Rhythms. What could Enron do?

It could shift the risk associated with the Rhythms stock off its own financial statements and onto the financial statements of another entity. And Enron had a history of creating Special Purpose Entities to hold risk.

At the same time, Enron had a gain on forward contracts on its own stock that it had purchased from UBS, a large investment bank. A forward contract is an agreement to purchase something on a future date at a price that, the buyer hopes, will turn out to be a bargain. Buying these forward contracts on stock is a common tactic that companies use to hedge against a surge in their own stock prices; this is useful because companies often buy back their own stock to minimize the impact created by employee stock option programs (which can effectively result in the company's equity being divided into many more shares, and therefore each share being worth a little less). Because of a rise in Enron's stock, its forward contracts had gains on paper for the Enron stock it would own. But accounting rules prohibit a company from recognizing gains on its own stock as income. Chief Financial Officer Andrew Fastow had the idea of putting the appreciated Enron stock forward contracts into a limited partnership special purpose entity. This SPE, named "LJM" (after the initials of Fastow's wife and two sons), would then hedge the Rhythms position, allowing Enron to offset losses if Rhythms' stock price fell. Fastow would serve as general partner of the SPE.

Fastow had actually come up with the LJM concept in the spring of 1999, and approached Enron Chief Accounting Officer Richard Causey at the time about the idea of forming a private equity fund. Causey's initial reaction was that the basic idea of LJM was okay, and that it was unusual but conformed to accounting rules. The idea of Fastow managing LJM raised eyebrows from the start. A member of Arthur Andersen's professional standards group wrote to Andersen partner David Duncan, "Setting aside the accounting, idea of a venture entity managed by CFO is terrible from a business point of view. Conflicts galore." Duncan wrote back that given the conflict issue, approval from the board of directors would be a requirement for forming LJM.

Enron's internal research group, originally set up for the trading operation and still run by Vincent Kaminski, was by then a part of the Risk Assessment & Control (RAC) Group; as such, it was sometimes called upon to look over investment deals and other complicated transactions not directly related to Enron's trading. Skilling came into Kaminski's office on June 10 with an "urgent" request that required immediate attention. He asked Kaminski to price a put option on Rhythms stock—an option allowing the holder to sell the stock in the future at a predetermined price. Skilling almost never came into Kaminski's office, so this was clearly a high-priority assignment. Kaminski got more information on the idea from a Causey lieutenant: The company wanted to know how it could price a put option on its Rhythms stock in order to hedge its exposure. Valuing this option was difficult because there was no public market for such a contract.

The research team brainstormed on the proposed Rhythms deal, and laughed about the idea of transferring the Enron forward contracts into a partnership. Kaminski didn't like the idea of handing over Enron assets to a third party, as it seemed more like a giveaway than a sale. The group did come up with a valuation of a Rhythms option, which it gave to Causey. But on June 11, Kaminski also went to Rick Buy, the head of the RAC Group and his boss, to present his concerns about the proposed deal. Inside Enron, ideas were critiqued in blunt and dramatic terms, and Kaminski said the SPE option idea was "so stupid that only Andrew Fastow could have come up with it."

Buy replied that not only did Fastow conceive of this SPE hedging deal, but Fastow proposed that he would run the SPE. Kaminski said the obvious conflict of interest—Fastow running a partnership that would engage in a transaction with Enron—should keep Enron from entering into this deal. At Buy's urging, Kaminski agreed to analyze the entire deal.

Kaminski and a colleague worked separately on the LJM idea over the weekend, then compared notes. On Monday, Kaminski told Buy that Enron shouldn't proceed with the Rhythms hedging deal both because of the conflict of interest and because the SPE was unstable from a credit standpoint—its ability to honor the put option and buy the Rhythms stock value depended on the value of Enron's stock, so if Rhythms' and Enron's stocks both declined, Enron could wind up with nothing. At the time, Kaminski believed the deal would be stupid, but he didn't think it would be illegal.

Buy was surprised by Kaminski's analysis, but he was able to joke, "Next time Fastow is going to run a racket, I want to be a part of it." Buy assured Kaminski that he'd pass on his objections to upper management before Enron's board of directors reviewed the deal, and Kaminski trusted him to do so. Kaminski then went off to an energy conference.

Whether or not Buy passed on the objections, the momentum behind the idea was too strong to stop. On June 18, Fastow presented the Rhythms idea to Lay and Skilling, and they approved pitching it to Enron's board of directors.

Before facing the board, Causey consulted on the concept with Enron's main accounting firm, Arthur Andersen. Andersen believed the deal met accounting rules, including the requirement that any SPE have at least 3 percent of its equity from an outside investor in order to qualify as a separate entity, and thus to not be consolidated into Enron's financial statements. Andersen also decided that Fastow's running of LJM would pose no problem in terms of the accounting treatment.

On June 28, Fastow presented the LJM concept to the board's finance committee, noting that while he would serve as general partner, he wouldn't benefit from gains on the Enron stock. He assured the board that an outside accounting firm would verify that Enron's value from the Rhythms hedges would exceed the value of the Enron forward contracts contributed to LJM. With those assurances, the overall deal seemed fairly standard. Enron's code of ethics barred employees from running separate partnerships, so the board approved waiving that rule to allow Fastow to form and manage the LJM partnership. The board also gave its okay on the Rhythms hedge.

Waiving the ethics code to allow Fastow to manage a partnership that would do business with Enron seemed like a red flag. But Enron's board didn't act as though the situation required vigilance. A few years later, a special committee of the board would regret this decision in the Powers Report, saying, "After having authorized a conflict of interest creating as much risk as this one, the board had an obligation to give careful attention to the transactions that followed. It failed to do this. . . . In short, no one was minding the store."

The formation of LJM and a complicated transaction to hedge the Rhythms stock closed on June 30, 1999. LJM included $15 million invested by two limited partners, affiliates of the investment banks Credit Suisse First Boston and U.K. bank NatWest. Enron restructured the UBS forward contracts, allowing it to transfer 3.4 million shares, worth about $276 million, to LJM. Enron put a condition on those shares, prohibiting LJM from selling or transferring them for four years and barring LJM from hedging them (by purchasing options on the stock, for example) for one year. These restrictions on the use of the stock effectively lowered the value of the shares, turning them into an "encumbered asset" for the life of the restrictions. This allowed LJM to value the stock at 65 percent of its full value, or roughly $168 million. In exchange for this stock, LJM gave Enron a down payment of $64 million in the form of a note. The restrictions on the stock may have been created solely to allow it to be transferred to LJM at a discount.

LJM then sold some of the unrestricted Enron stock for $3.75 million in cash, and transferred that cash, plus 1.6 million shares of Enron, to a vehicle known as Swap Sub, an SPE created just for this deal. Swap Sub gave Enron a put option—an option to sell stock in the future—on the entire 5.4 million shares of Rhythms; this meant Enron could require

Swap Sub to buy its stake in Rhythms at $56 per share in 2004, essentially putting a minimum value of $56 per share on that Rhythms stock. The put option itself was valued at $104 million. Rather than get an option directly from LJM, Enron apparently went through Swap Sub so that the option's liabilities didn't fall upon LJM. This looked like a tactic designed solely to protect LJM (and, therefore, Fastow's investment).

The outside accounting firm vetting this deal was Pricewaterhouse-Coopers. The firm figured that what LJM received—the 3.4 million shares of restricted Enron stock that was transferred at a discounted value—was worth $170 million to $223 million. It also figured that what Enron received—the put option combined with the $64 million note—was worth $164 million to $204 million. Therefore, Enron was receiving fair value in this deal.

The use of Swap Sub could have raised accounting questions because Swap Sub also had to meet the rule that 3 percent of its equity had to come from an outside investor in order to be a stand-alone partnership. But when the Rhythms deal was closed on June 30, Swap Sub had a $104 million liability in the form of the Rhythms put option, versus assets of nearly $84 million in the form of the $3.75 million of cash and about $80 million worth of Enron stock. Therefore, Swap Sub started its life with negative equity of about $20 million. This apparently didn't raise any concerns at the time.

But even this intricate setup didn't do the trick. Once the Rhythms hedge was in place, Enron found that the complex deal between Enron, LJM, and Swap Sub was not doing a good enough job in hedging the volatility related to the Rhythms investment. So on July 13, Enron and Swap Sub put a new set of hedges on the Rhythms stock using options, which were modeled by the research group.

The overall use of LJM in the Rhythms deal did not create a true "hedge" of the risks involved in the Rhythms investment. Typically, a company seeking to hedge its risk pays an outside entity so that the entity will take on some of the company's risk in an investment, such as buying an option on electricity prices. But in this case, Enron transferred its own stock to LJM, and that stock would be the source of payment if the Rhythms investment declined in value; in other words, Enron's own stock was essentially hedging its investment in Rhythms. A committee of Enron's board later concluded, in the Powers Report, that this "did not involve substantive transfers of economic risk" because either way Enron was at risk.

That was the research group's last such involvement. Although Kaminski's objections to the LJM-Rhythms deal were ignored, they did have one effect—they highlighted his group's role as internal critic. Later in July, Skilling told Kaminski that he'd received complaints about his research group; people had told Skilling the group operated "like cops" and Enron employees didn't want to work with it. So Skilling moved Kaminski and his group out of the RAC Group and back inside Enron Capital & Trade. While the move was not a demotion for Kaminski, it did take him out of the loop on deals involving LJM or other partnerships, thus removing his group from further opportunities to criticize the use of partnerships.

■ ■ ■

With Chewco and LJM, Andrew S. Fastow had taken Enron into new territory regarding partnerships and SPEs. If to outsiders he seemed comfortable doing so, it may have been because Enron employees knew him as confident, bordering on cocky. In his early days at Enron, Fastow once thanked an outside banker by saying, "I'll remember that when I'm CFO." In March 1998, he was indeed promoted to chief financial officer. The promotion was not a surprise to those who knew the determined Fastow.

Born in December 1961 in the Washington, D.C., area, Fastow was the middle of three children. His father, a buyer for a drugstore chain, soon moved the family to New Jersey. Andy was popular at New Providence High School, where he first displayed his quiet ambition by becoming president of the high school's student council and then the first student representative to the New Jersey State Board of Education. He went to Tufts University, where he finished his studies a year early and graduated with honors in 1983 with a degree in Chinese and economics.

Even as a child he'd taken an interest in the stock market, so it was no surprise when he went to Northwestern University to earn an MBA, and then went on to work for the Continental Bank in Chicago. Along the way he married Lea Weingarten, the daughter of a prominent supermarket-chain owner, whom he'd met at Tufts. Skilling recruited him from the bank to join Enron in 1990, and he was always viewed as Skilling's man.

Outside the company, Fastow was a family man who liked to coach his two sons' sports teams and shied away from socializing with Lay and Skilling; he was known as generous and a low-profile participant in a handful of civic causes including his local synagogue. But inside the company, Fastow's reputation was that of a smart but hot-tempered executive on the rise, focused on his own advancement. He seemed to like putting subordinates on the spot, in order to show them up as ignorant. People who worked with him also got used to being screamed at, although Fastow's flashes of anger usually faded quickly without lasting grudges. Jeff McMahon, a Fastow lieutenant, recalled that when Fastow chewed him out for the first time, in 1995, he'd never experienced anything like it and thought he was going to be fired. The next day, though, Fastow acted as though nothing had happened; eventually, McMahon was promoted to treasurer.

One reason Fastow gravitated toward finance was his weakness at running a business. In 1996, Rick Kinder had chewed out Fastow over Fastow's business plan for EES (this was before Fastow became senior vice president of finance). Fastow had devised a business plan that essentially called for EES to react to events as they occurred, which was really no business plan at all. Kinder yelled at him to come back with an actual strategy. In early 1997, Fastow moved to finance.

Although Fastow became known for devising complicated financing vehicles—what the business world calls "financial engineering"—some inside Enron felt that Fastow's strength was really in sales and relationships with banks and other firms, and that he wasn't that good with numbers (which, according to this thinking, may have been why some of his financial structures didn't work). According to one widely circulated story that may be apocryphal, Fastow tried to convince a credit rating agency that it should upgrade Enron's bond rating because then Enron would be able to borrow money more cheaply, enhancing its capital structure, and thereby justifying a higher bond rating. If not true, it was the sort of story many Enron employees found believable.

His heavy-handed method of dealing with colleagues could occasionally bleed into his dealings with outside parties. When Fastow was trying to attract investors in LJM, some banks felt pressured to participate. McMahon said two banks called him to express worries that they'd lose Enron investment banking business if they didn't invest in LJM. Fastow reportedly called the banks and assured them that wasn't the case. But big banks weren't blind to the fact that Enron conducted a lot of deals, and so Fastow controlled tens of millions of dollars in annual investment banking fees; it was in the banks' interests to remain on Fastow's good side.

As CFO, Fastow was one of the most powerful executives at Enron. In part, this stemmed from Enron's unique needs, as the company had become as much an investment bank as an energy company. It also stemmed from the rise in importance of American CFOs in the 1990s. They controlled their companies' purse strings, so they helped determine whether business moves made sense. But they'd also become responsible for revenue and income forecasts, and by the time Fastow became CFO, many were involved in corporate strategy. As the stock market became a more popular participatory sport in the 1990s, CFOs also became more visible to Wall Street as the financial faces of companies; often, when a company failed to meet financial expectations, it looked to fire the CFO rather than the CEO—the way a disappointing sports team might fire one of its senior coaches before going after the head coach.

This meant the CFO job carried a lot of pressure. It was clear that some of Fastow's partnerships were not monitored as closely as they should have been. But even under ideal circumstances, Fastow would have been difficult to oversee because it was difficult for management to understand all the things he was doing. Despite all their smarts, many executives lacked the financial background. Ken Lay, for example, had studied economics and finance in the 1960s, before derivatives revolutionized the business world in the 1980s and 1990s.

Enron understood Fastow as the wizard who somehow juggled accounting rules so that the company could preserve its credit rating. The purchase of Wessex Water was one example: Not only did he set up the SPE structure of Marlin Water Trust to keep the debt used in buying Wessex off Enron's books, but by promising to issue stock he secured a very favorable rating on that debt from rating agencies. Keeping the debt from Azurix, Dabhol, JEDI, and other ventures off Enron's books was important: At the end of 1998, Enron Corp. had $7.36 billion in long-term debt, but its "unconsolidated" ventures and partnerships had a total of $7.6 billion in long-term debt. If Enron had been forced to put all that debt on its own books, its credit rating would have been wrecked.

To effectively juggle Enron's capital needs, Fastow transformed the finance department much the way Skilling had transformed Enron's sales department. He more than doubled the finance staff, loading it with experts in investment banking, commercial banking, and corporate finance. Rather than just raise debt or issue stock, Fastow's finance department became a manager of risk; it sold securitizations, parceled out the company's risk into other vehicles, took on investing partners, and marketed debt as a way to participate in the sure growth of everything that Enron touched. "Essentially, we would buy and sell risk positions," Fastow explained.

Fastow's team designed the complicated structure for buying Wessex Water. Similarly, it bought Brazil's Elektro with low-cost debt that kept most of the utility's debt off Enron's books. Fastow combined securitization with SPEs so that the SPE-based acquisition of the Cogen power plants was essentially a securitization of the stream of income from the plants' long-term power contracts. In October 1999, *CFO* magazine gave Fastow its 1999 excellence award for capital structure management. "We needed someone to rethink the entire financing structure at Enron, from soup to nuts," Skilling told the magazine. "We didn't want someone stuck in the past, since the industry of yesterday is no longer. Andy has the intelligence and youthful exuberance to think in new ways."

Fastow had a taste for extremely complicated transactions. One example was an SPE called Whitewing Associates, formed in December 1997, and initially funded with $579 million from Enron and $500 million from an unnamed outside investor. Enron later altered Whitewing so that it was an independent SPE not controlled by Enron; the alteration also meant that Whitewing was funded by Osprey Trust, another SPE. Osprey raised a total of $2.4 billion in debt; that debt was backed by the assets in Whitewing, which included Enron preferred stock (a form of equity paying guaranteed dividends). In this case, the preferred stock could be converted into regular common stock in Enron, and Enron backed it by promising to issue more stock if its stock price fell below $28.

The goal of this convoluted structure was to set up Whitewing as an entity that could occasionally buy stakes in power plants, pipelines, stocks, and other investments from Enron. Whitewing would go on to buy hundreds of millions of dollars' worth of assets from Enron, getting them off Enron's balance sheet. But much of the details of Whitewing and Osprey were not disclosed in Enron annual reports.

Fastow's success with SPEs and partnerships emboldened him to push the envelope further on off-balance sheet deals. Unfortunately, the incestuous structures of Enron's partnerships almost inevitably created conflicts of interest—or at least the appearance of conflicts of interest. For example, when the JEDI partnership was being reorganized in 1997 to include the newly formed Chewco as a limited partner, Michael Kopper negotiated the terms on Chewco's behalf. Fastow contacted Enron's negotiator in the deal, who was also an employee working under Fastow, and pressured him to accept Kopper's terms. Fastow reportedly told his subordinate he "was pushing too hard for Enron, and that the deal had to be closed," according to the Powers Report. With his boss telling him to close the deal, the negotiator did so—even though he believed that further negotiating would have earned Enron better terms.

■ ■ ■

Conceivably, Enron's board of directors could have objected to LJM and Chewco. After all, a company's board, elected by investors, is supposed to represent the interests of shareholders by providing independent oversight of management. Andersen told the board that it rated Enron's accounting policies "high risk." Andersen personnel also claimed that they intended to convey to the board that the use of multiple SPEs and complex overlapping transactions ran the risk of violating accounting rules if just one element in the complicated structure failed. The accountants may have failed to convey that sense of risk, because Robert Jaedicke, then head of the board's audit committee, said that when Andersen spoke of these accounting strategies, "the usual expression was one of comfort."

But Enron's board went along with its risky accounting strategies. In one presentation to the board's audit committee in February 1999, David Duncan—Andersen's lead partner on the Enron account—included a handwritten note that read: "Obviously, we are on board with all of these, but many push limits and have a high 'others could have a different view' risk profile." In the discussion that followed that meeting, Andersen didn't recommend changing any accounting practices, and board members didn't advocate a more prudent approach or even a second opinion. Board members didn't characterize Enron's accounting structures as high-risk, but as "leading edge" or innovative—the sort of innovation they expected given the big fees they paid Andersen.

The apparently trusting attitude of the board created a problem, however. Fastow's finance ideas may have exhibited ingenuity, but in some cases they violated accounting rules. They also had a tendency to create conflicts where Enron employees had to serve two masters. And if the Chewco transaction raised questions about conflicts of interest, even larger conflicts would emerge in the Rhythms-LJM deal.

The lockup provision on the Rhythms stock, which was supposedly the original cause of all the maneuvering with LJM, expired in October 1999, but Enron held onto the stock. That year, thanks to LJM, Enron recognized $95 million in after-tax income from the Rhythms transaction. In the first quarter of 2000, the stock had begun to decline, so Enron decided to liquidate its position in Rhythms NetConnections. In addition, Kaminski's group estimated that the Rhythms structure had a 68 to 70 percent chance of defaulting, thus providing further impetus to liquidate, or unwind, the transaction.

So on March 8, Enron gave Swap Sub a put option on 3.1 million shares of Enron stock, allowing it to sell the stock at $71.31 per share. That day, Enron's stock closed at $67.19 per share, so the put was immediately worth a pretax gain of about $12.8 million. Swap Sub didn't pay Enron anything for this lucrative put option. Instead, according to Causey, it was given to Swap Sub to stabilize the structure by boosting its assets, so that the Rhythms deal could be unwound. If Enron had been dealing with a truly independent party for this hedge, it likely would have sold the put option rather than given it away.

Fastow proposed to Causey that Swap Sub receive $30 million from Enron in connection with unwinding the deal. Causey and others analyzed this, and thought it was fair. So on March 22, Enron and Swap Sub entered an agreement to liquidate the deal. Although Fastow was a senior Enron executive, in this transaction he was representing LJM and Swap Sub. The agreement called for: the original put options to be terminated; Swap Sub to return the 3.1 million Enron shares it got from LJM, but for Swap Sub to keep the $3.75 million in cash; Enron to pay Swap Sub $16.7 million—which was the $30 million fee, minus $10 million that Enron loaned to Swap Sub (plus interest) and the $3.75 million. The letter agreement was negotiated by Causey for Enron, and by Fastow for Southampton L.P., which was described in the letter as the owner of Swap Sub.

Although the unwinding of the Rhythms deal was very profitable for LJM and Swap Sub, Enron didn't seek a fairness opinion from an outside accountant. There was no evidence Enron's board knew of this unwind, even though it was negotiated in part by Fastow under a waiver of the ethics code.

There was another twist to this, in that the Rhythms deal eventually enriched several Enron employees. This occurred because one of LJM's limited partners—an outside investor besides Enron—wanted to cash out and that partner's investment was acquired by a newly formed partnership called "Southampton Place L.P." Southampton Place was formed by Fastow and by Michael Kopper, who was still managing Chewco.

The exact workings of Southampton are not known. Nevertheless, Southampton Place became the indirect owner of Swap Sub (technically, Swap Sub was owned by Southampton L.P., a partnership of which Southampton Place L.P. was the general partner). Whether Southampton bought out the LJM limited partner, and how Southampton came to own Swap Sub were not uncovered by the board's investigation that was written up as the Powers Report.

But what is clear is that through Southampton, several Enron employees made money off the unwinding of the Rhythms deal because of the $30 million Enron was paying Swap Sub for its hedging services. Southampton investors included Fastow; Kopper; Ben Glisan, an accountant who later became treasurer at Enron; Kristina Mordaunt, an in-house lawyer at Enron; Kathy Lynn, an employee in the finance area; and Anne Yaeger Patel, another employee under Fastow. The employees had various justifications: for instance, Mordaunt thought LJM was not doing any new business with Enron, while Glisan was assured by LJM's outside counsel, Kirkland & Ellis, that Southampton's involvement was not a "related party transaction" with Enron. Still, there was no evidence that these employees sought clearance from Lay or Enron's board before investing in a partnership that would be involved in a deal with Enron, which was frowned upon by the company's code of ethics. But invest they did, to the tune of $70,000. That investment included a $25,000 investment by something called "the Fastow Family Foundation"; a $25,000 investment by an entity called Big Doe, which was linked to Kopper; and investments of $5,800 each by Glisan and Mordaunt.

Interestingly, Fastow gave other investment opportunities to friends beyond LJM. In 1997, Fastow proposed having his wife, Lea, organize a group of Houston investors for the Chewco partnership, but Skilling nixed that idea. Still, starting with Chewco, Fastow did allow occasional friends to invest their money in Enron partnerships; this not only rewarded friends but also made it easier for Enron to control these supposedly independent partnerships. Within the company, these people came to be known as the "Friends of Enron," and being included in that list (which was never made public) was a lucrative honor. Among those who made the Friends of Enron list were Kathy Wetmore, Fastow's real estate agent, and Patty Melcher, a friend Lea Fastow. The Friends of Enron formed an informal pool of outside investors Enron could draw on when needed.

It may be fitting that the name "Southampton Place" has a posh ring to it, because the Enron employee-investors profited handsomely from their involvement. According to the Powers Report, the Fastow Family Foundation received $4.5 million on May 1, 2000, which was 180 times the initial investment of $25,000. Glisan and Mordaunt each received about $1 million for their investments of $5,800—a return of 17,200 percent. In the end, Enron did wind up earning substantial accounting profits on its investment in Rhythms NetConnections, but not returns as lucrative as those earned by Glisan and Mordaunt.

Another interesting twist emerged in unwinding the Rhythms transaction, involving NatWest's investment in LJM. In late 1999, before Enron terminated the hedge, NatWest became the subject of competing takeover offers from other banks; this prompted NatWest to consider selling the division that had negotiated the LJM deal, Greenwich NatWest, to boost its finances. An FBI affidavit filed in federal court laid out the scheme: Giles Robert Hugh Darby, a managing director at Greenwich NatWest, apparently began scheming with two colleagues— their jobs now seemingly up in the air—to pocket some of NatWest's profits off Swap Sub. In January 2000, David John Bermingham, a subordinate of Darby's, e-mailed Darby to say that NatWest's stake in Swap Sub was valuable due to the appreciation of the Enron stock in Swap Sub. The e-mail said: "The trick will be in capturing it [the value]. I have a couple of ideas but it may be good if I don't share them with anyone until I know our fate!!!" Over the next several weeks, the plan coalesced. In March, NatWest directors meeting in the Cayman Islands approved a deal whereby Enron bought out the bank's stake in Swap Sub for $1 million. That proposal had been put together by Darby and another of Bermingham's bosses, Gary Steven Mulgrew. The U.S. Justice Department claimed that the three of them knew that NatWest's stake was worth more than $1 million; for example, CS First Boston was negotiating to sell Enron its stake in Swap Sub for $10 million.

In April, Darby, Bermingham, and Mulgrew, as investors in an entity called Southampton K Co., bought what had been NatWest's stake for $250,000. According to the affidavit, the three worked out this deal with Fastow and Kopper. At the end of April, Enron terminated the Rhythms agreement with Swap Sub; Fastow then called the three bankers and told them they'd just made $7 million. Around May 1, the entity owned by Darby, Bermingham, and Mulgrew received about $7.3 million for their stake in Swap Sub; by that time, all three had left NatWest.

In effect, the three bankers had convinced their employer to sell its stake in Swap Sub at an artificially low price, then bought it themselves and immediately sold it to Enron for what it was really worth, thus splitting $7 million in profits that should have gone to NatWest. This violated NatWest's internal policies about employees' investments and partnerships. The transaction came to light two years later, and on June 27, 2002, the U.S. Justice Department charged Darby, Bermingham, and Mulgrew with wire fraud. Justice's legal documents didn't contain any charges against Fastow or Kopper.

■ ■ ■

Rhythms NetConnections was really just a financially motivated investment, and not the sort of hands-on involvement with the Internet that Enron wanted. The company liked to size up a market and start making financial deals and trades in it. Because the company already had a fiber network selling bandwidth, Enron decided to try trading bandwidth as a commodity. It already traded electricity, after all, and bandwidth's only difference lay in the fact that Enron would be trading the *capacity* to send something over lines, instead of electricity's model of trading the commodity that actually traveled over the lines. The company announced its plan in May 1999, claiming in its typically extravagant way that bandwidth trading would "revolutionize the Internet industry" by allowing companies to reserve the capacity needed for high-bandwidth software programs and computer applications.

Enron liked to burnish its own myths, and chief among its favored narratives was the independent employee hatching new ideas. So, according to Enron, an Enron executive named Thomas Gros thought of bandwidth trading when he tried to set up a regular videoconferencing link between New York and Houston and found the price to be excessive for a high-speed connection that would be used only a couple of hours each day. Why did he have to pay monthly rates for the high-speed connection? Why not pay for bandwidth as it was needed? So Gros, with corporate backing, set up bandwidth trading. To be honest, bandwidth trading was in the backs of executives' minds when they decided to develop Portland General's fiber network, and Enron even mentioned it as a possible business as early as July 1998, so Gros wasn't the only person at Enron with this idea. But Gros did spearhead Enron's efforts and he became vice president for global bandwidth trading.

The prevailing model for bandwidth was the multiyear contract, in part because building high-speed networks cost tons of money, so the builders liked to lock up customers in advance. Enron figured that telecommunications could be more efficient if bandwidth could be sold in small chunks under standard contracts, much the way Enron broke long-term gas contracts down into smaller pieces that could then be managed with options and other derivatives.

Enron proposed two initial bandwidth contracts: first, for use of a T1 line—a high-speed connection often used in offices and large companies—between New York and Los Angeles; second, for use of a DS-3 line—a much higher-speed connection used by phone companies and Internet service providers—between Washington, D.C. and San Francisco. The idea was to set two widely used standards, then expand the market from there. "We are creating a benchmark where none existed," Gros told the *Wall Street Journal*.

Enron worked with Sun and Cisco Systems to develop the hardware and software, including pooling points (switching and interconnecting facilities) that would act just as hubs served in natural gas—points where prices could be set and trades conducted. Because telecom capacity is a truly global system with e-mail seamlessly flying from New York to Moscow, Enron hoped its market would eventually connect to Asia and Europe for international bandwidth trading.

The first bandwidth trade finally occurred in December 1999, when Enron bought a forward contract on DS-3 bandwidth between New York and Los Angeles from Global Crossing, a telecom company. In 2000, Enron brokered more than 300 bandwidth trades between buyers and sellers, and it continued to envision bandwidth as a potential multibillion-dollar market to rival electricity. Although Enron was losing money on its bandwidth business, by mid-2000 Enron internally estimated that its Enron Broadband Services unit (encompassing both the fiber network and the bandwidth trading) would eventually be worth $29 billion—an optimistic projection at a time when Enron as a whole had a market capitalization of under $50 billion. Skilling also hyped the broadband unit to Wall Street analysts, who were impressed but skeptical of his claims that it justified a much higher stock price for Enron.

Enron wasn't the only firm to think this bandwidth thing would be a good idea. Several other companies, including Arbinet and Band-X, emerged to trade bandwidth. There was even a company called RateXChange, based in San Francisco, which arose in 1999 to provide a neutral exchange for trading bandwidth using both online trades and traditional telephone trades. The company began trading on its exchange in February 2000 with one-month spot and one-year forward contracts for telecom capacity between New York and Los Angeles. Later that year, RateXChange collaborated with financial publisher Dow Jones & Co. to create bandwidth commodity price indexes.

Bandwidth trading was small and grew slowly, but Enron had high hopes and Skilling took a big interest in the business. The company developed a sophisticated trading operation, quoting deals in dollars per DS-0 (representing capacity of 24 kilobytes per second); the smallest traded unit of bandwidth was DS-3, equaling 672 DS-0s (or roughly 45 megabytes per second). So if Enron sold three times DS-3 at 0.85 cents per DS-0, it would charge $18,901 per month for that bandwidth. Enron also sold and bought options and swaps on bandwidth, and advised companies on how to manage their bandwidth risks, including price changes and whether access to a network was available. Not surprisingly, Williams Cos. later entered bandwidth trading, as did Dynegy; the two companies didn't want to miss the boat if bandwidth did turn out to be a big market.

Trading bandwidth was just a warm-up for Enron's grandest entry into the Internet: trading commodities online.

A few companies had already insinuated the Internet into the energy-trading business. Williams advanced the furthest, developing an online system of displaying gas prices. In 1996, Williams combined its Internet price-display system with similar efforts at Duke Energy, and named the combination Altra Energy. In 1997, they sold a majority stake in Altra to Battery Ventures, a venture capital firm best known for investing in small Internet-related software firms; later, the rest of Altra was sold to Battery and Austin Ventures, a Texas-focused venture capital firm, making the company independent of Williams and Duke. That transaction garnered little fanfare, as the Internet mania of the moment was still fixated on business-to-consumer sites such as Amazon.com, and had yet to seize upon the business-to-business market.

Altra already hosted a limited amount of trading of gas and electricity— it facilitated more than $2 billion worth of trades in 1997—but its personality had been split between an electronic trading system and a trading software firm. Freed from its energy-company founders, Altra honed in on becoming a neutral online marketplace where customers could buy and sell energy. Altra merely hosted the marketplace, where energy traders anonymously posted bid and offer prices, and Altra didn't act as broker to any of the deals. Altra achieved some success charging energy traders a fee for using its marketplace, and it soon added electricity to its products.

By 1999, the Internet world had discovered business-to-business markets, and realized that they might be larger and more lucrative than any online retail businesses. Altra had the biggest name among online energy exchanges, but it was soon joined by others. In July 1999, HoustonStreet.com launched, offering a neutral exchange for electricity traders, and in its first four weeks its system hosted trades totaling 270,000 megawatt-hours. Quicktrade emerged as another energy exchange, although Altra bought it in 1999.

Enron was certainly technology-savvy, and it had an extensive computer system. But it saw no great advantage in using the Internet. Its traders were virtuosos at working the phones to hammer out deals and exchange information. Why use the Internet to open up its cozy trading business?

Well, the key reason was efficiency. As early as 1996, Enron had looked into creating an online system for posting energy prices, which might save customers and Enron staffers a few phone calls. After some delays, senior management gave the okay to use the Internet to display prices, but not to conduct transactions. In 1997 Enron's first such system went live in Oslo, displaying electricity prices for the Norwegian power-trading group. In computer-savvy Scandinavia, customers liked it. Soon,

Enron launched a similar system in Germany, where the energy-trading staff was relieved that they didn't have to overwork their German-speaking salespeople on customer calls.

By early 1999, the Internet was clearly too big for Enron to ignore; the growth of online stockbrokers such as E*Trade and Charles Schwab illustrated the demand for online transactions. "With all the success of the Internet and all the publicity, it became clear to me that we were moving too slowly," recalled John Sherriff, who headed European trading at the time. Greg Whalley, a senior trading executive in Houston, agreed with him. Fortunately, Sherriff had an employee in London who was hot to implement Internet trading—Louise Kitchen, the head of European gas trading. Sherriff tapped Kitchen to work full-time leading the online-trading project, giving her an initial budget of $15 million. Soon she was working on the effort with 25 to 30 other employees in London and Houston, and traveling frequently to Texas. The people involved kept the effort low-key because it was still in its formative stages.

Another reason Kitchen and her crew didn't trumpet what they were doing was Enron's skepticism of the Altra Energy model. Enron had made its money as a market maker, which involved taking one side of a trade (either buying or selling) and thus influencing pricing and volume. It had little interest in creating a neutral marketplace that would depend on other companies to provide a steady stream of trades, and where trades would occur without its involvement as a principal in any of the transactions; it might as well stick to cutting all its deals over the phone. "I was on record as being opposed to automated trading systems," Skilling explained. "Bulletin boards don't work very well. I believe you have to have a principal position to get liquidity in the market."

But the Enron idea solved that problem: The company would create an online exchange where Enron took one side of every trade. If someone wanted to buy gas from EnronOnline, he'd be buying it from Enron; and if someone wanted to sell electricity on EnronOnline, she'd be selling it to Enron. Rather than create an online market as a Switzerland of energy, Kitchen was leading the charge to create an online market that was an extension of Enron's existing market-making business.

In addition to the core group of roughly 30 employees, more than 100 other Enron employees worked on the idea part-time; finding help was not a problem, as Enron's culture trained employees to gravitate toward the next big idea. The team grappled with legal issues arising from the need to conform to different laws in the United States, United Kingdom, Germany, and other countries. They had to make sure the online exchange didn't meet the definition of a regulated exchange, like the New York Mercantile Exchange, or else the added paperwork and administrative requirement might have killed it. Enron had to craft standard online contracts for each commodity that every side could live with. Financial and software people had to install a system to cut off trades with a counterparty that exceeded its credit limit. Tech crews had to make sure the network functioned seamlessly so that with one click, the trade was entered in London, then sent to the main computer system in Houston, then back to the trader (where the books were kept), then back to Houston and back to the customer.

After spending more than $30 million (much of it bootlegged out of various departments' budgets), Sherriff, Kitchen, and others conducted a "beta" test of the system on a Saturday, just using pretend trades of U.S. natural gas, and it worked. At a business review meeting, Sherriff told Skilling about the project.

As Skilling recalled it, Sherriff sat down with him and said, "Look, this automated trading stuff, I really do want to talk to you about it." And Skilling rolled his eyes and said, "Aw, not again."

Sherriff explained, "Well, this is different. This is a principal-based system where we stand on each side of the transaction."

Skilling said, "Oh great, sounds good to me."

When a relieved Sherriff went "Whew," Skilling asked why he had that reaction. And Sherriff explained, "Well, that's good, because we're rolling it out next week."

The truth wasn't quite that dramatic, although it became part of Enron's legend that the whole system was developed behind Skilling's back and then sprung on him as a fait accompli. Sherriff recalled that Skilling was immediately supportive of the idea, and "he got genuinely excited about it." Also, it took a couple of months to roll out the system after getting Skilling's approval.

In October 1999, Kitchen gave a presentation on the planned system to all the company's top vice presidents at a management conference in San Antonio. EnronOnline went live on November 29, 1999. The first products offered were more than 20 different contracts for U.S. natural gas—still Enron's biggest market. Swaps pegged to NYMEX gas futures proved the most popular. Then Enron gradually added more products, so as not to overload the system. After U.S. gas came Canadian gas. In December, Enron added coal, U.S. electricity, Nordic electricity, pulp and paper, and plastics. The online platform tempted Enron to quickly expand the range of commodities it traded well beyond the energy world.

True to its conception, EnronOnline satisfied the company and put a great deal of trading on the Internet in a faster, more open design. While other online exchanges sought to make money by charging market participants to join or use the exchange, EnronOnline didn't have to do that. Instead, it made money from the transactions themselves. If a company sold Enron options to buy natural gas for $100,000 in the morning, Enron might sell those same options in the afternoon in two separate deals for a total of $105,000. The deals themselves were the source of profit, and those companies seeking to trade with Enron didn't have to pay any entry fee or a small cut of each trade. In addition, energy traders didn't have to wait for another counterparty to wander into the exchange—Enron usually made the trade happen instantly.

EnronOnline wasn't some new third party trying to host a piece of the energy trading business. It was an electronic extension of existing relationships between Enron traders and energy producers, energy users, and other trading firms. This was especially important for energy producers, who like to stabilize their prices rather than speculate in the energy markets, because they were assured of an ongoing relationship in which they knew they had a buyer for their gas or electricity.

It also helped that the core of EnronOnline was electricity and natural gas, which were already very large and liquid markets. There were critics who preferred Altra's neutral marketplace, worried that Enron's proprietary system gave it too much knowledge about the market. To counter these fears, EnronOnline always displayed the bid (offers to buy) and ask (offers to sell) prices on each contract, so customers didn't think they were getting conned. And the strategy of providing liquidity attracted users, drawing many away from using the phone for simple trades and instead using the Net. By January 19, 2000 (the day before Enron hosted a big meeting with Wall Street analysts), EnronOnline had more than 450 customers and had completed more than 10,000 transactions, trading contracts worth well over $100 million each day. Overall trading volumes rose.

Displaying prices so openly gave customers a better handle on what energy markets were doing, and so, thanks to EnronOnline, the spreads (gaps) between the bid and ask prices slowly narrowed. Where once Enron might have bought gas for $2 and sold it for $2.05, now it might buy gas for $2.02 and sell it for $2.04; the five-cent spread became a two-cent spread. But these spreads had been narrowing already as the gas and power markets matured, and more competitors entered the energy trading business. At Enron, Sherriff explained that the thinking was, "Let's drive down the spread but increase our volume."

EnronOnline continued to grow. In May 2000, it added bandwidth trading. By the end of June, nearly 60 percent of Enron's wholesale trading volumes had migrated to the Internet. From November 1999 through June 2000, EnronOnline had executed trades representing $100 billion in total value (not the income that went to Enron). In just eight months, EnronOnline had become the most important business in the corporation.

But there were subtle negative consequences from the success of the Internet trading business. EnronOnline slowly made Enron's trading operation more dependent on volume—in other words, as each trade on average became less profitable, Enron had to make that up in growth. The nature of EnronOnline also favored short term contracts (which were easier to standardize and deal with on the Internet), which were by nature less lucrative. So the trading operation also became even more short-term oriented.

At the same time, Enron had taken on a huge pile of risk, and the risk was still growing. Because Enron was the counterparty to every trade, the company tried to balance all the buy orders and sell orders each day, a nearly impossible task. It was as if one company ran the New York Stock Exchange *and* was involved in every trade on the exchange. Enron now made markets in dozens of commodities, as well as ran its retail energy business, operated pipelines, structured more complex financial deals that weren't suited for the Internet, and developed and managed overseas projects. If Ken Lay didn't stay on top of what Enron did with LJM, was it any wonder? As CEO, his hands-off management style may not have provided sufficient oversight to this sprawling corporation. Yet no one complained that Enron was spreading itself too thin.

9

POWER AND GLORY

Enron had a busy year in 1999, and not just because it created an Internet trading exchange. In February of that year, Germany opened its electricity market to competition at both the wholesale and retail levels. That sparked a scramble among German utilities, including number one RWE, number two Veba, and number three Viag, to get bigger and more competitive in response to falling power prices. So Veba entered serious talks with Enron about a merger, which could have based the merged company in Veba's base of Düsseldorf. The two companies kept the talks secret, although they retained advisers to look at the idea of combining.

The process began in late 1998, when then-struggling Veba brought Jeff Skilling to a management meeting as a guest speaker to talk about the need to embrace change. As they say in showbiz, Skilling killed. "If your managers aren't waking up at 3 A.M. sweating, you're doing something wrong," Skilling told the audience at one point, and his speech earned a standing ovation. Skilling kept in touch with Veba chief Ulrich Hartmann, and the two companies contemplated a joint venture in trading. In 1999, that turned into talks of a full-blown merger, although one of the sticking points was who would be in charge: Veba had been thinking about a merger of equals, while Enron, with the larger capitalization and more aggressive culture, visualized a takeover of Veba.

A bigger obstacle emerged when Veba looked into Enron's financial condition and, although the negotiations hadn't advanced to the point where the companies opened their books to each other, Veba got a glimpse of the array of partnerships that enhanced Enron's balance sheet. One Veba executive told the *New York Times* that Enron's "aggressive accounting practices" bothered the German company. Pricewaterhouse-Coopers, one of the advisers in the talks, told Veba that Enron used partnerships to sweep tens of millions in debt off its books, and so Enron's credit rating wasn't as solid as it appeared.

Whether control worries or accounting concerns served as the final straw, Veba backed away from the deal before even presenting it to its board of directors. The German company eventually merged with Viag to form a new utility company, E.On.

Another major change for the company had its roots in December 1998, when a company that Enron didn't identify offered to buy its majority stake in Enron Oil & Gas. At the time, low oil prices were inspiring consolidation among oil producing companies, and EOG seemed attractive because more than 80 percent of its assets were natural gas, not oil. The unsolicited offer started Enron examining its alternatives for its 53.5 percent stake in EOG; investors seconded the decision by sending Enron's stock higher the day that the bid hit the news. Enron Oil & Gas no longer served the strategic purpose it once did in providing a secure supply of natural gas for Enron Corp., because by the end of 1998 energy marketing had become so widespread and liquid that Enron didn't have to worry about gas supplies.

The board of EOG formed a special committee and hired outside advisers to study a possible change in ownership, and Enron Corp. began looking for potential buyers of its stake. But months passed without Enron Corp. and Enron Oil & Gas being able to hammer out a deal acceptable to both companies. In May 1999, Enron Corp. canceled plans to sell its EOG stake to a third party, but still wanted to do something with its investment as part of its move toward an asset-light company.

In July the two companies finally hit upon a solution: Enron Corp. agreed to sell most of its stake in Enron Oil & Gas Co. back to EOG in a deal valued at about $1.2 billion. Enron traded 62.3 million of its 82.3 million shares of Enron Oil & Gas back to EOG in exchange for $600 million in cash and EOG's assets in India and China (where Enron Corp. felt its hard assets still held strategic value). The transaction cut Enron's stake in EOG down to about 16 percent, and left Enron Oil & Gas as a truly independent company. The deal closed a month later, and Enron Oil & Gas changed its name to EOG Resources.

Enron's reorganizing didn't end there. The company had submitted a proposal to Oregon regulators for selling all of the power plants owned by Portland General, turning the electric utility into a pure distribution company. In many ways, the plan embodied Enron's vision of how the entire U.S. electric industry should restructure, dividing itself into power generation companies and power distribution companies. The proposal included selling the utility's hydroelectric plants, which accounted for about half of its generating capacity, to a state-controlled trust. But in January 1999, the Oregon Public Utility Commission rejected the idea, deciding that it was too risky to turn Portland General's 650,000 customers over to the open market to buy electricity the way consumers shopped for long-distance phone service. In addition, the Commission said it would allow the utility to sell its fossil-fuel power plants, but didn't want Portland General to sell its hydroelectric plants for fear that Oregon consumers would lose the benefits of their low-cost power.

Of course, even Portland General chief Ken Harrison admitted that consumers hadn't generated a "groundswell" of support for deregulation. After months of debate, the state passed a power deregulation law that called for the state's two big private utilities—Portland General and Pacifi-Corp's Pacific Power & Light—to allow business and industrial customers to buy directly from competing energy suppliers by October 1, 2001; meanwhile, residential customers would continue to buy electricity from their local utilities. The new law frustrated Enron. Speaking at an energy conference in August, Ken Lay admitted to the crowd that Oregon's pace of deregulation disappointed him. That started rumors flying that Enron wanted to just sell Portland General. Observers pointed out that Enron had no qualms about shedding an underperforming asset.

Meanwhile, morale at Portland General began to decline as the utility felt buffeted by Enron's different restructuring plans. In October, after releasing third-quarter results, Enron Corp. said it would "entertain alternatives" for Portland General—meaning the business was for sale a little over two years after the company bought the electric utility. This marked a big change of course, but California hadn't exactly turned out the way Enron had planned, and neither had Oregon's electric market.

In November, Enron reached a deal under which Sierra Pacific Resources, the owner of energy utilities in Nevada and California, would buy Portland General for $3.1 billion, including a $2.1 billion purchase price and the assumption of $1 billion of the utility's debt. Sierra Pacific would get a utility that had been consistently profitable under Enron, and Enron would unload one of its hard assets. The parties expected the sale to close in late 2000. "We have been very pleased with the performance of Portland General," Ken Lay said in a statement. "However, the rapidly evolving competitive electricity market allows us to deliver commodity services and risk management products to our customers without requiring the ownership of a regulated electric utility."

Enron executives explained the sale of Portland General by noting that the company bought the utility to learn about the electricity business, and having learned the market didn't need the utility anymore. But even some Enron employees doubted that strategy. As one former managing director said, "We didn't need to buy a company to get a few electricity traders. That's like if you want a glass of beer, you buy a brewery."

So 1999 served as another transforming year for Enron. The company traveled further down the asset-light path by unloading its oil and gas producing business and its regulated electric utility. Enron reported 1999 revenues of $40.1 billion (up from $31.3 billion in 1998), making it the 18th-largest company in the United States as measured by revenues and as ranked by *Fortune* magazine. Net income was $893 million, up from $703 million the year before.

As 1999 proved to be a good year for Enron's numbers, it was also a good year for Enron's stock. The stock price ended the year at $44.375 after a two-for-one stock split, posting a 50 percent increase between January 4 and December 31; that far outpaced the healthy 19.6 percent rise in the S&P 500 index, the leading gauge for the U.S. stock market, over the same time frame.

Not surprisingly, Enron's executives did well. Chairman and CEO Ken Lay received a cash bonus of $3.9 million on top of his $1.2 million salary. The company justified the bonus as being "in recognition of Enron's extremely strong performance during 1999 relative to targeted recurring after-tax net income." Lay's right-hand man, Jeff Skilling, got a cash bonus of $3 million on top of his $850,000 salary.

But the real value came in stock options. In this respect Enron mirrored most of the rest of corporate America, which decided to link top executives' compensation to the companies' earnings and stock performance—purportedly to tie CEOs' interests more closely to the interests of shareholders. Throughout the 1990s, stock option grants continued to grow. So in 1999, Lay was granted options on 1.3 million Enron shares at an exercise price of $37.1875, meaning that the options could be cashed in once Enron's stock rose above $37.1875—which it already had, given that it ended 1999 at $44.375. As common practice dictated, the options weren't all exercisable at once, but vested over a period of several years. Still, the 1.3 million options meant that if Enron stock appreciated at 5 percent a year, the options would be worth $30.4 million.

Enron granted Skilling options on 1 million shares at an exercise price of $41.0625. If Enron's stock appreciated at just 5 percent a year, Skilling's options would be worth $25.8 million.

Enron's top executives benefited even more from the options they'd been granted in the past. In 1999, Lay exercised past options to buy a little over 1.9 million shares of Enron. This resulted in a paper gain of $43.8 million. The same year, Skilling exercised options to buy roughly 2.36 million shares, resulting in a paper gain of $46.4 million. At the end of 1999, Lay still had options he hadn't exercised that were worth up to $130 million. And Skilling had unexercised options worth up to $20 million.

They weren't the only highly compensated executives at Enron. In 1999, Enron Europe CEO Mark Frevert exercised options to buy a little over 305,000 shares, giving him a paper gain of $5.5 million, and Stanley Horton, CEO of the gas pipeline group, exercised options to buy a little over 290,000 shares, giving him a paper gain of nearly $5.8 million.

If these compensation figures seemed inflated, they were only keeping up with the larger trend in boardrooms across the United States. Lay's compensation was high, but still less than that received in 1999 by General Electric CEO Jack Welch, Citigroup chairman Sandy Weill, or IBM chief Lou Gerstner (who, for example, exercised existing stock options for a paper gain of more than $87 million). Companies were happy to hand out stock options to employees at many levels—Enron awarded more than 30 million of them in total in 1999—because they didn't have to be booked as an expense the way salaries were. Some observers felt this accounting rule created misleading financial results, and the Financial Accounting Standards Board (FASB) proposed overturning this rule and making options a cost in the early 1990s. But it backed off in 1994 after

intense lobbying by industry and even some politicians. As a result, options remained a no-cost proposition, and corporations felt they could
hand out boatloads of options without dire consequences.

Did the potential rewards of options encourage Enron executives or
managers at other companies to fudge their earnings? Did the knowledge
that an extra $1 in stock price might translate into an extra $5 million
through the calculus of options contribute to Enron's willingness to bury
debt in off-the-books entities? It's impossible to know. But Enron and hundreds of other companies had argued for years that employee stock options
created important incentives for employees to perform better, so there *was*
a widespread belief that options grants influenced what employees did.

■ ■ ■

On the surface, Enron did very well in 1999. But underneath, there were
subtle signs of trouble. Enron expanded, but it sometimes jumped
through strange hoops to log that growth. For example, in order to land
a contract with a large paper company to supply its mills with electricity,
Enron agreed to buy an option from the company for several million
dollars. The deal would also have allowed Enron to supply electricity to
any new mills built by the paper company. According to a former Enron
employee, Enron bought an option structured as a contract on its right
to future business with the paper company, but in effect it worked like an
up-front payment for the company's future business. Thanks to mark-to-
market accounting, Enron was able to book the entire future value of the
deal at once as a profitable transaction—on paper. But the deal really
amounted to Enron paying out cash to the paper company in exchange
for hoped-for profits in the future.

Indeed, the flow of cash in and out of Enron told a less spectacular
story than its soaring revenue. In 1998, Enron actually had a negative
cash flow of $59 million, which meant it used more cash than it took in
through its operating and financing activities. In 1999, Enron had a positive cash flow of $177 million—but that came from a rise in short-term
borrowing, while the net cash generated by operating activities fell 25
percent from 1998 levels. Also, Enron generated a "return on equity" of
more than 15 percent in the middle of the 1990s, but that measure
dropped to 9.9 percent in 1998 and 9.3 percent in 1999. So Enron was

getting bigger, but it was becoming less profitable at the same time. Investors might have started to wonder about Enron had they paid closer attention to these subtler measures of efficiency and profitability rather than to earnings, or to "operating earnings," which Enron touted as a measure of its net income excluding one-time gains and charges. But analysts were recommending Enron, growth was obvious, and the stock continued to rise—the clearest confirmation of success.

In one sense, Enron was becoming more streamlined, with its online trading platform and its moves to shed hard-asset businesses such as oil and gas production and the electric utility. To accommodate the swelling trading operation, in mid-1999 Enron began building a gleaming new 40-story office tower across the street from its existing headquarters, which would include four state-of-the-art trading floors of 55,000 square feet each. But even as Enron slowly consolidated around its trading business, behind the scenes the company was becoming more complex as its web of off-balance sheet partnerships began to expand beyond Chewco and LJM.

In October 1999, Andrew Fastow proposed to the finance committee of Enron's board of directors that the company create a second, larger partnership, LJM2, to buy assets from Enron in the same way LJM did. Fastow proposed raising at least $200 million for LJM2, and managing it. The board's finance committee discussed the proposal on October 11, at a meeting also attended by Lay and Skilling. Fastow acknowledged that serving as CFO and managing the new partnership could create conflicts of interest, so he proposed that deals between Enron and LJM2 require the approval of Chief Accounting Officer Richard Causey and Chief Risk Officer Rick Buy, and that Enron review LJM2 annually. With those controls in place, the finance committee recommended the LJM2 deal, and Finance Committee Chairman Herbert S. Winokur Jr. proposed the idea to the rest of the full board. The board approved, and waived the company's ethics code to allow Fastow to manage LJM2.

Ken Lay never investigated whether the controls were followed. Enron had a "hands-off" management style, he later explained, and if someone identified a problem then he and Skilling fixed it. Skilling was responsible for ensuring the controls were in place, according to Lay.

Enron then began looking for outside investors for LJM2, and retained the help of several investment banks to do so. The documents prepared to market the new partnership (which were shown only to institutional investors) noted that LJM2 intended to generate an internal rate of return on investments of at least 30 percent, after fees. It also noted that LJM2 would benefit from being run by Fastow and two of his Enron lieutenants, Michael Kopper (a managing director) and Ben Glisan (a vice president)—although there's no record that the board knew of the involvement of Kopper and Glisan when it approved LJM2. Glisan later told investigators that his name appeared in the prospectus by mistake. Still, LJM2 promised investors that the principals—Fastow and his cohorts—would, as senior financial officers of Enron, "typically be familiar with the investment opportunities LJM2 considers. The Principals believe that their access to Enron's information pertaining to potential investments will contribute to superior returns." The offering documents went on to say that "investors in the partnership should benefit from Mr. Fastow's and the other Principals' dual roles."

One could interpret the references to the "dual roles" as implying that Fastow would use his knowledge of Enron to benefit LJM2 in its dealings with Enron, which could raise questions about conflict of interest. However, Enron's in-house lawyers and its main outside counsel, Vinson & Elkins, approved the documents. And Enron's board didn't see the offering documents at all. Directors didn't ask to see them. One director, Robert Belfer, remembered receiving a copy of the offering memorandum in the mail providing him the chance to invest in LJM2, but he threw it away without looking at it.

LJM2 was marketed as another example of Enron's innovative financing strategies using off-balance sheet entities. After all, Enron listed $34 billion of assets on its books as of June 30, 1999, but the company owned or controlled $51 billion of assets when off-balance sheet deals were included; in other words, one-third of Enron's assets were off its books. And investment opportunities promised to be abundant, because of Enron's stature as a major player in a growing global energy market and its entry into the booming communications industry (with its fiber network and bandwidth trading).

Merrill Lynch helped sell LJM2, and eventually it attracted roughly $386 million in investments from such firms as American Home Assurance Co., First Union Investors, Kleinwort Benson Holdings, the State of Arkansas Teachers Retirement System, and Travelers Insurance Co. and Citicorp—both arms of Citigroup. In addition, many of the investment banks that arranged deals for Enron invested in LJM2: Lehman Brothers invested $10 million; CIBC Capital Corp. invested $15 million; J.P. Morgan Chase invested $15 million; and Merrill invested a total of $22 million. Some of the investment banks felt pressured to put money into LJM2 in order to stay in the running for investment banking business from Enron. Interestingly, several top officials at Merrill made personal investments in LJM2 (which was legal and not uncommon), but some Merrill executives reportedly turned down the chance to invest because they were uncomfortable with LJM2's potential investments.

LJM2 immediately began buying assets from Enron. Two months after formation, LJM2 paid Enron $30 million for a 75 percent equity interest in a power project in Poland; Enron had been unable to find another buyer before year-end. Enron recognized a $16 million gain in 1999 on the sale. Enron paid $750,000 to LJM2 as an equity placement fee. In March 2000, Enron repurchased 25 percent of the equity in the Polish power project from LJM2 for $10.6 million, and Enron's Whitewing partnership acquired the remaining 50 percent from LJM2 for $21.3 million. In other words, LJM2 made a cool $1.9 million for simply holding the equity interest in the Polish plant for about four months.

Separately, Enron was trying to sell a 90 percent equity interest in MEGS, a company that owned a natural-gas gathering system in the Gulf of Mexico. Enron wanted to sell this before year-end, so that MEGS didn't have to be consolidated into its financial statement. So in December, Enron sold the stake to LJM2, in a combination of debt and equity, for roughly $26 million. Again, Enron bought back the stake in MEGS in March 2000, paying what LJM2 paid plus enough extra money to provide LJM2 with a 25 percent return. Enron Treasurer Jeff McMahon signed the approval sheet to buy back the MEGS interest, but under his signature he wrote: "There were no economics run to demonstrate this investment makes sense." McMahon didn't see a reason for Enron to buy back the MEGS interest. However, the round-trip transaction resulted in a nice profit for LJM2.

While the deals involving MEGS and the Polish project might suggest that LJM2 made some easy money from its Enron dealings, LJM2 also appeared to fill the need of a buyer for hard-to-sell assets. In December, Enron bundled together a bunch of loans it had made into a trust, so that the trust was now owed the money. It sold $324 million of notes and stock to institutional investors. The lowest-rated securities in the trust—those securities that would be repaid last in case of loan defaults—were difficult to sell. These securities were sold to Whitewing and LJM2. Two days before LJM2 bought notes and stock from the loan trust for $32.5 million, a Whitewing affiliate loaned $38.5 million to LJM2. The entire transaction took the loans, and their possible liabilities, off Enron's books.

Meanwhile, the first LJM partnership (now called LJM1) continued to do deals beyond the Rhythms transaction. In September 1999, LJM1 acquired from Enron for $11.3 million a 13 percent equity interest in a company owning a power plant in Brazil. Enron recognized a $1.7 million loss on the sale of these interests to LJM1. However, the sale allowed Enron to alter its accounting treatment of a related contract to supply gas to the plant, resulting in Enron recognizing mark-to-market revenues of $65 million in 1999.

If these didn't seem like the kinds of deals Enron would conduct with true third parties, that's because transactions with both LJM partnerships were "related party" deals. Looking back at the LJM deals, the Enron special committee that investigated Enron in late 2001 and early 2002 concluded in the Powers Report that the LJM partnerships *did* provide Enron with a "purported third party" to which it could quickly sell assets, thus avoiding the need to consolidate those assets into Enron's books and sometimes making a profit for Enron. However, the report went on: "Events after many of these sales—particularly those that occurred near the end of the third and fourth quarters of 1999—call into question the legitimacy of the sales themselves and the manner in which Enron accounted for the transactions." Among the eyebrow-raising details? There was evidence that in some of the deals, Enron agreed in advance to protect the LJM partnerships against a loss. And the LJM partnerships made a profit on *every* transaction, even when the asset purchased seemed to decline in market value.

In addition, Fastow's role in managing the LJM partnerships begged the question of whether they were independent entities. On the one hand, Fastow worked for Enron when he served as the general partner for LJM1 and LJM2, suggesting that Enron controlled the LJM partnerships. Should they therefore have been consolidated into Enron's books? On the other hand, the partnership agreements allowed the limited partners to remove the general partner (Fastow) under certain circumstances. So did this mean the LJM partnerships were independent enough to be treated as separate entities? The Powers Report didn't choose either side on this question, concluding: "There are no clear answers under relevant accounting standards."

Enron mentioned the two LJM partnerships in its 1999 annual report, which came out in early 2000. In a section on "Related Party Transactions," Enron disclosed that it entered a series of transactions with LJM1 (which it described as being run by "a senior officer of Enron") that involved forward contracts on Enron stock, and it disclosed that in the fourth quarter of 1999 it sold about $360 million worth of assets and investments to LJM2. The section ended with the note: "Management believes that the terms of the transactions with related parties are representative of terms that would be negotiated with unrelated third parties."

In a section on "Minority Interests" and one on "Unconsolidated Equity Affiliates," the annual report listed both JEDI partnerships (the second one formed with CalPERS, and the first one now a partnership with Chewco), the Whitewing entity, joint ventures such as Teesside and Dabhol, and its 34 percent stake in Azurix. But the report gave little detail on the nature of the many transactions, and didn't name the investments involved in the deals, such as Rhythms NetConnections and MEGS.

Why weren't investors more worried? Maybe because descriptions of the partnerships were so vague. Even a close reading of the report didn't reveal the full scope of Enron's off-balance sheet transactions. The Powers Report called the disclosures such as those in the 1999 annual report "fundamentally inadequate." And a U.S. Senate investigation in 2002 said Enron's initial public disclosures of its dealings with JEDI, Whitewing, and LJM "are nearly impossible to understand."

The 1999 annual report ended, as usual, with a note from Arthur Andersen verifying its audit of Enron's financial statements. Using language that's standard in annual and quarterly reports, Enron's accounting firm said, "In our opinion, the financial statements referred to above present fairly, in all material respects, the financial position of Enron Corp."

And that was that. The financial reporting system designated appropriate accounting firms to act as outside auditors of publicly traded companies, and Andersen and other such accounting firms had the responsibility to serve as corporate watchdogs. The accounting industry regulated itself. The Securities and Exchange Commission had oversight authority over accountants' audits of public companies, but the SEC never had enough manpower to read through more than a tiny sample of annual and quarterly reports. This staffing crunch worsened in the late 1990s, as the SEC had to devote more time and resources to the large number of Internet-related IPOs; this took efforts away from criminal oversight. Andersen had to make sure that Enron obeyed the law in its accounting. Without outside monitoring, Andersen's incentive to act as a watchdog was the threat of investor lawsuits, and the slim possibility that damage to its reputation would hurt its business.

■ ■ ■

Enron's accounting firm, Arthur Andersen, was known for its work in the energy industry. Founded in 1913 as Chicago's Andersen, DeLany & Company, the firm changed its name to Arthur Andersen in 1918. The firm rose to worldwide prominence under Leonard Spacek, who led it for 16 years after the 1947 death of founder Arthur Andersen.

Arthur Andersen thrived in the 1990s, its income growing by more than 10 percent each year, and its revenue rising from $3 billion in 1992 to $7.4 billion in 1999. In addition to traditional audit work, the firm stoked that growth by expanding its consulting work. Its consulting practice, formally established as a separate unit in 1989, included management advice and consulting on tax-reduction strategies.

Andersen was not alone in its consulting work—all of the so-called Big Five accounting firms had consulting arms, as part of the evolution of the accounting industry. Accounting firms were no longer the quiet conscience of business, stocked with professional introverts obsessed with numbers (one traditional industry joke said an extroverted accountant was one who stared at the client's shoes while speaking instead of staring at his own shoes). In 1973, the U.S. government set up the Financial Accounting Standards Board to oversee accountants and accounting rules. But FASB undid a lot of the restrictions that had kept big firms from competing with each other. Accountants started advertising, and as the industry became more cutthroat, the firms became more aggressive and started merging; over time, the original Big Eight accounting firms consolidated into the Big Five. In the 1980s, globalization and the increasing complexity of business—accentuated by the rise of complicated finance and derivatives use—brought new challenges to the accounting profession. Not surprisingly, this time period saw accounting firms rush into consulting. In 1999, consulting made up half of the Big Five's revenue, up from 13 percent in 1981.

One lucrative business consisted of taking over the internal accounting functions within a company, which Andersen did for parts of Enron; in that role, Andersen tried to ensure the accuracy of business records and identify any internal control problems. Other big accounting firms acted similarly, persuading companies that they could more easily provide internal auditing than the internal corporate employees that had traditionally done that job. For Andersen and other firms, this internal auditing was done while serving as the external auditor as well, even though serving as both external and internal auditor might have raised conflict-of-interest questions; the external auditor typically provided independent oversight of the company's books, which could include any internal auditing. Because of those conflict questions, the SEC adopted a rule in 2000 barring an external auditor from conducting more than 40 percent of the internal auditing at a client if that company has more than $200 million in assets. But throughout the 1990s, Andersen expanded its business as an internal auditor.

Despite its reputation, by 1999 Andersen sometimes walked a fine line between accounting creativity and impropriety. In 1998, the SEC began investigating the books of Sunbeam, an appliance maker and audit client of Andersen's. Later that year, Sunbeam restated some of its results to remove inflated profits. In 2000, Andersen would pay $110 million to settle a lawsuit brought by Sunbeam shareholders accusing Andersen of signing off on a company audit that included fake profits.

Meanwhile, Waste Management, a leading garbage-hauling company and another auditing client of Andersen's, also shocked Wall Street in early 1998 when it revealed that it had to restate several years of financial results. This sparked an SEC inquiry of both Waste Management and Andersen, charging that the former played tricks with its books to hide expenses from 1992 to 1997. In late 1998, Andersen and Waste Management agreed to settle shareholder lawsuits for a combined total of $220 million. In 2000, Andersen would also pay a $7 million fine for its role in the Waste Management debacle.

So in 1999, Andersen already faced embarrassing challenges of its auditing judgment for two clients. But the accounting firm still raised no objections over Enron's use of Special Purpose Entities. The cooperation of Andersen was no surprise. The accounting profession had been criticized for growing too cozy with the companies it audited. As Baruch Lev, a well-known professor of accounting and finance at New York University's Stern School of Business, said: "The auditing of public companies by external auditors is in many cases an 'all in the family' affair. Auditors are in too many companies *effectively* appointed and reappointed by managers, who also have a significant say in the audit fees."

Business like Enron's was like winning the lottery for an accounting firm, given its complexity. The derivatives revolution of the 1980s and 1990s created more business for accounting firms, because it meant that corporations could do more things with their books. Special Purpose Entities, securitization, synthetic leases—all these tools could help companies reduce borrowing costs and make their finances look better. If an oil refinery wanted to build a pipeline, it needed an outside investor to put up just a tiny bit of money to set up a partnership, and then the partnership would finance the project, thus taking the risk off its books. If a department store needed to raise some cash, it could sell bonds backed by the payments it had yet to collect from customers. If a company wanted to buy an airplane, it could sell it to a special purpose entity and then lease it back to the company for a tax break. And accounting firms provided both advice and consent for the use of these tactics. Their judgments could be somewhat subjective because they had to interpret the accounting rules, seeing as how those rules were formulated long before the advent of complex derivatives and asset-backed securities.

The problem, at bottom, was having some 100,000 pages of bookkeeping regulations known as "generally accepted accounting principles." With so many rules that were so specific, the details could obscure the bigger tenets. This allowed companies to follow the letter of the law even while violating the larger principle. So if Andersen couldn't show Enron a specific rule prohibiting what it wanted to do, Enron would do it.

On the other side of the equation, corporations were attracted to these complicated financial tools because they provided legal means to boost their reported profits. They simply responded to the pressure of the stock market. Over the course of the 1980s and 1990s, various factors combined to put more and more emphasis on quarterly results. For one thing, more Americans became shareholders, and they increasingly wanted to see quarter-to-quarter performance at the companies in which they invested. At the same time, more corporations paid their executives in the form of stock options, with the awarding of options tied to both long-term performance and quarterly results. In addition, the technology boom of the 1980s and 1990s created a new emphasis on growth: If household names such as Microsoft and Intel could rack up earnings growth of 50 percent per year, why couldn't "ordinary" companies grow their earnings by at least 15 percent per year?

Of course, for the vast majority of companies, achieving consistent growth of 15 percent per year is achingly difficult, especially when the U.S. economy rarely tops 6 percent growth in its best years. So companies looked for ways to cut interest costs, tax burdens, and everything else. Just about every company told Wall Street to expect growing profits—and if the company didn't meet the growth targets when it reported quarterly results, the stock would get slammed. It sounds both merciless and unrealistic, yet under this financial carrot-and-stick system, the U.S. stock market rose in 1995, then rose in 1996, and again in 1997, and more in 1998. And 1999 would eventually mark another up year for the stock market. In everyday conversation, "bull" means deceit, but in market terms, "bull" means optimism and rising values, and this was the greatest bull market in a generation. If companies had to strain to reach their growth targets, and if financial engineering made some annual reports hopelessly undecipherable, too bad. The market went up and so the system must have been working.

Enron was among the companies that frequently gave predictions of future earnings growth. For example, appearing at an investment conference in February 1997, Lay told an audience of fund managers and other professional investors that the company targeted annual earnings growth of 15 percent a year, on average, through 2000. Audaciously projecting out several years, he said Enron should reach $1.1 billion in net income in 2000. However, a shorter-term view was more typical. Like most companies, Enron provided private guidance to the Wall Street analysts who were estimating what the company would earn in the coming quarter. Those analyst estimates were published for the investing public, and quarterly results were then compared to them; analysts lavished praise on companies that consistently met or exceeded estimates. Throughout the Enron offices, employees knew of the company's desire to meet quarterly earnings estimates. Lay and Skilling set the bar high. And they knew that Wall Street wouldn't like it if they fell short.

■ ■ ■

At the same time that the company worried about earnings and revenue growth, it continued to keep close watch of its credit rating. This became even more important with the introduction of EnronOnline. Because Enron was the counterparty to every trade, Enron's financial sturdiness and credit rating backed EnronOnline. If Enron's credit rating were to fall too low, the huge Internet exchange trading $1 billion of commodities per day would collapse. This meant that keeping Enron's balance sheet healthy carried more importance than ever.

Enron kept reserves to provide for credit risks (in case a counterparty defaulted on a contract) and "prudency" reserves to cover trades gone bad. At the end of 1999, Enron had $337 million in such reserves. But those reserves, created based on equations related to Enron's various trades, covered just a fraction of Enron's trading activity. In addition, Enron traders sometimes trimmed the reserves on a trade a bit in order to boost its profitability and thus convince managers to approve the deal.

In addition, Enron worried about the previously mentioned disparity between trading income and cash. In 1999, the buying and selling of power amounted to a $137 billion market, according to technology research firm Forrester Research. But was it really such a great business? It entailed mass reserves of cash, which often translated into debt. But debt is supposed to be supported by inflows of cash, not by the accounting construction of "net income." The result? An increasingly rickety financial structure.

Though electricity trading generated big profits on paper, it actually brought in questionable amounts of cash. Mark-to-market accounting allowed Enron, Dynegy, Williams, and others to book all the profits up front from 2-year, 5-year, and even 20-year deals, while their clients could conceivably pay their cash share in small amounts over those long time periods. In addition, changes in market prices were virtually assured when dealing with volatile power prices over long stretches, which meant that the economics of the deals could change so much that clients might never be required to pay the cash that Enron had already accounted for as profits years earlier.

Volatile cash flows didn't help Enron's credit rating. And as the company's expansion rose to a new level, it once again worried about its creditworthiness, which was crucial to funding its investments and maintaining its trading business. Starting in autumn of 1999, Enron lobbied rating agencies to upgrade its long-term credit rating. In addition to calls and visits from CFO Andrew Fastow, this included at least one phone call from Ken Lay to Standard & Poor's credit analyst Ronald Barone. In the late 1990s, S&P kept Enron at a BBB+ rating, the low end of the investment grade spectrum, even though other large corporations had higher debt ratings: Boeing, for example, had an AA– rating. After Enron's collapse, critics wondered why the credit rating agencies hadn't discovered Enron's problems more quickly. But, according to the agencies, Enron's campaign for a rating upgrade depended on leaving out some of its off-balance sheet financings.

In presentations to S&P in 1999, for instance, Enron claimed to explain to the agency its full range of off-balance sheet affiliates. But the presentation made no mention of the Chewco partnership, or LJM1 or LJM2. In presentations the following year, Enron again failed to tell S&P about these partnerships, and also failed to mention that Michael Kopper of its finance department managed Chewco. Had S&P known of these arrangements, it would have discovered that Enron had more debt and looser risk management controls than it had realized, and that would have undermined the basis of its debt rating.

Moody's, the most august of the three main credit rating agencies, asked Enron to provide more information to justify an upgrade. Enron gave the firm what it called the "kitchen sink" disclosure, including all financial information and unconsolidated assets and debt. In March 2000, the agency, based on the information, upgraded Enron's rating from Baa2 to Baa1, which put Enron "at the upper range of the lowest investment-grade category," as Moody's described it. But, as Moody's later learned, what Enron had given it resembled a soap dish more than the kitchen sink. The information didn't mention the numerous partnerships with names like Rawhide and Braveheart. It also turned out that some of the information it did provide was inaccurate.

■ ■ ■

Enron may have had persistent worries about debt and its credit rating. But on the bright side, EnronOnline, even with its credit risks, was a mounting phenomenon that helped to boost Enron's growth. Using the Internet, Enron had turned energy commodities into easily traded products, like bonds or stocks. What's more, Enron's role as market maker on its Internet market assured it of liquidity—that crucial ability to buy or sell an asset easily without affecting its price—where many other online exchanges had trouble generating consistent liquidity. It seemed that it would only be a matter of time before the other commodity materials, such as chemicals, were ready for online trading. After all, those were no less difficult to price and trade over the Internet. Surely someone was going to be, for example, the Enron of chemicals. Enron felt it should be that someone, so it added chemicals to EnronOnline. And it added carbon-dioxide emissions trading. And aluminum and copper.

Enron's concerns about credit led the company to seize on it as an opportunity. The company had been a pioneer of energy derivatives, and then weather derivatives, so next up were credit derivatives. These were derivatives designed to hedge credit risk, and had been around for a few years. Banks had been in the business of selling credit protection as an insurance-like product, but credit derivatives characteristically attracted Enron as a market-based solution. But Enron was unhappy with the existing credit derivatives market for a number of reasons. First, with 100 participants (mostly banks) using customized contracts, the market lacked liquidity. Second, the market only did a good job covering bond defaults; in other words, if Enron had purchased a "credit default swap" from a bank on $10 million in bonds, when the bonds dropped in value to $4 million it was then up to the bank to make up the $6 million.

So in February 2000, Enron launched EnronCredit.com, an adjunct to EnronOnline that allowed customers to hedge their credit exposure instantly using tradable credit derivatives. EnronCredit.com utilized the software system Enron had been using to analyze credit exposure in real time for EnronOnline, where the thousands of trades each day required fast credit calculations. The outside world didn't know it at the time, but the launch of EnronCredit.com carried immense irony coming from a corporation with such a precarious credit situation. Adding to the irony, Enron soon developed bankruptcy swaps, a new product, as part of EnronCredit.com.

John Sherriff, the president of Enron Europe and the leader of the effort, figured that credit derivatives weren't much of a stretch from energy derivatives given that Enron relied on credit in its trading business. After all, if Enron traded $500 million worth of commodities each day via EnronOnline, most of that was done on credit without $500 million in cash changing hands. "Every part of our business involved granting and receiving credit," Sherriff explained. "Really, we were in the credit business more than we were in gas or electricity or oil."

Large banks with sterling credit ratings dominated the credit derivatives market, so Enron, with its mediocre credit rating, fought an uphill battle to break in. But Enron offered more liquidity, and Enron itself generated a lot of business for EnronCredit.com. By this time, Enron really operated more as an investment bank or a hedge fund (an unregulated investment fund that's often run like a mutual fund on steroids). Enron saw EnronCredit.com as a more sophisticated way to manage its own risk. But at the same time, it also loaded more and new risks on Enron. Unlike the banks that provided the bulk of credit derivatives, regulations didn't require Enron to maintain large capital reserves. This quirk was another consequence of the decision by the CFTC, under Wendy Gramm, that energy derivatives didn't fall under its regulatory jurisdiction (as mentioned in Chapter 3). Thanks to that ruling in 1992–1993, Enron didn't answer to the CFTC. Because it wasn't a bank, Enron didn't answer to the Federal Reserve, either. As a result, Enron's derivatives trading answered to no federal agency.

This allowed Enron to expand into new trading markets with no obstacles but customer demand and capital. So in mid-2000, Enron bought London's MG PLC, a leading metals-trading firm, for roughly $413 million in cash; the company also assumed some $1.6 billion of MG debt. MG, a spin-off from Metallgesellschaft, employed 330 people in 14 countries. The deal would provide Enron with the base of expertise it needed to seed its metals-trading business, much the way Portland General seeded its electricity business. "Enron has been monitoring the global metals market for several years, and we believe now is the time to enter this $120 billion market," Ken Lay said in a statement.

Enron completed its first metals trade on EnronOnline in July. The exchange's first metals contracts offered trades in aluminum from the Midwest and two kinds of U.S. copper. But integration of MG, which had a poor balance sheet, with Enron took a lot of time and energy. Sherriff recalled having 50 to 70 people working full-time integrating the different systems in risk management, technology, and cash management. In addition, metals prices began to slowly decline, sapping the profitability of metals trades (and hinting at the developing global economic slowdown). Because metals purchases tend to be large, costly transactions, metals trading used a lot of cash. "It was never all that profitable for us based on the capital we were using," Sherriff said.

Enron had already entered the paper and pulp business in 1998, and now it decided to add that to its Internet lineup, too. So Enron bought Garden State Paper, a recycled newsprint company in New Jersey, for $72 million. And in September, Enron launched Clickpaper.com, an online trading exchange like EnronOnline dedicated to pulp, paper, and other forest products. Trades for physical delivery dominated the site, as the paper industry had yet to embrace derivatives. Clickpaper.com would go on to have its biggest success in newsprint.

Enron may have been buying lots of companies to flesh out its Internet trading business, but in that respect it just fit in with the times. The acquisitions took place during a merger boom. Companies with rising stock prices used their shares as currency to buy other companies in stock-for-stock deals. In the early 1990s, the annual value of mergers in the United States didn't rise above $800 billion, but that soared in the late 1990s, peaking in 2000 with $1.7 trillion worth of mergers.

As EnronOnline spread out, it attracted even more notoriety to Enron. In February 2000, *Fortune* magazine's survey of America's most admired companies named Enron the most innovative U.S. company for the fifth straight year. In the same survey, Enron also topped the "quality of management" category, coming in just ahead of General Electric.

By the middle of 2000, Enron had come to be seen as the utmost example of an "old-economy" company that succeeded by embracing the Internet zeitgeist. Many newspapers and magazines hailed Enron and its stock. In its August 14, 2000, issue, *Fortune* magazine included Enron in its list of "10 Stocks to Last the Decade." *Fortune* wasn't being irresponsible or uniquely positive; rather, the huzzahs for Enron (the article noted that it had transformed itself into "a middleman for the new economy") were typical of the time. The business press and Wall Street believed the image that Enron presented to the outside world. It was a terrific story.

Enron managers began believing their own press. A Wall Street saying observed that if a company's stock doubled, its managers' egos would quadruple. While some pride may have been justified by the excellent performance of Enron's stock, Skilling and other executives exuded a conceit that even research analysts noticed. As research analyst John Olson noted, "Call it overconfidence, arrogance, or whatever; Enron's trading and adrenalin-driven culture began to sound dangerously invincible in 1997 and after. . . . Its rhetoric seemed to rise much faster than its business realities."

Enron's vision clearly went beyond being a natural gas major or being the world's leading energy company. It went beyond energy. The vision consisted of core skills that embraced innovation, markets, and creativity. In 2000, Enron gathered the executive committee to brainstorm a way to articulate Enron's new vision. "The voted favorite was 'world's coolest company,'" Skilling said.

Skilling had become an oracle of the New Economy, a souped-up information age marked by a rising stock market and a reliance on the Internet. This wasn't the flimsy act of a snake-oil salesman, as EnronOnline really did work as an online marketplace for trading commodities (mostly energy). Thanks to Enron's perceived success, Skilling joined Michael Dell, Charles Schwab, and other executives in touting the use of the Web. And it sounded good. Many people were looking for examples of how to profit from the Internet, which made sense.

Skilling opined to the press and public that business in general was changing because of the Internet's ability to drastically reduce "interaction costs," or the expense of dealing with, both financially and verbally, outside suppliers and partners. As Skilling would go on to tell *Business 2.0* magazine: "I believe the old model of rigid, asset-intensive, vertically integrated companies is becoming less viable. When the costs of transacting between organizations are high, it's logical to bundle more activities in a single entity because you have more control and it's easier to transfer information. You reduce the costs of interaction. But now interaction costs are collapsing because of the Internet. And as those costs fall, you're going to see the horizontally organized company—one that concentrates on a specific activity that it excels at—gradually beat out the old vertically integrated one that practices many activities but excels at few."

■ ■ ■

In early 2000, Enron was reaching a new peak of public influence. Enron already had a reputation for civic involvement, regularly donating money to the Houston Ballet, the Alley Theatre, and the KIPP Academy (a local charter school). Lay served as the chairman of the local United Way, and he encouraged Enron employees to donate time to such causes. Sometimes, the company even paid employees their regular salary while they donated time to building homes for Habitat for Humanity. But Lay and Enron reached a true pinnacle of local renown in baseball.

Houston's major league baseball team, the Astros, had been looking for a friendlier home than the cavernous Astrodome. Negotiations began between Astros owner Drayton McLane Jr. and city and state officials on building a new ballpark. Lay headed a consortium of local businesses that successfully pushed for the new stadium to remain in the downtown area, part of a goal to revitalize downtown Houston. In 1997, the various parties struck an agreement to finance a new stadium, including $180 million from a publicly funded sports authority, $52 million from the Astros, and $18 million from the consortium.

In April 1999, Enron agreed to pay the Astros an annual fee so that the new stadium would be named "Enron Field." In addition, Enron Energy Services signed a contract to manage the new stadium's energy needs, heating, ventilation, and air-conditioning. Both contracts ran for 30 years, with Enron paying a total of more than $100 million over that time to attach its name to the stadium. Enron now joined dozens of companies that had their names on sports arenas, such as Qualcomm Stadium, Continental Airlines Arena, and Coors Field. "This is a fitting partnership, given Enron's long-standing support of the Astros," said McLane.

Enron Field opened in April 2000. At the opening-day game, Lay threw out the first pitch. Enron would go on to host various employee trips to the stadium, and the company's offices soon filled with baseballs, bats, and baseball caps emblazoned with the "Enron" logo.

Meanwhile, Enron's political influence, or at least its reputation for political influence, continued to grow. Helping matters was Ken Lay's connection with George W. Bush, who was then the governor of Texas. Despite the fact that after Enron's collapse Bush tried to distance himself from the company, he was friendly enough with Ken Lay that they corresponded regularly. And while Lay often wrote to Bush to argue in favor of certain legislation, the letters went beyond a CEO lobbying a politician. Part of that may have been due to their shared tenure in Texas, the fact that Bush had also worked in the energy business, and the simple fact that they often had similar views—both men, for example, were suspicious of government regulation and were more comfortable with the concept of a free market determined by supply and demand.

Lay and Enron donated a lot of money to Bush's political campaigns. As far back as 1994, Ken and Linda Lay had donated $47,500 to Bush's gubernatorial campaign, with the Enron Corp. political action committee kicking in another $20,000. Other Enron executives also gave a total of $79,000 to the 1994 Bush effort, including $6,000 from Jeff Skilling and $6,000 from Thomas White, an Enron executive who would eventually become Secretary of the Army under President Bush. The Lays hedged their bets a bit in 1994, also contributing $12,500 (and Enron contributing another $5,000) to the campaign of incumbent Ann Richards. But it was clear that Lay was backing Bush. In Bush's 1998 re-election campaign, Ken Lay, Enron, and Enron executives upped the ante a bit, contributing a total of $166,000.

While there's no indication that Bush and Lay were best buddies, their relationship had a genuine friendliness to it. Lay felt close enough to Bush to write him letters on a range of subjects, including energy legislation, business conferences, and charity events. By 1995 the letters were addressed not to "Governor Bush" but to "George," although some of the letters were addressed to George Bush and his wife, Laura. In a September 1995 letter, Lay invited the couple to attend the CARE World Leadership Dinner honoring Bush's father, former president George H. W. Bush. In December 1997, Lay wrote to the Bushes thanking them for a State of Texas Christmas ornament the couple had given Ken and Linda Lay. "It was a thoughtful gift and one our family will enjoy hanging on the tree each year," he wrote.

In January 1997, Lay felt enough of a personal tie to send a handwritten letter to Bush about the governor's upcoming arthroscopic knee surgery. "I also want you to know that at least one jogger . . . got past 50 without surgery," Lay's note teased. Bush replied in an April note, "Thanks for your note. . . . My only regret is that I will be benched from jogging for about a month." Later that month, Bush sent a teasing letter to Lay about the CEO's 55th birthday, writing with Bush's characteristic casualness, "55 years old. Wow! That is really old. Thank goodness you have such a young, beautiful wife."

Business and trade interested both men, in ways that extended beyond issues directly affecting Enron or Texas. In March 1999, Lay sent Bush a *New York Times* article by Thomas Friedman that, he wrote, provided "an excellent overview" of globalization.

But Lay was also not shy about stumping for issues dear to Enron's heart. In February 1995, Lay wrote to "call your attention to the importance of allowing additional competition in Texas' wholesale power market." He went on to argue that such competition would reduce electricity rates for consumers. Understandably, opening the Texas wholesale electricity market to competition—in a word, deregulating it—was a key issue for Lay. Three months later, another Lay letter urged Bush to sign a Texas Senate bill that would have opened the state's wholesale power market to competition. The bill did not become law, and Lay returned to this theme in subsequent years. In addition, Lay wrote to Bush in 1997 to urge him to lobby Texas' congressional delegation to support the reauthorization of the U.S. Export-Import Bank for another four years. And in 1997, before Bush met with Uzbekistan Ambassador Sadyq Safaev, Lay wrote to the governor to remind him that Enron was negotiating a $2 billion joint venture with Neftegaz, an Uzbekistan company.

■ ■ ■

Back on Wall Street, the success of EnronOnline and the promise of its broadband business added some dot-com patina to Enron's stock. The shares kicked off 2000 at $43.44, and ended June at $64.50. Enron generated a robust $16.9 billion in revenue in 2000's second quarter, up sharply from the $9.7 billion in revenue it had in 1999's second quarter. Enron had long been a popular stock, but now it was a star stock favored by many fund and pension managers.

The Internet boom infected Wall Street analysts, whose purported job was to "analyze" stocks and then recommend that investors either buy them or sell them. Many of these analysts turned into unabashed cheerleaders. The investment banks employing these analysts all wanted to get business from these companies underwriting stock and debt offerings and advising on mergers. And the analysts were in a position to be perfect salespeople. If the problem had been created years earlier, then the overall bull market for stocks, and in particular the Internet boom, perfected this problem.

By the mid and late 1990s, research analysts were able to make $1 million or $2 million a year, and a few stars could make as much as $10 million. Analysts knew their compensation was based in part on the investment banking business they helped bring in, even if this connection was never explicitly calculated. And management encouraged them to bring in banking business. For example, according to charges by the New York State Attorney General that Merrill Lynch later settled, Merrill Lynch's Internet research group was supposed to objectively analyze Internet companies but the companies were instead given special treatment. Sometimes officers of potential client companies were allowed to edit Merrill's research reports on their companies, inserting quotations into the analysts' reports and suggesting analyst ratings (such as "buy" or "accumulate," which were separate ratings) on their own stocks.

Wall Street had long grappled with the conflict of interest inherent in serving both the corporations that raised capital and the investors who provided the capital. But amid the investment-banking mergers and soaring stock market of the time, the lines between research and banking blurred even more. This was the backdrop against which Enron's stock became a favorite of research analysts. And this was helped by the huge gobs of money that investors were pouring into mutual funds: These fund managers had to buy something with that cash, and they sought out growth stories like Enron (or Cisco Systems, or Microsoft Corp., or many other popular stocks).

Enron spread around its investment banking business to enough firms—by picking six or eight underwriters for one offering of preferred stock, for example—that many investment banks could have felt that they had something at stake when it came time to analyze Enron's stock. Enron as a company obsessed about its stock price, and as a result it paid close attention to what analysts were saying about the stock. As one analyst put it, according to an unspoken rule Enron was happy to provide banking business if the firm's analyst recommended its stock.

Enron executives made their displeasure clear to analysts who were too negative on the stock. "Enron's top management was not remotely interested in objectivity. You were either for them or against them," said Olson, an analyst who covered Enron for Merrill Lynch and then for Sanders Morris Harris. "In one telephone call . . . the then CEO told me quite succinctly, 'We are for our friends,' and proceeded to itemize the monthly history of my own 'unfriendly' Enron ratings over the prior two years."

The company's aggressive managing of analysts produced results—not just in terms of positive coverage but in influencing the profit estimates that analysts are supposed to calculate to help them value stocks. From 1998 to 2000, analysts' projections of Enron's earnings were unusually similar and changed little during the course of the year. "This pattern is highly suggestive that the analysts were being spoon fed as to what Enron expected earnings to be," said Chuck Hill, director of research at Thomson Financial/First Call, a firm that tracks analyst estimates. "One reason that analysts may have been more willing than normal to accept company guidance for Enron was that it was becoming increasingly difficult to understand how Enron was achieving its revenue growth and profitability. Extensive use of derivatives, particularly when the company is using mark-to-market accounting, is extremely difficult in the best of situations."

Enron's short-term focus on its stock followed the larger business trend. With the rise of the Internet, something had happened to the investing world. It had developed a reaction time as fast as electric impulses, and just as knee-jerk. Analysts' views could spread through the market in an hour or so. Thousands of online day traders jumped in and out of stocks in matters of hours or minutes just to squeeze out 25 cents of profit per share with the barest risk. Even commodities markets, dominated by professionals, reacted so quickly to news that a surge in oil prices in the morning inspired by rising tensions with Iraq would correct itself in the afternoon, reducing oil prices. In the late 1990s, markets simply moved faster. What used to take weeks now took days, and what had taken days now took hours.

In retrospect, a large portion of the stock market had been taken over by a "bubble" of unsustainable optimism and self-justifying momentum. Whereas stocks once rose on healthy earnings reports or news of a major contract, now it wasn't uncommon for a stock to rise on the news of its previous day's rise. Internet chat rooms and bulletin boards for regular-Joe investors sprang up, creating virtual support sessions for shareholders to cheer on each others' gambles on Amazon.com, America Online, Cisco Systems, and other high-risk stocks. In playing to this built-for-speed zeitgeist, Enron wasn't alone, and it didn't even run that far ahead of the pack.

10

CALIFORNIA DREAMIN'

L ong before Enron's confusing accounting raised the ire of investors or its
bankruptcy angered employees and politicians, the company had become
the target of criticism over energy deregulation. In California, electricity
deregulation precipitated a crisis in power prices and supply in 2000, and
Enron symbolized the opportunistic energy traders that profited from the
state's woes. After the California power crisis, Enron would forever be
known as "controversial" in addition to "successful" and "innovative."

To fully understand what happened in California, it's necessary to
backtrack a couple of years. Wholesale electricity trading sprang up
quickly in the mid-1990s, and even by 1998 it retained a touch of the
Wild West in its lightly regulated, pioneer spirit. In just a few years, more
than 400 power marketers had licenses from FERC to buy and sell electricity; none of them had to post collateral. While many of these players
were associated with electric utilities, the majority were independent
power marketers.

Traffic jams of electricity on transmission wires, called bottlenecks,
sometimes slowed down the interstate system. Even when traffic
flowed perfectly, heat waves could cause an upward spike in demand
and therefore in spot electricity prices. For example, in July 1997,
scorching weather in the Midwest and East caused some wholesale
power prices to triple to over $300 per megawatt-hour (MWh). And
in May 1998, a worse spike briefly lifted prices on some wholesale

power to $500 per MWh; in this case, the hot weather's effects were worsened by the fact that several power generating units had been shut for routine maintenance.

But the price spike of the following month was historic in magnitude. During the week of June 22, heat waves broiled the Midwest and East, causing wholesale power prices to surge as high as $6,000 per MWh, or 200 times the normal asking price. The end of June featured day after day of sky-high prices. In a handful of instances, trades occurred at $7,500 per MWh. Temperatures were higher than expected, driving unusually busy use of air conditioners and straining the supply capabilities of the Midwest. At the same time, more than a dozen major power plants happened to be shut for routine maintenance, taking even more electricity out of supply. Not until July 1 did power prices cool off to levels of $50 or $70 per MWh.

Other factors conspired to create the June price spike. Some transmission lines had been damaged by storms, curtailing the ability to move power around the region. At some utilities, senior managers told their traders to buy power at any price in order to avoid blackouts. The trading inexperience at some utilities caused them to pay higher prices than necessary. FERC also received complaints that traders manipulated the market to boost prices, although manipulation was never proved.

The June 1998 spike caused dramatic fallout. At the request of a few utilities, the FERC investigated. Some critics called for a re-regulation of wholesale power markets or at least the institution of price caps on wholesale electricity (which didn't happen). Federal Energy Sales, an independent power marketer that essentially sold contracts on power that it didn't have, simply defaulted on contracts, costing Ohio utility FirstEnergy $27 million; Federal went out of business. Oregon's PacifiCorp lost $13 million in trading because it made wrong-way bets on prices. And Kentucky utility LG&E Energy, which at the time was the seventh-largest power marketer in the United States, lost an undisclosed number of millions of dollars and decided to quit electricity trading— LG&E said it couldn't handle the high volatility.

Enron, the country's biggest power marketer, didn't disclose how it performed in the June crisis, but one news wire reported that the company made at least $50 million from it. The company apparently jumped in and out of the market to make its profits, rather than bet on one direction in prices. It was one more example of Enron's uncanny ability to read the energy market, and avoid losses like those rung up by competitors.

Similar price spikes did not occur later that year or the next. So the market may have been complacent in 2000, when electricity prices started to rise in California. Of course, the state didn't expect price spikes when it passed its electricity deregulation law in 1996. Back then, politicians and utilities expected deregulation to eventually result in lower power prices. The deregulation plan reflected that view: Utilities were required to sell off all their power plants and buy electricity from a centralized wholesale pool called the California Power Exchange, but they were forbidden to sign any long-term electricity supply contracts for fear that they'd be locked into higher prices. The utilities were then to buy their electricity from the Power Exchange, which would reflect the ups and downs of market prices. Small businesses and residential customers were given a 10 percent cut in electric rates, which went into effect in 1998.

To make sure electricity flowed smoothly from the third-party suppliers to the utilities and then to customers, the electric grid was turned over to a state-created Independent System Operator (ISO) for managing. The utilities still had to pay off their uneconomic old investments—their stranded costs. So California froze the prices that the utilities charged consumers through March 2002; the state's two largest utilities, Pacific Gas & Electric (PG&E) and Southern California Edison, lobbied hard for this rate freeze. At the time, the freeze was seen as an obstacle to utilities being forced to lower their prices, as utilities were paying far less to buy wholesale power than they were charging customers for it on the retail end. The state approved the freeze, assuming the profits on retail power sales would pay off the stranded costs in a few years.

The system worked well at first, in large part because California had an excess of power supply when it passed its deregulation law. From April 1998 to April 2000, the utilities paid an average of about $30 per MWh. But overall electricity demand grew as a result of the economic boom in California, which produced a surge in power-hungry computer equipment. Then unusually warm weather hit. In May 2000, the ISO declared the first alerts of possible power shortages because the state's power reserves, ideally maintained around 15 percent of total capacity, dropped below 5 percent. In June, prices began to spike, as several power plants were shut for maintenance. San Francisco was hit by "rolling" blackouts—typically, blackouts that last one hour for each city block, a tactic to ensure the grid doesn't overload. Just as the Midwestern utilities had been in 1998, California utilities were a captive audience that needed to buy power even at unreasonable prices. Wholesale prices topped $100, then $120 per MWh. During a hot spell from June 12 through June 16, state utilities paid an estimated $850 million for electricity, or triple the costliest five-day period in 1999. More than $600 million of that cost was spent on power the utilities purchased in the day-ahead market. Suddenly, the idea of prohibiting utilities from signing any long-term contracts and instead requiring them to buy *all* their power from the short-term market didn't look so smart.

Power prices continued to rise along with the mercury. By August 2000, as temperatures topped 100 degrees, the ISO warned of imminent power shortages. Businesses sent workers home early, and turned down air conditioners. But consumers had no incentive to change their power-using habits: Thanks to the deregulation law, their rates were frozen even as wholesale prices soared for the utilities. Also, a quirk of the deregulation law often required the utilities to buy power at high prices.

The high power prices also made it clear that not enough new power plants had been built in California to keep pace with demand; people in the energy industry explained that California's environmental laws and the low wholesale prices for power in 1998 and 1999 discouraged the building of new plants. From 1996 to 1999, electricity demand in the state grew by 5,500 megawatts, while supply increased by just 672 megawatts. Outside supplies were also of little help; in the past, California had been able to buy some power from sellers in Nevada, Oregon, and other nearby states, but those states were now grappling with their own record demands, too.

California Governor Gray Davis called for a probe into potential price manipulation in the wholesale market. Many observers suspected that energy traders were gaming the system a little—by, say, withholding power they could deliver in the morning until the prices rose further in the afternoon—but also figured that however sneaky or unfair these maneuvers were, they were legal tactics exploiting a poor market system.

"Designed to work in an environment of abundant power supplies, California's market structure has not served customers well under short supply conditions," said PG&E vice president Steven Kline.

Around Enron's offices, Lay liked to say, "An imperfect market is better than a perfect regulator." But California felt otherwise. The state's beleaguered utilities lost billions: They estimated that over the summer and early fall, their total cost to buy power was $6 billion more than they were allowed to charge for it. In contrast, traders such as Enron and Dynegy were doing very well. When Enron reported its results for the July-through-September quarter, it announced that income in its Commodity Sales and Services business rose to $404 million, up from $172 million the previous year. The company didn't specify how much money it made off California's volatility, but it clearly boosted profits. "Prices are rising, and I know that's hurting consumers—but it certainly has been beneficial for Enron," said Jeffrey Skilling. The power crisis generated much ill will, and Enron provided the most obvious target for this wrath because it was the nation's largest electricity trader—at times, it traded 50 percent more electricity than the number two player. California residents, and especially politicians, bridled at the profits that Enron and others seemed to be making off their troubles. But the troubles were not over.

■ ■ ■

Even as Enron enjoyed the fruits of its energy-trading savvy in California, the company was really flexing its muscles in the area of Special Purpose Entities. At Fastow's urging, the company decided to create a series of SPEs called "Raptors" after the vicious dinosaurs in the *Jurassic Park* movie. The Raptors would sell hedges for Enron investments, much the way LJM1 hedged the company's stake in Rhythms NetConnections as described in Chapter 8. The idea was to insure Enron against losses on various investments where the investments were so large or unique that traditional hedging deals weren't available.

Fastow and company created the first Raptor, Raptor I (also known as "Talon"), in April 2000. LJM2 invested $30 million in Raptor I, and through a series of agreements became the effective manager of the SPE. Enron contributed $1,000 in cash, Enron stock and stock contracts worth about $537 million, and a $50 million promissory note (a kind of guaranteed loan). The Enron stock and stock contracts came from forward contracts with UBS, just like with LJM1. The Enron stock contributed to Raptor I was valued at a 35 percent discount because the SPE was restricted from selling or hedging the stock for three years—again, a tactic used in forming LJM1. The restrictions on the stock lowered its value, and the restrictions may have been placed on the stock for the sole purpose of limiting its value; once the three-year restriction expired, the SPE would feasibly have an automatic gain. Enron consulted heavily with Andersen in setting up Raptor I.

With the $30 million from LJM2, Raptor I had the outside equity needed to qualify as an independent SPE. The partnership's deal with LJM2 also had an unwritten understanding that Raptor I wouldn't engage in any derivatives deals until LJM2 received an initial $41 million return on its $30 million investment, thus guaranteeing LJM2 at least a 30 percent annualized rate of return. The idea was that Raptor I would pay LJM2 its initial investment and a profit, but LJM2 would technically still keep its $30 million invested in the SPE. "These terms were remarkably favorable to LJM2, and served no apparent business purpose for Enron," the Powers Report would later criticize.

To generate the money needed to give LJM2 its return, Raptor I sold Enron a put option on 7.2 million shares of Enron stock for a $41 million premium; this meant that if Enron's stock price fell below $57.50 (it was at $68 when the put option was sold), Enron could demand that Raptor I buy 7.2 million shares at $57.50 a share. The put option was odd for two reasons. First, it amounted to a bet by Enron that its own stock price would decline. Second, the $41 million price of the put option was excessive given that Raptor I had very little capital at hand, and thus was at risk of not being able to fulfill the option if Enron's stock did drop. As it turned out, Richard Causey (negotiating for Enron) and Fastow (negotiating for Raptor I and LJM2) settled the option early, in August 2000: The settlement allowed Raptor I to keep $37 million of the option premium. However, it still gave $41 million to LJM2.

Although the documents that closed the Raptor I deal were dated April 18, Enron management formally approved the creation of Raptor I in May. Enron procedures required a deal approval sheet, or "DASH," for each big deal, and each DASH had to be signed by a series of high-level executives. Ben Glisan, Rick Buy, and Causey signed the DASH for Raptor I. There was a line for Skilling's signature as well, but he never signed it; he later claimed his approval wasn't necessary.

Enron's senior managers okayed Raptor I, with the structure that would ultimately place its control in the hands of Fastow, even though several senior employees were already concerned about conflicts in the LJM partnerships. Jeffrey McMahon, then Enron's treasurer, approached Fastow about inherent conflicts of interest, and then McMahon talked to Skilling about the LJM entities on March 16, 2000. The two men's memories of the conversation differ, however. McMahon said he told Skilling he was uncomfortable with Fastow "wearing two hats" as Enron's CFO (and therefore McMahon's boss) and as the manager of the LJM partnerships. According to handwritten notes McMahon had prepared for the meeting, "I find myself negotiating with Andy on Enron matters and am pressured to do a deal that I do not believe is in the best interests of the shareholders." As McMahon recalled it, Skilling ended the meeting by saying he understood his concerns and he'd remedy the situation. Other Enron employees knew of McMahon's worries about the conflicts of interest inherent in LJM2.

But according to Skilling, the conversation centered on McMahon's concerns that his role as an occasional negotiator across the table from Fastow might affect Fastow's opinion of McMahon when it came time for the PRC review. "Jeff felt he was being put in an awkward position in having to negotiate with Andy [Fastow] and that that might—this is my recollection—that it might impact his compensation package," Skilling explained. Whatever was actually discussed that day, it was followed by action. In April, McMahon accepted a new job at Enron's Internet operations. Skilling recalled the move was sparked by the need for good senior executives at what was yet another new business unit in the company.

Causey and Glisan presented Raptor I to the Enron board's finance committee on May 1, with Lay, Skilling, and Fastow in attendance. "Mr. Glisan stated that Project Raptor involved establishing a risk management program to enable the Company to hedge the profit and loss volatility of the Company's investments," the minutes of the meeting read. Before presenting Raptor, however, Fastow updated the committee on the success of LJM1 and LJM2: They had made seven investments so far, all in Enron assets, thus generating $229.5 million in earnings for Enron. Using the LJM entities, he added, had saved Enron $2.3 million in fees that would have been paid to bankers to arrange the same deals.

After directors heard these rosy data on the other SPEs, they took up the topic of Raptor.

One problem with Raptor I that had cropped up with LJM1 was the fact that it was funded mostly by Enron equity. In effect, this meant that even if Enron hedged an investment with Raptor I, it was hedging risk with itself because Enron still bore all the risk. Directors may have grasped the idea that Raptor I couldn't provide true "economic" hedges, as notes on the presentation documents made by the corporate secretary said: "Does not transfer economic risk but transfers P&L [profit and loss] volatility." Even if Enron directors understood this, it's possible the finance committee felt that Raptor I was acceptable as an accounting hedge. In any event, the committee approved the deal, and the full board signed off the next day.

Even before Fastow put Raptor I to work, he proposed a couple of similar SPEs: Raptor II and Raptor IV. An entity known as Raptor III would be created later. Again, Enron funded both Raptor II (also known as Timberwolf) and Raptor IV (also known as Bobcat) with restricted stock and stock-delivery contracts like the ones used in LJM1 and Raptor I. The restricted stock was straightforward, but crucial. The "contingency rights" contracts called for the Raptors to receive Enron stock if the shares remained above certain price levels on March 1, 2003. LJM2 also made similar $30 million investments in the new Raptor entities. Raptor II was authorized by the board in June, and Raptor IV was approved in August. As with Raptor I, each newer Raptor sold a put option on Enron stock to Enron for $41 million, enabling it to "return" $41 million to LJM2 although LJM2 still retained its stake in each Raptor.

By early autumn, Enron used Raptor I to hedge its investments with derivative contracts known as "total return swaps." These swaps basically required Raptor I to pay Enron for any losses on its investment, and in exchange, Raptor I could keep any gains on the Enron investments; the contracts acted as insurance that was paid for by swapping the potential downside for the potential upside. By the end of September, Raptor I hedged investments with a total value of $734 million, including Enron's investment in Avici Systems, a maker of data networking equipment; Enron had invested in Avici when it was private, and at one point after Avici's stock was publicly traded and benefiting from the Internet mania, the value of Enron's investment in Avici rose to $178 million.

Although the deals were finalized in September, the documents were dated as of August 3. Why August 3? It may be because on August 3, Avici, in which Enron had a large stake (and which counted Enron as one of its biggest customers), hit its all-time stock price high of $162.50. By dating the swaps as of August 3, Enron was able to lock in the biggest mark-to-market gain on Avici stock, thus enabling it to book investment gains of nearly $75 million in the quarter ending September 30.

The use of Enron stock to capitalize Raptors I, II, and IV not only meant that the hedges relied on Enron's stock doing well, but may have violated accounting rules. Under nearly all circumstances, a company may not book gains or losses based on changes in its own stock price; this rule is necessary so that companies don't create iterating loops of artificial growth in which a company's stock price boosts earnings, which boosts the stock price, which boosts earnings, and so on. However, in one instance Enron reportedly machinated to benefit from a rise in its own stock price. In January 2000, as Enron planned to announce its big alliance with Sun Microsystems (detailed in Chapter 8), Enron executives wondered how their company could cash in on the stock price rise they expected would be generated from the news. So they lifted hedges that had been placed on Enron stock held by the JEDI partnership; as is typical with hedges, these contracts protected the Enron stock from losses but also limited their potential gains. The announcement of the Sun deal, coupled with Enron's quarterly earnings results, boosted Enron shares 26 percent in one day. Removing the hedges allowed JEDI to book that full increase in the value of its Enron equity, and from its share of JEDI's gains Enron Corp. recorded $126 million in income. As was typical of Enron executives' cloak-and-dagger approach to its complex deals, this JEDI scheme was named Project Grayhawk after the Arizona golf resort where it was devised. (According to an April 2002 article in the *New York Times*, the FBI later began an investigation into Project Grayhawk.)

As summer crept into autumn, some of Enron's investments began to drop in value; for example, on September 15, Avici's stock price was down to $95.50. Would the Raptors have to deliver on their hedges of these investments? The question took on importance because of worries that Enron's stock, which provided most of the Raptors' capital, might decline, too. Enron's stock hit an all-time high of $90.75 on August 23, 2000, but it began to slip—and, although Enron officials couldn't know it, the stock would rarely see $90 again. So Enron executives decided to hedge the capital in the Raptor entities with Enron Corp. They did this using a popular derivative structure known as a "costless collar." Using a combination of options, each Raptor set a floor on how low the value of its Enron equity could fall; if the price of Enron's stock (as traded on the New York Stock Exchange) fell below that price, Enron Corp. would pay the difference in cash. In exchange, each Raptor also set a ceiling on how high the value of its Enron equity could rise; if Enron's stock rose above that price, the Raptor would pay Enron Corp. the difference in cash. The collar is "costless" because the money collected by setting a ceiling pays for the cost of the options used to set a floor. So in the case of Raptor I, the collar guaranteed that the SPE's Enron stock would fall no lower than $81 and rise no higher than $116. Raptor II's collar guaranteed its Enron stock would remain between $79 and $112, and Raptor IV's collar (actually completed in January 2001) set parameters of $83 and $112.

In and of itself, the costless collar provoked no controversy. Companies, trading firms, and even wealthy individuals use costless collars frequently. But the restricted stock in each Raptor included the provision that it could not be hedged for a three-year period. Hedging that stock with the costless collars directly violated that provision—the provision that had allowed the Enron equity to be transferred to the Raptors at a reduced value, and thus served as the basis for PricewaterhouseCoopers to deem the transactions fair. And with the restricted stock hedged, it likely no longer justified a 35 percent discount in value. Enron personnel did nothing to address that matter. And to execute the costless collars, Causey signed a document waiving the no-hedging restriction. By November 2000, Enron had hedged $1.5 billion worth of investments with the Raptors.

■ ■ ■

Enron created a Raptor III entity in the fall, but it differed from the other three Raptors because its goal was to hedge one specific investment: Enron's stake in the New Power Company.

Enron formed New Power in 1999 with IBM and America Online in another attempt to create a nationally branded provider of electricity and natural gas to residential and small business customers. Rather than go it alone, as it did in California, Enron signed contracts with AOL to market to its online customers and with IBM to handle the company's payment and billing systems. Enron installed Skilling loyalist Lou Pai as the chairman, and Lay and Causey took seats on the board.

In January 2000, Enron incorporated New Power in Greenwich, Connecticut, as a separate company, and transferred into it whatever residential energy business it had in Enron Energy Services. In subsequent months, Enron convinced outside investors to put a total of $204 million into New Power: CalPERS put in $40 million, and GE Capital and Donaldson, Lufkin & Jenrette also invested.

In July, New Power acquired the residential and small commercial retail energy business of pipeline company Columbia Energy Group. This gave it 285,000 natural gas customers and 20,000 electricity customers in eight states. Together with former EES customers, the company had a customer base topping 325,000.

New Power's strategy for selling energy hinged on marketing through the Internet, especially through AOL. As a start-up, the company naturally expected to incur substantial losses initially, and projected that its first-year operating costs would exceed $140 million. Those costs included the AOL agreement, under which Enron committed to pay the Internet service $49 million over six years for its marketing help. It also included the IBM contract, which New Power expected would cost at least $65 million. The company's risks included the fact that only a few states had opened residential power and gas markets to competition at that point. Still, Enron envisioned New Power would grow into a company with over $10 billion in revenue by 2005.

Enron guided New Power in its early days, and outside investors liked that. "It was all Enron people, which was a good thing because those people had great risk management skills," said Ron Chernin, who worked at GE Capital. As for the plan to turn a profit, New Power embraced the prevailing dot-com strategy of collecting a group of customers and then figuring out how to make money off them. The valuation and logic came straight from the era's Internet bubble.

New Power went public in October 2000 at $21 a share, raising about $473 million for the company. True to what were then the waning days of the dot-com boom, New Power rose $6 in its first trading day, giving the fledgling company a multibillion-dollar market value. And Enron retained a 44 percent stake in it.

Before the IPO, Enron took steps to hedge its investment in New Power. First, it sold a portion of its stake in New Power in the form of stock warrants (contracts to buy stock at a later date). The buyer was another SPE called Hawaii 125-O, a name that played on the old TV series *Hawaii Five-O*; New Power warrants were later hedged with SPEs named after McGarrett, the fictional star of the show.

Enron then created Raptor III (also known as Porcupine) with $30 million from LJM2. Instead of providing Enron stock to serve as the bulk of Raptor III's capital, Enron transferred into it New Power stock—24 million shares of New Power valued at $10.75 per share. Enron received a $259 million promissory note in return. Enron created Raptor III in September, and because the structure didn't involve Enron stock, Fastow didn't present it to the board of directors. Just a few weeks later, New Power went public at $21, much higher than the $10.75 price Raptor III had set on the stock; this meant Raptor III had an immediate paper gain of $246 million, giving it the capacity to do at least $246 million worth of hedging. On October 5, when New Power went public, Raptor III gave $39.5 million to LJM2 as the guaranteed "return" on its investment. Enron then entered into a total return swap with Raptor III on 18 million New Power shares at $21 per share. Between this swap and the Hawaii 125-O deals, Enron locked in a gain of $370 million on New Power stock.

But there was a problem. Enron used Raptor III to hedge potential declines in New Power stock. Yet the capital that Raptor III used for this was almost entirely New Power stock. Even casual observers would think this was poor business practice, like loaning money to yourself. The board's special committee, in the Powers Report, would later conclude that this was not a true hedge. The structure also set up a double reliance on New Power's stock price. If New Power's stock declined, Raptor III would have a hard time coming up with the money needed to pay Enron for declines in *its* New Power stock. Not surprisingly, New Power's shares began to decline immediately after going public. Its first-day closing price of $27 would prove to be the stock's all-time high, and by mid-November the stock had fallen below $10. And this would endanger the $370 million gain Enron had already booked on the New Power stock.

■ ■ ■

Over in California, the power situation calmed down a bit in the fall, but then prices started soaring again in late November, when a cold snap hit. Once again, California's poorly designed deregulation plan was allowing energy traders to make large profits off the state's desperate need for electricity.

Unknown to state regulators or senior executives at California's utilities, the screwed-up deregulation plan wasn't the only cause of rising power prices. Behind the scenes, Enron traders engaged in complex tactics to unfairly manipulate power prices, tactics with nicknames like "Death Star" and "Get Shorty" and that had been in use since the summer shortage. Enron lawyers claimed that they alerted senior company executives to these tactics in October 2000, partly out of fear that Enron would be sued.

California had two wholesale power markets: the real-time market and the day-ahead market. One strategy took advantage of the fact that the California ISO sometimes paid firms not to use power that they had scheduled for use in the real-time market, which involved same-day deliveries of electricity. So Enron would schedule excess purchases of power (also known as "load") in the day-ahead market, which worked exactly as the name implied. Then Enron would decide the next day not to buy that electricity after all, earning a real-time market payment for giving up power it never needed to begin with. This was known as "inc-ing" (short for increasing) the load.

Also, when the amount of power scheduled for delivery into California exceeded the capacity of some of the transmission lines, the ISO would pay traders "congestion fees" to either reduce the power they were selling into the state's system or to transmit power away from California. Enron would schedule power deliveries it never intended to make just so the state grid would seem like it would get congested in certain areas; the ISO would then ask it to reverse those deliveries and pay Enron congestion fees. Because the congestion fees could be as high as $750 per MWh, it occasionally made sense for Enron to sell some electricity at a loss in order to create the appearance of congestion, then reverse the trade to get the congestion fee. A similar technique Enron called "Death Star" routed power around the ISO to send power away from a transmission jam, also to collect congestion fees. In some views, Death Star did relieve congestion on parts of the electric grid, but in other views the tactic never sent power into the grid or took it off.

In the Get Shorty tactic, Enron would contract in the day-ahead market to provide ancillary services besides actual power. Then, when the day arrived, Enron would buy the ancillary services at lower prices in the real-time market. In effect, Enron was selling these services short—a technique used often in the securities business, when a trader sells something he or she doesn't own yet at a high price and then buys it later at a lower price when it's time to consummate the original sale. In a later analysis of how the deals were made, Enron lawyers explained in a memo that "in order to short ancillary services it is necessary to submit false information that purports to identify the source of the ancillary services."

Enron used a tactic called "Ricochet" to play the difference in prices in California's day-ahead and real-time markets. Enron would buy energy on the day-ahead market and sell it to an out-of-state trader. The next day, Enron would buy that electricity back and sell it into the real-time market, which was often dominated by power-hungry utilities willing to pay higher prices. This helped artificially boost electricity prices without helping supply or demand.

In early December, California officials tried to damp electricity prices by setting a cap of $250 per MWh on wholesale prices. But by then power shortages were affecting surrounding states. This allowed Enron to use another tactic, in which it bought power in California and sold it at higher prices in neighboring states. For example, on December 5 Enron was able to buy wholesale power in California at the $250 price and sell it in Oregon at $1,200 per MWh.

In early December, more than a month after Enron lawyers first warned executives of these trading tactics, an outside law firm, Stoel Rives LP, prepared detailed memos on these tactics for Enron in-house attorney Richard Sanders. The memos pointed out that if the ISO found out about Death Star and other maneuvers, it could impose penalties on Enron; Stoel Rives also worried that the tactics might be illegal (although it never came to a firm conclusion on their legality). Jeff Skilling, according to a spokesperson, did not give his approval of any illegal activity. Enron executives finally ordered a stop to these tactics on December 10. Still, the power crisis continued in California. Utilities felt such ire that on December 26, Southern California Edison sued the FERC for not ensuring that wholesale power was sold at reasonable prices.

Enron was not the only energy trader indulging in sneaky tactics. Xcel Energy and Mirant Energy also admitted that their traders sometimes schemed to "game" California's market. This included deals to get congestion payments and to make "ex-post" trades, which sent power into the grid at the last minute to meet shortages.

A transcript of traders' conversations on July 18 (released by Xcel) revealed how typical these maneuvers seemed:

Mirant trader: I like it okay. Yeah. Um, it's working out all right so far. And, uh, I hope it will work out even better this afternoon. You want to try to get something going?

Xcel trader: Yeah.

Mirant: You want to do an ex-post type of game or you want to do a congestion type of game plus ex-post or um . . .

Xcel: Either/or. Maybe we can.

Mirant: Either/or.

Xcel: Okay. It doesn't matter. We can figure something out.

Mirant: How about, um, let's see, I don't want to crush the market too bad. How about if we try to do a total of 50 [megawatts per hour].

Xcel: M'kay.

Mirant: Twenty-five of it we'll keep in SP15; and 25 of it we'll shoot up north to NP. Um, and try to benefit from trying to relieving [*sic*] some of that Path 26 congestion.

Xcel: M'kay.

Mirant: Does that sound all right? And, um, I don't know how we're gonna split the money up, yet.

Xcel: We'll figure it out.

Although California officials suspected that trading companies were gaming the system, they had no proof in 2000. Williams Cos., Reliant Energy, and other companies also later admitted to overscheduling power deliveries and other minor infractions. The memos and transcripts revealing traders' exploits at Enron and elsewhere did not surface until 2002. In hindsight, they cast a pall over claims from Enron and other companies that California's problems were entirely of its own making.

■ ■ ■

Even without knowing of Death Star, inc-ing, and other tactics, states that had yet to deregulate looked askance at the California electricity situation. The zeal to deregulate faded quickly. So the market lost even more faith in New Power Company, which saw its stock fall to $6.50 by December 1 as it ambled toward losses of $170 million for 2000. In addition, the dot-com bubble continued to deflate, sending Avici and other Enron investments lower in value. At the same time, Enron's stock price had slipped, eroding the capital of each Raptor even as the entities' obligations grew. In December 2000, the Raptors were in trouble.

If the Raptors didn't have the capital, and therefore the credit capacity, to cover the hedges they had sold, then Enron would have to book a credit reserve for the deals that would lower the corporation's fourth-quarter earnings. But not all the Raptors were in dire straits. So Enron, working with Andersen accountants, decided to use the excess credit capacity of Raptors II and IV to shore up the credit of Raptors I and III. This is a common and legal strategy known as cross collateralizing: In effect, it acted as though Raptors II and IV provided their guarantees on loans for Raptors I and III, making the healthy Raptors liable to help cover for the troubled ones.

To figure out how to pull this off, Andersen's partner in charge, David Duncan, consulted with the firm's Professional Standards Group, a core of accounting experts whose job was to make sure Andersen accountants hewed to accounting rules in their work for clients. Carl Bass, the primary contact between the Professional Standards folks and Enron, told Duncan that the four Raptors would essentially have to merge their credit capacities permanently. But Fastow didn't like that idea. While it would have protected Enron, it would have permanently lowered the values of the Raptors, thus lowering the values of LJM2's investments in them—and managing LJM2 was providing Fastow with lots of money.

Fastow proposed a cross collateralization that he could rescind at will. "I did not see any way that this worked," Bass wrote in an e-mail. "In effect, it was heads I win, tails you lose." Bass insisted that permanent cross collateralization provided the only means to structure the deal.

So Andersen accountants working on the Enron account ignored Bass. Without informing the Professional Standards Group, they engineered a cross collateralization that lasted only 45 days. Enron signed documents creating the temporary cross collateralization on December 22, and paid

LJM2 $50,000 for its role, even though LJM2 had no direct role. This temporary fix allowed Enron to avoid recording a credit reserve in the fourth quarter. The result? The Raptors added $462 million to Enron's fourth-quarter earnings.

Unfortunately, the transitory credit deal violated accounting rules. But it seemed that Andersen's Enron team inaccurately wrote that Bass and others had agreed with this solution, according to a December 28 memo in which they wrote: ". . . the assets of each entity . . . were cross collateralized for the benefit of the creditors of each entity for a 45 day period. . . . We discussed this conclusion with the Professional Standards Group (PSG) in Chicago, Carl Bass and John Stewart, and Mike Odom, Practice Director, who concurred with our conclusion." Had Enron followed the rules, it would have taken a short-term hit on the Raptors but that problem would have been over. Instead, the temporary hiding of the losses allowed the problem to fester.

Getting the stamp of approval from David Duncan and his coworkers involved more than just an okay from some outside accounting firm reviewing deals that Enron had worked out internally. Enron worked very closely with Andersen. At one point, Andersen had more than 100 employees leasing space in Enron's Houston headquarters. Richard Causey, as chief accounting officer, often included Andersen early in discussions and consulted with it on most projects. Andersen "gets all documents and they walk down the path with Enron all the way. Ultimately, AA [Arthur Andersen] signs off with an audit opinion and reports to Enron's audit committee," according to a later summary of an interview with Causey. In a promotional video for Andersen, Causey explained: "Arthur Andersen's penetration of involvement in the company is probably different than anything I've experienced. . . . They are kind of everywhere and in everything."

This ubiquity served Arthur Andersen's needs. The firm had hit a turning point in 2000, when the Andersen Consulting business acrimoniously split off into an independent company, leaving the original firm smaller and weaker. Andersen partners chose as their new CEO Joseph Berardino, a serious-looking and understated New York native who came up as an auditor. Once in charge, Berardino aggressively pursued revenue growth to beef up the accounting firm. That meant rebuilding the consulting practice, and working closely with clients. Some within Andersen felt the renewed consulting emphasis came at the expense of the quality of audits. And Andersen may have been more willing to bend accounting rules in order to bend to its clients' wishes.

Causey's position enabled him to exercise control over the use and potential abuse of accounting rules. But within Enron, managers viewed him as loyal to Skilling (Causey became chief accounting officer in 1997 after spending five years at Skilling's ECT division). And Skilling, either through backing Fastow or through his own generalized knowledge of the LJM and Raptor deals, seemed to support the aggressive accounting.

Causey had originally worked for Andersen in Houston before joining Enron, and he sponsored the hiring of other Andersen personnel as full-time Enron employees. Within Enron, this group developed a friendly Andersen network. Causey had a reputation for being detail-oriented and smart. Soft-spoken, he didn't like making snap decisions. But Causey was sharp enough to understand Fastow's deals; indeed, Fastow couldn't have conducted his SPE deals without Causey's approvals, according to one former Enron vice president, Allan Sommer.

Working extremely closely with Causey, Chief Risk Officer Rick Buy often had responsibilities that overlapped with Causey's. Skilling hand-picked Buy for his role, and within Enron Buy was viewed as Skilling's man; some Enron managers questioned whether Buy rose to his position because Skilling felt his loyalty would make him pliable. Within Enron, Buy developed the nickname "Muffin Man," partly for his round features but perhaps because he had a conciliatory attitude. A former Enron employee who worked with Buy and liked him admitted that Buy was "not confrontational." Others took a harsher view. Sommer said Buy "seemed out of his depth" in the intricate world of risk management.

But Causey and Buy got along very well. The result was that Enron's two most powerful accounting police were essentially loyal to Skilling and therefore, by association, inclined to favor Skilling protégé Fastow. So Causey and Buy didn't stop Enron from forming increasingly complex layers of SPEs.

LJM2, for example, invested in the Raptors and in other Enron-created SPEs like Osprey Trust, Rawhide, and Apex. This multitiered wedding cake of a partnership eventually invested over $430 million in various assets, including some money LJM2 borrowed to invest. The complexity didn't hurt LJM2's financial performance. At an annual meeting of LJM2 partners in October 2000, Fastow told investors that LJM2 was on track to produce a whopping 51 percent rate of return, with 63 percent of the investment capital put into deals lasting 12 months or less. In May, Fastow had told Enron's board the LJM2 entity would generate an 18 percent return—far below 51 percent. Although the returns may have been changed by deals after May, Fastow never told the board of LJM2's newly increased profitability.

That October meeting, held in a hotel in Palm Beach, Florida, raised questions about how much Skilling knew of LJM2's deals. The Power-Point document listing LJM2's finances included Skilling as one of the meeting's attendees. And according to the meeting agenda, Skilling addressed the group after the presentation on the strategy and structure of the LJM partnerships. But Skilling's attorney said Skilling put in only a brief appearance at the meeting, speaking for 10 to 15 minutes and then leaving without seeing the PowerPoint presentation.

LJM2 also helped Enron businesses when they were ailing. Despite the hoopla Enron created surrounding its fiber network and bandwidth trading initiatives, business was far from brisk for those operations. So in June 2000, LJM2 paid Enron roughly $100 million for strands of dark fiber-optic cable stretching from Salt Lake City to Houston. "Dark" fiber is line capacity that isn't connected yet to the lasers and switching equipment that route Internet traffic, and so is worth less than operating fiber. LJM2 paid Enron $30 million in cash and the rest in an interest-bearing note for $70 million. Enron recognized $67 million in pretax earnings in 2000 on the sale. LJM2 also paid Enron $20 million for marketing the fiber to other companies. LJM2 succeeded in selling a portion of the fiber to industry participants for $40 million. In December 2000, LJM2 sold the remaining dark fiber assets for $113 million to another SPE created by Enron. With the $113 million sale, LJM2 was able to pay off the note it had given Enron. But because Enron provided the credit to the SPE that paid $113 million for the remaining fiber, Enron was left with $61 million in credit exposure while LJM2 made a $2.4 million profit off the fiber deal.

The June 2000 deal approval sheet carried Ken Lay's signature for some reason. While Lay didn't have to approve individual deals between LJM2 and Enron, his signature on the fiber sale indicates that he knew at least some of the deals that Fastow's partnerships conducted.

■ ■ ■

As hard as Enron worked on creating and nurturing off-balance sheet partnerships, it also worked hard on lobbying to prevent regulations that would hamper its business. One example was derivatives regulation. The financial community had been considering stricter regulation of derivatives; at the end of 1998, over-the-counter (OTC) derivatives (those not traded on regulated exchanges) carried bets on $80 trillion of underlying assets, including bonds, commodities, currencies, and stocks. In 1999, the issue was taken up by the President's Working Group on Financial Markets, an irregular foursome in existence for 12 years and consisting at the time of Treasury Secretary Larry Summers, Federal Reserve Chairman Alan Greenspan, SEC Chairman Arthur Levitt, and CFTC Chairman William Rainer. One of the sparks for a new look at derivatives was the 1998 collapse of Long-Term Capital Management (LTCM), a multibillion-dollar hedge fund run by a klatch of Wall Street veterans and Nobel laureate economists.

Hedge funds are unregulated investment funds that can accept money only from millionaires and institutions, and unlike mutual funds, they're allowed to borrow massive amounts of money and take very risky positions. LTCM borrowed tons of money and used derivatives to grow the size of its investments; interestingly, LTCM (like Enron) felt it had developed an unmatched expertise in risk management, given its team of Ph.D.'s and savvy traders and its use of sophisticated computer models. The fund had a few years of success, but then the markets turned against LTCM, and the size of its investments made attempts to adjust or limit losses like trying to turn an 18-wheeler truck on a dime. It became clear that LTCM would sink with several billion dollars in losses, but its derivatives were connected to more than $1 trillion of underlying securities. Worried that LTCM's collapse might roil financial markets around the globe, the Federal Reserve orchestrated a $3.5 billion bailout by 14 investment banks in late 1998, so that LTCM failed, but did so slowly and without wider repercussions. LTCM had thrown a scare into the power centers in New York and Washington, just as the 1994 oil-trading fiasco at Metallgesellschaft had scared energy companies.

Washington decided it was time to update the laws regulating derivatives. Did these financial contracts deserve the same scrutiny that stocks got from the SEC? From the start, it seemed clear that regulators had little taste for that kind of close monitoring of derivatives trades between banks, corporations, and trading firms. That decision may have been helped by the fact that in 1999 Enron lobbied the President's Working Group on Financial Markets. The group—Summers, Greenspan, Levitt, and Rainer—issued a report in November 1999 that actually recommended that electronic exchanges trading derivatives be excluded from regulatory legislation, although the exemption *shouldn't* extend to energy commodities. It also recommended that any "clearing" system for derivatives—essentially a system that does the grunt work of validating and settling transactions—be regulated by the CFTC or another agency.

In 2000, Congress took up the issue of revising the regulation of commodities and derivatives trading. The legislation that began to wend its way through the Capitol became known as the Commodity Futures Modernization Act (CFMA). Enron's team of more than two dozen lobbyists snapped into action, encouraging lawmakers to water down the CFMA's provisions related to OTC derivatives.

Although Enron's critics overstated the company's impact on the legislation, Enron did have a big influence on the CFMA. "Everyone knew that," said Randall Dodd, director of the Derivatives Study Center. The CFMA didn't follow the recommendation that energy commodity derivatives face more regulation. And as it went through congressional committees, the CFMA included language that exempted what it called "bilateral" electronic trading exchanges from the CFTC's regulation. EnronOnline was just such a bilateral trading exchange, because Enron served as a counterparty to every trade on it. Although it didn't mention Enron by name, the CFMA's definitions of what didn't need regulation were so close to describing EnronOnline that in the derivatives community the definition became known as "the Enron exclusion."

The CFMA passed through the hands of Senator Phil Gramm (R-Texas), as he was the senior Republican on the Senate Banking Committee. Critics claimed the CFMA had Gramm's fingerprints all over it. The suspicions were natural: Gramm's wife, Wendy, was the CFTC chairman who later joined Enron's board in 1993. And Enron had long supported Gramm, a proponent of deregulation; between 1996 and 2002, Enron's employees and political action committees contributed $233,000 to the senator's campaign war chest. But Gramm said that he had no hand in the provision exempting EnronOnline. With or without his support, the CFMA was made into law in December 2000.

Enron fought another crucial regulatory battle that came to a head in 2000: changes to accounting rules that would require companies to disclose more information about off-balance sheet deals. Starting in the mid-1990s, FASB floated proposals to require a company to consolidate an SPE into its financial statements if the company controlled the assets in the SPE. The idea was shouted down by banks, accounting firms, and other interested parties. But FASB revived the idea of greater SPE regulation in late 1998 with a proposal to demand that companies report all their affiliates on their financial statements and balance sheets as though they were all controlled by the companies. It would end the use of the "unconsolidated affiliates" section of financial reports.

The following year, Enron sent a letter to the agency arguing that including full information on SPEs in financial statements, even in footnotes, would "contribute to disclosure overload." Andersen joined Enron in lobbying against the proposal, as did dozens of other companies, the Bond Market Association, and lobbying firms. In mid-1999, *CFO* magazine postulated that if FASB's rule were enacted, Enron's debt would balloon by $10 billion, raising its debt-to-capital ratio from 40 percent to a suffocating 70 percent.

After the barrage of criticism, the FASB issued rules in September 2000 requiring more data about SPEs in financial statement footnotes. But the agency didn't require all SPEs to be consolidated into earnings. Enron had dodged a bullet.

■ ■ ■

The California power crisis dragged on into 2001. In January, state regulators allowed Southern California Edison and PG&E to raise their retail rates between 7 and 15 percent. California's troubles became a regional problem, as the state pulled electricity from the Western power grid, forcing up prices in Oregon, Utah, and even Idaho. President Clinton, just weeks before leaving office, had his staff convene a meeting of various parties involved in the crisis. Ken Lay attended that meeting—to provide a voice for incoming President George W. Bush, according to a *Wall Street Journal* article. After that meeting, and a few other similar confabs, Clinton ordered electricity sales to cash-starved California utilities.

On January 17, the state ISO ordered rolling blackouts, cutting off power for homes and businesses for hours at a time. State utilities still racked up huge losses. This prompted California Governor Gray Davis to blame "out of state profiteers" for the state's woes; state Attorney General Bill Lockyer began inquiries into power markets.

In February, Davis signed into law a provision allowing utilities to enter long-term electricity contracts in order to steady their supplies. Once the deregulation-minded Bush took over the White House, he rejected the idea of FERC intervening to place permanent price caps on California's wholesale electricity. "A short-term delay of a needed solution," he called it, pointing to his belief that a market-based solution would be best. Lay offered advice in a column he penned for the *San Francisco Chronicle*, in which he argued against price caps and suggested more power generation be built. "The situation in California is the result of continued regulation, complicated by a series of natural and man-made factors," he wrote.

In early March, California reached an agreement to spend $40 billion buying electricity on behalf of its utilities over 10 years. The state then pushed through a large electric rate increase, and started buying the transmission systems of the utilities. On March 16, FERC staff recommended price caps on California electricity, despite the opposition of the U.S. energy secretary. On April 6, 2001, PG&E—California's biggest utility—filed for bankruptcy, claiming it had run up a deficit of $8.9 billion due to the power crisis.

Bush officials remained opposed to price caps. Indeed, Vice President Richard Cheney told a newspaper that "California is looked on by many folks as a classic example of the kinds of problems that arise when you do use price caps"—referring to the fact that California originally freed wholesale prices but capped retail prices. But Cheney also admitted that in April he'd met with Ken Lay, and that during their half-hour conversation they talked about energy policy, including the California crisis.

It's also not clear how much the Bush administration's stance on California was influenced by Enron's pleas. In addition to their face-to-face meeting, Lay gave Cheney a memo listing its energy policy ideas. The memo included this appeal: "The Administration should reject any attempt to re-regulate wholesale power markets by adopting price caps or returning to archaic methods of determining the cost-base of wholesale power. Price caps, even if imposed on a temporary basis, will be detrimental to power markets and will discourage private investment by significantly raising political risk." The memo didn't come to light until 2002, and when it did it underscored how much access Enron had to the White House—more access than Governor Davis, it seemed.

California officials, facing economic and political pressure, continued to point fingers at energy marketers. Lockyer, who had offered millions in rewards about information on lawbreaking in the power business, accused energy suppliers of creating "unconscionable profits." The attorney general said his office would inevitably file civil charges against energy trading companies, and he would love to add criminal charges. Lockyer expressed his anger bluntly, saying: "I would love to personally escort Lay to an 8 × 10 cell that he could share with a tattooed dude who says, 'Hi, my name is Spike, honey.' " Lockyer didn't know about Death Star and other tactics at the time—the memos outlining Enron's secret trading maneuvers weren't released until May 2002.

Enron's characteristic arrogance throughout the ordeal didn't win it any friends in California. At a conference in Las Vegas on June 12, Skilling joked to the audience that the difference between California and the *Titanic* was that at least the *Titanic* had the lights on as it went down. A little more than a week later, just as Skilling was about to address the Commonwealth Club of California in San Francisco, he was hit in the face with a pie by a protester. Skilling wiped the pie from his face and went on with his speech.

Finally, on June 19, FERC imposed price caps on electricity prices in California and 10 neighboring states. The FERC decision, coming after months of resisting such a move, appeared to be a resignation to the fact that the situation in the West would not be solved by market forces soon enough. The order permitted power sellers to charge 10 percent more in California than in other Western states, to compensate them for credit worries. Energy trading companies warned that the price caps, by removing market signals regarding demand and supply, might worsen electricity shortages.

But the price caps marked the beginning of normalization for California's power market. Southern California power prices averaged $234 per

MWh from January through May, but they averaged just $59 in July and August. California also benefited from conservation measures that reduced electricity demand by 10 percent and from unusually mild weather. So while price caps alone didn't solve the problem, they did seem to deter market manipulation.

In an interesting twist to the California story, Enron booked unusually large and secret reserves for its trading profits during the California energy crisis. The company put as much as $1.5 billion into undisclosed reserves, hiding massive profits while denying accusations that it generated excessive profits by price-gouging Californians. Of course, Enron regularly created credit and prudency reserves related to trading. But the $1.5 billion reserve may have been "cookie jar" reserves—rainy-day funds the company could draw from to boost quarterly profits.

Despite doubts about whether cookie jar reserves comply with accounting rules, they're not uncommon as another tool corporations use to smooth their quarterly earnings. But the reported size of Enron's reserves was notable. And whether they were proper or not, these reserves showed just how much money Enron made off California. If only Enron's other businesses performed so well.

11

POWER
OVERLOAD

Enron had an historic year in 2000. For the year, Enron reported revenue of $100.8 billion. That would put it at number seven in the Fortune 500 list of the country's biggest companies, above such blue-chip stalwarts as AT&T and Philip Morris. This represented a tremendous growth leap from the previous year, when revenues totaled $40.1 billion. Put another way, Enron's revenues had grown by more than 650 percent since it posted a mere $13.3 billion in revenue in 1996. That meant Enron's revenue grew more quickly over that five-year period than either Cisco Systems (the Internet equipment maker that came to embody the dot-com boom) or Intel (the maker of the brains of nearly all the world's personal computers).

How did Enron grow so quickly, vaulting into the upper echelons of corporations such as IBM and Wal-Mart? In a dubious but legal accounting method, the company often booked the full value of each trade as revenue, rather than just Enron's slice of the transaction. So if Enron bought $100,000 worth of natural gas, then sold it an hour later for $101,000, Enron booked the full $101,000 as revenue rather than the $1,000 in gross profit it made on the deal.

In this way, Enron was not like Wall Street investment banks. There, the traders booked as revenue either the commission made on each trade for a client or the gross profit on each transaction (that $1,000 on the gas deal, for instance). For example, if a Merrill Lynch client sold $3,000 worth of stock and paid Merrill a $50 commission, Merrill would book only the

$50 as revenue, not the $3,000. The larger revenue figures looked great, as they implied that each of Enron's 19,000 employees in 2000 generated a whopping $5.24 million in revenue on average. By contrast, oil giant Exxon Mobil generated a measly $2 million of revenue per employee.

Helping inflate the revenue figure was the fact that Enron could trade the same bunch of energy over and over, selling it and buying it and selling it again. The accounting rulemakers never specified how to account for energy trading, so Enron was free to report the value of each trade as revenue. On Wall Street, the revenue figures were not a priority anyway, so analysts and fund managers concentrated on earnings and cash flow. But to the outside world, it didn't hurt that Enron rose up the ranks of corporate size charts. It was more impressive to say that Enron was the seventh-largest company in the United States.

At year-end, the company had assets worth $65.5 billion (listed on its balance sheet). While revenues more than doubled in one year, net income for 2000 rose to just $979 million from $893 million. Still, the board was pleased with Lay's performance and for 2000 gave him a $7 million bonus (on top of his $1.3 million salary) that was based partly on the company's improvement in net income. The company also granted Lay options on 782,000 shares of stock, worth a potential $15 million if the stock rose by 5 percent a year. And Lay exercised options on 2.29 million shares, giving him a gain on paper of $123 million. This made Lay one of the highest-paid CEOs in the nation.

Skilling did well, too. His compensation included a base salary of $850,000, a bonus of $5.6 million, and the granting of options on 868,000 shares—more options that Lay received. Skilling exercised options on 1.19 million shares, giving him a gain on paper of $62 million.

Among the other executives who profited handsomely, Mark Frevert, the head of Enron's wholesale energy business, got $2.5 million in salary and bonus, and options on 1.1 million shares. Kenneth Rice, head of the still unprofitable broadband division, received $2.2 million in salary and bonus, and options on 1.8 million shares.

In early 2001, Skilling reached a pinnacle in his career. On February 12, at the age of 47, he took over as CEO of Enron. Ken Lay remained the chairman. "Jeff is a big part of Enron's success and is clearly ready to lead the company," Lay said in a statement. "With Jeff's promotion, succession is clear."

The promotion had been announced before the end of 2000, when rumors circulated that Lay might take a cabinet post in the Bush administration. "I am particularly happy that Ken and I will continue running the company together and that he has put the rumors of his possible departure to Washington, D.C., to rest," Skilling said.

Wall Street welcomed the news of Skilling's move up into the CEO role. As Prudential Securities analyst M. Carol Coale explained, "There is a huge premium in Enron's stock related to management quality and Jeff is at the helm."

Lay, in a different way, reached a personal peak of his own. He'd promoted Skilling as his successor, putting the company in good hands. At a party for Enron executives in early January, Lay told the champagne-and-cigar-stuffed ballroom that Enron's new mission was simply to be "the world's greatest company."

On the political front, Lay's clout had never been higher. His friend George W. Bush, who referred to Lay as "Kenny Boy," had been elected president in November 2000, and Lay had indeed been rumored as a possible cabinet member—perhaps Secretary of Energy. Lay, Skilling, and Enron donated a combined $300,000 to the cost of the inaugural. On January 20, when Bush took the oath of office, Lay watched from the elite "Pioneers" box reserved for the biggest movers and shakers from the Bush campaign. The next day, he attended an exclusive luncheon at the White House.

Lay had become a mover and shaker in the political world, apparently trying to influence who would head FERC—the agency where Lay worked in the 1970s back when it was the Federal Power Commission. It began in January, when Bush named Curtis Hebert Jr., a FERC commissioner for several years, as the agency's new chairman. Hebert said Lay called him and implied that Enron would urge the newly installed Bush administration to keep Hebert in the job—if he changed his views to support Enron's position for faster electricity deregulation. (Lay disagreed with that version of events and contended that Hebert called him to ask for support.) Hebert said he wouldn't play ball.

Later in the year, Lay gave the White House personnel director a list of people he'd advocate to serve as one of five commissioners of FERC. "As I recall, I signed a letter which in fact had some recommendations as to people that we thought would be good commissioners," Lay said in a PBS television interview. One of the names was Pat Wood III, an acquaintance of Lay's who had served as chairman of the Texas Public Utility Commission under Governor Bush. In August 2001, Hebert resigned from FERC and Bush named Wood the new chairman. There was no proof that Bush had replaced Hebert with Wood at Lay's urging, but many in Washington perceived the move as evidence of Enron's influence.

Enron was no stranger to politics. In addition to former regulator Wendy Gramm, Enron's board included Lord John Wakeham, Britain's former energy minister. Thomas White, who had run Enron Energy Services, joined the Bush administration as Secretary of the Army. And while Lay contributed much more money to Republicans, he was also friendly with Democrats, playing golf in Colorado with President Bill Clinton. In May 1999, when Robert Rubin stepped down as Treasury Secretary, Lay sent him a note urging him to join Enron's board, writing, "If you are considering joining any corporate boards, I would like very much to talk to you. . . . I think you would find serving on our board intellectually and otherwise interesting." Rubin didn't become an Enron director. The company angered some Republicans, though, when it did succeed in hiring Linda Robertson, a Democrat who served in Clinton's Treasury Department, to run its Washington office. "We . . . don't discriminate based upon political preference," Lay explained. Enron spent millions on lobbying the Clinton White House and Congress, including $1.9 million of lobbying expenditures in 1999 and $2.1 million in 2000.

And the company was used to relying on government help. From 1992 through 2001, Enron projects in dozens of countries received billions of dollars in public financing. This included $3.6 billion in risk insurance and other aid from U.S. agencies including the Overseas Private Investment Corporation (OPIC), the Export-Import Bank, the Maritime Administration, and the Trade and Development Agency. The World Bank, which counts the United States as a key backer, also provided more than $700 million to several Enron projects. While some of this financial support was promised but never delivered, and some of the loans and insurance were actually requested by the host countries, Enron did display an aggressive bent toward soliciting government help. These agencies exist in large part to help private companies develop businesses outside the United States, and Enron clearly understood what an important partner Washington, D.C., could be.

That's why Lay eagerly met with Vice President Dick Cheney as the

Bush administration put together its energy policy. Cheney formed a task force in January to assemble an official Bush energy strategy, and Enron officials met with the task force six times; this included the April 17 meeting between Lay and Cheney. Lay and Cheney knew each other at least as far back as the mid-1990s, when Cheney served as CEO of Houston-based Halliburton, a large oil-services and engineering firm; a division of Halliburton built Enron Field. The two men may have been different types in that Lay's affable demeanor diverged from Cheney's mix of gruff confidence and arrogance, but the politically conservative Cheney agreed with many of Lay's beliefs about the value of markets over regulation. And although Cheney could be single-minded, such as when he stormed ahead with an energy plan without consulting Congress, that trait echoed Enron's tendency to dismiss critics and hew to its trading-centric worldview. While many companies and environmental groups wanted Cheney's attention—and the task force did hear from representatives of the energy and transportation industries, state and local regulators, academics and policy analysts, and others—Lay got a full half hour of face time with the vice president. Cheney said he wanted Lay's thoughts because "Enron has a different take than most energy companies."

Cheney and company didn't just listen to Enron and then adopt everything the corporation wanted. For instance, Enron argued in favor of fighting global warming by requiring reductions in carbon dioxide emissions (which could have helped Enron's fledgling emissions credit trading business), but the Bush administration backed away from that idea. But when the task force released its report, it contained more than a dozen policy stances that could benefit Enron. Among the more significant recommendations in the task force report was its suggestion that "the U.S. government should continue to support the development of efficient derivatives markets," because they help mitigate energy price volatility. Obviously this corresponded with Enron's goals of having a larger and unfettered energy derivatives market it could dominate.

Other policy agreements abounded. Enron had argued for federal control of electric transmission lines, to ensure open access to competing power suppliers, rather than local utility control of them. The national energy policy report backed that view, with a recommendation that "the President encourage FERC to use its existing statutory authority to promote competition . . . in transmission facilities" and that federal agencies "take actions to remove constraints on the interstate transmission grid." The task force's position was not a universally held view; electricity cooperatives, for instance, opposed moves to place them under FERC's jurisdiction.

The task force also supported the repeal of the Public Utility Holding Company Act (PUHCA) of 1935, legislation that governed public utilities and what kinds of business decisions they can make. Enron had long advocated repeal of PUHCA, which would have given it a free hand to invest in various electric utilities.

Enron had encouraged the federal government to use the power of eminent domain to seize land for use in transmission facilities, even over the state's objections. Despite Bush's public support of states' rights, the task force report agreed with Enron, urging the Bush administration to "develop legislation to grant authority to obtain rights-of-way for electricity transmission lines." Similarly, as part of its desire for an expanded, standardized electricity grid that would ease the trading and transporting of power, Enron had long called for the establishment of a nationwide electricity grid—which it saw as a "highway for interstate energy in electricity." The task force's report asked Bush to "examine the benefits of establishing a national grid," and, in language similar to Enron's, called the electric grid "the highway system for interstate commerce in electricity."

U.S. Representative Henry Waxman (D-California), the senior Democrat on the House Committee on Government Reform, questioned whether the task force's plan gave the appearance that a large contributor had special access to top officials and obtained favorable results in energy policy. "The policies in the White House energy plan did not benefit Enron exclusively. And some of the policies may have independent merit," Waxman wrote. "Nevertheless, it is unlikely that any other corporation in America stood to gain as much from the White House energy plan as Enron."

The similarities between Enron's proposals and the task force report, and Waxman's comments, did not surface until January 2002. And that occurred after several months during which Cheney's office resisted appeals from Waxman to disclose how much contact his task force had with Enron. When the details did surface, the White House defended Cheney's task force. "In fact, if you really want to take a look at some things, some of the things that Enron wanted the most, they didn't get, such as a global warming agreement by the United States. The previous administration, of course, did enter into an agreement on global warming, which

I think was very pleasing to Enron," White House spokesman Ari Fleischer said. Referring to the call to repeal PUHCA, he added the law "prevents more efficient operation in the energy market, as companies work with each other or are able to purchase other electricity companies. That PUHCA measure has been passed previously by House committees in overwhelming bipartisan votes." Despite the White House's spin, many critics saw Bush's energy strategy as a document that had been influenced by Kenny Boy and Enron.

■ ■ ■

David Duncan graduated from high school with honors and attended Texas A&M University, developing a reputation as a respectful, hardworking student. The good-looking Duncan, who grew up in a close-knit family, also displayed ambition early on. Teachers sometimes thought of him as a young man who was going places. Some elders also saw in his politeness a possible tendency to avoid confrontations and not rile authority.

He joined Arthur Andersen in 1981 right out of college, and working in Andersen's Houston practice he eventually met future Enroners Rick Causey and Jeffrey McMahon. He interrupted his Andersen career to work for Freeport-McMoRan, a global natural resources company, but he didn't like it and returned to Andersen nine months later. Resuming his place as a rising star within the accounting firm, Duncan made partner in 1995. In 1997, he became the "global engagement partner" for one of Andersen's most valued clients: Enron.

Andersen earned $47 million in fees for its Enron work in 1999, and that total rose to $58 million in 2000. Duncan made more than $1 million a year now, and was a valued partner at the firm. But people who knew Duncan had a sense that he struggled with Enron's persistent desire to push the envelope on accounting rules. In the end, the deferential side of Duncan won out, and he helped Enron construct its elaborate partnerships.

Duncan's job evolved to include defending Enron against the strict accounting interpretations of Andersen's Professional Standards Group (PSG), the expert accountants charged with defending the accounting rules. It was the PSG that advised in December 2000 that the Raptors' credit capacities would have to be permanently merged, a recommendation that Duncan overruled. But Duncan's wrangling with PSG dated back to December

1999, when PSG member Carl Bass disagreed with him over how to account for an Enron partnership's options sales. Bass even admitted to a colleague by e-mail, "I do not know if he [Duncan] knows how much we cannot support this." But Duncan went over Bass's head to Michael Odom, Andersen's practice director in Houston. Odom backed Duncan on how to account for the sale, thus saving Enron over $30 million.

Bass, based in Houston, raised questions from time to time about Enron's accounting. Commenting on a proposed deal in which LJM wanted to make an investment and hedge it with options, Bass wrote in a February 2000 e-mail: "Going back to the Enron income effect, this whole deal looks like there was no substance. The only money at risk here is $1.8 million in a bankrupt proof SPE. All of the money here appears to be provided by Enron."

A few days later, Bass criticized the same deal for in effect allowing Enron to profit from gains in its own stock price. He wrote: "I am still bothered with the transaction. . . . 1. The SPE is non-substantive. They receive no protection on the option, other than $3. 2. Any payments made on the appreciation of stock is [*sic*] in essence an equity transaction. They should realize no income on this. It looks like they have parked the shares there because they get it back one way or another."

Bass may have been the most vocal in his skepticism of Enron's transactions, but he was not the only one at Andersen who wondered about the innovative customer. Andersen partners debated whether to keep Enron as a client; the firm occasionally dropped clients based on the risks they presented to Andersen. This consideration peaked on February 5, 2001, at a meeting of the key partners working on Enron. Duncan, Odom, and six others attended in person, while six Andersen employees participated by speakerphone. According to a memo prepared the next day by Andersen employee Michael Jones, "significant discussion was held regarding the related party transactions with LJM including the materiality of such amounts to Enron's income statement and the amount retained 'off balance sheet.' "

Jones' summary of the meeting went on: "The meeting addressed Fastow's conflicts of interest in his capacity as CFO and the LJM fund manager. The amount of earnings that Fastow receives for his services and participation in LJM, the disclosures of the transactions in the financial footnotes, Enron's Board of Directors' views regarding the transactions and our and management's communication of such transactions to the Board of Directors and our testing of such transactions to ensure that we fully understand the economics and substance of the transactions."

Andersen partners acknowledged that Enron's use of mark-to-market income in its earnings constituted "intelligent gambling," and admitted "Enron is aggressive in its transaction structuring." They also spoke of Enron's reliance on its credit rating and its dependence on SPE transactions to meet financial targets. But, ultimately, the partners decided to retain Enron as a client. "It appeared that we had the appropriate people and processes in place to serve Enron and manage our engagement risks," according to Jones' memo. The group also discussed the possibility that Andersen's fees from Enron might eventually rise to $100 million per year.

Andersen later explained that the February 5 summit was a routine meeting consistent with firm policy to conduct annual risk assessments. The firm also explained that describing mark-to-market accounting as "intelligent gambling" referred to its reliance on future assumptions, and that the discussion of fees reaching $100 million per year related not to Andersen's desire to grow revenues but to the concern that the size of the fees might hurt perceptions of Andersen's independence. And Andersen noted that nothing in the meeting indicated the partners suspected illegal actions or improper accounting.

The February 5 meeting ended with the Andersen partners drawing up a to-do list of actions to mitigate any concerns. They decided they should suggest that Enron's board form a special board committee to review LJM's deals, and they should look further into whether the LJM partnerships qualified as separate entities. A week later, on the day that Skilling took over as CEO, Duncan and fellow Andersen partner Thomas Bauer met with the audit committee of Enron's board. But when directors asked them if they wanted to express any concerns, neither Duncan nor Bauer raised any issues.

Carl Bass's objections kept coming. On March 4, he e-mailed John Stewart, the PSG's director of accounting, to reiterate that he'd had some doubts about a number of Enron deals that resulted in the company boosting its reported income by about $150 million just before the end of 2000. Of the Raptors, Bass wrote, "I will honestly admit that I have a jaded view of these transactions." On a joint venture between Enron and video-store chain Blockbuster, Bass wrote that Duncan's team "did not follow our advice on this" and, instead, Enron's proposed accounting treatment "was sustained."

Although the PSG group dealt only with Duncan and other members of the engagement team, and not directly with clients, Bass complained in the same e-mail that people at Enron knew who he was and felt he opposed their accounting. "There appears to be some sort of assertion that I have a 'problem' with Rick Causey or someone at Enron that results in me having some caustic and inappropriate slant in dealing with their questions," he wrote. He contended that he had nothing against Enron, and wouldn't have asked to be the lead PSG person on Enron if he had, given the complexity of its accounting issues.

Bass concluded that part of the problem "stems from the client knowing all that goes on within our walls on our discussions with respect to their issues. . . . The PSG only gives advice. The engagement partners and practice directors then reach a decision based on that advice and other considerations."

The fallout? In handwritten notes, Duncan scrawled, "Negative view of Carl" and "Client sees need to remove Carl." Duncan relayed Enron's objections to Bass back to his bosses in Chicago. On March 12, Andersen reassigned Carl Bass out of the PSG, taking him out of the loop on Enron issues.

■ ■ ■

Thanks to declining stock prices, the Raptors' liabilities swelled again in early 2001. The cross-guarantees reached in December had been intended as temporary patches, and by late March the credit capacity had eroded further. With Enron's stock down to $68.68 on March 1, and New Power's stock down to $6.20, Raptors I and III had lost enough value that Enron might have had to take a $504 million charge against earnings. Employees said that Skilling, now the CEO, felt fixing the Raptors' credit problems was one of his priorities; Skilling later contended that he had only a general knowledge that the Raptors had some credit problems and that it was an accounting issue.

So Enron restructured the Raptors once more, and the transaction was dated as of March 26 in order to affect the first quarter ended March 31. The deal, not surprisingly, was complex. First, Enron transferred its right to receive any distributions from the two healthy Raptors to the sick Raptors. Then, Enron set about strengthening the two healthy Raptors that were supporting credit-impaired Raptors I and III. Enron agreed to deliver up to 18 million more shares of Enron stock to Raptors II and IV to shore up the value of the original equity, in exchange for $260 million more in notes from the Raptors.

Enron also sold Raptors II and IV about 12 million shares of Enron to be delivered in March 2005 at $47 per share. In return, the Raptors gave Enron $568 million more in notes. The 12 million shares were sold at a discounted value because they, like the original stock delivery contracts, were restricted so that they couldn't be sold, pledged, or hedged for three years. Despite the restrictions, Enron hedged that stock via costless collars.

The process capitalized the two healthy Raptors with even more shares of Enron stock, their excess credit intended to cover any losses in the weak Raptors. The four-step recapitalization resulted in Enron recording a $36.6 million credit reserve against its earnings, rather than a $504 million credit reserve, in the first quarter. Together with losses and gains on some of the Raptor-Enron transactions, the Raptors enhanced Enron's first-quarter earnings by a total of $255 million. Causey and Buy, who were supposed to oversee the Raptors and LJM deals, never told Enron's board about the Raptors' credit problems or of the restructuring—even though both involved sums of more than $500 million.

The recapitalization set up a potentially dangerous trigger, because the Raptors could only accept so many Enron shares if the stock price fell. If Enron's stock price plunged to $20 or below, losses would begin to accrue to the company's income statement. What's more, Causey would later tell Vinson & Elkins that Enron's top two executives knew about this danger. "All these consequences were known to Jeff Skilling and Ken Lay through discussions of this structure," he said. This implied that Lay and Skilling knew what was at stake in buoying Enron's stock price.

The dance steps may have been awkward, but Enron's SPE tango met its immediate goal of surpassing Wall Street's financial expectations. When Enron released its first-quarter results in April, it reported earnings excluding one-time items of 47 cents per share, topping the 45 cents that had been the consensus projection of analysts. Many inside Enron felt that if the company missed its quarterly earnings estimates, then analysts would hold its finances under a microscope—so making or beating quarterly estimates was a way to avoid scrutiny. In a vicious cycle, Enron depended on the Raptors to prop up earnings and therefore support its stock price, while the Raptors' financial health increasingly depended on Enron's stock price for support.

Also in March 2001, Enron bought out Chewco, the SPE formed in 1997 and described in Chapter 7. Although Fastow and others floated the idea to buy out Chewco in 2000, it didn't happen until near the end of 2001's first quarter. Enron agreed to buy Chewco's stake in JEDI for $35 million, which also settled most of the money Chewco owed to JEDI and accounted for guaranteed fees owed to Enron.

As a result of this buyout, Michael Kopper and William Dodson received a $3 million cash payment at closing. This came on top of $7.5 million in cash that they received during the term of the investment. So the total of $10.5 million was quite a payday in return for their original investment of $125,000 less than four years earlier. Kopper asked for supplementary money to cover tax liabilities from his large gains. Enron personnel debated this request for several months because the agreements governing Chewco didn't require such a payment. But Fastow backed Kopper, and in September, Enron paid Kopper an additional $2.6 million to cover tax expenses.

The Enron board's special committee concluded in the Powers Report in February 2002 that "Kopper reaped a financial windfall from his role in Chewco." Michael Kopper left Enron on August 1, 2001, and the company gave him a severance payment of $905,000.

The oddities of the Raptor and LJM deals piled up. One Enron employee who noticed was Jordan Mintz, a former tax attorney who was a general counsel and vice president in Enron Global Finance. Mintz had tried unsuccessfully to get Skilling to sign off on deal approval sheets for various LJM transactions—as CEO, Skilling's signature was supposed to be on the approvals, as Mintz understood the controls set up by the board. According to Mintz, he sent the approvals to Skilling's office in mid-May and after three weeks of trying gave up without getting the signature. His decision to drop it may have been influenced by the advice of Rick Buy, who reportedly told him, "I wouldn't stick my neck out." The LJM deals continued to be active; around the same time, Fastow even proposed that LJM buy Enron Wind Corp., a deal valued at about $600 million, but that sale never happened.

Mintz looked over the partnerships and felt uncomfortable with the structure surrounding LJM. As he said, "I brought to the attention of certain members—senior members of the company—concerns I had. And I went to Mr. [Thomas] Bauer and Mr. [Rick] Causey and met with them regularly and wrote them a memo about some of the problems I saw in the process and procedures associated with the LJM approval." He also got the feeling that questioning Fastow's judgment would be a bad idea because Skilling protected Fastow.

On May 22, Mintz finally retained the New York law firm Fried Frank Harris Shriver & Jacobson to review the LJM transactions. He didn't tell Vinson & Elkins or his bosses. "I wanted somebody that no linkage, no connections with the company, and just to take a fresh look at everything," Mintz explained. He had two concerns: the related party transactions between Enron and LJM, and the disclosures about LJM made in Enron's proxy statements.

Before Fried Frank finished its review, Fastow told Mintz that he intended to divest his interests in the partnerships. Mintz was elated by that news, feeling it would lift much of what he termed the "dysfunctionality" in Enron headquarters. Mintz asked Fried Frank for advice on how to terminate Fastow's interests in the partnerships and clean everything up. Fried Frank advised Mintz to "halt this practice" of conducting deals with related partnerships. The law firm also recommended that the board's audit committee review the LJM transactions, including the fairness of the deals and their disclosure in company financial statements, and said it could serve as independent counsel for the audit committee if desired. But these ideas never advanced within Enron, and Fastow's proposed divestment from the partnership dragged on well into the summer.

Mintz confided some of his concerns with J. Clifford Baxter, who served as a vice chairman at the time. They had lunch in April and discussed, among other things, the conflicts of interest arising from having Enron personnel negotiate both sides of deals between Enron and the LJM partnerships. Baxter wondered why Enron's board allowed it to continue.

In the spring, Baxter complained to Skilling, whom he regarded highly, about the conflicts he believed were inherent in the LJM setup. The two argued, but came to no resolution. Feeling burned out, Cliff Baxter resigned from Enron in May.

■ ■ ■

Whatever internal dissent existed within Enron remained inside the corporation. To the outside world, Enron did very well. Sure, the stock had continued to slip, closing at $58.10 on March 30, largely because valuations for telecommunications stocks were dropping everywhere and so Enron shares lost much of their telecom premium. Still, at the start of January, Enron had a market capitalization of $64 billion, making it the world's fifth most valuable energy company and worth almost five times as much as rival Dynegy. And Enron's earnings grew consistently, so its stock earned a high price-to-earnings ratio, a valuation measure that determined how much the market paid for each $1 of earnings power. As consulting firm McKinsey & Co., Skilling's old stomping grounds, noted approvingly: "Enron has convinced Wall Street of the favorable long-term prospects of its new businesses; about half of its current market cap is attributable to businesses that have yet to generate annual earnings. As a result of this persuasiveness, Enron trades at a price-to-earnings ratio of 60, in contrast to an industry average of 14."

EnronOnline ran smoothly and successfully, trading over 1,000 iterations of commodities from Henry Hub natural gas to cold-rolled sheet steel. The system also tried to create new markets, such as trading advertising space and data storage capacity. How much EnronOnline boosted Enron's earnings over the old phone-based trading system is hard to tell, but the company claimed that it lowered the cost of its trading business. It also succeeded as a trading platform, so while online exchanges like Chemdex struggled, EnronOnline attracted increasing liquidity. By late March, the system conducted over 4,500 transactions each day, trading more than $2.5 billion daily.

The success of EnronOnline prompted rivals to jump into online energy trading with new verve and a commitment to provide liquidity as trade counterparties—not just try to match other buyers and sellers. In March 2000, BP Amoco, Royal Dutch/Shell, Goldman Sachs, and a handful of other companies formed Intercontinental Exchange (ICE), an Internet market for trading energy and other commodities. Power marketers Aquila, American Electric Power, Duke Energy, Reliant, and Mirant later joined ICE, and in April 2001 ICE agreed to purchase the International Petroleum Exchange, an energy derivatives market in London that competed with NYMEX. And in September 2000, Dynegy, Williams Cos., Texas Utilities, and other energy companies teamed with eSpeed, an operator of business-to-business trading platforms, to create TradeSpark, an online exchange for trading gas, electricity, coal, and weather derivatives. The founding companies provided the core of the liquidity, and TradeSpark advanced to the point where it hosted $18 billion worth of trades in the first quarter of 2001.

Louise Kitchen continued to run EnronOnline. Loud and brash, Kitchen fit in with Enron's other high-strung managers. "She was a very intimidating person, and I don't say that lightly," said Allan Sommer, who worked for Kitchen in 2000. Her organization reflected her personality, so EnronOnline was a tense, competitive place. "It was famous, but it had its price," said Sommer. And the success of EnronOnline gave even more power to the traders within Enron Corp.

Some employees didn't mind the culture, enjoying instead Enron's famous penchant for giving young workers real responsibility. Jon Pope, a programmer who developed specific trading software for different commodities, could add a feature to the program and then see it in use on the site a few weeks later. "Very few places you could make that impact as just a lowly software developer," Pope explained. "It was pretty exciting. You felt like you could make a difference."

Enron placed EnronOnline under a new umbrella organization called Enron Net Works, which included Clickpaper.com. This e-commerce oriented division also included DealBench, which ran online reverse auctions for corporate procurement—taking bids from sellers rather than buyers to supply raw or finished goods to a business. Enron used DealBench to buy carpets, light fixtures, and other amenities for its new office building. Deal-Bench also provided a service for secure online viewing of legal documents. The document management combined with the reverse auctions when DealBench ventured into financial deals: In some instances, customers used DealBench to solicit bids on credit facilities from banks.

Enron Net Works also included CommodityLogic, a business aimed at online automation of back-office functions such as payroll and human resources. Enron Net Works in general had the feel of a dot-com, with talented and even cocky tech specialists banded together to work 11-hour days. "There were a lot of bright people. And it was a flat hierarchy so everyone could have a say, and that was impressive," recalled John Spitz, who worked on software development.

In May 2001, *Worth* magazine named Skilling the second best CEO, despite the fact that he'd only assumed the CEO title that February. The magazine ranked him right behind Microsoft's Steve Ballmer and well ahead of such luminaries as Steve Jobs and Michael Dell.

■ ■ ■

Despite the accolades, some of Enron's businesses were doing poorly. Azurix, the once-promising water business, provided one visible example as its stock dropped below $7. During the fourth quarter of 2000, Azurix lowered the value of its Argentine assets, resulting in a charge of approximately $470 million; Enron's portion of the charge was $326 million. In March 2001, Azurix shareholders approved a plan whereby Enron bought out the public shareholders for $8.375 per share, or a total of $326 million. The merger folded Azurix back inside Enron—although Atlantic Water Trust remained a part owner—and ended one chapter in one of Enron's biggest failed experiments.

The Dabhol power plant in India cropped up as a problem again. In January 2001, the state of Maharashtra found itself unable to buy the 30 percent stake in Dabhol that had been part of the agreement worked out in 1996. So Enron, planning to invest $1.2 billion to build phase two of the plant, obtained Indian government approval to increase its stake in Dabhol. Unfortunately, later that month, Maharashtra failed to make some $50 million in payments for Dabhol electricity. The missed payments portended larger controversy.

Critics had contended for years that the Dabhol project was overly expensive, with its high fixed costs and guaranteed electric rates. Those claims came home to roost. Even before January, the state had been buying just a portion of the plant's electrical output, even though it was contracted to buy all of it. Maharashtra had trouble making its payments because Dabhol's power had become so costly, due to high oil prices (raising costs of the naphtha fueling the plant) and lower power demand. Changes within India also resulted in the emergence of local industrial power plants that produced cheaper electricity—power from Dabhol was four times more expensive than that from domestic power producers. According to one report, the payments due to Dabhol would be more than Maharashtra's education budget.

On January 31, five days after an earthquake rocked the neighboring state of Gujarat, Enron said it would invoke the federal guarantees and would auction off government properties if it didn't get its money; Enron's timing was not a public relations coup. Invoking federal guarantees, Enron got a $17 million payment from Maharashtra in February for November's bill. Later, Maharashtra announced it would stop buying electricity from Dabhol and wanted out of the contract. In April, Enron began arbitration proceedings and stopped construction of phase two. In May, it idled the plant.

Enron was now saddled with a huge, inactive power plant in India. Just as it had relied in the past on the diplomacy of U.S. ambassadors, commerce secretaries, and at least one energy secretary to help push its cause in India, the company again tapped its political connections. In April, U.S. Secretary of State Colin Powell raised the Dabhol issue as part of talks with India's foreign minister. In June, Vice President Cheney lobbied the leader of India's opposition Congress Party, Sonia Gandhi, on behalf of Enron. Still, the legal dispute continued.

Enron, which still controlled 65 percent of Dabhol, reversed course and tried to scale back its stake in the troubled project. But Dabhol, looking more and more like a white elephant, did not attract investors. Enron finally decided that it would try to sell Dabhol for some $2.3 billion, even though the company contended its legal claims relating to the plant totaled more than $4 billion. Dabhol remained for sale in December when Enron eventually declared bankruptcy.

After years of losses, in 2000 Enron Energy Services finally reported income before interest and taxes of $103 million, excluding one-time items. The division continued to sign up customers for its energy outsourcing services, with annual revenue more than doubling to $4.6 billion. However, even people within Enron questioned the quality of that income. EES relied heavily on mark-to-market accounting, so much of its earnings came from the immediate recognition of profits on long-term deals rather than through actual cash coming in. Actually, the division sometimes spent more cash in initial outlays for its outsourcing contracts than it received in the initial year.

"It was well-known that it was cash-negative and the goal was to make it profitable through mark-to-market," explained a former Enron executive. One former EES employee said the division never made any real profits, just mark-to-market profits based on internal projections.

Although EES had several years to figure out what was really a new business for Enron, even in 2000 the unit was flying semiblind. Much of the business relied on assumptions about when states would deregulate retail electricity and gas markets, which would then lower Enron's costs of providing energy in the EES contracts. But those regulatory changes were nearly impossible to predict. State deregulation happened at a slower pace than Enron projected, and then hit a standstill after the power crisis erupted in California in 2000. "There was a lot of guesstimating going on in those models," recalled Beau Ratliff, a former EES analyst.

One deal Ratliff worked on changed by $10 million per day because the manager in charge kept changing the projections. But the volume of deals rose steadily. "Clients loved it. With the California crunch, everyone wanted fixed-price contracts," Ratliff said. So there were many nights when the EES staff worked past midnight.

The biggest symbol of the division's internal contradictions came in 1998. Enron executives were touting EES, then still relatively new, to Wall Street analysts. Leading the analysts through a tour of Enron's headquarters, the company pulled about 75 EES workers—including sales reps and secretaries—from their actual jobs and had them pose in a fake trading center on the building's sixth floor. The goal was to show the analysts that EES was a real and busy business. The company moved phones, computers (some not working), and family pictures to the desks of the fake trading floor. Lay and Skilling reportedly helped orchestrate the ruse, and even led a rehearsal the day before the analyst tour. When Lay and Skilling led the analysts through the area, the EES team "at work" gave the impression of a busy, dynamic operation. It was one more example of Enron's emphasis on appearances and spin.

Margaret Ceconi, an EES employee who was laid off from the division in August, later fired off an angry letter to Ken Lay describing the poor business practices in the operation. EES underwent five internal restructurings in nine months. Most deals were signed at an initial loss to Enron. Customers threatened to sue to get favorable terms in their contracts. New managers came in and changed the price projections, so that some deals estimating $15 million in client savings dropped to $2 million in savings. "EES has knowingly misrepresented EES' earnings," she wrote. "This is common knowledge among all the EES employees, and is actually joked about." She claimed that EES sat on a total of $500 million in losses, but hid them in the complex trading books of Enron Wholesale Services (formerly known as Enron Capital & Trade Resources). EES later responded to Ceconi's charges by saying, "This letter is, unfortunately, not based on all the facts."

The highest-profile Enron business encountering financial troubles was Enron Broadband Services, which including the fiber network and bandwidth trading. "Broadband could potentially be our highest area of growth," Lay told listeners at PaineWebber's Annual Energy Conference in February 2000. "We intend to become the world's biggest buyer and seller of bandwidth, just as we have become the world's biggest buyer and seller of electricity and natural gas." But Enron Broadband Services lost $60 million in 2000 and had no profits on the horizon.

It started with the fiber network, which Enron eventually spent over $1 billion to assemble. Although Enron claimed its "intelligent network" connected to most major cities in 1999, according to allegations in a lawsuit, Enron really had access to only a small number of lines that were "lit" and had access to very few bandwidth pooling points. Enron also claimed that its Broadband Operating System could meter and direct the flow of traffic through the network, but the Operating System never developed beyond some rudimentary building-block software. In 2000, Enron claimed that its network included 25 pooling points in Tokyo, Brussels, Paris, Amsterdam, and 18 U.S. cities—but internal Enron documents showed that as of December 2000, only Las Vegas, Los Angeles, New York, and London had pooling points up and running. Enron's network couldn't make a broadband connection between Portland and Seattle, and used Internet service providers to carry content that it claimed went over Enron's video-streaming network, according to the lawsuit.

Enron's reach in broadband consistently exceeded its grasp. In July 2000, Enron signed an agreement with video-store chain Blockbuster to stream movies over high-speed lines, with the intent of eventually streaming concerts, video games, and other entertainment. The 20-year venture aimed to compete with pay-per-view services offered on cable television systems and with video rentals. Enron wouldn't connect directly to customers' homes, but would transmit the movies to the local telecom company, which would then send the film over high-speed DSL phone lines to the homes. The two companies envisioned the new service starting in late 2000 or early 2001.

Despite the embryonic nature of the project, Enron put its stake in the

Blockbuster venture into an SPE—which, drawing from the love of code names, was called "Project Braveheart." Through Braveheart, Enron booked $110.9 million in income from the Blockbuster venture in the fourth quarter of 2000 and the first quarter of 2001. This apparently represented future income from the venture, even though it had yet to come close to generating profits. This was either a sign of Enron's optimism or another accounting trick to make Enron Broadband look healthier.

The companies did launch tests of their service in four cities, covering some 1,000 homes. But in March 2001, the companies ended their venture. Both Enron and Blockbuster said at the time that they would seek comparable deals with other partners: Blockbuster claimed it lacked confidence in the security of the Enron network, while Enron complained that Blockbuster had signed up too few movie studios to license their films for the service.

The broadband business stumbled on the problem plaguing many telecom companies: There was too much bandwidth. The rush to build high-speed networks had created a glut of broadband capacity. This produced little demand for the capacity on Enron's network, and little incentive to trade bandwidth to lock in prices. One of the division's largest deals was the June 2000 sale of dark fiber to LJM2 (described in Chapter 10). In addition, Enron reportedly engaged in useless bandwidth trades in 2001 with companies such as Qwest in order to boost the value of the division. Enron and its counterparties would essentially swap equal amounts of network capacity with each other—transactions known as "wash" trades—to create the illusion of an active trading market. And Enron could inflate revenue figures and asset values by booking these "trades" at ever-higher values: For instance, Qwest and Enron could agree to take fiber originally worth $1 million per mile and book wash trades at $10 million per mile, so the assets' value rose without any cash changing hands.

Skilling put his best spin on the broadband situation as a potential opportunity for Enron, telling analysts in a March conference call: "This marketplace is going through a very tough time. I look at this as the natural gas business in the mid-80s all over again. There is a meltdown in prices. There is way too much supply. . . . So I think this is going to accelerate the opening of the markets."

Even as Skilling gave those reassurances, many employees in Enron Broadband knew that the company had quietly been trying to sell the entire 18,000-mile fiber network. By that time, the broadband business had become a dumping ground for employees from other Enron divisions. In April 2001, when Enron Broadband reported a loss of another $35 million in the first quarter, Enron said it didn't expect the division to generate profits for another two or three years. That news disappointed Wall Street, and whatever extra zip broadband had added to Enron's stock disappeared.

Then in July, Enron hit Wall Street with its second-quarter results: Enron Broadband lost $102 million in the quarter. Enron said it would shift more personnel out of the division, after cutting its workforce by 250 positions in April. "This is just a recognition of reality," one analyst said. But the facts couldn't be ignored. Broadband was another experiment that had cost Enron millions and millions of dollars.

■ ■ ■

Equity analysts at the investment banks and brokerages covering Enron remained loyal, even after the buyout of Azurix, the setbacks at Enron Broadband, the struggles of Dabhol, and the Blockbuster deal gone bust. Merrill Lynch analyst Donato Eassey, for instance, reiterated his "buy" recommendation on Enron stock in an April 18, 2001, report titled "Raising the Bar—Again!" The report said that Enron's stock, then at $60, could rise above $100 over the next 12 months "as tech market psychology and valuations ultimately rebound." Eassey raised his projections for Enron's earnings and said, "We reiterate our Buy opinions."

The rift between Enron's cheerleaders on Wall Street and the gradual accumulation of stumbles and bad news created some cracks in Enron's glistening facade. Most research analysts continued to praise Enron's tradition of innovation, but open skepticism began to appear elsewhere in late 2000 and early 2001.

One skeptic was James Chanos, president of Kynikos Associates, a hedge fund specializing in selling short. Selling short follows the dictum of "buy low, sell high," but in reverse order, so the investor sells borrowed shares of a company at high prices, then replaces the stock by purchasing it later at a lower price—if the strategy works correctly. Chanos looked at Enron's annual report and saw that it used mark-to-market accounting, which raised a red flag for him, and so he studied the finances more closely. "Enron's return on capital, a widely used measure of profitability, was a paltry 7 percent before taxes. That is, for every dollar in outside capital that Enron employed, it earned about seven cents. . . . For this type of firm a 7 percent return on capital seemed abysmally low, particularly given its market dominance and accounting methods," he said. Chanos also figured that Enron's *cost* of capital exceeded its 7 percent return on capital, which meant that Enron wasn't really earning money. Based on this analysis, Chanos started short-selling Enron stock in November 2000.

Further inquiry only confirmed Chanos' view that Enron was over-hyped. In early 2001, several Wall Street analysts he spoke with admitted they couldn't really analyze Enron. One analyst told Chanos Enron was an inscrutable "black box" of earnings, but as long as the company delivered he wouldn't argue. After Kynikos Associates discussed its opinion of Enron at its February conference, overall short-selling of Enron stock slowly rose.

Press coverage turned mixed as Enron's stock lost some of its froth. The first in-depth article questioning the greatness of Enron appeared in a March issue of *Fortune* magazine under the headline "Is Enron Overpriced?" The writer, Bethany McLean, described analysts' difficulties in breaking down the company's business to assess what it was really worth, and noted that they didn't know what was in the division labeled "Assets and Investments" even though it produced wide swings in profits.

"But for all the attention that's lavished on Enron, the company remains largely impenetrable to outsiders, as even some of its admirers are quick to admit," McLean wrote. "Start with a pretty straightforward question: How exactly does Enron make its money? Details are hard to come by because Enron keeps many of the specifics confidential for what it terms 'competitive reasons.' And the numbers that Enron does present are often extremely complicated." She quoted an analyst at Goldman Sachs who recommended the stock even though he confessed that analyzing it was difficult "with as little information as we have." One strategist and Enron fan admitted in the article that if the company missed earnings targets its stock could implode.

Enron didn't like to be challenged. And as problems mounted in 2001, Enron's management appeared to become more irritable. In an April 17 conference call with analysts to discuss the first-quarter earnings Enron had just released, Skilling called the results "outstanding" and discussed the status of some of Enron's businesses. Then he opened the call up to questions from analysts and institutional investors. After several other exchanges, Richard Grubman of investment firm Highfield Capital asked for the assets and liabilities from price risk management. Skilling told him Enron didn't have its balance sheet completed, and that Grubman would have to wait until Enron filed its 10-Q quarterly report with the SEC.

Grubman didn't like that answer, and said, "You're the only financial institution that cannot produce a balance sheet or a cash flow statement with their earnings."

Skilling replied testily, "Thank you very much, we appreciate that." Then he muttered "asshole" to his colleagues, but the slur was audible to everyone on the call. Skilling was having trouble tolerating dissent even outside Enron.

■ ■ ■

Skilling had reason to feel testy. In addition to falling telecommunications valuations and setbacks in the broadband strategy, Enron's stock was jabbed by worries that the recently ended energy crisis in California would mean an end to Enron's huge trading profits. The shares, which started the year above $75, were down to $45.61 by August 1. Meanwhile, Skilling's personal life had grown busier. He was in a serious relationship with Rebecca Carter, Enron's corporate secretary. In what seemed an unusual move for Enron, he'd asked the board of directors for permission to date her in the spring of 1998. Skilling and Carter would get engaged later that summer.

On a Friday afternoon in August, Skilling sprang a surprise on Lay when he told his mentor that he wanted to resign. As Skilling explained it, he had three children, two of whom were teenagers approaching college age and, as a divorced father with joint custody, he felt that if he didn't take the opportunity to spend time with them then, that he never would be able to do so. Lay pressed him, and Skilling admitted that Enron's stock was dropping and he couldn't do anything about it. Skilling took the stock decline personally and couldn't sleep at night.

The following Monday, Lay tried to talk Skilling out of resigning. Several board members also tried to persuade Skilling to stay. But he insisted on leaving, and on resigning from the board as well. Skilling also asked that Enron's announcement of his departure eschew any mention of his desire to spend more time with family, because he didn't want his children to think they were responsible for him quitting Enron after all those years.

On Tuesday, August 14, Lay sent an e-mail to Enron employees revealing Skilling's resignation, saying: "Jeff is resigning for personal reasons and his decision is voluntary. . . . I want to assure you that I have never felt better about the prospects for the company."

Later that day, after the stock markets closed, Enron officially announced that Skilling had resigned after just six months as CEO. The company said he resigned for personal reasons. Lay would assume the duties of CEO again, in addition to being chairman. "In terms of timing, I feel the company is in good shape," Skilling said. In a conference call with investors, Lay said there were "no accounting issues, trading issues, or reserve issues."

Within Enron, employees reacted with shock and worry. "Everyone was in awe. No one thought it was for family reasons," recalled one former Enron trader. Ex-Enron employee John Allario said people were disappointed to be losing the company's most articulate spokesman. "It caught us all off guard," he said; rumors began to fly that the company might try to bring Richard Kinder back.

The business world also took notice. James Chanos saw the resignation as another reason to bet against Enron. "In our experience, there is no louder alarm bell in a controversial company than the unexplained, sudden departure of a chief executive officer no matter what 'official' reason is given," he said. A research executive at another hedge fund, which sometimes traded with Enron, said he was flabbergasted. "This is one of the most driven men in history. At the peak of his career, he finally had everything he wanted," this executive said, "and he left!" His hedge fund stopped trading with Enron almost immediately, and the next month sold Enron's stock short.

Skilling had complained of being under unusual pressure, and it sometimes looked that way to other Enron officials. Only a week or two before his resignation, Skilling alarmed fellow executives at a breakfast to celebrate the company's aid to the United Way in Houston. Skilling appeared with a black eye. Called upon to make an impromptu speech, he started by jokingly explaining that he'd recently had minor eye surgery and that rumors that Rebecca Carter had hit him were not true, according to an executive who'd been there. Among the several dozen Enron bigwigs in the audience, more than a few eyed each other in silent disbelief, wondering if Skilling had actually alluded to real anger from Carter over his rumored womanizing. Was this a stressed-out Skilling letting slip a personal problem, or another inappropriate comment from the same Skilling who joked about California being worse than the *Titanic* and called an analyst an asshole?

Either way, Skilling's abrupt departure seemed to be a black eye for Enron, and as such it raised the eyebrows at credit rating agencies. Moody's called Enron soon after the news and asked senior management if they anticipated any major charges, write-downs, or other one-time financial adjustments. Enron assured the agency that none were coming.

Skilling, for whatever reason, couldn't seem to fade away quietly. The day after Enron revealed his exit, he gave an interview to the *Wall Street Journal* in which he admitted Enron's plunging stock price was the chief reason he left. "I put a lot of pressure on myself" for the poor stock performance, he told the paper. Skilling's comments displeased Lay, who felt that Skilling had undercut the company.

Skilling's exit displeased the stock market, too. Markets dislike uncertainty, and the CEO's quick exodus cast a pall of doubt over Enron. The stock dropped from $42.93 to $40.25 the day after his resignation. A day later, when Skilling's interview was published, Enron's stock fell to $36.85.

On August 16, Lay held an all-employee meeting to calm any fears, which was simulcast to all offices. When he took the stage, wearing a shirt and tie but no jacket, Enron workers gave him a standing ovation. As ex-Enron employee Francisco Duque remembered it, "At the beginning of the meeting he was received like a rock star. I was really impressed."

Lay spoke for roughly an hour, standing in front of a lectern, showing slides, and exhibiting a passionate and occasionally folksy demeanor. "I'm excited. I think we've got a lot of great stuff going on," he said. "The next several months, the next few years, are going to be great for Enron, great for Enron employees." Lay discussed various challenges, including California and Dabhol, but ventured, "I think the worst of that's behind us."

He admitted that Enron Broadband had developed slowly—"We have had to redeploy and lay off about 500 people; about half of those have been redeployed," he said—but then he assured the crowd that he expected Enron Broadband to break even by the end of 2002.

"I'm concerned about the value of our stock options. And the stock," he said. He noted that the last round of stock options carried exercise prices of $83, far out of range of Enron's stock price. To offset that, he revealed that the board recommended a special one-year award of new stock options equivalent to about 5 percent of each person's salary.

In closing, Lay told his employees that Enron's vision was to be the world's leading company, and he felt it could possibly reach that goal within five years. Lay either didn't suspect or didn't reveal the true extent of the company's troubles. Enron would have less than five months, let alone five years.

12

DOWNWARD SPIRAL

"**H**as Enron become a risky place to work? For those of us who didn't get rich over the last few years, can we afford to stay?"

So began a blunt and prescient letter that an anonymous Enron employee sent to Ken Lay on August 15, 2001, triggered by Skilling's sudden resignation. The writer obviously knew about Enron's extensive use of SPEs, and knew that the problems with these partnerships were cresting. "Skilling's abrupt departure will raise suspicions of accounting improprieties and valuation issues," the letter said. "Enron has been very aggressive in its accounting—most notably the Raptor transactions and the Condor vehicle. We do have valuation issues with our international assets and possibly some of our EES MTM [mark-to-market] positions."

The letter was a call to action in light of Skilling's exit and the understanding that Enron would be obligated to transfer large amounts of its own stock to the Raptor entities, and another SPE called Condor, over the next two or three years. "I am incredibly nervous that we will implode in a wave of accounting scandals," the note said. "My eight years of Enron work history will be worth nothing on my resumé, the business world will consider the past successes as nothing but an elaborate accounting hoax. Skilling is resigning now for 'personal reasons' but I think he wasn't having fun, looked down the road and knew this stuff was unfixable and would rather abandon ship now than resign in shame in two years."

It turned out that the letter writer was an employee named Sherron Watkins. Watkins, a maternal-looking blonde with a penchant for outspoken independence and straight talk, grew up in a small Texas town, went on to get bachelor's and master's degrees in accounting from the University of Texas, and went to work for Arthur Andersen. With Andersen, she had no trouble adjusting from small-town roots to the cities of Houston and New York.

Leaving Andersen, she spent three years at MG Finance, and then took a job at Enron in October 1993. Watkins worked under Andrew Fastow, and her duties included helping manage JEDI, Cactus, and related projects. Typical of an Enron employee, she moved around within the company, working for a spell at Enron International, then Enron Broadband, and in the spring of 2001 wound up working for Fastow again. Back in finance as a vice president of corporate development, one of Watkins' duties was to list and evaluate assets that Enron might want to sell off—and this work sparked questions about the Condor and Raptor entities.

Looking further into the Raptor transactions, Watkins concluded that they looked bad: The SPEs owed Enron hundreds of millions of dollars due to their hedges on Enron investments, but they had no ability to pay and LJM had no requirement to put more money into the Raptors. The Raptors looked like pure manipulation of income statements because, with Enron's own stock supporting the Raptors, the true economic risk remained with Enron. "I was highly alarmed by the information I was receiving," she wrote. "My understanding as an accountant is that a company could never use its own stock to generate a gain or avoid a loss on its income statement." In her view, Enron engaged in "an increasing aggressiveness" in its accounting practices, and by 1999 the company "was pushing the edge."

What's more, colleagues she spoke with believed Fastow had an agreement with Skilling guaranteeing the LJM partnerships would never lose money. Watkins claimed to hear a manager at an Enron group that hedged some investments with Raptors say, "I know it would be devastating to all of us, but I wish we would get caught. We're such a crooked company." And, like Jeff McMahon, Watkins was troubled by the conflict of Fastow serving as CFO and managing LJM.

She had decided to leave Enron and tell Skilling what she'd found on her last day (when she'd have nothing to lose), but then Skilling resigned suddenly. So Watkins, described by friends and family as loyal, decided to put her thoughts in a letter to Ken Lay. She sent the letter anonymously, and it startled Lay. A few days later, Watkins came forward and identified herself as the author, then met with Lay in person on August 22 to discuss her concerns.

Her letter laid out some of the problems in detail: "How do we fix the Raptor and Condor deals? They unwind in 2002 and 2003, we will have to pony up Enron stock and that won't go unnoticed. To the layman on the street, it will look like we recognized funds flow of $800 million from merchant asset sales in 1999 by selling to a vehicle (Condor) that we capitalized with a promise of Enron stock in later years. Is that really funds flow or is it cash from equity issuance? We have recognized over $550 million of fair value gains on stocks via our swaps with Raptor. Much of that stock has declined significantly—Avici by 98 percent, from $178 million to $5 million; The New Power Co. by 70 percent, from $20/share to $6/share. The value in the swaps won't be there for Raptor, so once again Enron will issue stock to offset these losses. Raptor is an LJM entity. It sure looks to the layman on the street that we are hiding losses in a related company and will compensate that company with Enron stock in the future."

In addition to the original letter, Watkins wrote out for Lay what she felt were the key accounting issues for the future, among them: The contingent Enron stock given to the Raptors likely meant that Enron would be obligated to issue them shares in the future, and this would affect earnings per share in 2002, 2003, and 2004; with the Raptors technically bankrupt, they seemed to imply a loss of $500 million from inception to date; and Enron would probably have to write down the value of its interests in the Raptors, but could wait until 2002 or later.

Watkins expressed her concern about disclosure of the deals, writing: "I realize that we have had a lot of smart people looking at this and a lot of accountants including AA & Co. have blessed the accounting treatment. None of that will protect Enron if these transactions are ever disclosed in the bright light of day. . . . My concern is that the footnotes don't adequately explain the transactions. If adequately explained, the investor would know that the 'entities' described in our related party footnote are thinly capitalized, the equity holders have no skin in the game, and all the value in the entities comes from the underlying value of the derivatives (unfortunately in this case, a big loss) and Enron stock and [New Power]."

Watkins, seeking a way out for Enron, recommended to Lay that he hire an outside law firm to investigate Raptor and Condor—because Vinson & Elkins, as Enron's counsel, had advised on the LJM and Raptor deals, raising conflict issues. Enron seemingly would have to restate its past financial statements and take its lumps. She said Enron should clean up the transactions quietly if possible, or at least quantify the cleanup and develop public relations and investor relations plans to explain the deals. If Lay doubted her, she told him to quiz Jeff McMahon, Mark Koenig (an investor relations executive), Rick Buy, and Greg Whalley to determine, as she put it, "if I'm all wet." Months later, Watkins' warnings would cause her to be looked on as a whistleblower, but it seemed her main concern was cleaning up and spinning the problems, not exposing them to the public.

Lay listened to her, troubled at times—he winced when she relayed the comment from a fellow employee that Enron is "such a crooked company"—and said he would look into it. A little more than a week later, Fastow found out that Watkins had written the letter. According to Watkins, Fastow wanted to have her fired. Lay had her transferred out of Fastow's department.

Fastow, for his part, questioned Watkins' motives, because, as he would later explain to Vinson & Elkins, he considered her smart enough to know that the structure and all the transactions were reviewed by Andersen and found to be appropriate. Fastow also told the law firm he believed Watkins acted "in conjunction with a person who wants his job"—an apparent reference to Jeff McMahon.

Two days before her meeting with Lay, Watkins had called an acquaintance named James Hecker, an audit partner at Andersen who didn't work on the Enron account. She reached out to Hecker as a sounding board, informing him of her concerns about the propriety of how Enron accounted for some related-party transactions. She included her surprise that Enron could repeatedly use its own stock to add to the collateral of an obligation owed to Enron from a related party. Hecker told her she seemed to have some good questions, and he commended her "stand-up" attitude. He passed her concerns on to David Duncan and the rest of the Enron team.

Watkins' meeting with Lay produced another immediate result: Enron's legal department contacted Vinson & Elkins seeking advice for dealing with Watkins. It appeared that Enron considered firing Watkins. Carl Jordan of Vinson & Elkins wrote back to Enron that the corporation had asked about "the possible risks associated with discharging (or constructively discharging) employees who report allegations of improper accounting practices."

Vinson & Elkins' memo suggested the direction of the questions; it said, "Texas law does not currently protect corporate whistleblowers." But the firm also cautioned, "In addition to the risk of wrongful discharge claim, there is the risk that the discharged employee will seek to convince some government oversight agency (e.g., IRS, SEC, etc.) that the corporation has engaged in materially misleading reporting or is otherwise non-compliant."

The law firm sent a memo to Enron employee Sharon Butcher noting that Watkins' request to be transferred to another department was positive. The firm recommended that Enron keep Watkins' authorship of the letter private, and that Enron managers not treat Watkins "adversely in any way for having expressed her views." In the end, Watkins retained a position at Enron.

■ ■ ■

In late August, Ken Lay made a point of trying to restore credibility in the investment community. The stock had weakened to the $37 range, Skilling's resignation left a ream of unanswered questions, the planned sale of Portland General had fallen through when Sierra Pacific couldn't raise the money, and Wall Street felt less rosy about energy trading—particularly with bankrupt California utilities still owing Enron hundreds of millions of dollars. Lay also believed Skilling's April conference call muttered slur of an investor as an asshole (as described in Chapter 11) was unfortunate and continued to irk the company. So Lay promised that Enron would disclose more information about how the company made its money. He pledged to make the financial statements less opaque, and to start putting out more detailed information on the individual business segments.

Lay also announced that as of July 31, CFO Andrew Fastow had ended his ownership and management ties with what Enron referred to as "certain limited partnerships." Lay alluded, of course, to Fastow's role with the LJM2 partnership; Fastow had sold his interest in LJM2 to Kopper. Analysts had begun to wonder if Fastow's dual roles, alluded to cryptically in Enron's financial statements, meant that Fastow sometimes benefited from deals that hurt Enron. Lay told the press that Fastow's involvement with the partnerships had become a "lightning rod" for criticism, so Enron would be "better off not doing it."

Wall Street welcomed the promises of a more open Enron. "I'm not sure that Enron is exactly humbled," said one analyst, "but they're certainly under a new kind of pressure." Some analysts suggested that Enron shares' price-to-earnings ratio, which once soared above that of other energy traders thanks to the potential of its many new ventures, was not just lower but permanently lower.

After the flurry of news surrounding Skilling, Lay continued to defend Enron and its status to employees. In an August 27 e-mail to the company, Lay wrote, "As I mentioned at the employee meeting, one of my highest priorities is to restore investor confidence in Enron. This should result in a significantly higher stock price."

On September 26, Lay again told employees the company's stock seemed like a bargain and that the third quarter was "looking great"—only weeks before Enron would fall apart and its stock price plunge. "My personal belief is that Enron stock is an incredible bargain at current prices and we will look back a couple of years from now and see the great opportunity that we currently have," Lay wrote in reply to an employee question on Enron's "ethink" intranet site. Throughout the statements in the transcript, Lay reassured Enron workers that the company was doing well. In the transcript, an employee anxiously asked Lay how staffers could help the stock, which had fallen to about $25 per share. Lay advised Enron employees to "talk up the stock." He said, "The company is fundamentally sound. The balance sheet is strong. Our financial liquidity has never been stronger."

However, Lay made this series of comments touting Enron's stock not long after he and other senior executives had sold large amounts of their Enron shares. Between February 1999 and July 2001, Lay sold more than 1.8 million shares of Enron stock for total proceeds of $101.3 million. He sold his stock on more than 100 different dates in batches ranging from 500 shares to lots of 100,000 shares. To some extent this was an understandable strategy for diversifying a net worth tied up in Enron stock. Lay also claimed he sold some Enron stock to meet personal debt obligations to banks and brokerages. But given that Lay was privy to at least some of Enron's undisclosed problems in 2000 and 2001, his sales raise the question of whether he was dumping the stock before it could plunge. And when his sales became public months later, it didn't look good; a lot of the stock he dumped in 2001 fetched prices of $80, $78, or $70 per share, while he had urged Enron rank and file to hold onto their stock as it sank throughout 2001. His actions seemed to contradict his own cheerleading.

Lay was hardly alone. Lou Pai, who ran Enron Energy Services and was involved with several other Enron divisions, topped Lay's sales: Pai sold a total of $353.7 million of Enron stock from January 1999 through July 2001. The majority of Pai's sales occurred at high prices in the first half of 2000, but what seemed like fortuitous timing was really sparked by the divorce settlement with his first wife—reportedly over his affair with a former topless dancer. Rebecca Mark, long gone from Enron and now remarried and calling herself Rebecca Mark-Jusbasche, sold $79.5 million of Enron stock from February 1999 through May 2000. And Skilling sold $66.9 million worth of Enron stock from January 1999 through June 2001.

In all, Enron officers and a few directors unloaded a whopping $1.1 billion in Enron stock from January 1999 through July 2001. Because the senior executives' stock sales had to be reported to the SEC, observers were aware that Enron managers had been selling their stock—and for some short sellers, it further fueled their confidence that Enron was a slowly sinking ship.

Ken Lay and other top executives had written plans, executed by a broker, to automatically sell Enron stock at regular intervals regardless of news at the company. Before Skilling's exit, Lay had been contemplating retirement, so his stock sales in 2001 were an attempt to diversify his investments. Lay later said he thought the automatic stock-selling plan "did a lot of damage" because analysts viewed executives selling their stock as the sign of a problem.

■ ■ ■

Enron may have used SPEs such as the Raptors to enhance its earnings, but they weren't the only strategies the company used for financial results. Chief among the company's income-boosting tricks were two other important tactics: reducing tax costs, and hiding loans as derivative transactions known as "prepaid swaps."

Corporate America has a long tradition of using SPEs and other tactics to get tax breaks. After all, tax breaks associated with employee stock options provided one reason that companies had been attracted to their use as compensation. And in a world that emphasizes net income, reducing tax expenditures is equivalent to increasing after-tax income through sales or trades. So Enron applied its expertise in what the business world called "financial engineering" to taxes. In 1995, for example, the company created a structured transaction called Tanya: Enron formed a new unit to manage deferred compensation and retirement benefits; this unit issued preferred stock and transferred the stock to Enron; Enron sold the preferred stock back to the unit at a loss, creating a tax deduction. The new unit eventually transferred the stock back to Enron, but the IRS accepted the Tanya transaction. It generated a $66 million reduction in taxes.

Soon, Enron's tax department had an internal structured transactions group to assemble strategies that rivaled the JEDI and Cactus partnerships in complexity and ingenuity, and which involved both domestic and offshore partnerships. The group put together a series of transactions with code names such as Teresa (which added $229 million to net income over its life), Cochise (which added $110 million), and Valhalla (which added $20.2 million). Teresa, for instance, created a synthetic lease on Enron's Houston office building to fashion deductions not available had a traditional lease been used.

Enron worked with outside law firms and banks to create these tax strategies, which by all indications were legal and passed muster with the Internal Revenue Service. The company seemed to view tax reduction strategies as yet another way to manage its earnings. It's difficult to determine exactly how much Enron wound up paying in taxes each year, however: Enron's annual report for 2000 lists $434 million in income tax expenses for federal, state, and foreign obligations, but one newspaper account said that after refunds and deductions Enron actually paid just $62 million in taxes that year.

The *Washington Post* reported that the tax department's structured transactions increased Enron's reported profits from 1995 to 2000 by a total of almost $1 billion. This resulted in far lower tax expenses for Enron, even as it reported after-tax earnings of $703 million in 1998, $893 million in 1999, and $979 million in 2000.

Rather than deducting or eliminating outright some tax expenses, Enron deferred some of them—either for years or permanently. U.S. law allows companies to defer paying taxes on some income earned overseas until that income makes its way to the United States. So in its 2000 annual report, Enron stated that its foreign subsidiaries' cumulative undistributed earnings of roughly $1.8 billion were considered to be permanently reinvested outside the United States, and, accordingly, no U.S. income taxes had been paid on them.

Even with its structured tax strategies and offshore deferrals, it appears that Enron couldn't avoid all taxes. The company paid the alternative minimum tax, a separate tax aimed at guaranteeing that corporations pay some taxes when they earn profits despite deductions.

Separately, Enron used derivatives known as prepaid swaps to keep debt off its books. Swaps are derivatives in which two firms swap risks on a deal, often trading fixed-price risk for floating-price risk. Prepaid swaps, as explained in Chapter 4, are contracts that swap risk in a different fashion—one company gets paid up front for the risk, and the other party gets repaid over time. Enron's Volumetric Production Payments, which financed small exploration companies in exchange for future natural gas production, were a kind of prepaid swaps. They essentially function as loans, but when properly structured they can be counted on the books as hedges; the two companies don't need to even own the underlying assets being hedged. Prepaid swaps are sometimes called "Islamic financing," because they mimic loans in a way that doesn't violate Islamic law's prohibition against charging interest. In the prepaid swaps with the banks, though, Enron was the one getting the financing.

One instance of the prepaid swap occurred in 2000, when Enron entered a deal with Credit Suisse First Boston. The bank gave Enron $150 million and Enron had to pay it back over two years, the payments varying with the price of oil. Enron was thus able to book the deal as a hedge on oil prices, so it didn't have to add $150 million to its debt. Credit Suisse, interestingly, counted it as a loan on its own books. Like the tax structures, Enron's prepaid swaps appeared to be legal, even if some thought they were misleading.

Perhaps the biggest example of Enron's prepaid swaps surrounded Mahonia Ltd., an offshore entity based in the Channel Islands. In a complicated triangle of deals, Enron traded energy to J.P. Morgan Chase through Mahonia, and J.P. Morgan later traded the energy—through Mahonia—back to Enron at slightly higher prices. The energy didn't actually change hands, but the cash did. The slightly higher prices obtained by J.P. Morgan represented interest on the original cash outlay.

This circular trading went on from 1997 through 2001, resulting in roughly $1 billion passing from J.P. Morgan to Mahonia (a shell company set up by J.P. Morgan Chase) to Enron. Enron apparently entered its last Mahonia transaction in September 2001. In that deal, J.P. Morgan entered a prepaid swap in which it paid Mahonia $350 million in exchange for future payments that would vary based on gas futures prices. At the same time, Mahonia entered a prepaid swap with Enron for the same terms. The J.P. Morgan money flowed to Enron, and Enron's variable payments would ultimately flow through Mahonia to J.P. Morgan. Simultaneously, Enron entered a deal with J.P. Morgan: Enron agreed to pay the bank $356 million six months later in exchange for J.P. Morgan paying Enron variable sums based on gas futures prices. In this deal, Enron essentially got a $350 million advance from J.P. Morgan in return for repaying $356 million in six months—which looked a lot like a six-month loan with 3.4 percent interest. But because these were a series of derivative transactions, Enron didn't add the $350 million to its balance sheet.

The Mahonia deals later became the subject of litigation between J.P. Morgan Chase and Chase's insurers, who had provided a form of insurance on the prepaid swaps believing, they claimed, that they were actually contracts for delivering oil and gas. Although the bank continued to deny any wrongdoing, in March 2002, a U.S. District Court judge ruled that the transactions were a "disguised loan."

Enron used the prepaid swaps because they kept the financing from its official debt, allowing the company to retain a decent credit rating. Mahonia-type transactions aren't uncommon. Many companies use prepaid swaps using offshore accounts, because the "hedges" don't appear on their balance sheets and they also carry tax benefits. The involvement of J.P. Morgan Chase also wasn't unusual, as it fell into the gray area of lenders also acting to structure deals. This gray area had expanded since 1999, when the federal government repealed the Glass-Steagall Act, a Depression-era law that had mandated the separation of commercial banking and investment banking.

J.P. Morgan Chase dealt with Enron in other SPE-related transactions. One concerned Sequoia, an SPE created by Enron to buy from the company some of its electricity and gas receivables—bills due from customers for energy that Enron had sold them. When Sequoia bought a $1 million receivable from Enron, it meant that the $1 million Enron was due to receive from gas customers would instead be paid to Sequoia. Sequoia bought the receivables and then securitized them, bundling them and selling them in slices to investors.

In 1999, Choctaw Investors, an entity unaffiliated with Enron, borrowed $485 million from a group of lenders led by J.P. Morgan Chase, and got a $15 million equity investment from another investor. Choctaw then used this money to buy $500 million of preferred units in Cherokee Finance, an SPE controlled by Enron. Cherokee then bought senior notes issued by Sequoia.

The following year, J.P. Morgan Chase again led a group of lenders in loaning $482 million to Zephyrus Investments, another SPE "unaffiliated" with Enron. Zephyrus took the $482 million in loans, plus $18 million in equity contributed by investors, and bought $500 million worth of preferred units in an entity called Enron Finance Partners. Enron Finance Partners, an SPE controlled by Enron, used that money to buy senior notes issued by Sequoia.

Senior notes and preferred units function as debt, so the two Sequoia transactions acted as though they funneled loans from J.P. Morgan Chase and other banks to Enron, with the loans being backed by the energy bill receivables.

J.P. Morgan received $11.5 million in fees for its Sequoia work, and the bank explained, "The Sequoia Transactions were designed to raise financing in the form of minority interest equity financing, a well-established means used regularly by large corporations to meet their capital needs. Such financing has attributes of debt for tax purposes and attributes of equity under Generally Accepted Accounting Principles."

■ ■ ■

Ken Lay thought Sherron Watkins was credible and referred her concerns to both Andersen and Vinson & Elkins. Although Watkins recommended that an outside law firm conduct a review of the SPEs, Lay decided that outsiders wouldn't be able to quickly grasp Enron's transactions, so he had Vinson & Elkins conduct the investigation. Lay agreed with Enron's general counsel, James Derrick (who'd joined Enron from Vinson & Elkins), that it would be a preliminary investigation anyway, aimed to determine whether a full probe would be needed.

In late August and early September, Vinson & Elkins looked at documents, including deal approval sheets and financial statements, and interviewed a variety of Enron employees, including Watkins, Fastow, Causey, Buy, McMahon, Mintz, and Greg Whalley, who'd been promoted to chief operating officer following Skilling's exit. V&E also interviewed Andersen partners David Duncan and Deb Cash.

But V&E proceeded within restricted parameters. Enron and V&E decided the probe would *not* second-guess the accounting treatment of the partnerships or the advice of Andersen. The reason for setting this condition isn't clear, seeing as how the accounting treatment lay at the root of Watkins' concerns. The investigation also wouldn't analyze each transaction in detail. The firm didn't interview anyone beyond Enron or Andersen, such as bankers who dealt with the company or outside finance experts. Instead, V&E's preliminary investigation would see if the issues demanded a fuller inquiry.

In the V&E interviews, McMahon and Watkins both expressed concern that Fastow pressured banks into participating in LJM2 with the understanding that their cooperation (or lack thereof) would be linked to their ability to win investment-banking business from Enron. In one V&E interview, Fastow defended the LJM and Raptor structure, noting although the structures were in a "gray area," they had been approved by Andersen and fully disclosed to investors. The LJM partnerships, he reasoned, offered greater speed and confidentiality for Enron's asset deals than a third party would.

On September 21, V&E reported back to Lay and Derrick with the conclusions of its "preliminary" investigation, although they didn't turn in a written report until October 15. The firm looked at the setup of LJM1 and LJM2, and at the approval, disclosure, and review requirements aimed at avoiding conflicts, and determined that "it appears that the approval procedures were generally adhered to." It did say the conflicts of having Fastow and other Enron staff working for LJM partnerships raised employees' concerns, but concluded "much of this awkwardness" would disappear with Fastow's selling his interest in LJM2. The firm also said that while the accounting for the Raptor and Condor transactions was "creative and aggressive," no one they interviewed had reason to judge it as inappropriate.

Vinson & Elkins told Lay that their findings didn't show a need for a further, independent investigation. Given what the firm deemed the "bad cosmetics" of the related-party dealings, V&E concluded that the only risk involved "a serious risk of adverse publicity and litigation."

In hindsight, the special board committee that investigated Enron opined in the Powers Report that the preconditions of the V&E investigation—not challenging the accounting treatment or analyzing each deal in depth—hamstrung the operation. "The scope and process of the investigation appear to have been structured with less skepticism than was needed to see through those particularly complex transactions," it stated.

When Watkins later found out about the report, and that V&E had been directed to accept the accounting treatments of the partnerships, she was disappointed. "It all appears to be somewhat of a whitewashed report to me," she said, noting that this only delayed Lay from grasping the gravity of the situation. "The reason I think Mr. Lay didn't 'get it' was he gets this report from V&E on October 15th saying it's all okay, the optics are bad and he just decided let's unwind it, let's write it off, let's get it behind us. If he truly understood the magnitude of manipulating your financial statements, I think he—you know, if it were me, I'd do a lot more contingency plans."

■ ■ ■

By September, the situation with the Raptors became untenable. Their underlying capital had eroded dramatically, due to further declines in Enron's stock (it was down to $35 on September 4) and New Power's stock (down to $4.15 on September 4). Also, their hedging obligations had risen because the investments they were protecting had also declined sharply; for example, Avici's stock, transferred to Raptor I at $162.50 per share, had plummeted to $3.20 on September 4. The Raptors were credit deficient by hundreds of millions of dollars, again. And the costless collars on the Enron stock within the Raptors were a problem for Enron Corp., because they obligated the company to pay loads of cash given that Enron's stock had dropped below the floor set by the collars; so, for instance, Enron would have to make up the difference between Enron's $35 stock price and the guaranteed minimum price of $79 on some of the stock in Raptor II.

In September, Lay, Causey, and Whalley met to discuss what to do about the Raptors. They decided to terminate them. So on September 28 Enron bought them out. The company paid LJM2 $35 million for its interest in the Raptors—a sum settled upon by Kopper, no longer with Enron but negotiating for LJM2, and Fastow, negotiating for Enron.

The company computed the Raptors' combined value at $2.5 billion, consisting of Enron stock hedged at higher-than-market prices. The Raptors' combined liabilities totaled about $3.2 billion. The difference between liabilities and assets, plus the fee to LJM2, came to a grand total of $710 million—or a charge to earnings of $544 million after taxes. The special board committee that probed Enron later noted that this accounting treatment might have been improper because Enron had already recorded $1.1 billion of income in 2000 and 2001 from the Raptors. The committee wondered if Enron should have reversed that $1.1 billion in gains as well.

Andersen and Enron also decided that they'd accounted incorrectly for a feature of Raptors I, II, and IV. Enron had sold Enron stock to the three Raptors in exchange for promissory notes from the SPEs, and then booked the transactions as increases to "notes receivable" and "shareholders' equity." These decisions boosted Enron's shareholder equity—total assets minus total liabilities—by $1 billion in 2001. But Andersen and Enron now believed the notes transactions should have been recorded as *reductions* of shareholder equity.

Around that time, research head Vince Kaminski had figured that the Raptors were more than just a bad business decision—they were an accounting scam. Kaminski had several problems with the Raptors. First, the restricted Enron stock that had been "sold" to the Raptors at a discount supposedly earned that discount because they couldn't be resold or hedged. Yet Enron went ahead and hedged their value with the collars, which meant the restrictions were moot and therefore the stock was worth more than its discounted value. This implied that Enron had given value for free to the Raptors. Second, the structures provided no effective transfer of risk from Enron to LJM, so the Raptors were not hedges but means to manipulate profits and losses. The hedges on the Enron stock, in his view, were attempts to cover up the lack of an effective transfer of risk. He called it "an act of economic self-gratification." Third, Kaminski looked at the cash payouts that had been made to LJM2 and couldn't figure out where the money came from.

He grew worried about questions his research group had been asked to work out, questions that were narrow or vague, so the team couldn't tell their work was related to LJM or the Raptors. On October 2, Kaminski e-mailed Andersen for the first time, telling a partner there that the Raptors could either have the collar on Enron stock or have the stock at a discount, but not both. The next day, Kaminski notified Enron's global finance group that even if it meant he'd be fired, he would no longer sign off on anything related to LJM or the Raptors. On October 4, Kaminski ordered his group to stop work on LJM- or Raptor-related issues. He e-mailed Buy to say that he wouldn't sign off on any of the work his group had already done on LJM and Raptors in 2001 without first seeing all the legal documents. The e-mail never received a reply.

Enron had some good news to report. It had been looking for a new buyer for Portland General to replace Sierra Pacific, and on October 8 the company announced it had reached an agreement to sell the utility to Northwest Natural Gas. Northwest, Oregon's largest gas utility, would pay $1.88 billion for the company and assume $1.1 billion of its debt. This came on top of an earlier pledge by Lay that Enron would sell $4 billion to $5 billion of assets—mostly overseas assets—over the next two years. But that news would soon be overshadowed by Enron's bad news.

On October 16, the company released its third-quarter results. Surprising Wall Street, it reported a loss of $618 million, including a one-time charge of $1 billion. The charge included lowering the value of certain Azurix assets by $287 million; $180 million for restructuring Enron Broadband, including layoffs and losses on inventory; and $544 million for terminating the Raptors. The press release explained that last part as "related to losses associated with certain investments, principally Enron's interest in The New Power Company, broadband and technology investments, and early termination during the third quarter of certain structured finance arrangements with a previously disclosed entity." In a statement, Lay said the bundle of charges would "clear away issues that have clouded the performance and earnings potential of our core energy businesses."

Years earlier, Enron finessed its J-Block mishap with one bunch of charges and earned kudos. This time, the press coverage was anything but kind. In explaining the charges, the press described how the "structured finance arrangements" related to two partnerships that had until recently been run by Fastow. The *Wall Street Journal* said the charge "raises anew vexing conflict-of-interest questions."

Enron also reduced shareholder equity by $1.2 billion, as warranted by the corrected accounting treatment for the notes given by the Raptors. Shareholder equity fell to $9.5 billion. But, in a bad public-relations move, the company hadn't included this charge in its October 16 press release. Instead, company management disclosed it later in the day in a conference call with analysts and investors. Lay explained in the call that the charge covered the company's repurchase of 55 million shares of Enron stock from the Raptors (although he didn't mention them by name) as the company unwound the transactions. An Enron spokesman justified excluding the shareholder-equity reduction from the initial press release by saying it was "just a balance-sheet issue" and therefore not significant enough for disclosure.

But it seemed significant enough to rating agency Moody's, which put Enron debt on review for a possible downgrade because of the valuation write-downs and charges. Enron said the $1 billion reduction in shareholder equity raised its debt-to-equity ratio to 50 percent from 46 percent.

All the news about Fastow and the partnerships finally spurred Enron's board to inquire into how much money Fastow had made from managing the LJM entities. According to Lay, the board had trusted Fastow and couldn't imagine that he was making substantial sums of money from his LJM involvement. Fastow told directors that over the lives of the partnerships, he had made roughly $45 million from them. It's not clear how much of that came from management fees and how much from investment gains.

Lay described himself as "shocked." As he understood it, Fastow spent only three hours a week on LJM matters, and he believed Fastow had created LJM out of an obligation to the company. But Fastow made more from his involvement with LJM than from his position as CFO of Enron. Lay questioned whether Fastow lived up to his fiduciary duty to Enron.

Making matters worse, the *Wall Street Journal* broke the news on October 19 that Fastow had made substantial profits from managing the

LJM partnerships. The article didn't have the $45 million figure, but it did note that over the past year Fastow, and possibly some partnership associates, realized $7 million in management fees and $4 million in capital gains. The story pointed out that the partnerships had been set up to do business with Enron, and they sometimes profited from renegotiating existing deals with the company. Investors began to speculate that maybe Enron let Fastow make money from the partnerships as an incentive to stay with the company, even though that risked conflicts of interest. Enron's stock had been at $33.84 before the release of quarterly numbers, but three days later it closed at $26.05. Vinson & Elkins had been right after all about the serious risk of adverse publicity.

■ ■ ■

On October 22, Enron revealed that the SEC had asked for more information regarding the "related-party transactions." The company said it would cooperate fully and it looked forward to putting to rest any more concerns about the partnerships.

Given that Enron had been including allusions to related-party deals in cryptic footnotes in its financial statements for a while, why hadn't the SEC called sooner? It's the job of the SEC to review company financial statements and other investor disclosure documents, like stock offering prospectuses. But with over 10,000 public companies to monitor, the agency tried to review the annual reports of significant companies at least every three years. Enron's 2000 annual report came close to being reviewed, but SEC staff postponed it to allow Enron time to get used to new reporting requirements regarding derivatives. So the SEC had last done a thorough review of Enron's 1996 and 1997 annual reports.

Wall Street began to wonder about what other bad news lurked in Enron's finances. Analysts buzzed about the possibility that Enron might have to issue even more stock to other entities to cover deals pegged to Enron's stock price. Following news of the SEC inquiry, Enron's stock fell to $20.65—a drop of 21 percent in one day. And trading partners began to slowly back away from Enron.

Perhaps the stock market would have been more forgiving if Enron had released this news a year earlier. But in October 2001, the markets were in a sour mood. The bull market of 1996–2000, led by technology stocks, had been over for months. The Dow Jones Industrial Average and other leading stock indexes were all depressed. And on September 11, two hijacked U.S. airliners had crashed into New York's World Trade Center, destroying the two skyscrapers and killing thousands. Wall Street, a stone's throw from the Twin Towers, only became more nervous after the horrendous tragedy.

What caused Enron's downward spiral? The business world slowly lost confidence in Enron, and confidence may have been its most prized asset. As with any trader, only the assurance that Enron could back up its deals persuaded others to trade with it. But with confidence eroding, the liquidity started to disappear. Enron seemed liquid enough when it had a market capitalization of more than $60 billion—it could always, as it had in the past, issue some more stock. But as the stock price fell, and Enron's market capitalization shrank to roughly $17 billion, the stock market was no longer a viable option. Stock market value of $60 billion was not the same as assets of $60 billion, so suddenly Enron's large liabilities loomed even larger. The truth is, trading companies don't back up their business with their stock as Enron had. Nothing had gone fatally wrong, but Enron's cushion had shrunk.

The partnerships weren't the only details worrying Enron and investors. Enron revealed in its third-quarter earnings that its Global Assets division—which included such hard assets as Azurix, Enron Wind, Dabhol, and Brazil's Elektro utility—had generated just $12 million of income before interest and taxes in the first nine months of 2001, despite producing revenues of $1.1 billion. The company's profligate spending had come back to haunt it in the form of assets that were unprofitable or actively losing money. Enron had put most of those assets up for sale, and temporarily put them under the guidance of Stan Horton, the head of the pipeline group.

Clearly, the low returns on so many of the overseas investments only put more pressure on Enron's earnings and financial status. Observers speculated about Enron's ability to manage its far-flung portfolio of businesses and proceed with much-needed sales of underperforming assets amid the cloud of controversy gathering around it.

The same day that Enron disclosed the SEC inquiry, Lay oversaw a meeting of several dozen top executives. It had been scheduled weeks in advance to review the third quarter, but the agenda had changed. Now,

Lay said the meeting intended to unite management behind the board of directors. He also said that while Enron didn't do anything wrong, the company would never again do what it had done. When a tax department executive asked, "How can you say we didn't do anything wrong, but would never do it again?" he was met with stony silence. Derrick said the board approved the partnerships, so management should protect the board. Kaminski, attending the meeting, interrupted to say that management should protect the company, not the board. Lay countered that the board's approval implied that the partnerships were proper. But Kaminski said he had to disagree because the partnerships were improper. "The only fighting chance we have is to come clean," Kaminski said. Whalley calmly stopped Kaminski, saying, "Enough, Vince." No one at the meeting rose to agree with Kaminski, but afterward several managers called him to thank him for speaking up.

On October 23, Enron hosted a conference call with analysts and investors to discuss the partnerships. Lay said Enron's stock price disappointed him because the company's businesses were performing well and the company continued to conduct business as usual. Lay reiterated Enron's commitment to maintain its credit ratings. On the call, Fastow assured listeners that Enron had enough liquidity to conduct normal operations, and had billions of dollars of credit lines it could tap if necessary. "We have spoken to our key banks . . . and we expect to have their continued support," he said.

Once the conference dived into question-and-answer format, the call featured some testy exchanges. Richard Grubman, the investor Skilling had called an asshole, was back and this time he asked how Enron would pay the debt on the Marlin Water Trust when Enron had just lowered the valuation of assets owned by Azurix, Marlin's chief asset. When Enron personnel didn't answer the question to Grubman's satisfaction, Lay interrupted to say, "Now, I know you want to drive the stock price down, and you've done a good job at doing that, but I think that's that. Let's move on to the next question."

"That's pointless," Grubman replied. When Lay said Grubman was monopolizing the call and implied that his question wasn't real, Grubman said, "I would appreciate an answer to the question. That's fine if you move on. I think everybody understands why."

Several participants asked questions about other transactions in which

Enron might have to issue stock to cover obligations. John Olson, the analyst with Sanders Morris Mundy, asked for Fastow to explain his role as manager of the LJM partnerships. Lay explained that he'd rather Fastow not answer the question because the SEC had started looking into it.

The call exuded an overall tone of ambivalence from the investment community. "There is the appearance that you're hiding something," said David Fleischer, an analyst at Goldman Sachs. "I, for one, find the disclosure is not complete enough for me to understand and explain all the intricacies of those transactions. And that's why there are so many questions here. And I think you're now in a position where you really have to give us a lot more information."

Despite assurances to be more open, Lay seemed defensive and guarded throughout the call. Perhaps it was the pressure he was under, or perhaps Enron's years of protective aloofness took a while to wear off. Whatever the cause, it came out most explicitly in his defenses of Andrew Fastow. At one point, Lay said, "We're very concerned about the way Andy's character has been kind of loosely thrown about over the last few days in certain articles, as well as, of course, the integrity of the company." And he also said: "I and the board of directors continue to have the highest faith and confidence in Andy, and believe he is doing an outstanding job as CFO."

The next day, Enron put Fastow on a leave of absence and named Jeff McMahon the new chief financial officer.

13

RACING THE CLOCK

Enron executives thought the removal of Fastow from the CFO post—he would never return to the company, as it turned out—would soothe Wall Street's jangled nerves. "In my continued discussions with the financial community, it became clear to me that restoring investor confidence would require us to replace Andy as CFO," Lay said.

The blockbuster move, however, looked like the biggest red flag Enron could hoist, and so it scared the business community more than it appeased it. Enron never had the kind of top-notch credit rating typically awarded to big banks or huge corporations like GE. As a result, the company's trading business relied to a great extent on the business world's faith in Enron management, and any dip in that faith shook the company's standing as a trader. For weeks, utilities, trading firms, manufacturers, distributors, and banks had been withdrawing their trading from Enron in a small but steady trickle, but dumping Fastow turned that retreat into a flood of lost business. "The minute we fired him, people were backing out left and right," recalled a former trader.

Any weakness in Enron's massive trading operation would prove critical, because that business generated the bulk of its profits. In the most recent fiscal quarter, wholesale trading business accounted for 97 percent of the company's income before interest and taxes, or $754 million.

While traders still worked out complex deals by phone, the bulk of that trading business occurred on EnronOnline, a platform that had quickly expanded the volume Enron traded. The extent to which Enron-Online helped turbocharge the trading business can be seen in the company's assets and liabilities related to price risk management activity (i.e., trading). In 1999, Enron had trading-related assets of $2.2 billion and liabilities of $1.8 billion; but in 2000 it had trading-related assets of $12.2 billion and liabilities of $10.5 billion. "These numbers are staggering," opined Frank Partnoy, a professor of law at the University of San Diego Law School.

And even with the company's expansion into metals and other commodities, the majority of EnronOnline's trades dealt with gas or electricity. By the fall of 2001, EnronOnline handled $15 billion or more per month in trades, and all of that used trade credit. Counterparties such as Shell Oil, SoCal Gas, and others sold Enron energy on credit, and all the trades wouldn't have to be settled until four to six weeks later. In the past, getting that trade credit proved easy for Enron because the company controlled such a large portion of the gas and power markets: 25 percent of North America's gas and electricity by some accounts.

"People were granting us a lot of credit—probably more than we deserved with a BBB+ rating—because we were so big and so important in the markets," explained John Sherriff. "In hindsight, we never talked about how much trade credit we were being extended."

The founders of EnronOnline had anticipated all sorts of concerns, from growing the database to adding software to tracking all the credit and trades. But they hadn't thought about how much the online trading system would rely on credit given that Enron would be a counterparty to every trade. And that looked more and more like a fatal flaw as EnronOnline grew to use $5 billion, then $10 billion, then $20 billion in trade credit. "What would happened if we needed to come up with that in cash? Nobody had ever thought about that," admitted Sherriff.

In late October, counterparties gradually stopped extending credit to Enron. They wanted to be paid up front. That meant Enron could either come up with $20 billion in cash to back its monthly trading tab, or Enron could trade less. The company traded less. "That killed us," said Sherriff.

The outside world didn't know about this. Other traders suspected that EnronOnline's volumes declined, but no one firm had the full picture. And Enron didn't tell anyone, especially not Wall Street. So equity analysts continued to rally behind Enron's stock. Lehman Brothers analyst Richard Gross, for example, wrote in a report that the October 23 conference call with Lay "deteriorated into an inadequate defense of the balance sheet," but Gross still rated the stock "strong buy" because "the stock should recover sharply." Credit Suisse First Boston analyst Curt Launer, a longtime Enron fan, said, "I don't think my analysis has been as wrong as the stock has performed." And David Fleischer of Goldman Sachs, after his plea for greater disclosure on the conference call, kept recommending Enron stock.

If one believed that Enron shares would rebound, then the analysts had a point, because Enron's stock had fallen so far that it was now cheap on a price-to-earnings basis. Of course, that was a big "if," because a rebound could occur only if investors decided the newly unreliable Enron was worth more than the contrition-loaded, cheap stock price. At the same time, though, investors may have noticed that analysts (like Gross and Fleischer) had consistently supported the stock, even on its way down. In September, Enron's research coverage consisted of "buy" ratings from 16 analysts and a "hold" rating from one. By October 26, only Carol Coale of Prudential Securities downgraded Enron stock to "sell," and she lamented it was "too little, too late."

In retrospect, "what was missing in the case of Enron was skepticism," said William Mann, a senior analyst at The Motley Fool, an investing web site. Mann pointed out that equity analysts were predisposed to look for the positive in a stock, because that's what generates investment banking income.

Enron executives also sought to relieve those who worried about the company's debt and possible future obligations. Enron admitted that over the next 20 months, more than $3 billion worth of notes sold by Marlin Water Trust, Osprey Trust, and several other entities would come due. But the company said planned asset sales, including the sale of Portland General, would raise the money needed to repay those notes. In a worst-case scenario, Enron said it would have to issue about $1 billion in new stock to cover these obligations—and given the lower market value of the company, that would dilute the value of existing shares by more than 5 percent. Enron also drew $1 billion of cash from its bank credit lines to substantiate its claims of having enough short-term liquidity. "We are making it clear that Enron has the support of its banks and more than adequate liquidity to assure our customers that we can fulfill our commitments in the ordinary course of business," McMahon explained.

Inside the company, Lay had a harder time selling Enron's stability and promising future. On October 23, he held another all-employee meeting, but this time no one greeted him like a rock star. Instead of charming the crowd, Lay apologized. "I am absolutely heartbroken about what happened. . . . Many of you who were a lot wealthier six to nine months ago are now concerned about the college education for your kids, maybe the mortgage on your house, maybe your retirement," he said. "And for that I am incredibly sorry, but we are going to get it back."

Lay then read aloud employees' written questions and tried to answer them, and at one point he read this comment: "I would like to know if you are on crack. If so, that would explain a lot. If not, you may want to start because it is going to be a long time before we trust you again." To which Lay answered, "I think that's probably not a very happy employee and that's understandable." NBC News would get a tape of that moment the following January and show it over and over.

As October crawled to a close, Enron staffers may not have trusted Lay anymore, but they still believed, Enron-style, in their ability to outwit the market. So when Enron's stock hit $15 per share, more than a few saw it as a buying opportunity. Enron had spent a lot of time touting its stock to its employees. Vice presidents in the trading operation bought the stock, and junior employees who believed these savvy traders knew what they were doing followed suit.

It turned out to be a wrong bet. By November 6, Enron shares dropped below $10 a share. "We wound up selling at $7 or $7.50," recalled one former trader. John Spitz, the software developer, bought Enron stock as it went down and even past the $7 level. "People said it would go back up," he said.

■ ■ ■

People at Arthur Andersen also worried about Enron's decline. Four days before Enron issued the October 16 press release with the $1 billion in earnings charges, Duncan had a chance to see it. He questioned Enron's decision to characterize the charges—the charges for buying out the Raptors, restructuring Enron Broadband, and lowering the value of some Azurix assets—as "non-recurring." "We did not advise the use of 'non-recurring' as a description and were concerned it could potentially be misunderstood by investors," he wrote to a handful of colleagues. But Rick Causey told Duncan that the press release had gone through Enron's "normal legal review," and the phrase "non-recurring" stayed in the press release.

The day the press release hit the public, Nancy Temple, an in-house lawyer for Andersen, wrote back to Duncan (and Houston practice director Michael Odom) suggesting that Duncan delete references to "consultation with the legal group and deleting my name from the memo." She also recommended "deleting some language that might suggest we have concluded the release is misleading."

Temple's October 16 e-mail would later prove very significant. But Duncan and others at Andersen quickly turned their attention to the news that the SEC had begun an informal inquiry into Enron. On October 23, Duncan convened a conference-call meeting of Temple and other members of the "core consultation team," to discuss Enron, technical matters, legal issues, documentation, and Andersen's role. According to Andersen, Duncan on that day ordered Andersen personnel to begin destroying Enron-related documents—despite knowing about the SEC's inquiry.

No one disputed the fact that Andersen began shredding documents. But Duncan would later point to an October 12 e-mail from Temple as a nudge to start shredding. Her e-mail, sent to Odom, stated: "It might be useful to consider reminding the engagement team of our documentation and retention policy. It will be helpful to make sure that we have complied with the policy."

At Andersen, the documentation policy called for destroying many audit-related records once they were no longer needed; this meant disposing of drafts, personal notes, and other papers not necessary to support the audit report, leaving behind just the paperwork that supported the accounting judgments ultimately reached. Duncan believed this e-mail provided the green light to get started destroying the proper Enron-related documents, according to an assistant to Duncan.

Andersen employees working out of Enron's headquarters began shredding papers and deleting computer files. Andersen's paper shredder at Enron's building worked overtime, so employees sent trunks of documents to Andersen's Houston office for shredding. They erased computer files and e-mails. Similar document-destruction orders were given to Andersen employees attending to Enron matters in Portland, Chicago, and London.

On October 31, Enron disclosed that the SEC had upgraded the inquiry to a "formal investigation." But the shredding apparently continued. On November 8, the SEC served Andersen with a subpoena relating to its work for Enron. The next day, Andersen alerted employees that as a result of the subpoena there could be "no more shredding."

■ ■ ■

To many people, the term "accounting crisis" seems like it would be an oxymoron. Yet that's exactly what Enron faced. As its financial condition grew more precarious, Ken Lay alerted top federal officials. On October 26, Lay called the Federal Reserve chairman, Alan Greenspan, to inform him of Enron's problems.

And on October 28, Lay called U.S. Treasury Secretary Paul O'Neill—himself the former CEO of aluminum maker Alcoa—to notify him that Enron's problems "were mounting." Lay didn't ask for government help. Instead, he offered to have Enron executives speak with Treasury officials about the extent of Enron's troubles. O'Neill directed the Undersecretary of the Treasury to talk with Enron officials to gauge the potential impact of Enron's woes on the U.S. economy.

Lay's desire to keep Bush's cabinet in the loop on Enron's difficulties was understandable. The company was huge, and had thousands of contracts and trades worth billions of dollars, in addition to billions owed to banks. Given its broad web of connections, would a sudden collapse of Enron inflict wide-ranging damage on the financial markets? And on the economy? One parallel was the 1998 downfall of Long-Term Capital Management. The Federal Reserve's arrangement of a bailout of LTCM had been a very unusual move, but the financial world had evolved to the point where a large trading firm's problems could snowball into a market crisis. In the case of Long-Term Capital, the bailout averted any potential economic catastrophe, and now experts worried that Enron might be facing a similar situation. Lay even mentioned the LTCM analogy to O'Neill.

O'Neill told Undersecretary of the Treasury Peter Fisher to keep tabs on Enron and figure out what might happen if Enron went bankrupt. Fisher was a natural choice for this task, because his job involved monitoring financial markets. In addition, as an official with the Federal Reserve Bank of New York in 1998, Fisher played a key role in the LTCM rescue. So in late October and early November, Fisher spoke six or eight times with Enron president Greg Whalley. Recollections about those calls differ. According to the Treasury Department, Enron was trying to convince its banks to advance it more money, and Whalley asked Fisher to call the banks to support Enron's case. Enron, however, claimed that the calls were "informational," and not attempts to get federal help. Either way, Fisher by then didn't see Enron as having the same potential spillover effect as LTCM, and he made no effort to help the energy trader.

Enron later appealed to the Treasury Department through Robert Rubin, who had been the Treasury Secretary under President Clinton and was then a top executive at Citigroup, the parent of Citibank and one of Enron's two biggest lenders. On November 8, Rubin asked Fisher what he thought of calling the debt rating agencies and asking them to work with Enron's banks to prevent a downgrade of Enron's debt rating. Fisher said it wouldn't be appropriate for him to make those calls, and Rubin agreed with his position. Fisher never made the calls.

Enron also worked another angle. On October 29, Lay called U.S. Commerce Secretary Donald Evans, telling him that Moody's would likely downgrade Enron's debt rating. Lay said that if Evans could do anything to help Enron deal with Moody's it would be welcome. But Lay didn't ask Evans specifically to intervene with Moody's. Evans then told O'Neill about the call. "I don't think there was anything for us to do," Evans explained months later on a CNBC television program. "Secretary O'Neill agreed with me there was not so we didn't do anything." President Bush wasn't even told of the calls until the following January.

The same day as the call to Evans, Moody's went ahead and lowered its rating on Enron's debt a notch and placed its ratings on review for a possible further downgrade. The agency said the revelations of Enron's partnerships and equity charges "led to a substantial loss of investor confidence that has led to a more than halving of Enron's share price and difficulties in . . . [renewing short-term corporate notes known as] commercial paper." Lay's calls, if they were intended to obtain help, didn't do anything. Lay's access to Bush officials may have been impressive, but it didn't guarantee actual help. And although Moody's was still rating Enron's debt investment-grade, the company's situation clearly grew worse.

Sherron Watkins, who had warned all too prophetically about the accounting scandal, stepped in again with new advice for Lay: that he "come clean and admit problems." She suggested that she help with public relations and investor relations efforts. She met with Lay on October 30, and advocated that he "admit that he trusted the wrong people" and that he fire both Andersen and Vinson & Elkins. She also suggested that Enron restate its 2000 financials and Lay meet with top SEC officials.

If Enron took these steps, Watkins believed Enron's problems would be public knowledge and the company would face numerous shareholder lawsuits, but the speculation would die down. As she put it in a memo, "Nobody wants Ken Lay's head. He's very well respected in the business community. The culprits are Skilling, Fastow, Glisan and Causey as well as Arthur Andersen and V&E."

Lay didn't adopt Watkins' recommendations. What he and Enron's board *did* do, however, was finally arrange for an outside investigation of LJM and the other outside partnerships. On October 31, the board added William Powers Jr., the dean of the University of Texas Law School, as a new director. The rest of the board immediately appointed Powers to head a special board committee that would look into Enron's accounting issues. The committee included Frank Savage, who ran his own investment firm; Paulo Ferraz Pereira, an executive at a Brazilian investment bank; and Herbert S. Winokur Jr., who also headed an investment firm. To steer clear of Vinson & Elkins and Andersen, the committee retained Wilmer, Cutler & Pickering as its law firm, and Deloitte & Touche to provide accounting advice. Lay said the committee would "take a fresh look at these transactions."

The company then focused on the difficult task of assuring the markets that Enron had access to cash. The danger was that otherwise, trading counterparties would flee from Enron's signs of financial weakness, thus weakening Enron even more. It's a cruel irony of the financial markets that the more a company obviously needs cash, the less a bank is willing to provide it—the company's desire brands it as a poor risk. This catch-22 ensnared Enron.

Enron didn't find a perfect solution, but on November 1 it got a lifeline. Citigroup's Salomon Smith Barney brokerage business and J.P. Morgan Chase extended a $1 billion line of credit to the company. Unfortunately, as collateral for the $1 billion, Enron had to pledge its best pipelines, Transwestern Pipeline and Northern Natural Gas. In the third quarter of 2001, those two pipelines had generated a healthy $85 million in pretax profit on revenue of $450 million. Enron used $250 million of the $1 billion to refinance some of its debt that was going to mature soon, and then had the remaining $750 million to increase liquidity. It said the new credit line was intended to "restore investor confidence."

Yet, Standard & Poor's lowered the credit ratings a bit on the two pipelines, and also lowered its rating on Enron's long-term debt. S&P wondered if Enron would take on too much debt, and expressed skepticism that the company would regain its previous credit quality. And the new credit line did not appease the stock market; potentially mortgaging its safest assets smacked of desperation. Enron's stock fell 14 percent that day to $11.99 per share. By November 1, more than a dozen separate shareholder lawsuits had been filed against Enron.

With Enron's stock price so low, the business world began to speculate if the company was a candidate for a takeover by a stronger enterprise engaged in energy or trading. Would Enron, once a bold acquirer of assets around the world, become someone else's discount purchase?

■ ■ ■

At the behest of Enron's board, Andersen personnel were looking at the Chewco transaction again. As recounted in Chapter 7, Enron created Chewco as an independent SPE to buy out CalPERS' stake in the JEDI partnership. The outside equity in Chewco was $16.6 million contributed by Barclays. But on reviewing that detail, Andersen and Enron accounting employees decided that because Enron backed the Barclays contribution with $6.6 million in collateral, the $16.6 million was not "at risk" in case of a loss. For Chewco to have been considered independent, the 3 percent of outside equity had to be at risk. As a result, Chewco should have been consolidated into Enron's financial statements in 1997—and, therefore, JEDI should have been as well. That meant more than three years of financial statements were wrong.

Enron filed restated financial results with the SEC on November 8. Including the losses incurred by JEDI in Enron Corp.'s finances reduced Enron's reported net income by $96 million in 1997, $113 million in 1998, $250 million in 1999, and $132 million in 2000, but increased net income by $5 million in the first three quarters of 2001. In all, Enron revealed that it had overstated its earnings by a total of $586 million over four and three-quarters years.

In addition, Enron had to include JEDI's debt with its own. This meant that Enron's debt should have been $711 million higher in 1997, $561 million higher in 1998, $685 million higher in 1999, and $628 million higher in 2000.

In one day, the restatement added $2.59 billion of debt to Enron's books and wiped away roughly 20 percent of its earnings for the prior five years. Enron's 1998, 1999, and 2000 earnings all should have been lower, and its 1997 results should have shown a loss of 1 cent per share rather than net income of 16 cents.

Enron also said it had discovered that employees other than Fastow had invested in the controversial partnerships—Kopper, Anne Yaeger, Kathy Lynn, Ben Glisan, and Kristina Mordaunt. The first three no longer worked at Enron, and the company said it was firing Glisan, the company treasurer, and Mordaunt, an in-house lawyer.

"We believe that the information we have made available addresses a number of the concerns that have been raised by our shareholders and the SEC about these matters," Lay said in a press release.

Fitch credit analyst Ralph Pellecchia said the latest SEC filing might further hurt Enron's credit rating. "It's bad," he said flatly.

Enron's restatement of its results was only the most famous incident in an era when restatements had mushroomed. The early and mid-1990s never featured more than 59 earnings restatements in any one year. But there were 204 restatements in 1999, 163 in 2000, and 158 in 2001. Restatements blossomed in the late 1990s because of the rise in the uncertainty and volatility of the business environment at the time, and because of the pressure from Wall Street to meet or beat the earnings forecasts of financial analysts; this led managements such as Enron's to try to "manage" their quarterly numbers, only to see many of these efforts inevitably reversed.

Enron's restatement may have shot any remaining investor confidence in the company. If the buyout of the Raptors were strike one, and disclosing Fastow's involvement with LJM were strike two, then the restatement stemming from the mistaken accounting of Chewco was a swinging strike three. On the day Enron unveiled its restatement, its battered stock fell another 7 percent to $8.41.

Enron had its back to the wall, and regaining the trust of Wall Street would be daunting, even doubtful. "It is not possible to recover from a loss of investor confidence by some quick management actions," said Bala Dharan, an accounting professor at Rice University. He said the "process of rebuilding trust often takes place through several quarters of reliable financial disclosures." With a massive trading business that lived or died on credit, Enron just didn't have that kind of time.

■ ■ ■

If Ken Lay gave the impression of being a well-read uncle, Chuck Watson had the air of being a gregarious fraternity president. Watson was born in 1950 and, as the son of a Navy man, lived snatches of his childhood in nine different states. But even as an adult, rooted in Houston, he was always in motion. After years as a gas trader for Conoco, in 1985 he became the head of Natural Gas Clearinghouse and led it to its transformation to NGC and then to Dynegy.

Watson hooked his company up with well-heeled investor/partners in Chevron Corp. and Nova Corp. He bought gas processing plants and power plants, and then bought an electric utility in Illinois. Dynegy became one of the largest gas and electricity traders behind Enron. But while Enron pursued its asset-light strategy, the strategy of Dynegy chairman and CEO Charles Watson was to be asset-medium: exploiting the assets for trading purposes, but also owning the assets just in case.

Dynegy had assembled an impressive combination of energy trading ability, pipelines, and power plants, yet to an extent Dynegy lived for years in Enron's shadow. Enron landed on magazine covers as the energy pioneer, while NGC/Dynegy appeared to safely follow into markets after Enron scouted them out. And while Lay aspired to hobnob with Nobel economists and diplomats, Watson indulged his love of sports. He owned a minority stake in the Houston Texans National Football League team, and he owned the Houston Aeros, a minor-league hockey team. "He's a bright, fun guy to be with," said Raymond Plank, founder and head of the Houston-based oil and gas company Apache. "He's a human dynamo—lots of energy."

Watson's opportunity to finally top Enron arose in late October. That was when Stan Horton, head of Enron's gas pipelines group, had revealed

Enron's problems to Dynegy's second in command and the two discussed the concept of a merger. Their informal talks led to a meeting between Lay and Watson in Lay's home on the last weekend in October. On November 7, Enron's board tentatively approved a deal to merge with Dynegy. Rumors of the deal had begun to leak out. On Friday, November 9, the two companies made an official announcement at a joint press conference. Enron would merge with Dynegy.

In truth, the "merger" would actually be the purchase of Enron by Dynegy. Dynegy agreed to pay 0.2685 shares for each share of Enron, which worked out to roughly $9.80 per share, for a total purchase price of about $9 billion. Dynegy shareholders would own 64 percent of the new company, Chuck Watson would remain chairman and CEO, and Dynegy's Steven Bergstrom would retain the post of president and chief operating officer. Lay would not have a role in day-to-day operations. Assuming that Enron had aired all of its problems, the deal would be a steal for Dynegy: Just $9 billion would get it EnronOnline and Enron's vaunted trading operation, in addition to its solid pipeline business.

Importantly, ChevronTexaco, the oil giant that remained a longtime shareholder of Dynegy, agreed to invest $2.5 billion of equity into the combined company—$1.5 billion into Dynegy immediately, then another $1 billion into the bigger Dynegy once the Enron acquisition closed. As evidence of how shaky Enron's finances were, Dynegy announced that it would use the $1.5 billion to provide financing to Enron by purchasing preferred stock in Enron's Northern Natural Gas pipeline.

The merger would require the approval of shareholders of both companies. On completion, the new Dynegy would have over $200 billion in annual revenue—making it one of the largest companies in the world—and over $90 billion in assets. "The merger protects Enron's core franchise and enables the stockholders of both companies to participate in the tremendous upside of the combined enterprise," Lay said in a statement. "The company we are creating will have a strong balance sheet, a world-class merchant energy operation, and ample liquidity."

If anything framed the depth of Enron's problems, the merger did. The proud company had agreed to be taken over by its longtime smaller rival, like Pepsi taking over Coca-Cola, because it saw no other way out. It needed Dynegy, a white knight, to rescue it. Combined with Dynegy, the larger company could handle Enron's $13 billion of balance-sheet debt, as well as the possible obligations of some $4 billion in off-balance sheet debt that Enron had disclosed.

Dynegy was taking a chance. Companies open their books to each other before signing merger agreements, but Enron's books were particularly complex, and many of its problems were hidden off its books. Although Watson confidently claimed that Enron had bared its financial soul to Dynegy, Enron could still have more skeletons in its closet. Dynegy took the risk because the merger would make it the biggest energy trader and the biggest pipeline company, and would, by the company's calculation, provide an immediate boost to its earnings.

Under normal circumstances, a proposed marriage of Enron and Dynegy might have been a tough sell to regulators because of the market dominance the combination would have in energy trading—no other company would have half as much market share in wholesale gas and electricity trading. But Enron and Dynegy expressed no concerns about gaining the needed government approvals for their merger. That indicated the level of concern that had gripped the gas and electricity markets in the previous few weeks; other companies, and a few government officials, worried that a sudden collapse by Enron would wreak havoc on wholesale energy markets. There were many people outside of Enron and Dynegy hoping that the companies' merger would work.

That day, Lay sent a mass voice mail message to Enron employees announcing the deal. "Together, we will be a new merchant energy powerhouse. This transaction confirms the substantial value of Enron's core businesses," he said. "We have an enormously bright future as a combined company."

■ ■ ■

The merger deal staved off what could have been debilitating action from the credit rating agencies. On October 29, Moody's Investors Service had lowered its rating on Enron's debt from Baa1 to Baa2, and placed its ratings on review for a possible further downgrade. By November, it was worried that Enron no longer warranted an investment-grade rating. If it had lowered the credit rating to junk status, doing so would have mostly shut down Enron's trading business because other companies would not trade with a counterparty whose rating was junk grade. But with Dynegy's agreement to buy Enron, Moody's held off lowering the credit rating and looked at the new situation: Enron was going to be bought by the more stable Dynegy, and the deal included an additional $1.5 billion in equity from ChevronTexaco. If all this did happen, then Moody's decided that a merged Dynegy-Enron would deserve a "marginally" investment-grade rating. This decision would later inspire critics to claim that Moody's and its peers waited too long to downgrade Enron.

The opinion of Moody's and other credit rating agencies was extremely important. Although these agencies are private, for-profit companies, they were designated by the Securities and Exchange Commission to serve in their unique roles as quasi-public judges of credit quality. In addition to rating the debt of corporations, they rate the debt and credit quality of nations; and by judging what is "investment grade" debt, they determine what bonds banks can hold. Through industry consolidation, as of late 2001, there were three such agencies whose ratings were acceptable by the Securities and Exchange Commission—in order of importance, Moody's, Standard & Poor's, and Fitch Investor's Service. The agencies are registered with the SEC as investment advisers, and regulated as such. There were times—such as when huge investment losses led Orange County, California, to declare bankruptcy in 1994—when the SEC thought about closer regulation of these agencies, given their almost royal authority. But the SEC never reached consensus on changing its oversight of the credit rating agencies. So they retained their special roles as independent yet quasi-government agencies.

And the power of the credit rating agencies would prove to be decisive. Although Moody's decided to wait on the Dynegy acquisition, the agency had some concerns about the terms of the purchase agreement. The merger contract allowed Dynegy to pull out of the deal if Enron's credit rating fell to junk status, although the pending merger was the only thing keeping the rating above junk status. These and other provisions suggested that the merger might fall apart. Moody's wanted to downgrade Enron's rating to junk status, and called Enron on November 8 to say so. Enron convinced Moody's to hold off by disclosing that another $1 billion in investment would be coming, that the merger deal had been amended so that a rating downgrade couldn't trigger Dynegy's pullout, and that the lead banks had promised to put in another $500 million. The next day, Moody's downgraded Enron's long-term debt rating from Baa2 to Baa3, which was only just investment grade, and also downgraded its short-term debt rating. This mini-downgrade aimed to signal that Enron's short-term debt was not investment grade but its long-term rating was still barely investment grade.

Standard & Poor's had also been monitoring Enron's debt rating, and worried that the company was unable to calm investor fears about the core trading business. On November 9, S&P downgraded Enron's debt rating to BBB– from BBB, and said Enron's rating was being monitored for further downgrades. S&P explained that the pending Dynegy merger kept Enron's rating from dropping to junk status.

The S&P downgrade had one outcome that outsiders hadn't anticipated: It triggered a clause in one of Enron's loan agreements suddenly making a $690 million note come due. The note, originally due in 2003, related to one of Enron's off-balance sheet partnerships, which explained why rating agencies hadn't known about it. The company had until November 27 to repay the $690 million unless it posted collateral; if not, investors in the note had the right to liquidate the partnership. Enron revealed this $690 million obligation in SEC documents it filed November 19, which surprised the credit rating agencies.

Lay tried to help damp the outrage over Enron's dire straits; on November 13, he announced that he'd forgo a severance payment of $60.6 million that could be triggered by Dynegy's planned acquisition of Enron. But trading companies continued to pull back from Enron and place their trades elsewhere. Intercontinental Exchange, the rival Internet marketplace to EnronOnline, reported a sharp rise in activity in energy and metals trading on its platform.

On November 14, Lay and Whalley held another conference call with analysts and investors, this time to explain the transition strategy. Enron had reviewed its many assets, and now had a much larger category of noncore assets. "We have over $8 billion invested in these businesses and the return from these businesses and investments is terrible," Whalley said. So, he explained, Enron hoped to sell these assets, which included the Dabhol plant, Portland General, nonenergy wholesale businesses (like pulp and paper), and the broadband business.

Lay also took the opportunity to acknowledge Enron's missteps, and provided a surprisingly apt explanation of a large part of the cause of Enron's downfall. "In hindsight, we made some very bad investments in non-core businesses," he said. "Our investments in various international assets . . . performed far worse than we could ever have imagined when we made these investments. Because of the investments and other matters, Enron became over-leveraged. While the poor performance of our investments was bad enough, the negative impact of these investments on the company has been exacerbated through the extensive use of debt capital, both on and off the balance sheet. We entered into related-party transactions that produced various conflicts of interest, both real and perceived. . . . And on top of it all, we discovered and disclosed errors in our financial statements, which will require restatement of our previously reported financial statements. We fully understand and regret that the combination of these events has resulted in the complete loss of investor confidence."

Still, Enron's financial situation continued to deteriorate. In a November 19 filing of its third-quarter report with the SEC (the same one in which it revealed the $690 million note), Enron warned that continuing credit worries, a decline in the value of some of its assets, and reduced trading activity could hurt its fourth-quarter earnings. Enron said it was seeing less trading with its counterparties, and fewer long-term trades in particular. In addition to those potential ill effects on its fourth quarter, Enron said investors should expect some hits on its income from the company's scramble to shore up its finances. In the filing, Enron put it bluntly: "The fourth quarter of 2001 will likely be negatively impacted by severance, restructuring, and other charges resulting from the repositioning of many of Enron's businesses consistent with the restructuring plan, as well as potential writedowns."

The quarterly filing contained yet another small bomb: Enron had financial arrangements—beyond the $690 million note—tied to maintaining specific credit ratings. If its credit rating fell below investment grade and its stock were to drop "below a specified price," that could trigger the need to repay or provide collateral for $3.9 billion of debt— the bulk of which was $2.4 billion of debt in Osprey Trust and $915 million in Marlin Water Trust. It gave Enron more reason to be paranoid about its credit rating.

The filing also revealed that Enron had a cash balance of $1.2 billion as of November 16, meaning it had burned through roughly $2.5 billion in the seven weeks since the end of the third quarter. With the company perilously close to owing additional billions, it was a bad time to be going through money so quickly. The news soured investors further. Analysts withdrew their support. Enron's stock plummeted from $9.06 to $6.99, a staggering drop of 23 percent.

The November 19 filing stunned people. It even stunned executives at Dynegy, who hadn't known of the $690 million note. Also, the acquiring company had expected the quarterly report to show $3 billion in cash, but it showed just $1.2 billion. "Despite assurances that Enron's liquidity situation had stabilized, the cash [the $1.5 billion Dynegy had provided] was gone in less than three weeks, and Enron has had difficulty providing accounting as to where it went," Watson would later say.

With Enron's stock slide, Dynegy's agreement now called for it to pay more than double Enron's stock price, a hefty premium for a company that was so plainly tottering. Nevertheless, Dynegy put out a cheery announcement on November 21 to say that it closed the remaining $450 million of the $1 billion line of credit provided by J.P. Morgan Chase and Citigroup and secured by Enron's Northern Natural Gas pipeline. Dynegy also noted that J.P. Morgan and Citigroup agreed to give Enron a three-week extension to mid-December to repay the $690 million note. Of course, because most of Enron's debts to banks were not secured by any assets, it was in the interests of the banks to do everything possible to keep Enron afloat. Dynegy reiterated its commitment to the acquisition, saying in a statement: "We are working . . . to accelerate the regulatory approvals required to complete the merger in accordance with the previously announced agreement." Dynegy's comments didn't reassure the market; Enron's stock fell to $5.01.

■ ■ ■

Inside Enron, the mood darkened. Trading activity eased up so much that traders were bored. Some employees were coming in at 10 A.M. and leaving at 3 P.M. Others packed boxes and spent their time looking for other jobs. "There was nothing to do. Every day you just sat there wondering if this would be your last day," said Beau Ratliff.

On November 23, the day after Thanksgiving, Enron gathered Dynegy executives and both companies' platoons of bankers and lawyers in Houston. Enron executives admitted to their Dynegy counterparts that Enron's core trading businesses in North America and Europe were practically shut down. Enron needed several billion dollars in immediate liquidity and balance sheet restructuring. So began a series of talks between the two companies to rework, and thereby save, the planned merger.

Agreements needed to be reached quickly, because further erosion of Enron's financial status could spark credit rating agencies to cut Enron's debt to junk grade. And Enron knew the merger agreement allowed Dynegy to walk away from the deal if Enron's debt fell below investment-grade rating. The talks, shielded from the public, continued over the weekend in the New York area. Enron expressed a willingness to reduce its selling price by half. Enron and Dynegy tentatively reached a new deal by November 26. But Watson explained that he needed his board's approval.

Moody's, still monitoring the situation, didn't like what it saw. Enron continued to burn through cash. The agency had found out that banks were reluctant to provide $1 billion in credit lines that Enron had trumpeted. And the new merger terms being discussed by the companies no longer included an equity infusion of $1 billion, but an investment below that figure. Around Thanksgiving the firm figured that the odds of the Dynegy merger happening had grown much slimmer. Moody's decided on November 27 to downgrade Enron's credit rating to B2, below investment-grade status, and made its announcement the next morning.

Also on November 28, S&P determined that the Dynegy merger was unlikely to come off. That merger had been the only thing buoying Enron's debt rating, so that agency, too, downgraded Enron; in this case, it lowered the company to a B– rating, which was noninvestment-grade. "A collapse of the Dynegy deal would create enormous pressures on Enron's credit profile," S&P said in a statement. "A move by Enron to seek protection from creditors through a voluntary filing under Chapter 11 of the U.S. Bankruptcy Code is a distinct possibility if the merger falls through."

By now, Enron employees were using their computers to search the Internet for news on their company; web sites offering news updates and television sets tuned to market news provided much more information than Enron itself did. The news of the credit rating downgrades flashed across Enron computer and TV screens, and the workers knew it was over. "People just stopped working," Francisco Duque recalled. Louise Kitchen ordered EnronOnline employees to shut the service down. One trader said, "Traders went out and bought a bunch of vodka and beer and got drunk on the trading floor."

As expected, Dynegy notified Enron that it would terminate the merger agreement. Dynegy would explain that Enron's "breaches of representations" forced it to back out. Enron announced the merger termination and said that it would temporarily suspend all payments, other than those necessary to maintain core operations. With the merger's failure, Lay said, "We are evaluating and exploring other options to protect our core energy businesses."

At the New York Stock Exchange, Enron shares rode a whirlwind. A total of approximately 181.8 million shares changed hands at the exchange, setting a new record for the busiest trading session by any single stock in the NYSE's history. Enron's stock, which had been worth more than $80 not 12 months earlier, ended the day at 61 cents per share, just a fraction of the cost of a soda at Enron Field.

Enron had essentially collapsed, but the collapse didn't hurt wholesale electricity and gas prices as many had feared. Volatility increased, but the markets continued trading just as before. That's because well before Enron declared bankruptcy, other traders in the markets began adjusting their positions to essentially eliminate Enron from trades—in other words, they began trading around Enron, avoiding it as a counterparty. As Dynegy's Bergstrom explained in a conference call later that day: "Fortunately, because this has drug on for awhile, the industry has had several weeks to prepare for this event. It has adjusted to neutralize its position and is spreading the risk, working with many industry players. The market as a whole has shown no signs of degradation, just shifting of business between players. Dynegy and its industry peers have been absorbing liquidity demand for energy, supply and logistics, and risk management needs."

Without the merger, Enron had nothing to fall back on. Following Skilling's philosophy, the company had emphasized "virtual" assets, such as intellectual property, a talent to innovate, financial acumen, and reputation. But, unlike a factory or a pipeline, those intangible assets can decrease in value suddenly. That's what happened to Enron. Suddenly, all those intangible assets seemed worthless.

Enron's next steps were obvious. Enron gathered its lawyers to assemble a list of creditors. Then on Saturday, December 1, Enron's board met and approved a motion to declare bankruptcy. The next day, using the Internet, Enron electronically filed for Chapter 11 bankruptcy protection. Lay's dream of creating the world's leading company was dead.

14

ENDGAME

In filing for bankruptcy, Enron listed assets of roughly $62 billion, making it the largest bankruptcy in U.S. history at that time. Even that milestone would be erased in July 2002, when WorldCom filed for bankruptcy with over $100 billion in assets. But it was still an unusually dramatic defeat for a company that had once been valued at more than $100 billion by the stock market.

In its filing, Enron specifically blamed the failure of the Dynegy merger, which it claimed made it unable to rework its obligations and secure more funds outside of court. Rather than file in Houston, Enron filed Chapter 11 in New York bankruptcy court, which had expertise in complicated bankruptcy cases. And it would be a complicated process, thanks to Enron's dense morass of SPEs and partnerships. The company had many SPEs, including: Osprey Trust; Whitewing Associates; LJM; LJM Cayman; Condor; Raptors I, II, III, and IV; Chewco Investments; Firefly; JEDI; Rawhide Investors; Ponderosa Assets; Zephyrus; Choctaw; Timberwolf; Porcupine; Cornhusker; Slapshot; Marlin Water Trust; and others. Poring over the financial documents also revealed that Enron made ample use of U.S. companies' ability to incorporate subsidiaries in Aruba, Bermuda, and other offshore locations as a way of reducing tax costs. But, while a corporation such as AT&T had 36 offshore subsidiaries, Enron had a staggering 2,800 offshore units.

The combined list of people and companies owed money by Enron filled 54 pages. Filing for Chapter 11 also meant Enron didn't have to immediately liquidate the company: Chapter 11 bankruptcies allow the debtor to remain in possession of the business while sheltering it from debt collection efforts so that the bankrupt company can restructure its obligations. In practice, creditors usually have to accept far less than what they are owed, sometimes as little as 20 cents on the dollar. Common shareholders, who have the lowest priority in a bankruptcy case, often wind up with nothing.

Technically, although the main corporation filed for bankruptcy, not all of Enron Corp. filed. Enron had roughly 3,500 companies and subsidiaries. Only 68 subsidiaries filed for bankruptcy, so there were still many Enron companies that were not bankrupt—the main one being its pipeline business. Enron set to work right away to arrange financing in order to keep its healthy businesses breathing.

Within a day, Enron arranged up to $1.5 billion in "debtor-in-possession" financing from J.P. Morgan Chase and Citigroup. The so-called DIP financing gave Enron a line of credit it could use to keep its business operating. The banks handed Enron the first dollop of the new money, $250 million, later that week. The DIP financing, in addition to becoming higher priority than Enron's other debt, fetched sizable fees for J.P. Morgan and Citigroup—immediate fees of $6.25 million, plus the promise of similar fees as Enron borrowed more from the credit line.

Enron being Enron, it couldn't go down without a fight. At the same time that the company filed for bankruptcy, it also filed a lawsuit against Dynegy for terminating the merger—and also for claiming ownership of the Northern Natural Gas pipeline, which Dynegy had essentially bought with its $1.5 billion infusion into Enron. In a suit filed in U.S. Bankruptcy Court in New York, Enron claimed that Dynegy breached its merger agreement by terminating the deal when it didn't have the right to do so and that Dynegy had no right to the pipeline, and asked for $10 billion in damages. "Dynegy knew that Enron was in precarious financial condition, was on the verge of dropping to a noninvestment-grade credit rating, and was in no small measure dependent on the successful completion of the Merger for its very survival. In executing the Merger Agreement, Dynegy obligated itself to complete the Merger," Enron's suit stated. It further claimed that Dynegy undermined public confidence in its commitment to the merger as an excuse to back out of the deal and keep the pipeline.

Dynegy, not surprisingly, saw things differently. "Enron's lawsuit against Dynegy has no merit whatsoever in law or fact, and is one more example of Enron's failure to take responsibility for its demise," Watson said in a statement. "Enron's rapid disintegration is the result of a general loss of public confidence, fueled by the startling disclosures on November 19 of new and adverse information."

Enron may have declared an unprecedented bankruptcy, but it was one of many, many Chapter 11 cases. The year 2001 set a record for bankruptcies by public companies, with 257. That record total represented $258.5 billion in assets held by those companies. Although each company obviously had its own reasons for declaring bankruptcy, it was clear that Enron was not the only corporation to overreach during the bull market of the 1990s.

■ ■ ■

While sorting out that legal tangle with Dynegy and obtaining funds, Enron also had to deal with its staff. On December 2, Enron still employed 25,000 people around the world. That number shrank the next day, which inside the company came to be known as Black Monday. That day, Enron laid off roughly 4,000 employees, the bulk of whom worked in Houston. The company had already laid off some 1,100 in the United Kingdom the day before. Most of the Houston layoffs were announced in the morning. First, the computer network and e-mail went down, then employees were gathered in conference rooms and auditoriums and laid off in bunches.

Diana Peters recalled being told that the entire headquarters had a half hour to evacuate, and then people could call back to find out the status of their jobs. "As employees left, they carried out desk supplies, printers, and even computers, and security guards didn't stop them," she said. Vice president Allan Sommer had to collect his entire technology staff of around 290 and tell them they were being let go. "It was the hardest thing I had to do professionally," he said. A week later, Enron would lay off Sommer, too.

On top of everything, the layoffs not only occurred during a slowdown in the U.S. economy characterized by a tight job market, but also featured a surprising twist in that the fired employees didn't receive the severance pay they'd expected. The Enron benefit plan called for employees who were laid off due to company reorganization to receive a severance check with one week of salary for each year of employment at Enron, plus one week of salary for each $10,000 of base pay. So, many employees expected to receive severance payments of $10,000, $15,000, or more. Instead, Enron gave every laid-off worker a severance payment of just $4,500.

"It was a nightmare. I'd hung in there because I had seven or eight months' severance coming to me. But I got nothing," said John Allario, who'd worked at Enron for more than five years. "It was heartbreaking."

In 2002, a coalition of over 400 laid-off Enron employees filed a class action lawsuit against Enron and won status as a creditor in the bankruptcy proceedings. And in June, Enron committed another $30 million to its laid off, meaning severance could rise to $7,900 per employee, which still fell far short of their original expectations.

Despite the infighting, the uncertainty, and the intense pressure of Enron's corporate culture, many laid-off Enron employees were sad not just because they were leaving regular paychecks. Many missed the autonomy they were given, the camaraderie of smart, driven colleagues, and the freedom to be creative. "There were just a lot of bright people in one place," explained John Spitz. "I came up with an idea to try to commoditize air cargo. Based on a 15-page proposal I put together, they let me try it," Allario recalled fondly. Then he said with a mix of wistfulness and embarrassment: "We really believed anything could be done."

The layoffs were bad enough, but even Enron employees who remained with the company had to contend with retirement savings plans that had been wrecked by the company's collapse. Like many companies, Enron offered its workers a 401(k) retirement savings plan that allowed them to invest a portion of their salaries in mutual funds or in company stock, and these investments represented a tax-deferred plan for retirement. Enron encouraged its employees to invest these funds in Enron stock, and, again like many other companies, it also matched employee contributions with Enron stock.

The result was dreadful. The value of the plans plummeted along with Enron's stock price. Worse, Enron happened to be changing administrators of the plan, so it "locked down" the 401(k) plan from October 17 to November 19. During that time, plan participants couldn't change their holdings or sell their Enron stock.

In late November, members of the 401(k) plan filed two separate lawsuits against Enron, claiming that the lock-down period—which isn't uncommon—forced employees to remain invested in the plunging stock. The suits also claimed that Enron failed to advise employees to diversify their holdings and failed to adequately warn employees about the risks of investing so much of their savings in Enron stock; some employees put all their 401(k) plan money into Enron shares. About $1.3 billion of the $2.1 billion of assets in Enron's 401(k) plan was invested in Enron stock by the end of 2000, according to one of the lawsuits.

Among the victims was Charles Prestwood, who worked for Houston Natural Gas and then Enron, and who had retired October 1, 2000. "I had all my savings, everything in Enron stock. I lost $1.3 million," he said. "When we were locked down, we couldn't get to our stock, and we couldn't get to our broker to move that stock out because it was in the process of being transferred to another company."

Another victim was Robert Vigil, an electrical machinist working for Portland General. When Enron bought Portland General in 1997, Enron converted all the Portland General stock in the utility's 401(k) plan to Enron stock. This sank large portions of his savings—and the savings of many of his coworkers—into Enron stock. And as the company made more matching contributions, their exposure to Enron stock rose. According to Vigil, the company's matching contributions (made in Enron stock) couldn't be traded if the employee was under age 50; employees over 50 could trade only 25 percent of the company's contribution each year. As a result, even those employees who had tried to bail out of Enron stock before the October meltdown began were often stuck in Enron stock. "It is estimated that Enron's collapse resulted in employee pension plan losses of up to $1 billion," Vigil said. But he noted, "If my eight coworkers alone lost $2.8 million, that estimate is low."

Why didn't Enron employees simply diversify their investments more? Enron's active touting of its stock to its own workforce apparently worked. Employees who were filled with pride about working for Enron also proudly invested 401(k) money in Enron's stock—and, after all, it had been a terrific investment until 2001. "They were always talking about the stock price," explained John Spitz. "They always said the stock was undervalued."

So Diana Peters saw her 401(k) savings drop from $22,000 to $4,000 as Enron's stock collapsed. "It's like psychologically and financially we've been assaulted," she said.

■ ■ ■

At Enron, the pain continued. Although the company was back in oper ation and even conducting a little trading, on December 7 it laid off another 200 employees at its power trading business. That brought total layoffs to 5,300.

But some of those who remained at Enron benefited from the company's desperation. Around the time of the latest round of layoffs, the press publicized the fact that just before declaring bankruptcy Enron paid out $55 million in special "retention" bonuses to roughly 500 employees it deemed critical. Enron needed top employees to remain if the company would survive, so it justified the payments as "necessary to maintain and protect the value of the estate." The payments averaged $110,000 apiece, although they varied widely.

Just what kind of company these crucial employees would help survive became clearer on December 12, when Ken Lay unveiled Enron's reorganization plan to the company's eager but skeptical creditors. Giving the presentation to hundreds of creditors in a ballroom at the New York Hilton Hotel, Lay said Enron hoped to restructure its way out of bankruptcy court protection within 12 months, which would include some $6 billion worth of asset sales that would help pay off creditors.

The plan called for Enron to sell control of its vaunted trading business to a partner with a strong balance sheet and the remaining company to focus on pipelines and power plants. Lay envisioned a surviving Enron that owned the same interstate pipeline system, Portland General, a few international projects, Enron Energy Services, and a wholesale energy sales business. The challenge: Enron had, according to this plan, some $39 billion in debt and other obligations, only $22 billion of which was carried on its books. As a result, the plan spelled out bluntly: "Enhancing cash flow is a top priority." Lay said after the meeting that he was "committed" to seeing the restructuring through to its end.

The trustee overseeing the bankruptcy case appointed a 15-member committee to represent Enron's creditors in negotiations over the Chapter 11 process. The creditors committee included J.P. Morgan Chase, Citigroup, and Duke Energy, among other firms. Enron's 10 biggest bank lenders, with J.P. Morgan and Citigroup leading the way, accounted for more than $7.5 billion of Enron's debt.

Meanwhile, investigations into Enron proliferated. Several congressional committees held hearings, and another half dozen announced that they planned to hold hearings in 2002. Legislators and Wall Street professionals began to wonder why research analysts hadn't caught any of the problems at Enron, and whether Andersen's consulting work compromised the integrity of its audit work at Enron. Newspapers also reported that the U.S. Justice Department began its own inquiry into Enron.

Dynegy, Mirant, and other Enron rivals weren't left untouched by the widening scandal. Enron's woes made investors nervous about energy-trading companies in general, and put credit rating agencies on high alert about credit issues among energy traders. Not two weeks after Enron filed Chapter 11, Dynegy had to issue a statement that it was confident it had enough capital for its trading operation and that it was reviewing its debt structure. That announcement followed a downgrade by Moody's, which cut Dynegy's credit rating to Baa3, just one notch above junk status. El Paso Corp., a pipeline company and big energy trader, quickly disclosed plans to sell $2.25 billion of assets and cut capital spending by $900 million. El Paso noted that "the credit requirements in our industry have changed," and pledged to rejigger two off-balance sheet financing entities.

Mirant, the energy trader spun off from electric utility Southern Co., announced plans to raise $759 million in a stock offering. Despite that move, Moody's lowered its rating on Mirant's debt to junk status. And after several days of consideration, Dynegy announced plans to shore up its balance sheet by selling $500 million in stock and $750 million in assets. Nevertheless, Moody's struck again, downgrading Dynegy's credit rating to its lowest investment-grade rating. Dynegy's stock plunged by 22 percent over one week. During that same time, Mirant shares dropped by 40.5 percent. Enron had focused everyone's eyes on balance sheets, and the energy-trading sector would never be the same again.

But Dynegy did get one piece of good news. On January 3, 2002, Enron settled its dispute with Dynegy over ownership of the Northern Natural Gas pipeline. The pipeline is a prize asset, capable of transporting roughly 8 percent of total U.S. natural-gas production from Texas to Canada. Enron agreed to drop its objections, and Dynegy exercised its option to buy the pipeline for $23 million—the pipeline that essentially served as collateral for Dynegy's $1.5 billion investment in Enron before their merger collapsed. Enron did not drop its $10 billion suit against Dynegy.

■ ■ ■

Enron limped into 2002, still functioning but weighted down by concerns, issues, and complications. Then, as the press bored deeper and discovered Enron's ties to Bush and other politicians, the story broke open. Three days into the new year, Senate Democrats said they would subpoena documents from Enron and look into connections between the company and the Bush White House. A week later, the Justice Department formed a special Enron Task Force, made up of prosecutors from across the country, to investigate the company. On January 11, Enron for the first time took up more space on the front page of the *New York Times* than the military action in Afghanistan. Enron was now a bona fide scandal. It was the subject of jokes on late-night television shows and cropped up in comic strips.

President Bush even included an oblique reference to the Enron collapse in his State of the Union address. "Through stricter accounting standards and tougher disclosure requirements, corporate America must be made more accountable to employees and shareholders and held to the highest standards of conduct," he said.

Enron became a real political football. Suddenly, every utterance on the matter was loaded with political freight. When asked about Enron's sudden collapse, Treasury Secretary Paul O'Neill said, "Companies come and go. It's part of the genius of capitalism." Some took his view as a typically blunt truism about the business world. However, the comment was criticized as "cold-blooded" by Senator Joseph Lieberman (D-Connecticut), chairman of the Committee on Governmental Affairs, one of the committees investigating Enron. It may have been a bit much to suggest that O'Neill (a longtime voice for worker safety) didn't care about the Enron collapse's impact on its employees, but it was in keeping with the tenor of the time.

If there was any mudslinging, perhaps it was inevitable given that Washington was equally awash in mud. Lieberman said he received $2,000 from Enron in his 1994 Senate campaign; one focus of his committee's investigation was "whether any of the influence" from Enron money affected the administration's handling of the Enron collapse or oversight by federal agencies. At the same time, Senator John McCain, a champion of campaign finance reform, told CBS' *Face the Nation* program in January: "We're all tainted by the millions and millions of dollars that were contributed by Enron executives, which again creates the appearance of impropriety." McCain admitted receiving $9,500 in Enron contributions in two Senate campaigns.

Several lawmakers vowed to return the contributions they received from Enron. But the fact remained that Enron had spread the money around Capitol Hill so well that dozens of sitting lawmakers in the House and Senate had taken campaign money from the company.

By the end of January, language pundit William Safire observed that "Enron" had entered the American vocabulary. In politics, Democratic Congressman George Miller derided Bush's proposed 2003 budget as an "Enron budget," and Senate Majority Leader Tom Daschle said, "I don't want to Enron the American people. . . . I don't want to see them holding the bag at the end of the day." As with Daschle's comment, "Enron" became popular as a verb, as in "they were Enroned" or "you've been Enroned, pal."

It wasn't just Enron that was the butt of jokes. The Enron scandal tarnished Arthur Andersen, and by implication the whole accounting industry. Even President Bush joked at a late January dinner that he received good news and bad news from Iraqi dictator Saddam Hussein: "The good news is that he's willing to have his nuclear, biological, and chemical weapons counted. The bad news is he wants Arthur Andersen to do it."

Wall Street began talking regularly about Enronitis infecting stocks, as pundits ascribed various declines in the broad market to worries about corporations' accounting. This bookkeeping disease emerged mightily the week of February 4, as U.S. stocks declined four days in a row due to Enronitis, or the fear that another accounting blowup could occur at any moment. Newspapers and magazines said that investor anxiety, centered on Enronitis, had caused downturns in stocks. In Europe, market strategists said stocks there were hurt by a combination of worries about Argentina's financial problems and, of course, Enronitis. Ordinary investors' faith in the stock market had already been shaken by the dot-com implosion. In a larger sense, Enronitis was an investor loss of faith in the stock market and in corporate integrity, as Enron had proven that stocks are still risky and markets remain untamed.

■ ■ ■

Enron had been looking for a partner for its trading operation, but as the search wore on it became clear that the taint of scandal clung too tightly and Enron would have to sell the business. After several weeks of bidding and negotiations, Enron picked a buyer in UBS Warburg, a division of the large Swiss bank UBS AG. On January 18, the bankruptcy court judge approved the sale of Enron's North American trading business to UBS Warburg. The sale price? Nothing. Well, Enron got no cash up front. Instead it agreed to receive one-third of all future profits. The deal was for 10 years, but UBS could start buying out Enron's interest in the third year. In all, the terms must have been a disappointment for Lay and Enron—a virtual giveaway of the trading business they had pioneered and built into a dominant force around the globe.

UBS was expected to lease Enron's Houston office and retain several hundred of Enron's trading staff. UBS didn't take on any of the trading business' liabilities. Instead, the business had almost a clean slate, now belonging to a large, deep-pocketed bank with an AA+ credit rating. The big question was whether UBS would be able to revive Enron's trading business with any substantial volume.

One of the tricky aspects of the sale was the fact that UBS didn't buy Enron's "book" of trades when it acquired Enron's trading operation. Enron didn't auction its trading book as part of its trading business because bidders didn't want the book—it had too many exposures, and those had the potential to decline. That meant long-term trading positions were left out there to be unraveled by Enron and the various counterparties.

The real value of that trading book wasn't even clear. According to court testimony, Enron estimated its trading book had more than $13 billion worth of in-the-money contracts, or contracts that met the criteria to be enforced, and $8 billion of out-of-the-money contracts, or positions that were not yet in force but could be—for instance, an option on electricity where the exercise price had not yet been met. One way to value the trading book would be to offset those two figures for a total value of $5 billion (13 minus 8). But Enron also estimated that it had $1.3 billion worth of open physical contracts (contracts to receive or deliver a commodity), in which Enron was carrying the full price risk—for instance, if Enron had a contract to buy gas at the Permian Basin without an offsetting contract to sell gas at the Permian Basin. The value of open contracts can be highly volatile. Other energy experts informally estimated the Enron trading book had much more than $5 billion worth of deals that would have to be closed out. It was clear that Enron had a massive amount of contracts that needed resolving.

A group of trading companies, including Aquila, Mirant, PG&E, and Reliant Energy, were not happy with the deal. They felt that Enron's former trading staff, now at UBS and with no allegiance to Enron, would be free to use their knowledge of Enron's existing positions to trade against the Enron trading book. For example, if an ex-Enron trader knew Enron had signed a deal to buy natural gas at $2.10 per 10,000 cubic feet and sell it at $2.20, the trader could jump into the middle of it and buy the gas at $2.12 and then sell it at $2.18, sucking most of the profit out of Enron's deal. To guard against the Enron trading staff using its knowledge of Enron deals unfairly, UBS developed policies banning its new traders from using their knowledge of Enron to the detriment of Enron, and from contacting counterparties about Enron deals.

Further doubt would be cast on the value of Enron's trading operation. In April, Enron reported to the SEC it suspected the value of its trading book—or, as the company put it, "certain price risk management assets"—could have been overestimated by $8 billion to $10 billion. This related to mark-to-market values of trading positions, many of which changed after the Chapter 11 filing. In addition, Enron said that if a thorough financial review were done, the estimated value of the company's assets would likely have to be lowered by roughly $14 billion, caused in part by "accounting errors or irregularities."

■ ■ ■

It may have seemed like a perfunctory move, but on January 17 Enron fired Arthur Andersen as its auditor. That move came six days after Andersen admitted that its personnel disposed of a "significant but undetermined number" of documents relating to Enron—an admission that would prove critical months later. The day before Enron severed its relationship with Andersen, the accounting firm had fired David Duncan. Duncan had been the firm's lead partner on the Enron account, but now Andersen blamed him for shredding Enron-related documents.

The job losses didn't stop there. On January 23, Ken Lay, under pressure from creditors, resigned as chairman and chief executive of Enron. "This was a decision the board and I reached in cooperation with our Creditors' Committee," said Lay, who explained that the litigation and investigations hampered his ability to run Enron. "I want to see Enron survive, and for that to happen we need someone at the helm who can focus 100 percent of his efforts on reorganizing the company and preserving value for our creditors and hard-working employees." Some felt Lay was falling on his sword to help preserve Enron, while others simply saw the move as too late.

A few days later, Ken Lay's wife, Linda, defended him on television. Appearing on NBC's popular *Today* show, Linda Lay said, "My husband is an honest, decent, moral human being, who would do absolutely nothing wrong. . . . There's some things he wasn't told."

Linda Lay went on to say that the millions Lay made from Enron were gone. "There's nothing left. Everything we had mostly was in Enron stock," she said, adding that three of the family's four properties were up for sale, while they kept the luxury condominium in Houston. "We're fighting for liquidity. . . . We don't want to go into bankruptcy." Her TV appearance sparked a lot of speculation about how bad off she and her husband really were, but not a lot of sympathy.

Enron picked a new interim CEO, hiring Stephen F. Cooper, a turnaround expert. Cooper was the managing partner of Zolfo Cooper, LLC, a corporate recovery and crisis management firm, and had more than 30 years' experience leading companies through operational and financial reorganizations. Cooper's experience included helping turn around Federated Department Stores, the owner of Macy's, and Laidlaw Inc., the owner of Greyhound bus lines. Enron also promoted Jeff McMahon to president and chief operating officer; he replaced Greg Whalley, who left for a position with UBS.

"Enron is a very good candidate for a successful restructuring," Cooper told reporters in a conference call the next day. In restructuring, Cooper said he looks at four factors: the organization, the businesses involved, the customer base, and liquidity. He added: "My sense is Enron has a tremendous, tremendous organization. . . . This company has some tremendous businesses. In the markets that it serves, it's got strong leadership positions." In his view, the core Enron likely to survive would have lower revenues but would be in steadier, regulated businesses such as pipelines. "We will be a company based on businesses with hard assets, very predictable revenues, and cash flow," Cooper said.

Separately from the ousting of Ken Lay, the human toll from Enron's collapse widened in a tragic way in late January. On January 24, the body of J. Clifford Baxter—the former Enron vice chairman who had resigned months after complaining about the LJM partnerships—was found in his Mercedes-Benz in the Houston area. Baxter, 43, was dead of a gunshot wound.

Police ruled his death a suicide. Months later, they released the suicide note he'd written, addressed to his wife and found in his wife's car. "Carol, I am so sorry for this," the note said. "I feel I just can't go on." The handwritten note went on to say: "I have always tried to do the right thing, but where there was once great pride now it's gone. . . . Please try to forgive me."

Although the note didn't mention Enron by name, Baxter had apparently been tormented by problems at Enron and the publicity surrounding them. He had recently been subpoenaed to testify before Congress, and, as a former senior officer, he was also named in some lawsuits against Enron. Friends and colleagues remembered him as a likable and assured family man. Enron issued a statement that it was "deeply saddened" by his death.

Jeff Skilling, who described himself as a close friend of Baxter's, said, "I don't think there's anyone that knew Cliff and spent time with Cliff toward the end that didn't realize—and I don't think this is betraying any confidence with the family—there's no one that knew Cliff toward the end that didn't realize that he was heartbroken by what had happened." He said Baxter likened the public drubbing of Enron executives to being called a child molester. Skilling explained, "He believed that his reputation, my reputation, the reputation of the board of directors, the reputation of Ken Lay, people that we had worked with for a long time and his own personal reputation were ruined by what had happened to the company."

■ ■ ■

The bankruptcy process continued, and it wasn't cheap. It required several law firms and some attorneys who charged more than $600 per hour. More than two dozen law firms handled various parts of Enron's bankruptcy case.

Enron's main law firm was Weil, Gotshal & Manges of New York, which charged Enron $6.2 million for legal fees for December 2001. Also, other law firms charged Enron millions for their services. For example, Andrews & Kurth charged Enron $1.93 million for legal fees for December 2001 and January 2002. Leboeuf, Lamb, Greene & MacRae charged Enron $704,000 for legal fees in December 2001. Cadwalader, Wickersham & Taft charged $284,000 for its services to Enron in December 2001 and January 2002. And Wilmer, Cutler & Pickering charged Enron $2.17 million for legal services in January 2002.

Indeed, the bills piled up so quickly that some expected Enron's bankruptcy to beat the record for a Chapter 11 case's legal fees, which was previously set at $120 million by Federated Department Stores. Whether that would happen was unclear. But if Enron spent $8 million per month on legal fees, and the company stayed in bankruptcy for 12 months as Lay had suggested, then Enron's total legal bill for its bankruptcy could certainly have approached $100 million when all was said and done.

The bankruptcy judge oversaw efforts to wrap up loose ends and sell assets. For example, the court approved a deal whereby the Houston Astros bought back the name of their baseball field so that it would no longer be called Enron Field. The Astros had asked that Enron's license agreement for Enron Field be resolved, arguing that the allegations swirling around Enron tainted the city of Houston and its residents. The team also explained, "The Astros' business relationship with Enron leaves the Astros burdened with Enron's considerable baggage. The Enron collapse has tarnished the reputation of the Houston Astros." After the deal, the stadium was named simply Astros Field, until it eventually took the new name Minute Maid Park (after signing a $100 million deal with the juice company).

Separately, Judge Melinda Harmon of the U.S. District Court in Houston named Milberg Weiss Bershad Hynes & Lerach to represent the class action lawsuit of shareholders against Enron. The firm's well-known securities lawyer, Bill Lerach, would lead the mass of securities fraud charges against Enron and Enron executives; Lerach is a famous class action lawyer, having won cases involving savings and loan institutions and junk bonds. The University of California, which lost $144.7 million, was named the lead plaintiff in the class action suit. Other major plaintiffs included the state retirement system of Georgia, which claimed $127 million in losses, and the New York City Pension Funds group, which claimed $109 million in losses. The class action suit claimed that Enron and Enron executives committed securities fraud by improperly inflating Enron's financial statements, thus affecting its stock price. The plaintiffs later expanded the suit to include some of Enron's banks and law firms.

■ ■ ■

On February 2, the special board committee investigating Enron released its findings after three months of investigations. Because William Powers chaired the committee, the 217-page report came to be known as the Powers Report. The report described the workings of LJM1 and LJM2, Chewco, and the Raptors, and judged the company—and the board—to have failed to implement controls throughout the process.

"What we found was appalling," Powers said. "We found that Fastow—and other Enron employees involved in these partnerships—enriched themselves, in the aggregate, by tens of millions of dollars they should never have received. Fastow got at least $30 million, Michael Kopper at least $10 million, and still two more amounts we believe were at least in the hundreds of thousands of dollars."

Powers went on: "We found that some transactions were improperly structured from an accounting point of view. It is important to note that, if they had been structured correctly, Enron could have kept assets and liabilities (especially debt) off of its balance sheet. But Enron did *not* follow the accounting rules."

And, Powers concluded, "We found a systematic and pervasive attempt by Enron's Management to misrepresent the Company's financial condition. . . . There was a fundamental default of leadership and management."

The report came down hardest on Andrew Fastow and Michael Kopper, but also chided Rick Buy and Rick Causey for appearing to rubber-stamp Fastow's deals. The report faulted Lay and Skilling for apparently being too uninvolved in overseeing the activity of the partnerships. And the report also blamed Andersen and Vinson & Elkins for approving many of the deals.

The report detailed Enron's improper accounting decisions, such as the choice to consider Chewco an independent entity when the 3 percent "equity" in it from Barclays was actually collateralized like a loan. But it also explained Enron actions that went beyond accounting misdeeds into the realm of just plain bad business decisions. Take, for example, the creation of the Raptor III entity to provide insurance on Enron's investment in New Power Company. Absurdly, Enron decided to back Raptor III's hedge of New Power stock with New Power stock. When Enron later cross collateralized Raptor III using the excess credit of Raptors funded with Enron stock, the company essentially doubled its bet on New Power Company instead of hedging it—because now Enron stock was backing both the hedge of New Power and the stock backing that hedge. The complicated transaction would end up doing just the opposite of its supposed intent.

Behind the partnership transactions, the report found, was "a flawed idea, self-enrichment by employees, inadequately designed controls, poor implementation, inattentive oversight, simple (and not so simple) accounting mistakes, and overreaching in a culture that appears to have encouraged pushing the limits."

Enron reacted to the Powers Report's findings by firing both Rick Buy and Rick Causey on February 14, "in connection with" the special board committee's probe. Stephen Cooper once again issued a statement saying he and the board were committed to restructuring the company and emerging from Chapter 11.

■ ■ ■

While Enron wrangled with the implications of its investigation and navigating the bankruptcy process, Congress busily held a series of hearings through January, February, and March to look into various aspects of the Enron collapse—the impact on employees, the impact on energy markets, and what Enron executives knew.

Unfortunately, two potential star witnesses decided to assert their Fifth Amendment rights against self-incrimination and not testify: Lay and Fastow. Andersen's David Duncan also took the Fifth. But Skilling, in a move that surprised some, agreed to testify. However, lawmakers met Skilling's testimony with skepticism and hostility. When asked whether anyone besides Baxter and McMahon had complained to him about Fastow's partnerships, Skilling replied, "I don't recall." Skilling's testimony before the House Committee on Energy and Commerce on February 7 was dominated by the explanation "I don't recall." He used that phrase, or variations on it, nearly 20 times.

"On the day I left, on August 14, I believed the company was in strong financial condition," Skilling said. At another point he said, "I did not do anything that was not in the interest of shareholders." He also said, "This was a very large corporation" and he couldn't be expected to know everything that went on.

"You are practicing plausible deniability," responded Representative Clifford Stearns (R-Florida). Another lawmaker, Representative Bart Stupak (D-Michigan), said, "Earlier witnesses put it that you were intense, hands-on. From what I've heard from your testimony today, you don't know what was going on."

Jeff McMahon and Jordan Mintz testified, describing an Enron where crossing Fastow was a dangerous career move. Herbert Winokur, who served on Enron's board, said his biggest regret was that many executives seemed to know something was fishy but no one came forward until Sherron Watkins did in August 2001.

Watkins appeared before several congressional committees, including a Senate hearing in late February where Skilling also appeared. They gave testimony that sometimes conflicted, although both agreed on what did Enron in—as Skilling put it, "it was a classic run on a bank," a reference to the phenomenon whereby all the depositors panic and withdraw their money simultaneously, making it impossible for the bank to remain solvent.

However, Watkins and Skilling differed on his role. She claimed that Skilling "duped" Ken Lay. "I never duped Ken Lay," Skilling replied. "I heard Ms. Watkins testify to her opinion; I have no idea what the basis is for that opinion." At this hearing, before a Senate panel, Skilling's favorite refrain was "I'm not an accountant." He also challenged legislators with slight sarcasm. Watkins was more critical of Lay. When asked if she thought Lay was "bright," Watkins retorted: "Not after this fall."

The various hearings helped illuminate some of what went on behind the scenes at Enron, and provided some entertaining theater, but they didn't resolve who was to blame for the huge bankruptcy.

■ ■ ■

For those waiting for the government to take some decisive action, March 14 must have come as a relief. That day, a federal grand jury charged Arthur Andersen LLP with obstruction of justice in the investigation into Enron. The charge stemmed from Andersen's admission that it had shredded numerous Enron-related documents even as it knew the SEC was investigating Enron.

The one-count indictment came after Andersen and the government failed in several attempts to settle the case, both sides knowing that an indictment would scare away so many clients that it could effectively terminate Andersen. Berardino had by then resigned from the accounting firm. Andersen, in a statement, called the indictment "without precedent and an extraordinary abuse of prosecutorial discretion." Andersen sent a memo to its employees warning that the indictment could destroy the firm.

Because Andersen admitted it shredded documents and tried to cast those actions as the work of rogue employees in its Houston office, obtaining a guilty verdict would have seemed to some to be a slam dunk for government prosecutors. But it wasn't. After a four-week trial, the jury came close to being deadlocked. The judge had to order the jury to continue pondering the evidence until it reached a verdict.

Finally, after 10 days of deliberations, the jury found Andersen guilty of obstruction of justice for impeding the probe by securities regulators. But the admitted shredding of documents was not the crux of the verdict. Instead, jurors said in interviews, they'd voted "guilty" based on Andersen actions regarding Enron's October 16, 2001, press release announcing third-quarter results. The jury took a dim view of the e-mail from Andersen lawyer Nancy Temple advising Duncan to delete from his paperwork any reference to his objections to Enron using the phrase "non-recurring." Jurors felt this was done to keep information from the SEC.

The conviction was the first ever of a major accounting firm. The SEC issued a statement that Andersen was giving up its ability to audit public companies in the United States: The SEC doesn't allow such audits to be conducted by firms convicted of felonies. The move seemed to assure the end of Andersen, which had already lost more than half of its employees and a huge chunk of clients since Enron's bankruptcy filing. Sentencing of Andersen was scheduled for October; as if to add insult to injury, the firm faces potential fines of up to $500,000.

The SEC issued a statement after the verdict, saying, "The Commission is deeply troubled by the underlying events that resulted in Andersen's conviction. . . . The Commission's investigation into Enron Corp., and Andersen's role in it, is continuing."

■ ■ ■

Where did all this leave Enron? As of August, when this book was being completed, the SEC had yet to file civil charges against Enron. And the class action lawsuit claiming securities fraud was still pending. On another front, Enron settled its lawsuit with Dynegy over the merger cancellation, with Enron receiving $25 million from Dynegy (which had agreed to sell the valued Northern Natural Gas pipeline to allay its own financial troubles).

And one of the most notable developments occurred on August 21, 2002, when former Enron executive Michael Kopper pleaded guilty to one count of money laundering and one count of conspiracy to commit wire fraud. The charges arose from Kopper's dealings with off-balance sheet partnerships, including Chewco and LJM. As part of the plea deal, Kopper agreed to cooperate with prosecutors and agreed to turn over $12 million acquired through criminal activity. It was the first criminal charge against an Enron insider obtained by the Department of Justice's Enron Task Force.

According to the cooperation agreement between Kopper and the Justice Department, Kopper admitted guilt involving three partnerships: he cheated Enron in managing Chewco, claiming he secretly kicked back some of his management fees to Andrew Fastow; in structuring the buyout of the Swap Sub in the LJM's Rhythms deal, he and Fastow maneuvered millions from Enron's payment into Southampton Place, an entity in which they were investors; and he, Fastow, and others convinced Enron to sell some wind farms to a little-known SPE called RADR that, without Enron's knowledge, funneled $4.5 million in profits to Fastow, Kopper, and their friends. Not only did Kopper's plea end his loyalty to Fastow, it suggested that some of Enron's accounting shenanigans were more than just errors—they were carried out with criminal intent.

Enron provided the biggest example of corporate malfeasance, but it marched at the head of a long parade of business misdeeds. In the months following Enron's bankruptcy, one scandal after another popped up in the business pages, among them: Allegations arose that telecom company Global Crossing (which filed for bankruptcy) illegally boosted its revenue figures with fake swaps, and top executives may have engaged in insider sales. Industrial conglomerate Tyco International, built on hundreds of acquisitions, saw its stock plummet on doubts about its accounting, and then its CEO was charged with tax evasion. Cable television company Adelphia (which also filed for bankruptcy) faced questions about transactions involving the founding Rigas family, including billions of dollars in off-balance sheet deals that the company's board didn't know about. The CEO of biotechnology company ImClone Systems was charged with insider trading for tipping family and friends off about a negative regulatory decision. The SEC began a probe of accounting at oil services company Halliburton for cost overruns incurred while the company was headed by Dick Cheney, before he became the U.S. vice president. Brokerage firm Merrill Lynch paid $100 million to settle charges from New York State that its research analysts knowingly issued glowing recommendations of Internet stocks that conflicted with their own internal—and decidedly dour—opinions. Xerox settled charges by the SEC that it misled investors by improperly recognizing $3 billion in revenue (later upped to nearly $6 billion) from 1997 through 2001. And in June, embattled telecom giant WorldCom, already facing an SEC inquiry into its accounting, admitted that it had improperly booked $3.8 billion in expenses, wrongly boosting cash flow and profit over the previous 15 months. The trail of charges and admissions sowed the population with a new cynicism toward corporate America.

Responding to this crush of scandal, the SEC in late June ordered the CEOs and CFOs of companies with at least $1.2 billion in revenue to personally certify in writing, under oath, that their financial reports are complete and accurate. The order, covering 945 companies, was intended to restore faith in financial reports, the SEC said. These executives had until August 14, 2002, to comply.

As for Enron, Stephen Cooper presented plans in May to reorganize as a smaller company that would have only around 12,000 employees. He said the new company, which at some point would change its name from Enron, would operate mostly in North, Central, and South America. If creditors accepted this plan, most assets outside of the Americas would be sold. Cooper estimated that, with asset sales and operating profits, perhaps $15 billion to $20 billion could be recovered for creditors. In August, Enron began the process of putting its assets up for auction to satisfy creditors, opening the possibility that there might not even be a surviving company.

If a company does endure, it would be an "energy infrastructure" firm with roughly $10 billion in assets focused on the transportation, distribution, generation, and production of natural gas and electricity. The heart of the new company would be its 15,000 miles of gas pipelines. In other words, after all the attempts to make Enron function more like an investment bank or a consulting firm, after all the machinations to get into energy trading, after years of pushing employees to innovate, and after Skilling's vision of a virtual company had seemingly won, now the hope was for a company that was in the hard-assets business.

The plan Cooper described for an ongoing firm sounded very much like Enron did before Lay brought Skilling on board to reinvent the company. If the plan worked, it would almost be as if the years between 1985 and 2001 hadn't happened. Almost, but not quite.

EPILOGUE

Looking back, the Enron saga can be seen as a fable of what happens when a company starts to believe the spin and hyperbole about its success that have been spread by the media, admiring consultants, Wall Street, and the company itself.

Enron wasn't a complete hoax. The company deserved admiration for its early forays into trading gas and electricity, and for its plunge into the innovative financing of energy projects. It outmaneuvered the old-line energy companies to expand the use of derivatives in the energy industry. This introduced new ways of managing risk, which lowered the costs of energy-related transactions for an array of businesses.

In energy, necessity served as the mother of invention, and Enron responded with expertise and market knowledge to conditions that were ripe for the birth of energy trading. But in expanding beyond energy into the trading of metals, bandwidth, paper, and other products, Enron didn't respond to market signals. The company arrogantly believed it could broaden its trading savvy unhindered, and Enron executives evidently dived into new markets with little research or sense of industry demand— otherwise, how else could Enron have thought that the telecom industry would want bandwidth trading at a time when experts were already warning of a glut of broadband capacity?

Similarly, Enron believed that its expansions into international projects were positive initiatives simply because they put the company in more potential markets. In truth, Enron made bad business decisions that weren't supported by the deals' economics. The bad business decisions piled up, stretching from India to Brazil, pressuring the company to do something about its finances.

At the same time, Enron had pushed the envelope in using Special Purpose Entities and other off-balance sheet financing strategies. As Enron's success continued, it bent the rules more and more, somehow staying within the loosely defined parameters of accounting. Eventually, it seemed like a small leap to make from bending the rules to breaking them. There was no single moment when Enron transgressed from rule bender to rule breaker: Rather, the transformation resulted from the gradual accretion of offenses, encouraged by a corporate culture that valued aggression.

Sometime around 1996–1997, Enron crossed the line. Richard Kinder's departure as the financial conscience of the company seemed to be a critical step in this transformation. So Enron, which until then had been a successful energy trading and logistics company, became an overconfident hedge fund that believed it was entitled to bend the rules to finance its trade-everything ambition. Along the way, Ken Lay, Jeff Skilling, and other executives failed in their duties to oversee how the company did business. Lay and Skilling professed ignorance of any accounting misdeeds, but records show they were briefed on many of the partnerships at board meetings. This may suggest that they either approved of plans to cook the books, blindly trusted the accountants and lawyers, kept themselves away from the details in case they'd need plausible deniability, or lacked the competence to monitor their company's financial dealings. The board of directors, the auditors, and the law firms failed to adequately police the company's decisions. Wall Street banks, too, appear to have willingly aided Enron's financial acrobatics with complex debt strategies. And research analysts didn't inquire about partnerships mentioned in the footnotes of the company's financial statements, happy instead to relax and watch the stock climb.

And the story really did end in, as Skilling put it, a "run on the bank." Trading partners fled for the exits because Enron's financial condition had suddenly been revealed as a rickety contraption with few safety nets. That destroyed the trading operation, which had become Enron's main engine of profits, and the company sank quickly.

■ ■ ■

All of this doesn't mean that Enron was wrong to pursue innovation. In *Fortune* magazine surveys, Enron was chosen as the most innovative U.S. company—beating out Apple Computer, eBay, and IBM—from 1996 through 2001. On the positive side, Enron accepted the occasional failure that inevitably comes from trying new things. Yet the company seemed to rely too much on innovation, eventually pursuing new ideas just for the sake of their newness. Some ideas worked out, such as EnronOnline, which proved that online exchanges could attract traders if liquidity were provided. Some ill-conceived ideas, like trading water, never got off the ground. And other ideas never developed into the big markets that Enron and others predicted: Weather derivatives, for instance, remained a niche product, overshadowed by weather insurance. Unlike Enron, successful businesses need to differentiate between good ideas, bad ideas, and ideas that only go so far.

Every corporation needs a firm board of directors to monitor the activity of management, but especially at an innovative company that is trying new things. Too many company boards are filled with the CEO's golfing buddies or fellow executives appointed to open doors for more contracts. As a result, boards function as rubber stamps, approving the decisions of strong CEOs.

Unfortunately, Enron's board rubber-stamped the practices of Lay, Skilling, and Fastow. The board included a couple of high-level officials from the University of Texas' Anderson Cancer Center, raising questions about whether they were qualified to scrutinize the company's complicated business model. But those two can't be blamed for Enron's collapse. In 2001, Enron's board also included an accounting professor, two former energy regulators, and four executives of financial and investment firms. Couldn't one of these directors have had the expertise to spot problems in Enron's use of SPEs? Shouldn't one of the directors—each getting $50,000 a year for serving on Enron's board—have had the confidence necessary to raise questions about SPEs? The lesson here is that companies need to have a few outside directors who can understand the business, but these outside directors must also be willing to ask probing questions.

New federal legislation goes some way in encouraging this. In July 2002, Congress passed (by overwhelming margins) and President Bush signed into law a bill on corporate oversight that includes the requirement that directors of a board's audit committee be independent and makes them responsible for hiring the company's auditor. A board's audit committee must also monitor the auditor's actions and create a process for handling complaints, or else have the company face removal from the stock exchange.

For boards of directors to properly function, they need company managers to be forthcoming with information, particularly where it concerns new and risky directions for the company. This openness flows from the top. Enron's secretive nature grew from its unique corporate culture, which cultivated a mix of caution and swagger. A corporate culture that promotes competitive spirit and performance-based job assessment can be productive. But the company that adopts this approach needs sturdy controls to ensure the culture doesn't go overboard. Enron had no such controls, and so even as its culture bred innovation and creativity, it also created a mercenary, short-term-oriented personality as a side effect.

■ ■ ■

In the wake of Enron's collapse, the investment community heightened its examination of the role of Wall Street analysts—such as the ones who had been rating Enron's stock a "buy" even as the company was slowly suffocating from its many off-balance sheet partnerships. The question seemed more relevant than ever: How trustworthy were analysts in analyzing companies when the analysts' employers were trying to get hired by those companies to advise them on stock offerings and mergers?

The positive slant that seemed to characterize Wall Street research raised more eyebrows than ever; for example, the vast majority of analyst ratings on stocks were variations on "buy" or "hold," and fewer than one percent of ratings were "sell." In February 2002, the New York Stock Exchange and the National Association of Securities Dealers—which regulates the Nasdaq Stock Market—proposed several rules to help clarify the roles of research analysts. These included: barring investment banking departments from supervising analysts; prohibiting analysts' compensation from being tied to investment banking transactions; and requiring clear disclosures in research reports of business relationships between the analyst's firm and the company being analyzed.

Enron's collapse was not single-handedly responsible for the new, harsher spotlight on analysts; the tide had begun to turn by early 2001, after the Internet boom went bust and many analysts' positive recommendations seemed laughable. But Enron, with its high profile and its history of favorable analyst coverage, was a lightning rod for concern over the independence of analysts. Helping the momentum were outraged members of Congress holding hearings and looking to take some sort of post-Enron action. The fine point was put on this issue in April 2002, when the SEC launched a formal inquiry into Wall Street's research analysts. This inquiry, the SEC explained, "will help determine the necessity of additional rulemaking and whether any laws have been violated."

Fortunately, some investment banks have already begun to implement new rules for their research analysts. Merrill Lynch, in settling charges from New York State's attorney general, agreed to create an analyst oversight committee and to increase the disclosures about banking relationships in its research reports. Investment banks Credit Suisse First Boston and Bear Stearns soon volunteered to adopt similar policies. But relying on self-policing is not enough. New rules to discourage analyst conflicts of interest must be adopted and enforced.

In avoiding future Enrons, investors can also help themselves. It's clear that many investors, including professional money managers, focused on net income and didn't pay close enough attention to cash flow when analyzing Enron. Because companies can legally manage net income and earnings, those measures by themselves don't provide the most accurate picture of a corporation's financial health. Also, a closer reading of Enron's financial statements would have raised questions about how aggressively the company used mark-to-market accounting. As Enron showed, a company can become too focused on the short term, and one possible warning sign is an overreliance on mark-to-market accounting, especially in illiquid markets where values are based on internal assumptions.

The final piece of this puzzle is beefing up the Securities and Exchange Commission. The SEC has operated for years with too little staff and too small a budget. From 1991 through 2000, corporate filings to the SEC rose by 59 percent, while the staff to review those filings grew by just 29 percent. Clearly, the SEC needs to have sufficient resources to do its job.

■ ■ ■

Enron's downfall also raises issues regarding energy deregulation and accounting. After Enron, politicians started to rethink energy deregulation. But energy deregulation wasn't responsible for Enron's collapse. In truth, deregulating the gas industry resulted in billions of dollars in savings. And in electricity, not every state suffered California's fate; some states that deregulated electricity saw benefits for consumers. In Pennsylvania, for instance, competitive power markets resulted in $562 million in savings for individuals by mid-2000.

The problem, as Enron and other trading firms demonstrated, is that energy deregulation can create opportunities to manipulate the market. Deregulation is not guaranteed to work, just as regulation isn't. But deregulation needs proper oversight if it is to have a chance. That requires that regulatory agencies have a sophistication they currently lack. Congress determined that the FERC, for one, "has not yet adequately revised its regulatory and oversight approach to respond to the transition to competitive energy markets." Upgrade the capabilities of regulators, and *then* see whether deregulation works.

As for accounting, the Enron story highlights the many flaws prevalent in the auditing industry. What many people find most frustrating about the Enron saga is that many of Enron's accounting tricks were legal. Enron executives may eventually be charged with and found guilty of fraud or insider trading, but off-balance sheet financing is legal deception. In lobbying to keep these accounting rules in place, Enron wasn't guilty of secret payoffs but of making the perfectly legal political contributions that were second nature to many corporations. In many instances, Enron may very well have followed the letter of the law while subverting the spirit of the law.

After the sobering example of Enron, other corporations tempted to engage in financial engineering will probably tone down their impulses to aggressively massage the books. But the fact remains that accounting rules are too pliable. Mark-to-market accounting needs to be clarified so that it isn't abused in illiquid markets, which is what Enron did. And the definition of what makes an SPE independent needs to be refined. These are just a few of the rules that need upgrading.

The accounting industry also needs greater oversight, and the United States took an encouraging step in that direction in July 2002 when it passed its massive corporate oversight bill. The legislation creates a five-member oversight panel that can investigate and discipline accounting firms. It also prohibits an auditor from offering nine different types of consulting services to a company it audits, which should cut down on conflicts of interest. And the legislation requires an accounting firm to rotate the lead partners on an auditing assignment every five years, which should provide fresh sets of eyes and deter auditors from getting too cozy with their corporate clientele.

The fallout, though, will stretch well into 2003. The SEC began investigating Merrill Lynch, and Congress began investigating Citigroup and J.P. Morgan Chase for their roles in the scandal, so it may yet be determined whether Enron's banks, which stand to lose billions of dollars on Enron's bankruptcy, violated any laws. The energy trading business has shrunk, with Dynegy and Williams cutting back their trading staffs and Aquila planning to exit the business altogether, and the business' rebound is uncertain. And the big question hanging over everything is whether any Enron executives will go to jail. Given how surprisingly difficult it was to obtain a guilty verdict against Andersen after admitting it shredded documents, no one should expect an easy victory in the more complicated matter of Enron's finances. The government will likely find it challenging to explain to a jury the ins and outs of Enron's books, and may have trouble making airtight cases against Enron's biggest icons, Lay and Skilling. But the criminal probes will be pursued, and well they should be.

In sum, whether dealing with securities laws or energy regulation, with corporate governance or corporate audits, the message is clear: Capitalism is a complicated enterprise, and the system won't work without referees. That much is clear from the Enron story, even through the dense thicket of Raptors and LJMs.

AUTHOR'S NOTE

In looking at the endnotes to follow, keep in mind that Enron did not authorize this book and that, despite my efforts, Enron didn't cooperate in the research. Rather, this was an independent examination of the events that led to the rise and fall of the company. The research began after Enron declared bankruptcy, and this hampered my access to former Enron executives. I tried to obtain interviews with many of the key players in this tale, including Kenneth Lay and Jeffrey Skilling, but their spokespeople, not surprisingly, declined.

Still, I managed to interview dozens of sources for this book. I appreciate the many former Enron employees who took the time to speak to me, both on the record and off. Given the nature of the story, I had to rely for many details on people who wound up being identified as confidential sources, and that's simply par for the course with this type of book. Fortunately, I also had many documents to draw from, including those made public by congressional committees. In the end, I stand by my reporting.

While I'm thanking sources for their time, there are just a few other people I'd like to thank by name. I am indebted to my partner, Hazel May, for her patience and advice. I am grateful to my editor, Bill Falloon, for his help with contacts and for being an early champion of this project, and to his assistant, Melissa Scuereb. And I thank my agent, Esmond Harmsworth, for his guidance and support, and his associate, Scott Gold.

NOTES

CHAPTER 1　Pipeline to Profit

Page 1: Details of Ken Lay's appearance before the Senate Commerce Committee come from the televised proceedings.

Page 3: "Lay's attorney had written to Congress . . ." is from a February 3, 2002, letter by Earl Silbert, Lay's attorney, to the chairmen of two congressional committees.

Page 4: Robert Smoot's reactions are based on an author interview with Smoot.

Pages 7–11: "His father, Omer, was a Southern Baptist minister . . ." Information on Ken Lay's childhood and life before Enron came from a variety of sources, including Ken Lay's spokesperson, Kelly Kimberly; Laura Goldberg and Mary Flood, "The Rise of Ken Lay As Dramatic As His Fall," *Houston Chronicle*, February 3, 2002; the Hickman Kewpie Classmates Association web site; Jeffrey Share, *The Oil Makers* (Rice University Press, 1995); Jeff Kunerth, "Enron Chief's Rise Began in Winter Park," *Orlando Sentinel*, December 23, 2001; and notes from Ken Lay's interview with Wilmer, Cutler & Pickering, as part of the Enron board's investigation in January 2002.

Pages 10–11: Managing Energy Price Risk (Risk Publications, 1995) was helpful for background on the natural gas industry.

Page 12: Lay's work on spot markets at Transco is from Ken Lay spokesperson Kelly Kimberly.

Page 12: The development of Natural Gas Clearinghouse is from two Natural Gas Clearinghouse press releases: one from March 4, 1985, and one from December 16, 1985.

Pages 13–14: Details of the HNG-InterNorth merger are from HNG and InterNorth press releases.

Page 14: The fact that HNG/InterNorth had $12.1 billion worth of assets and 15,000 employees after the merger is from the "Enron Milestones" section of Enron's web site.

Page 14: The story of "Enteron" and "Enron" is according to Enron spokesman Mark Palmer, and from William Safire, "Enroned," *New York Times Magazine*, February 10, 2002.

Pages 14–15: "The company had already cut 1,000 jobs . . ." is from an Enron press release of April 10, 1986.

Page 15: Enron's headquarters moving to Houston is from an Enron press release of May 12, 1986.

Pages 15–16: Discussion of Jacobs' and Leucadia's investments in Enron is from Matt Moffett, "Leucadia Buys Stake in Enron, Weighs Options," *Wall Street Journal*, July 29, 1986.

Page 16: Details on Enron's purchase of shares from Jacobs and Leucadia come from an Enron press release of October 20, 1986; a press release from T. Boone Pickens' United Shareholders Association of October 20, 1986; and from John Crudele, "Enron Buys Back Its Stock," *New York Times*, October 21, 1986.

Page 16: Lay's explanation of the stock buyback and information about Enron's cost cutting are from Steve Jordon, "Low Energy Costs Force Reductions: Enron Corp.'s Lay Outlines Future Cuts," *Omaha World-Herald*, December 9, 1986.

Page 17: "At the end of the year, Enron had $3.43 billion in long-term debt" is from Enron's 10-Q quarterly report for June 30, 1988. The raising of $585 million through a debenture sale is from an Enron press release of February 12, 1987.

Page 17: Moody's downgrade of Enron debt is from a Moody's press release of January 30, 1987.

Page 17: Enron's debt-to-capital ratio at the end of 1987 and Lay's comments at the 1988 shareholders meeting are from an Enron press release of April 28, 1988.

Page 17: The year-end debt-to-capital ratio of 65.7 percent and the reduction of take-or-pay claims are from an Enron press release of February 13, 1989, announcing 1988 results.

Page 18: "Small producers sometimes felt Enron . . ." is from an author interview with Apache Corp. chairman and CEO Raymond Plank.

Page 18: Enron's 1987 results are from Enron press release of February 13, 1989.

Page 18: Information on the unauthorized trading at Enron Oil comes from an Enron press release of October 22, 1987, and from Caleb Solomon, "Enron Expects an $85 Million Charge Because of Secret Trading by Oil Unit," *Wall Street Journal*, October 23, 1987. The broad details were also confirmed by Enron spokesman Mark Palmer.

Pages 18–19: Details on the investigation into Louis Borget and Thomas Mastroeni are from two unbylined articles: "Former Enron Execs Charged with Fraud," *Houston Chronicle*, December 21, 1989, and "Two Former Officials of Enron Plead Guilty to Conspiracy," *Wall Street Journal*, March 1, 1990.

Page 19: Information on Enron Oil & Gas is from Enron's 10-K annual report for 1988.

Page 19: Enron's minor involvement with a company run by George W. Bush is from an Enron Oil & Gas press release of October 16, 1986.

Page 20: Background on Richard Kinder is from Enron's SEC filings and a press release from KN Energy.

Page 20: "Kinder was open and approachable" is from an author interview with a confidential source.

Pages 20–21: The story of the "Come to Jesus" meeting is from Terry Maxon, "Enron Goes from Sleepy Utility to Global e-Commerce Leader," *Dallas Morning News*, July 2, 2000, and Michael Davis, "Enron: Making of the Market Maker," *Houston Chronicle*, April 15, 2001.

CHAPTER 2   Where the Money Is

Page 22: "In October 1989, Enron's Transwestern Pipeline . . ." is from Enron's web site.

Page 23: The relative size of the spot market, and the 1989 interest in Enron's long-term contracts, is from Sanjay Bhatnagar and Peter Tufano, "Enron Gas Services," Harvard Business School, Case 9-294-076, September 26, 1995.

Page 23: "In 1990 alone, Enron contracted to sell 190 billion cubic feet of gas . . ." is from Enron's 10-K 1990 annual report.

Pages 24–25: Information about the state of gas trading is from an author interview with John Sherriff, former CEO of Enron Europe.

Page 25: "Enron became a 'market maker' for gas . . ." is from an author interview with Edward Krapels, director at Energy Security Analysis Inc.

Page 27: "One signature hedging deal involved a Louisiana aluminum producer . . ." is from Sanjay Bhatnagar and Peter Tufano, "Enron Gas Services," Harvard Business School, Case 9-294-076, September 26, 1995.

Pages 27–28: Information about the Enron–Bankers Trust joint venture is from an author interview with a confidential source.

Pages 29–30: "One of the advantages to a gas futures contract . . ."   Some information about the gas hedging market and the use of NYMEX gas futures is from an author interview with Shannon Burchett, the CEO of consulting firm Risk Limited Corp.

Page 30: "There was some resistance to the NYMEX futures . . ." is from an author interview with Joseph Pokalsky, former Enron executive.

Page 30: "But by mid-1991, more than one-quarter of futures trading consisted of hedges . . ." is from Peter Fusaro and Roger Benedict, "Spot Price Plunge Spurs Growth of Price-Hedging in Gas Industry," *Oil Daily*, July 30, 1991.

Page 30: Information about Hub Pricing is from Enron's 1990 annual report.

Page 31: Information about Gas Bank and Enron's gas sales practices comes from Enron, including its annual reports of 1989 and 1990.

Page 31: Some information about VPPs and Gas Bank is from an author interview with Joseph Pokalsky, former Enron executive, and from Sanjay Bhatnagar and Peter Tufano, "Enron Gas Services," Harvard Business School, Case 9-294-076, September 26, 1995.

Page 32: The Forest Oil and Zilkha Energy VPP examples are from *Managing Energy Price Risk* (Risk Publications, 1995).

Page 32: "Enron was . . . the preeminent provider of this financing . . ." is from an author interview with Shannon Burchett.

Pages 32–33: Details of Enron's supply pact with Sithe are from an Enron press release of January 28, 1992, and from "Cogen Plant Sets New Technical—and Business—Standards," *Power*, April 1995. The Sithe deal's importance to Enron is from an author interview with Ed Krapels of Energy Security Analysis and an author interview with a confidential source.

Page 33: Enron hired Skilling on June 26, 1990, according to an Enron press release.

Pages 33–35: Information on Skilling's background and personality, as well as his "asset-light" strategy, comes from Mike Tolson and Alan Berstein, "Skilling Energized Enron but Draws Suspicion after the Fall," *Houston Chronicle*, February 10, 2002; Wendy Zellner, "Jeff Skilling: Enron's Missing Man," *Business Week*, February 11, 2002; a January 16, 2002, summary of an interview of Ken Lay for the Powers Report; and author interviews with confidential sources.

Pages 36–37: Enron's use of oil swaps and gas options is from interview with Pokalsky.

Pages 37–38: "Enron hired an internal research team in 1992 . . ." is from an author interview with Vincent Kaminski, former managing director of research.

Page 38: "Enron stood on the shoulders of the financial community . . ." is from an author interview with Edward Krapels.

Pages 38–39: "Skilling encouraged the three groups to view each other as competition . . ." Information about the internal competition between Enron divisions is from a confidential source.

Page 39: "Traders sometimes changed price assumptions to benefit their trading books . . ." is from a confidential source.

Page 39: The growth of the trading and finance business in terms of employees and income is from Sanjay Bhatnagar and Peter Tufano, "Enron Gas Services," Harvard Business School, Case 9-294-076, September 26, 1995.

Page 40: "In January 1991, Enron began using an accounting method known as 'mark-to-market' accounting . . ." is from Enron's 10-K annual report for 1991.

Page 41: "Enron traders sometimes used mark-to-market accounting to massage their results."   From an interview with a confidential source.

Page 41: "Derivatives are so flexible . . ." is from an author interview with Randall Dodd, director of the Derivatives Study Center.

Page 42: "You had to kill to eat." is from a confidential source.

Page 42: Enron's market capitalization at the start of 1990 is from *Forbes* magazine's Forbes 500 list of April 30, 1990; Enron's market capitalization at the start of 1994 is from the Forbes 500 list of April 25, 1994.

CHAPTER 3   Major Ambition

Pages 43–44: Enron Oil & Gas sales volumes, and tight sands tax credits, are from an Enron press release of January 26, 1993; background on tight sands tax credits and the related politics is from Margaret Kriz, "Fuel Duel," *National Journal*, September 19, 1992.

Page 44: The offering of EOG stock is from an Enron press release of October 4, 1989.

Page 44: Historical stock quotes for Enron Oil & Gas are from BigCharts.com.

Page 44: Information on Enron's Peruvian investment is from an Enron press release of February 13, 1987, and the 10-K annual report for 1993.

Page 45: "British Gas had sparked the competition . . ." is from a British Gas press release of December 17, 1990.

Page 45: Initial talks on Teesside are from an Enron press release of October 18, 1989.

Page 45: Enron's contracts for gas supplies and to sell electricity from Teesside are from Enron press releases of January 29, 1990, and of September 11, 1990.

Page 46: Enron's failed purchase of a stake in the J-Block is from Neil Buckley, "Enron Thwarted in North Sea Move," *Financial Times*, September 22, 1992.

Pages 46–47: Details related to the opening of Teesside, including Lay's quote, are from an Enron press release of April 1, 1993.

Page 47: "The Teesside plant was a showcase . . ." is from Deborah Hargreaves, "Gas-Fired Power Station Unveiled," *Financial Times*, April 2, 1993.

Page 47: Enron's other overseas projects comes from Enron press releases of December 3, 1992 and of April 2, 1993, and Charles Thurston, "Guatemala Is Site of Central America's First Privately Financed Power Project," *Journal of Commerce*, May 20, 1993.

Page 47: "Rather than resisting change . . ." and the anecdote about $50 bills are from Thane Peterson, "Natural Gas's Hottest Spot," *Business Week*, March 8, 1993.

Page 47: Lay's appointment to Bush's advisory panel is from Keith Schneider, "Bush Names Panel for Environment," *New York Times*, July 24, 1991; and

Lay's involvement with the 1992 Republican convention is from "Houston Raises $4.3 Million for Republicans," Associated Press, April 3, 1992.

Page 48: The hiring of Baker and Mosbacher, and Lay's quote are from "Baker and Mosbacher Are Hired by Enron," Bloomberg Business News, February 23, 1993.

Page 48: Wendy Gramm's hiring by Enron is from Jerry Knight, "Energy Firm Finds Ally, Director in CFTC Ex-Chief," *Washington Post*, April 17, 1993.

Page 48: Lay as a "relationship guy" is from an author interview with Sherriff.

Pages 48–49: Background on John Wing is from a Wing-Merrill Group Ltd. press release of December 11, 1991.

Pages 49–50: Background on Rebecca Mark is from an author interview with Diana Peters, and from Patricia Sellers, "Women, Sex & Power," *Fortune*, August 5, 1996, and Toni Mack, "High Finance with a Touch of Theater," *Forbes*, May 18, 1998. Reference to the rumored Mark-Wing affair is from the *Fortune* and *Forbes* articles.

Page 49: "We are a very eclectic bunch . . ." is from Louis T. Wells, "Enron Development Corp.—The Dabhol Power Project in Maharashtra, India (A)," Harvard Business School, Case 9-797-085, February 4, 1997.

Page 50: The December 1993 Dabhol agreement is from an Enron press release of December 8, 1993.

Pages 51–52: Dabhol's political effect is from Arundhati Roy, *Power Politics* (South End Press, 2001).

Page 51: The World Bank's opinion on Dabhol and LNG is from "Background on Enron's Dabhol Project," by the Minority Staff of the U.S. House of Representatives Committee on Government Reform, February 22, 2002, and from Louis T. Wells, "Enron Development Corp.—The Dabhol Power Project in Maharashtra, India (A)," Harvard Business School, Case 9-797-085, February 4, 1997.

Pages 51–52: The criticisms in Maharashtra are from Louis T. Wells, "Enron Development Corp.—The Dabhol Power Project in Maharashtra, India (B)," Harvard Business School, Case 9-797-086, February 4, 1997.

Page 52: The Dabhol financing is from an Enron press release of March 1, 1995.

Page 52: Entergy's investment is from an Entergy press release of April 3, 1995.

Pages 52–53: Information on Enron's foreign operations and Enron Global Power & Pipelines is from Enron press releases of September 8, 1994, and October 18, 1994.

Page 53: "But the good vibes didn't last long . . ." is from Arthur Max, "Review Begins on Power Project," Associated Press, May 5, 1995, and John-Thor Dahlberg, "This Power Game Has High Stakes for India," *Los Angeles Times*, June 22, 1995.

Page 53: The Dabhol cancellation is from an Enron press release of August 2, 1995. *Pages 53–55:* Information on the renegotiation of the Dabhol project comes from several sources: Sarayu Srinivasan, "Enron Development Corp.—The Dabhol Power Project in Maharashtra, India (C)," Harvard Business School, Case 9-596-101, December 16, 1996; Rebecca Mark, "Surviving the Challenge," *Independent Energy*, March 1996; and John F. Burns, "India Project in the Balance," *New York Times*, September 6, 1995.

Page 55: Opposition to Dabhol and claims of rights violations are from several sources: "The 'Enron Project' in Maharashtra—Protests Suppressed in the Name of Development," Amnesty International report, July 1997; "Background on Enron's Dabhol Project," the Minority Staff of the U.S. House of Representatives Committee on Government Reform, February 22, 2002; and Arundhati Roy, *Power Politics* (South End Press, 2001).

Page 56: Information about Enron's new global breadth is from "Natural Gas: Enter Enron," *Economist*, February 12, 1994, and Caleb Solomon and Robert Johnson, "Piping Up: Natural Gas Industry Is Reinventing Itself by Going International," *Wall Street Journal*, April 19, 1994.

Pages 56–57: The pricing problem with the J-Block pact is from "Enron Defends Gas Contract in North Sea," Bloomberg Business News, September 14, 1995.

Pages 57–58: Data on the legal battle over J-Block is from Hillary Durgin, "Enron Suit Challenges North Sea Gas Contract," *Houston Chronicle*, April 4, 1996; an Enron press release of October 10, 1996; and a Phillips press release of April 21, 1997.

Page 58: The competition between ECT and Enron International is from an author interview with a confidential source; resolution of the J-Block issue is from an Enron press release of June 2, 1997.

Page 58: The Qatar agreement is from Nelson Antosh, "Enron, Qatar Reach $4 Billion Natural Gas Deal," *Houston Chronicle*, January 20, 1995, and "Enron and Qatar Cancel a Gas Project," Bloomberg News, March 20, 1999.

Page 58: Earnings figures for ECT and Enron International are from an Enron press release of January 24, 1996.

CHAPTER 4   Electrifying Opportunity

Page 59: Enron's financial and operational results for 1993 are from an Enron press release of January 27, 1994.

Page 60: "According to Lay, the first decade of competition . . ." is from Jeffrey Share, *The Oil Makers* (Rice University Press, 1995).

Pages 60–61: Information on Enron's U.S. power plants is from an Enron press release of July 13, 1992.

Page 61: "Independent producers accounted for at least 5 percent of the nation's electricity-generation capacity . . ." is from Arthur Gottschalk, "US Energy Bill Likely to Boost Independent Power Projects," *Journal of Commerce*, September 18, 1992.

Pages 61–62: Background on the Energy Policy Act is from *Managing Energy Price Risk* (Risk Publications, 1995).

Page 62: Enron's estimate of the wholesale power market is from Jeffrey Share, *The Oil Makers* (Rice University Press, 1995).

Page 62: The Western Systems Power Pool's electronic trading experiment is from Peter C. Fusaro, *Energy Risk Management* (McGraw-Hill, 1998).

Pages 63–64: The combination of VPP contracts and swaps, and the success of Cactus are from Sanjay Bhatnagar and Peter Tufano, "Enron Gas Services," Harvard Business School, Case 9-294-076, September 26, 1995.

Pages 63–64: Cactus raising $340 million is from Enron's 1991 10-K annual report, filed with SEC March 31, 1992.

Page 64: Information on the separate classes of securities in Cactus is from Kurt Eichenwald, "Deals That Helped Doom Enron Began to Form in the Early 90s," *New York Times*, January 18, 2002.

Page 64: The sale of an Enron Oil & Gas interest to Cactus for $327 million is from an Enron Oil & Gas press release from September 30, 1992.

Page 64: That Andy Fastow was behind the Cactus vehicles is from a confidential source.

Page 65: Details on JEDI are from an Enron press release of June 30, 1993.

Page 65: The battle for Bridge Oil is from "Parker & Parsley Petroleum Officially Wins Control of Bridge Oil to End Takeover Battle," *Oil Daily*, July 13, 1994.

Pages 65–66: JEDI's list of deals is from various sources. The JEDI loan to Forest Oil is from a Forest Oil press release of April 18, 1995; the JEDI loan to Flores & Rucks is from Louise Durham, "The 10-Year, Overnight Sensation," *Oil & Gas Investor*, October 1995; the JEDI purchase of Coda Energy is from a Coda press release of October 31, 1995; and the JEDI purchase of Clinton Gas Systems is from a Clinton Gas press release of September 4, 1996.

Page 66: Details on the Coda investment are from an internal Enron manual on "Applied Finance," February 2000.

Page 66: Enron's credit sensitive notes are from Stephen Lynagh, "Enron Corp.—Credit Sensitive Notes," Harvard Business School, Case 9-297-099, July 25, 1997.

Page 67: Enron's trouble with oil trading is from an author interview with John Sherriff.

Page 67: The date of Enron's first electricity trade is from Enron's web site. Its power sales volumes by October 1994 are from an Enron press release of October 13, 1994.

Page 68: Enron's boast that it would grab 20 percent of the wholesale power market is from "New Kid on the Grid," *Journal of Commerce*, April 6, 1995.

Page 68: "Enron sold 7.8 million megawatt-hours of electricity—about the amount of electricity used in a city the size of Portland, Oregon . . ." is from Brent Walth, Jim Barnett, Gail Hulden, and Lovelle Svart, "Enron on a Mission to Reshape World Energy Business," *Oregonian*, December 8, 1996.

Page 69: Enron's deal with Oglethorpe is from Daniel Southerland, "You've Heard of Big Oil, This Is the Story of Big Gas," *Washington Post*, February 4, 1996.

Page 69: "When electricity trading started . . ." is from an author interview with Shannon Burchett.

Page 69: ECT's 1995 results are from Enron's 10-K annual report, filed on March 30, 1996.

Page 70: Skilling's quote on telemarketing, and the number of Enron power marketers are from Daniel Southerland, "You've Heard of Big Oil, This Is the Story of Big Gas," *Washington Post*, February 4, 1996.

Page 70: Lay's testimony to Congress is from an Enron press release of May 15, 1996.

Page 71: The terms of Enron's proposed acquisition of Portland General are from Benjamin Holden, "Enron Agrees to Buy Portland General," *Wall Street Journal*, July 22, 1996, and two Enron–Portland General press releases of July 22, 1996.

Page 72: Ronald Barone's quote is from Dwight Oestricher, "Enron Buy of Portland General Heralds Gas, Electric Industry Merger," Dow Jones News Service, July 22, 1996.

Page 72: The fact that the merger could serve as an example of restructuring the power industry is from an interview with a confidential source.

Page 73: Enron's filings with the OPUC and FERC are from Enron press releases of September 3, 1996, and September 20, 1996.

Page 73: Utilities' criticisms of the Portland General merger are from Bill MacKenzie, "Utilities: Enron–PGE Deal Stifling," *Portland Oregonian*, October 11, 1996, and Jim Barnett, "Enron Vows to Keep Utility Intact," *Portland Oregonian*, October 19, 1996.

Page 73: Shareholder approval is from an Enron press release of November 12, 1996. The utility's rate cut plan is from a Portland General press release of November 15, 1996.

Page 73: The promise of an open competition plan is from a Portland General press release of November 25, 1996.

Page 74: Enron's lobbying for support and the opposition to the merger are from Bill MacKenzie, "Forces Join to Fight Merger," *Portland Oregonian*, December 3, 1996.

Pages 74–75: Details on the Hanover deal are from internal Enron manual on "Applied Finance," February 2000.

Page 75: ECT's growth in 1996 is from Enron's 10-K annual report for 1996.

Pages 75–76: Quotes from Skilling's speech are from a transcript of remarks he made at the Arthur Andersen Oil & Gas Symposium on December 6, 1995.

CHAPTER 5 Culture of Creativity?

Page 78: Skilling's quote comparing selling gas to selling washing machines is from Peter Tufano, "How Financial Engineering Can Advance Corporate Strategy," *Harvard Business Review*, January/February 1996.

Page 78: The figures for Enron's return on equity are from Dennis Wamsted, "A Word to the Wise: Keep an Eye on Enron," *Energy Daily*, February 23, 1996; gas transportation's shrinkage as a percentage of Enron's revenue is from Gary McWilliams, "Enron's Pipeline into the Future," *Business Week*, December 2, 1996.

Page 78: Enron hiring Ogilvy & Mather is from Michael Davis, "Enron Hires an Ad Agency for Campaign," *Houston Chronicle*, August 27, 1996.

Page 78: Kenneth Rice's comments are from Samuel Bodily and Robert Bruner, "Transformation of Enron: 1986–2000," University of Virginia's Darden Graduate School of Business, October 6, 2000.

Page 78: Lay's quote on shaking up Enron's culture is from Gary Hamel, "Turning Your Business Upside Down," *Fortune*, June 23, 1997.

Page 79: Enron's four core values are from an internal Enron analyst program orientation guide, July 17, 2000.

Page 79: Companies recruiting from Enron are from a NorAm press release from September 22, 1997, and PG&E press releases from August 30, 1999, and September 24, 1999.

Page 79: Lay's quote about hiring and the salary data are from Daniel Southerland, "You've Heard of Big Oil, This Is the Story of Big Gas," *Washington Post*, February 4, 1996.

Pages 79–80: Lay's quote about compensation and Forrest Hoglund is from Jeffrey Share, *The Oil Makers* (Rice University Press, 1995).

Pages 80–82: Information on Enron's associate and analyst programs are variously from an author interview with Beau Ratliff; from an author interview with a confidential source; from an internal Enron analyst program orientation guide, July 17, 2000; and from "Enron 2001: An Inside View," a report by the consulting firm Global Change Associates, issued in July 2001.

Page 82: Skilling's views on flattening the management hierarchy and on new business development are from Samuel Bodily and Robert Bruner, "Transformation of Enron: 1986–2000," University of Virginia's Darden Graduate School of Business, October 6, 2000.

Pages 83–85: Basic information on Enron's PRC process comes from an internal Enron analyst program orientation guide, July 17, 2000; Samuel Bodily and Robert Bruner, "Transformation of Enron: 1986–2000," University of Virginia's Darden Graduate School of Business, October 6, 2000; "Enron 2001: An Inside View," a report by the consulting firm Global Change Associates, issued in July 2001; and author interviews with John Sherriff, Shannon Burchett, and Beau Ratliff.

Pages 85–86: Various information on the internal competition caused by the PRC process comes from Samuel Bodily and Robert Bruner, "Transformation of Enron: 1986–2000," University of Virginia's Darden Graduate School of Business, October 6, 2000; author interviews with ex-Enron employees Beau Ratliff, Diana Peters, and Jon Spitz; and interviews with several confidential sources.

Page 87: Figures on the characteristics of Enron's workforce are from "Enron Global Human Resources," an internal Enron report from October 15, 1999.

Page 87: Global Change's view of Enron culture is from "Enron 2001: An Inside View," a report by the consulting firm Global Change Associates, issued in July 2001.

Pages 88–89: Information on Enron's reorganizing and transferring of people is from Samuel Bodily and Robert Bruner, "Transformation of Enron: 1986–2000," University of Virginia's Darden Graduate School of Business, October 6, 2000; "Enron 2001: An Inside View," a report by the consulting firm Global Change Associates, issued in July 2001; and author interviews with Robert Smoot and Diana Peters.

Pages 89–90: Enron's restructurings causing selfishness and short-term priorities is from an author interview with a confidential source.

Page 90: Some information on Enron's fast pace is from Christopher Meyer, "The Second Generation of Speed," *Harvard Business Review*, April 2001.

Pages 90–91: Background on a typical trader's day, including the money involved and the stress, is from an author interview with a confidential source.

Page 92: Enron's lavish partying is from Neela Banerjee, David Barboza, and Audrey Warren, "At Enron, Lavish Excess Often Came before Success," *New York Times*, February 26, 2002, and author interview with Diana Peters.

Pages 92–93: Background on the affairs and sex at Enron, including Skilling's romance with Carter, are from author interviews with confidential sources, and from

Johnny Roberts and Evan Thomas, "Enron's Dirty Laundry," *Newsweek*, March 11, 2002. The Lipsticks anecdote is from a confidential source who was present.

Pages 93–94: Enron's tendency toward hype and emphasis on stock price are from an interview with a confidential source.

Pages 94–95: Enron's willingness to make big bets is from author interviews with Shannon Burchett and several confidential sources.

Page 95: Enron's use of Value at Risk is from Samuel Bodily and Robert Bruner, "Transformation of Enron: 1986–2000," University of Virginia's Darden Graduate School of Business, October 6, 2000, and an interview with a confidential source.

Page 96: The story of Metallgesellschaft and the consultant's quote are from Edward Krapels, "Paper Oil," Energy Security Analysis Inc., January 1996.

Pages 96–97: The Skilling-in-handcuffs rumor is from Daniel Southerland, "You've Heard of Big Oil, This Is the Story of Big Gas," *Washington Post*, February 4, 1996.

Page 97: Wall Street's worry about Enron's trading, and the $12 billion exposure are from Peter Fritsch, "Size of Enron's Trading Operation Worries Some Analysts," *Wall Street Journal*, December 29, 1995.

Page 97: The fact that employees viewed Enron as a "house of cards" is from author interviews with several confidential sources.

Page 97: The board's push for tighter controls is from author interviews with John Sherriff and several confidential sources.

CHAPTER 6 The Energy Buffet

Page 98: Kinder's departure and his quote are from Michael Davis, "Lay Staying, So Kinder Will Leave," *Houston Chronicle*, November 27, 1996. Kinder's 1996 compensation is from "Houston's Top-Paid Executives in 1996," *Houston Chronicle*, June 15, 1997. Kinder's strengths are from interviews with several confidential sources.

Pages 98–99: Kinder Morgan's origin is from an Enron Liquids Pipeline press release of January 9, 1997.

Page 99: Skilling's speech on Standard Oil is from Samuel Bodily and Robert Bruner, "Transformation of Enron: 1986–2000," University of Virginia's Darden Graduate School of Business, October 6, 2000.

Page 100: Results for Enron's divisions are from Enron's 10-K annual report for 1996.

Pages 100–101: Skilling's cool personality is from an author interview with Joseph Pokalsky.

Page 101: EI's atmosphere is from an interview with Diana Peters and an interview with a confidential source.

Page 101: Mark's comments on Dabhol are from "You Have to Be Pushy and Aggressive," *Business Week*, February 24, 1997.

Pages 101–102: The range of EI's activity is from Enron's 10-K annual report for 1996.

Page 102: The rivalry between Skilling and Mark is from author interviews with Diana Peters and a confidential source, and from Johnny Roberts and Evan Thomas, "Enron's Dirty Laundry," *Newsweek*, March 11, 2002.

Page 103: Skilling's appointment as president and Lay's comments are from an Enron press release of December 10, 1996.

Pages 103–104: Comments about Skilling's personality are from author interviews with confidential sources.

Page 104: The deal with the Northern California Power Agency is from Michael Davis, "Enron Plugs into California Market," *Houston Chronicle*, January 16, 1997.

Page 105: DeFazio's quote is from Brent Walth and Jim Barnett, "Enron on a Mission to Reshape World Energy Business," *Portland Oregonian*, December 8, 1996.

Pages 105–106: Enron's negotiations with the OPUC are from Bill MacKenzie, "State Conditions Displease Enron, PGE," *Portland Oregonian*, January 18, 1997; "Portland General Talks Hit Snag," Associated Press, January 25, 1997; Bill MacKenzie, "PUC Takes Hard Line on Utility Deal," *Portland Oregonian*, February 15, 1997; a Portland General press release of March 12, 1997; Bill MacKenzie, "Enron Merger Takes Step Forward," *Portland Oregonian*, May 7, 1997.

Page 106: Comments on spark spreads are from an interview with a confidential source.

Pages 107–108: The discussion of optionality and the quotes from Skilling and Tawney are from Samuel Bodily and Robert Bruner, "Transformation of Enron: 1986–2000," University of Virginia's Darden Graduate School of Business, October 6, 2000.

Pages 108–109: Background on Enron's Super Bowl ad campaign is from Allen R. Myerson, "Enron, Seeking to Be a Household Name, Plans to Start Its Campaign on Super Bowl Sunday," *New York Times*, January 14, 1997, and Michael Davis, "Enron Corp.'s New Logo Will Be Unveiled Today," *Houston Chronicle*, January 14, 1997.

Page 109: Enron's experience in New Hampshire is from Lisa Singhani, "Open Market Creates Rush for Electricity Customers," Associated Press, May 9, 1996, and Richard A. Oppel Jr., "New Hampshire Tryout Lets People Shop for Electricity," *Dallas Morning News*, April 6, 1997.

Page 111: "Enron estimated that half of the money invested in the U.S. electric industry" is from Samuel Bodily and Robert Bruner, "Transformation of Enron: 1986–2000," University of Virginia's Darden Graduate School of Business, October 6, 2000.

Page 111: Enron's federal-level political contributions from 1988 to 1996 are from Brent Walth and Jim Barnett, "Enron on a Mission to Reshape World Energy Business," *Portland Oregonian*, December 8, 1996.

Page 111: Enron's soft-money donations and the comparisons to other companies are from Charles Lewis, *The Buying of the President 2000* (Avon Books, 2000).

Pages 112–113: Background on Enron, DeLay, and federal deregulation bills is from Juliet Eilperin, "What Happened to Big Electricity Overhaul Bill?," *Roll Call*, October 20, 1997, and Brent Walth and Jim Barnett, "Enron on a Mission to Reshape World Energy Business," *Portland Oregonian*, December 8, 1996.

Page 113: Enron's connection to Bush's inauguration is from Shelby Hodge, "Bush Beginnings," *Houston Chronicle*, January 15, 1995.

Page 113: The story of Enron, Bush, and Kuwait is from "Report Says Bush Sons Lobbied for Kuwait Business," Associated Press, August 29, 1993, and Brent Walth and Jim Barnett, "A Wealth of Influence," *Portland Oregonian*, December 8, 1996.

Pages 113–114: Information on Texas' deregulation and Enron is from Michael Totty, "As Clock Ticks, a Push to Deregulate Electricity," *Wall Street Journal*, April 30, 1997.

Page 114: Skilling's stake in EES is from Enron's proxy statement of March 24, 1997. Background on Pai is from Peter Behr and Robert O'Harrow Jr., "$270 Million Man Stays in the Background," *Washington Post*, February 6, 2002; and an interview with a confidential source.

Page 114: Enron's involvement with the Toledo pilot program is from an Enron press release of March 27, 1997, and from Jennifer Scott, "Customers Stay with Columbia," *Columbus Dispatch*, June 4, 1997.

Page 114: EES' $14 million loss are from an Enron press release of April 11, 1997.

Page 115: EES losses and Wall Street's reaction are from Loren Fox, "Enron Paying Price for Entering Retail Energy Market," Dow Jones News Service, July 15, 1997.

Page 115: Enron's pacts with SMC Business Councils and Healthcare Services of New England are from Enron press releases of October 6, 1997, and November 20, 1997.

Page 116: Enron's complaints about California's deregulation plan are from "Is Enron Getting Cold Feet?," *San Francisco Examiner,* September 10, 1997.

Page 116: Enron's California offer is from an Enron press release of October 23, 1997.

Pages 116–118: Information about Enron's battle with Peco is from Kathryn Kranhold, "Rattling Cages: Utilities' Quiet World Is Shaken Up As Enron Moves on Philadelphia," *Wall Street Journal,* January 7, 1998; a Peco press release of November 10, 1997; and Jim Strader, "PUC Adopts Its Own Plan, Rejecting Peco, Enron Proposals," Associated Press, December 12, 1997.

Page 118: Skilling's quote about customers wanting functions is from Samuel Bodily and Robert Bruner, "Transformation of Enron: 1986–2000," University of Virginia's Darden Graduate School of Business, October 6, 2000.

Pages 118–119: The Pacific Telesis pact is from an Enron press release of January 15, 1998.

Page 119: EES having over $1 billion in contracts is from Loren Fox, "Enron Corp. Sees 1998 Oper Net of $2.20/Diluted Share," Dow Jones News Service, January 20, 1998.

Pages 119–120: Details of the Owens Corning deal, and other sale/leaseback arrangements, are from an internal Enron presentation on structured finance for Enron Energy Services.

Pages 120–121: The sale of a piece of EES is from an Enron press release of January 6, 1998; a CalPERS press release of January 6, 1998; Loren Fox, "Enron Corp. Sees 1998 Oper Net of $2.20/Diluted Share," Dow Jones News Service, January 20, 1998; the Ontario Teachers' Pension Plan 1999 annual report; and an author interview with a confidential source.

CHAPTER 7   Taking the Plunge

Page 122: The performance of JEDI is from Enron's 10-K annual report for 1997, filed March 31, 1998. CalPERS' return on JEDI is from a CalPERS press release of January 6, 1998.

Pages 122–124: Information on the formation of Chewco and its approval are from "Report of the Investigation by the Special Investigative Committee of the Board of Directors of Enron Corp.," chaired by William C. Powers, issued February 1, 2002 (henceforth known as "The Powers Report"), and minutes of a meeting of the executive committee of Enron's board of directors, November 5, 1997. Background on Michael Kopper is from Tami Luhby, "Local Boy Caught in the Mix," *Newsday,* February 12, 2002.

Pages 124–125: Information on Enron's dealings with Sharon Lay and Mark K. Lay is from Enron's proxy statements (schedule 14-A) filed on March 24, 1997, and March 24, 1998; David Barboza and Kurt Eichenwald, "Son and Sister of Enron Chief Secured Deals," *New York Times*, February 2, 2002; and "Enron Boss Defends Contracts with Companies Owned by His Kin," *Portland Oregonian*, May 7, 1997.

Pages 125–127: Information on Chewco and meeting the SPE rules is from the Powers Report. David Duncan's assertion that Andersen didn't know about Enron's side agreement with Barclays is from his court testimony in the 2002 trial of Arthur Andersen, as reported in Kurt Eichenwald, "How the Trial of Andersen Could Hurt a Fraud Case," *New York Times*, May 24, 2002.

Page 128: Enron's third-quarter 1997 earnings and analysts' estimates is from Loren Fox, "Enron 3Q Surprises Wall Street," Dow Jones News Service, October 14, 1997.

Page 130: "Reported earnings follow the rules and principles of accounting . . ." This quote is from Paradigm Associates Group, "Derivatives I: Introduction," an Enron Capital & Trade Resources training manual, 1996–1997.

Page 130: Information about Enron's compensation plan, relative stock performance of 1992 to 1997, and stock ownership is from Enron's proxy statements (schedule 14-A) filed on March 24, 1997, and March 24, 1998.

Page 131: Gas trading's shrinking profit margin is from a confidential source.

Page 131: The purchase of Zond is from an Enron press release of January 6, 1997.

Pages 131–132: The growth of Enron Renewable Energy is from Enron press releases of July 7, 1997, October 15, 1997, and December 8, 1999; "Green Power: Two CA Deals Promote Renewable Energy," *Greenwire*, July 8, 1998; and Loren Fox, "Enron Sees Wind Energy Leading Renewable-Power Growth," Dow Jones News Service, May 15, 1998.

Pages 132–133: The founding of Enron's paper-trading business is from an internal Enron analyst program orientation guide, July 17, 2000; "Risk Management for the Pulp and Paper Industry," an internal Enron Capital & Trade manual produced in 1997; and Agis Salpukas, "Firing Up an Idea Machine," *New York Times*, June 27, 1999.

Pages 133–134: Information on Enron's weather derivatives business is from Loren Fox, "Weather Hedging Gathers Steam with Boost from El Niño," Dow Jones News Service, December 1, 1997; Agis Salpukas, "Firing Up an Idea Machine," *New York Times*, June 27, 1999; an author interview with John Sherriff; and an internal Enron analyst program orientation guide, July 17, 2000.

Page 135: Enron's repurchase of Enron Global Power & Pipelines is from an Enron press release of November 18, 1997.

Page 135: Mark's promotion to vice chairman is from "Enron Names Mark a Vice Chairman," *Wall Street Journal*, May 7, 1998.

Pages 136–137: Information on the plan to buy Wessex Water is from Enron press releases of July 16, 1998, and July 24, 1998; Loren Fox, "Enron Dives into Water Business, and Market Reacts Coolly," Dow Jones News Service, July 24, 1998; and Kathryn Kranhold, "Enron to Acquire Wessex Water for $2.2 Billion," *Wall Street Journal*, July 25, 1998.

Pages 137–138: The financing of Azurix and Marlin Water Trust is from an Azurix S-1 registration statement filed March 15, 1999; a press release from Standard & Poor's from December 1, 1998; and Jeffrey Keegan, "Enron Goes to 144A Well to Fund New Water Business," *Investment Dealers Digest*, December 14, 1998.

Page 138: Background on Spottiswoode and Azurix is from Andrew Taylor, "Former Gas Industry Regulator to Leave Enron," *Financial Times*, February 25, 1999.

Pages 138–139: Azurix's two deals in early 1999 are from Azurix press releases of January 20, 1999, and March 26, 1999.

Page 139: Information on Azurix and its Buenos Aires concessions, and the IPO, is from Azurix press releases of May 19, 1999, and June 9, 1999; Jenalia Moreno, "Azurix Testing the Waters," *Houston Chronicle*, January 9, 2000; Rebecca Smith and Aaron Lucchetti, "Sink or Swim: Rebecca Mark's Exit Leaves Enron's Azurix Treading Deep Water," *Wall Street Journal*, August 28, 2000; and Brad Foss, "How a Fledgling Water Business Helped Sink Enron," Associated Press, February 3, 2002.

Page 140: Azurix's disappointing earnings and job cuts are from "Investors Unload Azurix's Shares after Company's Earnings Warning," *Dow Jones Business News*, November 4, 1999; and Christopher C. Williams, "Azurix Sees $30 Million–$35 Million Nonrecurring 4th Quarter Charge," Dow Jones News Service, November 16, 1999.

Page 140: Azurix's earnings compared with Wessex Water's earnings are from Azurix's 10-K405 annual report for 1999, filed on March 30, 2000.

Pages 140–141: Background on Azurix's Water2Water.com is from Azurix's 10-K405 annual report for 1999, filed on March 30, 2000, and Rebecca Smith and Aaron Lucchetti, "Sink or Swim: Rebecca Mark's Exit Leaves Enron's Azurix Treading Deep Water," *Wall Street Journal*, August 28, 2000.

Page 141: Information on Rebecca Mark's resignation is from Azurix press releases of August 8, 2000, and August 25, 2000, and Michael Davis, "High-Profile Executive Calls It Quits," *Houston Chronicle*, August 26, 2000.

Pages 141–142: Enron's effort to sell its wind business is from Enron motion filed in Bankruptcy Court on February 20, 2001, Document 1583.

CHAPTER 8   Enron Gets Wired

Page 143: Yahoo!'s stock rise was calculated with stock quotes from BigCharts. com.

Page 144: The Cogen deal is from Enron press releases of October 30, 1998, and August 13, 1999; East Coast Power's S-4 registration statement, filed June 25, 1999; a Duff & Phelps credit rating press release of April 6, 1999; and Ronald Fink, "Balancing Act," *CFO*, June 1, 1999.

Page 145: Details on Enron and Brazil's Elektro are from Enron's annual report for 1999, and from Kathryn Kranhold and Peter Fritsch, "Enron Accelerates Push into Brazil with Controlling Interest in Utility," *Wall Street Journal*, July 17, 1998.

Page 145: Enron's shift in California strategy is from George Raine, "Enron Drops Home Market," *San Francisco Examiner*, April 23, 1998.

Page 146: The end of EnergyOne is from Loren Fox, "Efforts to Sell Brand Name Energy to Homes Stumble," Dow Jones News Service, May 6, 1998.

Pages 146–147: The origin of Enron's data network, and quotes from Ken Rice, are from Samuel Bodily and Robert Bruner, "Transformation of Enron: 1986–2000," University of Virginia's Darden Graduate School of Business, October 6, 2000.

Page 147: Enron's plan to link Los Angeles and Portland, and background on Williams' strategy, is from an Enron press release of September 8, 1997; Loren Fox, "Energy Giant Enron Touting Plans for National Fiber Network," *Dow Jones Online News*, July 21, 1998; and Loren Fox, "Texas Utilities Eyes Bundling of Energy, Telecom Services," Dow Jones News Service, August 25, 1997.

Pages 147–148: Enron's further development of its fiber network is from Jeff Manning, "Enron Unit Buys Portland Company," *Portland Oregonian*, November 18, 1997; and Loren Fox, "Energy Giant Enron Touting Plans for National Fiber Network," *Dow Jones Online News*, July 21, 1998.

Page 148: The Scott McNealy anecdote is from an interview with a confidential source.

Page 148: Enron's network being open for business in April 1999 is from an Enron press release of April 19, 1999.

Pages 148–153: Information on LJM and the Rhythms NetConnections transaction is from the Powers Report; investigators' interview with Richard Causey on November 30, 2001, for the Powers Report; investigators' interview with Vincent Kaminski on December 19, 2001, for the Powers Report; "The Role of the Board of Directors in Enron's Collapse," a report by the U.S. Senate Permanent Subcommittee on Investigations, issued July 8, 2002; and an author interview with a confidential source.

Pages 154–155: Background on Andrew Fastow is from Wendy Zellner with Mike France and Joseph Weber, "The Man Behind the Deal Mchine," *Business*

Week, February 4, 2002; Peter Spiegel, "Enron Collapse: The Fastow Factor," *Financial Times*, May 21, 2002; Lois Romano and Paul Duggan, " 'Low-Profile Guy' Was Wizard behind Enron's Complex Books," *Washington Post*, February 7, 2002; and author interviews with confidential sources. The EES incident is from a confidential source.

Pages 155–156: The anecdote about banks' pressure to invest in LJM is from Peter Spiegel, "Enron Collapse: The Fastow Factor," *Financial Times*, May 21, 2002.

Page 156: Figures for Enron's debt and the debt of its unconsolidated affiliates are from Enron's 10-K annual report for 1998.

Page 157: The story of Fastow's transformation of the finance department, and Skilling's praise of him, is from Russ Banham, "The Finest in Finance: Andrew S. Fastow," *CFO*, October 1999.

Page 157: Information on Whitewing and Osprey are from Enron's 10-K annual report for 1999; Enron's 10-Q quarterly report filed November 19, 2001; and a Duff & Phelps press release of September 16, 1999.

Page 158: Details of Fastow's involvement in the Chewco-Enron negotiations are from the Powers Report.

Pages 158–159: The Enron board's willingness to accept "high risk" accounting strategies is from "The Role of the Board of Directors in Enron's Collapse," a report by the U.S. Senate Permanent Subcommittee on Investigations, issued July 8, 2002.

Page 159–162: Information on the unwinding of the Rhythms deal, including Enron employees' profits, is from the Powers Report. Information on the "Friends of Enron" is from Jim Landers, "Enron 'Friends' Told of Deals," *Dallas Morning News*, March 23, 2002.

Pages 161–162: Information on the three NatWest bankers' scheme to profit from Swap Sub is taken from the affidavit filed June 27, 2002, by FBI special agent C. Deanne Simpson, in connection with the Justice Department's charges against Mulgrew, Darby, and Bermingham.

Pages 162–164: Background on Enron's launch of bandwidth trading is from Enron press release of May 20, 1999, and December 2, 1999; Joel Kurtzman and Glenn Rifkin, *Radical E: From GE to Enron—Lessons on How to Rule the Web* (John Wiley & Sons, 2001); Kathryn Kranhold, "Enron Is Planning to Create a Market to Trade Communications Capacity," *Wall Street Journal*, May 20, 1999; Enron's 10-K annual report for 2000 (filed March 31, 2001); and an internal Enron analyst program orientation guide, July 17, 2000.

Page 164: Information on RateXChange is from RateXChange press releases.

Page 164: Examples of how Enron's bandwidth deals were priced are from "Introduction to Bandwidth Risk Management," an internal Enron manual prepared by Paradigm Strategy Group in 2000–2001.

Page 165: Information on the formation of Altra and other energy exchanges is from a Battery Ventures press release of August 20, 1997; an Altra Energy press release of December 11, 1997; a HoustonStreet.com press release of August 10, 1999; and "Altra Buys Electronic Trading Rival QuickTrade," *Gas Daily*, January 15, 1999.

Pages 166–169: The formation of EnronOnline is from an author interview with John Sherriff; Samuel Bodily and Robert Bruner, "Transformation of Enron: 1986–2000," University of Virginia's Darden Graduate School of Business, October 6, 2000; and Enron press releases of October 26, 1999, January 20, 2000, and July 24, 2000.

CHAPTER 9 Power and Glory

Pages 170–171: Information on the Enron-Veba merger talks is from Neal E. Boudette, "Once Seen as Prey for Likes of Enron, E.On Turns Nimble," *Wall Street Journal Europe*, February 7, 2002; and Edmund L. Andrews, Neela Banerjee, and Andrew Ross Sorkin, "Early Warning: '99 Deal Failed after Scrutiny of Enron's Books," *New York Times*, January 27, 2002.

Page 171: Background on the Enron-EOG deal is from Loren Fox, "Wall Street Votes for Sale of Enron Oil at Right Price," Dow Jones News Service, December 16, 1998; "Enron Corp. Scraps Plans to Sell Its Stake in Enron Oil & Gas," *Wall Street Journal*, May 10, 1999; an Enron press release of July 20, 1999; and "Enron Corp. Cuts Loose EOG Resources," *Houston Chronicle*, August 17, 1999.

Pages 172–173: The Enron–Portland General information is from Jeff Mapes, "PGE Deregulation Plan Zapped," *Portland Oregonian*, January 29, 1999; "As Usual, Budget Rules Legislature," *Portland Oregonian*, July 26, 1999; Fred Leeson, "Talk Swirls of Enron Plan to Sell PGE," *Portland Oregonian*, October 1, 1999; author interview with a confidential source; and an Enron press release of November 8, 1999.

Page 173: The comment about not needing Portland General "to get a few electricity traders" is from a confidential source.

Page 173: Enron's revenue and net income figures are from Enron's 1999 annual report; stock and S&P 500 information is from BigCharts.com.

Pages 173–174: Enron compensation data is from Enron's proxy (Schedule 14A), filed March 21, 2000. Data on Lou Gerstner is from IBM's proxy, filed March 13, 2000.

Page 175: Enron's paper company deal is from a confidential source.

Page 175: Cash flow and return on equity data are from Enron's 1999 annual report.

Page 176: The fact that Enron began building a new, 40-story office tower is from an Enron press release of July 13, 1999.

Pages 176–178: The formation and marketing of LJM2 is from the Powers Report; the LJM2 Co-Investment L.P. private placement memorandum circulated by Merrill Lynch & Co.; a list of limited partner groups for LJM2 Co-Investment L.P.; "The Role of the Board of Directors in Enron's Collapse," a report by the U.S. Senate Permanent Subcommittee on Investigations, issued July 8, 2002; and Charles Gasparino and Randall Smith, "Merrill Officials Invested Their Funds in Enron Partnership That They Sold," *Wall Street Journal,* January 30, 2002. Lay's comments about the controls being Skilling's responsibility are from notes of Ken Lay's interview with Wilmer, Cutler & Pickering, as part of the Enron board's investigation in January 2002.

Pages 178–180: Deals between Enron and LJM2, and LJM1, are from Enron's 10-Q quarterly report filed November 19, 2001, and the Powers Report.

Page 180: Details were taken and passages quoted from Enron's 1999 annual report, filed March 13, 2000.

Page 180: The U.S. Senate investigation's comment that Enron's disclosures were "nearly impossible to understand" is from "The Role of the Board of Directors in Enron's Collapse," a report by the U.S. Senate Permanent Subcommittee on Investigations, issued July 8, 2002.

Page 181: Background on Arthur Andersen's history is from Andersen's web site.

Page 182: Information on the rise of consulting among accounting firms is from Jeremy Kahn, "One Plus One Makes What?," *Fortune,* January 7, 2002.

Page 182: Background on internal auditing is from David S. Hilzenrath, "Enron's 'Outside' Accountants Also Did Inside Audit," *Washington Post,* December 14, 2001.

Page 182: Andersen's involvement with Sunbeam and Waste Management is from Kurt Eichenwald, "Waste Management Executives Are Named in S.E.C. Accusation," *New York Times,* March 27, 2002, and Kirstin Downey Grimsley, "Scandals Put Andersen's Future at Risk," *Washington Post,* January 16, 2002.

Page 183: Baruch Lev's views are from testimony of Baruch Lev to the U.S. House Committee on Energy and Commerce on February 6, 2002.

Page 184: Lay's earnings forecasts are from "Enron Corp. Sees Earnings per Share Up 10%–15% in 1997," Dow Jones News Service, February 12, 1997.

Page 185: Enron's reserves are from the 2000 annual report; traders' practice of occasionally trimming reserves on a trade is from an interview with a confidential source.

Page 185: Forrester's estimate is from Neela Banerjee, "Doubts Emerge on Business of Trading Electricity," *New York Times,* June 15, 2002.

Page 186: Enron's lobbying for a better credit rating, and what it didn't tell S&P, is from testimony of Standard & Poor's managing director Ronald Barone to the U.S. Senate Committee on Governmental Affairs on March 20, 2002.

Page 186: The role of Moody's is from testimony of Moody's managing director John Diaz to the U.S. Senate Committee on Governmental Affairs on March 20, 2002.

Pages 187–188: The birth of EnronCredit.com is from an Enron press release of February 23, 2000, and an interview with John Sherriff.

Pages 188–189: Information on Enron's entry into metals trading is from Enron press releases of May 22, 2000, and July 6, 2000; Enron's 2000 annual report; and an interview with John Sherriff.

Page 189: EnronOnline's entry into paper trading is from Enron press releases of July 13, 2000, and September 5, 2000, and an interview with John Sherriff.

Page 189: Data on the rise in mergers is from Thomson Financial.

Page 189: *Fortune* magazine's survey results are from Geoffrey Colvin, "America's Most Admired Companies," *Fortune*, February 21, 2000.

Page 190: John Olson's comments on Enron's arrogance are from Olson's prepared testimony delivered to the U.S. House Committee on Energy and Commerce on February 7, 2002.

Page 190: The "world's coolest company" anecdote is from Samuel Bodily and Robert Bruner, "Transformation of Enron: 1986–2000," University of Virginia's Darden Graduate School of Business, October 6, 2000.

Page 190: Skilling's quotes to *Business 2.0* are from "What I Learned at the Revolution," *Business 2.0*, August 2001.

Page 191: Some of Enron's local involvement is from Jim Yardley, "Fall of Enron Ends Its Dance with Houston," *New York Times*, January 14, 2002, and author interview with Diana Peters.

Page 191: Enron's involvement with the Astros is from John Williams, "A Ballpark Figure; Astros, City, County Approve Stadium Plan," *Houston Chronicle*, July 17, 1997; an Enron press release of April 7, 1999; and Todd Ackerman, "Enron Field: Grand Opening," *Houston Chronicle*, March 31, 2000.

Pages 191–192: Information on donations from Lay and Enron to Bush's gubernatorial campaigns is from Texans for Public Justice news release of January 11, 2002.

Pages 192–193: Letters between Bush and Lay are from: letter of September 21, 1995, from Lay to Governor Bush; letter of December 11, 1997, from Lay to Laura and George Bush; handwritten note of January 13, 1997, from Lay to Governor Bush; letter of April 2, 1997, from Bush to Lay; and letter from Bush to Lay of April 14, 1997, obtained from www.thesmokinggun.com.

Pages 192–193: Letters from Lay to Bush are from: March 31, 1999; February 15, 1995; May 30, 1995, July 15, 1996; and April 3, 1997.

Page 193: Enron's stock prices are from BigCharts.com; revenue figures are from an Enron press release of July 24, 2000.

Page 194: Information on Merrill Lynch's Internet research is from "Affidavit in Support of Application for an Order Pursuant to General Business Law Section 354," filed by New York State Attorney General in New York State Supreme Court.

Page 194: "Picking six or eight underwriters for one offering . . ." is from Enron's January 13, 1997, prospectus for Trust Preferred Securities, in which six underwriters were listed.

Pages 194–195: John Olson's comments, and the "unspoken rule" trading banking business for recommending the stock, are from Olson's prepared testimony delivered to the U.S. House Committee on Energy and Commerce on February 7, 2002.

Page 195: Chuck Hill's comments are from Hill's testimony delivered to a joint session of the U.S. House Subcommittee on Capital Markets, Insurance, and Government Sponsored Enterprises and the House Subcommittee on Oversight and Investigation on October 12, 2001.

CHAPTER 10   California Dreamin'

Pages 196–197: Information on the June 1998 power price spike is from "Staff Report to the Federal Energy Regulatory Commission on the Causes of Wholesale Electric Pricing Abnormalities in the Midwest during June 1998," a report by FERC staff delivered September 22, 1998.

Page 197: Fallout from the June 1998 power price spike is from Loren Fox, "Utilities Study Ways to Avoid Trading Losses," Dow Jones News Service, July 9, 1998; Rebecca Melvin, "LG&E Energy's Exit from Power Marketing Shows High Stakes," Dow Jones Energy Service, July 29, 1998; and Mark Golden, "Enron Seen as Big Winner in June Eastern U.S. Power Trading," Dow Jones Energy Service, July 6, 1998.

Page 198: Background on California's deregulation of power is from Jessica Berthold, "Pointing the Finger: Who's at Fault in California? It Depends on Whom You Ask," *Wall Street Journal,* September 17, 2001, and "Anatomy of a Jolt," *Wall Street Journal,* June 25, 2001.

Pages 198–200: The California power crisis in summer and fall 2000 is from Rebecca Smith, "California Ponders Lowering Price Cap on Power As Hot Spell Raised Tempers," *Wall Street Journal,* June 26, 2000; testimony from Steven

Kline, vice president for federal governmental and regulatory relations of PG&E Corp., delivered to the U.S. Senate Committee on Energy and Natural Resources on January 31, 2001; an Enron press release of October 17, 2000; Craig D. Rose, "Power-Company Profits Climb Along with Prices," *San Diego Union-Tribune*, October 18, 2000; and "Anatomy of a Jolt," *Wall Street Journal*, June 25, 2001. Lay's quote on markets is from a confidential source.

Pages 200–202: The formation and approval of Raptors I, II, and IV are from the Powers Report; handwritten notes by Jeff McMahon (released by the U.S. House Committee on Energy and Commerce); an October 22, 2001, summary of an interview with McMahon conducted by Vinson & Elkins; transcripts of the February 7, 2002, hearing of the Oversight and Investigations Subcommittee of the U.S. House Energy and Commerce Committee; and minutes of the May 1, 2000, meeting of the finance committee of the Enron board of directors.

Pages 202–204: Information on deals done by the Raptors comes from the Powers Report, and from Raptor Asset Inventory, an internal Enron document, from March 31, 2001.

Page 204: Details of Project Grayhawk are from Kurt Eichenwald, "U.S. Inquiry Tracks Insiders at Enron," *New York Times*, April 15, 2002.

Page 205: Information on the costless collars put on Raptors is from the Powers Report.

Pages 205–207: The formation of New Power is from an amended prospectus (Form S-1) for New Power filed October 2, 2000; Rebecca Smith, "New Power Saga Shows How Enron Tapped IPO Boom to Boost Results," *Wall Street Journal*, March 25, 2002; and an author interview with Ron Chernin.

Page 207: The creation of Raptor III and hedging of New Power stock is from the Powers Report, and from Rebecca Smith, "New Power Saga Shows How Enron Tapped IPO Boom to Boost Results," *Wall Street Journal*, March 25, 2002.

Pages 208–209: Various details of Enron's electricity trading tactics are from "Traders' Strategies in the California Wholesale Power Market/ISO Sanctions," a memo from Christian Yoder and Stephen Hall of Stoel Rives, December 6, 2000; Thomas S. Mulligan, "How Enron Manipulated State's Power Market," *Los Angeles Times*, May 9, 2002; "Status Report on Further Investigation and Analysis of EPMI Trading Strategies," a memo from Gary Fergus of Brobeck, Phleger & Harrison LP and Jean Frizzell of Gibbs & Bruns LLP, undated; and Richard A. Oppel Jr., "Enron Traded Amid Doubts, Senate Is Told," *New York Times*, May 16, 2002.

Page 210: Information on other energy companies' tactics in California is from Scott Thurm and Robert Gavin, "Energy Traders at Xcel, Mirant Discussed 'Gaming' California," *Wall Street Journal*, June 10, 2002, and a transcript con-

Kenneth Lay, the chairman and patriarch of Enron. Starting in 1985 he built the company into a powerhouse that included pipelines, power plants, and an impressive trading operation. (© Pam Francis)

Richard Kinder, Enron's president and chief operating officer until he left at the end of 1996. Kinder made the trains run on time, and the loss of his operational skill was a turning point for Enron. Kinder appears here in May 2002 in his new firm, a pipeline company that doesn't trade energy. (Carlos Antonio Rios/*Houston Chronicle*)

Corporate statesman Ken Lay had many political connections, but the most notable was his friendship with George W. Bush; his ascent to the presidency in 2001 seemed to give Enron special access to the White House, critics charged. Shown here is a casual letter Bush wrote to Lay on April 14, 1997, when he was governor of Texas. (*Source:* thesmokinggun.com)

STATE OF TEXAS
OFFICE OF THE GOVERNOR

GEORGE W. BUSH
GOVERNOR

April 14, 1997

Mr. Kenneth Lay
2121 Kirby Drive
Houston, Texas 77019

Dear Ken:

One of the sad things about old friends is that they seem to be getting older - just like you!

55 years old. Wow! That is really old.

Thank goodness you have such a young, beautiful wife.

Laura and I value our friendship with you. Best wishes to Linda, your family, and friends.

Your younger friend,

George W. Bush

Jeffrey Skilling, the former McKinsey consultant who masterminded the company's trading strategy and eventually rose to become, briefly, the CEO. (D. Fahleson/*Houston Chronicle*)

Andrew S. Fastow, the financial "whiz kid" who rose to chief financial officer at Enron. Fastow created and managed the controversial LJM partnerships that enriched him and helped lead to Enron's accounting scandal. (James Essrun/ *The New York Times*)

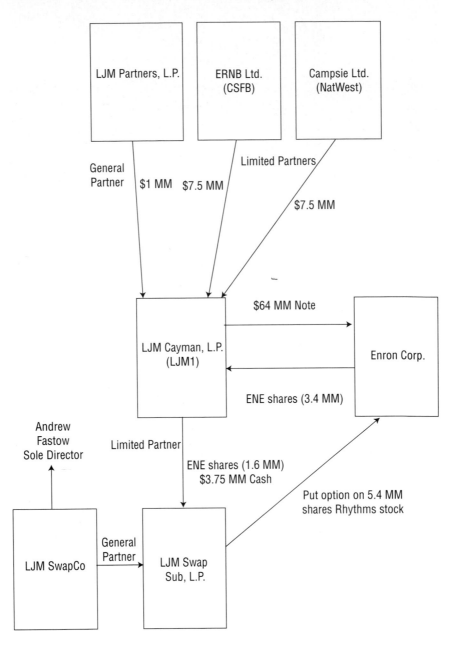

The Rhythms transaction, carried out in 1999 by a few of the partnerships Fastow created. The idea here was to protect Enron's investment in an Internet company, but the diagram illustrates the mind-boggling complexity that was used to keep the deal off Enron's books. (*Source:* The Powers Report)

Rebecca Mark and Joseph W. Sutton, the leaders of Enron International, pictured in their glory days in 1998. Mark's ability to land projects in England, India, and other foreign locales made her a possible successor to Lay, but Skilling beat her out as Enron moved away from the asset-heavy businesses she'd championed. (Ben Desoto/*Houston Chronicle*)

Richard Causey, Enron's chief accounting officer. Causey approved Fastow's partnerships and their deals with Enron. (© Pam Francis)

Enron Vice President of Corporate Development Sherron Watkins looks on as former Enron Chief Executive Officer Jeffrey Skilling testifies on Capitol Hill Tuesday, February 26, 2002, before the Senate Commerce Committee hearing on Enron. (AP Photo/Ron Edmonds)

Dear Mr. Lay,

Has Enron become a risky place to work? For those of us who didn't get rich over the last few years, can we afford to stay?

Skilling's abrupt departure will raise suspicions of accounting improprieties and valuation issues. Enron has been very aggressive in its accounting – most notably the Raptor transactions and the Condor vehicle. We do have valuation issues with our international assets and possibly some of our EES MTM positions.

The spotlight will be on us, the market just can't accept that Skilling is leaving his dream job. I think that the valuation issues can be fixed and reported with other goodwill write-downs to occur in 2002. How do we fix the Raptor and Condor deals? They unwind in 2002 and 2003, we will have to pony up Enron stock and that won't go unnoticed.

To the layman on the street, it will look like we recognized funds flow of $800 mm from merchant asset sales in 1999 by selling to a vehicle (Condor) that we capitalized with a promise of Enron stock in later years. Is that really funds flow or is it cash from equity issuance?

We have recognized over $550 million of fair value gains on stocks via our swaps with Raptor, much of that stock has declined significantly – Avici by 98%, from $178 mm to $5 mm, The New Power Co by 70%, from $20/share to $6/share. The value in the swaps won't be there for Raptor, so once again Enron will issue stock to offset these losses. Raptor is an LJM entity. It sure looks to the layman on the street that we are hiding losses in a related company and will compensate that company with Enron stock in the future.

I am incredibly nervous that we will implode in a wave of accounting scandals. My 8 years of Enron work history will be worth nothing on my resume, the business world will consider the past successes as nothing but an elaborate accounting hoax. Skilling is resigning now for 'personal reasons' but I think he wasn't having fun, looked down the road and knew this stuff was unfixable and would rather abandon ship now than resign in shame in 2 years.

Is there a way our accounting guru's can unwind these deals now? I have thought and thought about how to do this, but I keep bumping into one big problem – we booked the Condor and Raptor deals in 1999 and 2000, we enjoyed a wonderfully high stock price, many executives sold stock, we then try and reverse or fix the deals in 2001 and it's a bit like robbing the bank in one year and trying to pay back it back 2 years later. Nice try, but investors were hurt, they bought at $70 and $80/share looking for $120/share and now they're at $38 or worse. We are under too much scrutiny and there are probably one or two disgruntled 'redeployed' employees who know enough about the 'funny' accounting to get us in trouble.

What do we do? I know this question cannot be addressed in the all employee meeting, but can you give some assurances that you and Causey will sit down and take a good hard objective look at what is going to happen to Condor and Raptor in 2002 and 2003?

Enron accountant Sherron Watkins sent this frank warning letter to Lay on August 15, 2001, after Skilling's surprise resignation from the company. The letter presciently alerted Lay that Enron might "implode in a wave of accounting scandals."

On November 9, 2001, then Enron chairman Kenneth Lay appeared with Chuck Watson, chairman and chief executive officer of Dynegy, to announce that Dynegy would rescue Enron by acquiring it. The deal fell apart three weeks later. (Christobal Perez/*Houston Chronicle*)

The Enron headquarters in Houston, as seen at dusk in April 2002. Enron employees had routinely worked long hours in the building as they jostled for promotions in the competitive culture. (Andrew Innerarity/ *Houston Chronicle*)

Arthur Andersen's lead Enron auditor, David Duncan, is followed by the media after he pleaded guilty to obstruction of justice on April 9, 2002, in the Houston federal courthouse. (Steven Ueckert/*Houston Chronicle*)

Choosing not to testify about his role in Enron's demise, Lay asserts his Fifth Amendment right against self-incrimination before the Senate Commerce Committee on February 12, 2002. At those hearings, he was compared unfavorably to a carnival barker. (Paul Hosefros/*The New York Times*)

versation from July 18, 2000, "Sold 50 Megawatts to SCEM at Four Corners," released by Xcel Energy.

Page 211: The 2000 loss for New Power is from New Power's 10-K annual report for 2000, filed March 30, 2001.

Pages 211–212: The December cross collateralization of the Raptors is from the Powers Report; a memo entitled "Raptor Structures Update," from David Duncan, Deb Cash, Patty Grutzmacher, and Jennifer Stevenson, of Arthur Andersen, dated December 28, 2000; and Kurt Eichenwald, "Andersen Trial Yields Evidence in Enron's Fall," *New York Times*, June 17, 2002.

Page 212: Causey's explanation of how closely Enron worked with Andersen is from September 18, 2001, summary of an interview with Richard Causey conducted by Vinson & Elkins; and Ianthe Jeanne Dugan, Dennis Berman, and Alexei Barrionuevo, "People at Andersen, Enron Crowed on Camera about Their Close Ties," *Wall Street Journal*, April 15, 2002. Background on Joseph Berardino and Andersen is from John A. Byrne, "Fall from Grace," *Business Week*, August 12, 2002.

Page 213: Causey's Enron resume is from Enron's 10-K annual report for 1997, filed March 31, 1998

Page 213: Background on Causey and Buy is from author interviews with Allan Sommer and several confidential sources.

Page 214: Information on the LJM2 partnership meeting is from the PowerPoint presentation, "LJM Investments: Annual Partnership Meeting," October 26, 2000; the Powers Report; and Julie Mason, "Dingell Doubts Claims of Skilling's Ignorance," *Houston Chronicle*, February 12, 2002.

Page 214: The dark fiber sale is from Enron's 10-Q quarterly report filed November 19, 2001, and from an LJM approval sheet from June 2000 for "Project Backbone."

Page 215: The fact that OTC derivatives covered $80 trillion of underlying assets is from "Over-the-Counter Derivatives Markets and the Commodity Exchange Act," a report from the President's Working Group on Financial Markets, November 1999.

Page 215: The summary of Long-Term Capital Management's failure is from Nicholas Dunbar, *Inventing Money* (John Wiley & Sons, 2000).

Pages 216–217: Recommendations from the President's Working Group are from "Over-the-Counter Derivatives Markets and the Commodity Exchange Act," a report from the President's Working Group on Financial Markets, November 1999. Enron's lobbying of it is from Public Citizen, "Blind Faith: How Deregulation and Enron's Influence over Government Looted Billions from Americans," a December 2001 report.

Page 216: Enron's exemption in the CFMA is from Erin Arvedlund, "Mr. & Mrs. Enron," *Barron's*, December 10, 2001, and an author interview with Randall Dodd.

Pages 216–217: Gramm's denial of aiding Enron is from Toby Eckert, "Regulatory Exemptions Aided Enron," *San Diego Union-Tribune*, March 13, 2002. Enron's campaign contributions to Gramm are from the Center for Responsive Politics.

Page 217: Information on Enron and FASB's proposal on SPEs is from Glenn R. Simpson, "Firms Repeatedly Dodged Efforts to Rein in Off-the-Books Deals," *Wall Street Journal*, April 10, 2002, and Ronald Fink, "Balancing Act," *CFO*, June 1, 1999.

Pages 217–218: The continuation of California's power crisis into 2001 is from "Anatomy of a Jolt," *Wall Street Journal*, June 25, 2001; Jeanne Cummings, "Power Politics: Energy Crisis Offers Clues to the Workings of Bush Administration," *Wall Street Journal*, February 16, 2001; "Pacific Gas Files for Chapter 11," Associated Press, April 6, 2001; and Kenneth Lay, "Generating Ideas," *San Francisco Chronicle*, March 1, 2001.

Pages 218–219: Ken Lay's meeting with Cheney and his memo to Cheney are from Anthony York, "Enron's California Smoking Gun," Salon.com, January 16, 2002, and "Enron's Energy Policy Priorities," a memo from Lay to Cheney.

Page 219: Lockyer's accusations and his quote about Lay are from John R. Emshwiller, "California Blame Game Yields No Score," *Wall Street Journal*, May 22, 2001.

Page 219: Skilling's joke comparing California and the *Titanic* is from Peter Behr, "Skilling to Face Senators, Accusers," *Washington Post*, February 26, 2002. The pie-in-the-face incident is from "Enron Executive Takes Heat in California—with a Pie," *Houston Chronicle*, June 22, 2001.

Pages 219–220: FERC's setting of price caps is from Rebecca Smith and Richard B. Schmidt, "Electricity Price Controls in West Are Set," *Wall Street Journal*, June 19, 2001, and Peter Behr, "Why Did Energy Prices Fall?," *Washington Post*, September 2, 2001.

Page 220: Information on Enron's reserves on California profits is from David Barboza, "Former Officials Say Enron Hid Gains during Crisis in California," *New York Times*, June 23, 2002.

CHAPTER 11   Power Overload

Page 221: Data on companies' revenues and Enron's ranking in the Fortune 500 are from the Fortune 500 "Largest U.S. Corporations" list, *Fortune*, April 16, 2001. Enron's 2000 financial data is from its 2000 annual report.

Page 222: Compensation data is from Enron's proxy statement, filed March 27, 2001.

Pages 222–223: Skilling's promotion to CEO is from an Enron press release of December 13, 2000, and Michael Davis, "No Ordinary Jeff: Skilling Will Take Reins at Enron," *Houston Chronicle*, December 14, 2000.

Page 223: Lay's inauguration experience is from Kurt Eichenwald with Diana B. Henriques, "The Company Unravels: Enron Buffed Image to a Shine Even As It Rotted from Within," *New York Times*, February 10, 2002.

Pages 223–224: Lay's involvement with Hebert and FERC is from Dan Morgan and Juliet Eilperin, "Campaign Gifts, Lobbying Built Enron's Power in Washington," *Washington Post*, December 25, 2001, and Marcy Gordon, "Enron Chairman Gave List of Favored Names to White House," Associated Press, January 31, 2002.

Page 224: Enron's courting of Robert Rubin is from Marcy Gordon, "Lay Offered Rubin Enron Board Seat," Associated Press, February 20, 2002; Enron's hiring of Linda Robertson is from David Ivanovich, "They Get It: Enron Displays Political Savvy in Access to Decision-Makers," *Houston Chronicle*, April 15, 2001. Enron's lobbying costs are from the Center for Responsive Politics.

Page 224: Data on foreign-project aid to Enron is from Jim Vallette and Daphne Wysham, "Enron's Pawns: How Public Institutions Bankrolled Enron's Globalization Game," a report from the Institute for Policy Studies, March 22, 2002.

Pages 224–225: Enron's involvement with the Cheney task force on energy policy is from "How the White House Energy Plan Benefited Enron," a report of the Minority Staff of the House Committee on Government Reform, January 16, 2002, and Bob Davis and Rebecca Smith, "Power Politics: In Era of Deregulation, Enron Woos Regulators More Avidly Than Ever," *Wall Street Journal*, May 18, 2001.

Pages 226–227: Ari Fleischer's comments are from a White House press briefing on January 17, 2002, available at www.whitehouse.gov.

Page 227: Background on David Duncan is from Anita Raghavan, "Accountable: How a Bright Star at Andersen Fell Along with Enron," *Wall Street Journal*, May 15, 2002.

Pages 227–228: Carl Bass' questions about Enron accounting are from an e-mail from Carl Bass to John Stewart from December 18, 1999; an e-mail from Carl Bass to Debra Cash from February 1, 2000; an e-mail from Carl Bass to John Stewart from February 4, 2000; and Mike McNamee with Amy Borrus, "Out of Control at Andersen," *Business Week*, April 8, 2002.

Pages 228–229: Details of the Andersen meeting to discuss retaining Enron are from an e-mail from Michael Jones to David Duncan from February 6, 2001; an Andersen press release from January 17, 2002; and the Powers Report.

Pages 229–230: Carl Bass' defense of his views on Enron, and his removal from the PSG are from an e-mail from Carl Bass to John Stewart from March 4, 2001; handwritten notes from David Duncan dated March 12, 2001, released by the U.S. House Committee on Energy and Commerce; and Mike McNamee with Amy Borrus, "Out of Control at Andersen," *Business Week*, April 8, 2002.

Pages 230–232: The March restructuring of the Raptors is from the Powers Report. Causey's quote about Lay and Skilling knowing about the stock price trigger in the Raptors is from a September 18, 2001, memo summarizing an interview with Causey by Vinson & Elkins. The fact that Enron beat first-quarter analyst estimates is from Kristen Hays, "Enron Surges with Higher Gas Demands," Associated Press, April 17, 2001.

Page 232: Kopper's exit is from Kopper's separation agreement, July 23, 2001.

Page 233: Jordan Mintz's doubts and his hiring of Fried Frank are from a letter from Alan Kaden of Fried Frank to Mintz on May 22, 2001; an e-mail from James Schropp of Fried Frank to Jordan Mintz on June 8, 2001; Roe Tempest, "Enron Counsel Warned about Partnerhips," *Los Angeles Times*, January 31, 2002; and transcripts of testimony at a February 7, 2002, hearing before the U.S. House Energy and Commerce Committee.

Page 233: Cliff Baxter's opposition to the LJM deals is from Peter Behr and April Witt, "Ex-Enron Executive Related a Dispute," *Washington Post*, March 19, 2002; and transcripts of testimony at a February 7, 2002, hearing before the U.S. House Energy and Commerce Committee.

Page 234: Enron's market cap versus Dynegy's is from "Gas-Power Firms Dominate Energy 50 Ranking in 2000," *Oil & Gas Journal*, January 29, 2001; McKinsey's comment is from David Campbell and Ron Hulme, "The Winner-Takes-All Economy," *McKinsey Quarterly*, January 1, 2001.

Page 234: EnronOnline volumes are from the transcript of an analyst conference call with Enron on March 23, 2001.

Pages 234–235: Information on IntercontinentalExchange and TradeSpark is from ICE press releases of March 21, 2000, and April 30, 2001, and TradeSpark press releases of September 25, 2000, and April 10, 2001.

Page 235: Comments about EnronOnline are from author interviews with Allan Sommer and Jon Pope.

Page 235: Information on DealBench and CommodityLogic are from an author interview with John Spitz.

Page 236: Azurix's charge for Argentina is from Enron's 10-K annual report for 2000; the Azurix-Enron merger is from Azurix's 10-K annual report for 2000.

Pages 236–237: Maharashtra missing payments on Dabhol, and background on Dabhol's costs, is from "Indian Government Allows Enron to Raise Equity in Indian Power Project," Associated Press, January 24, 2001; "India State Pays

$17M to Enron," Associated Press, February 12, 2001; "Background on Enron's Dabhol Project," a report from the Minority Staff of the U.S. House Committee on Government Reform, February 22, 2002; and Arundhati Roy, *Power Politics* (South End Press, 2001).

Page 237: The legal dispute over Dabhol and Enron's decision to sell is from Al Hunt, "Enron's One Good Return: Political Investments," *Wall Street Journal,* January 31, 2002, and "Background on Enron's Dabhol Project," a report from the Minority Staff of the U.S. House Committee on Government Reform, February 22, 2002.

Pages 237–238: EES results are from Enron's 2000 annual report; its reliance on mark-to-market accounting is from an interview with a confidential source; comments from Ratliff are from an author interview with Beau Ratliff.

Page 238: The story of the fake EES trading center is from C. Bryson Hull, "Enron Built Fake Nerve Center," Reuters, February 21, 2002; Jason Leopold, "Workers Say Enron Had Them Pose as Energy Traders for Analysts' Visit," *Wall Street Journal,* February 7, 2002; and an interview with a confidential source.

Page 239: Margaret Ceconi's comments are from Ceconi's letter to Kenneth Lay and Enron's board of directors, dated August 29, 2001, and from Joe Stephens and Peter Behr, "Enron's Culture Fed Its Demise," *Washington Post,* January 27, 2002.

Page 239: Lay's comments and Enron Broadband's results are from "Enron's Lay Rolling Dice on Broadband Trading," *Gas Daily,* February 17, 2000, and from Enron's 2000 annual report.

Pages 239–240: Information about the misrepresentation of Enron's broadband network is from the amended class-action complaint (Civil Action No. H-01-3624) from Mark Newby, et al., suing Enron Corp., et al., filed April 8, 2002, in U.S. District Court, the Southern District of Texas.

Pages 239–240: The Enron-Blockbuster deal is from Rebecca Smith, "Blockbuster, Enron Agree to Movie Deal," *Wall Street Journal,* July 20, 2000; Gary Gentile, "Enron, Blockbuster End Their Movies-on-Demand Pact," Associated Press, March 13, 2001; and Rebecca Smith, "Blockbuster Deal Shows Enron's Inclination to All-Show, Little-Substance Partnerships," *Wall Street Journal,* January 17, 2002.

Page 240: The report of bogus bandwidth trading is from David Barboza, "Energy Trades Echoed in Broadband Market," *New York Times,* May 17, 2002.

Page 240: Skilling comments on the bandwidth market are from an Enron conference call with analysts on March 23, 2001.

Page 241: Enron Broadband's results and staff reductions are from Tom Fowler, "Broadband-Unit Hype Didn't Match Reality," *Houston Chronicle,* January 18,

2002; Brad Foss, "Enron's Stock Price Gets Whipped After Broadband Unit Falls Short," Associated Press, April 28, 2001; and Michael Davis, "Broadband Trims Down at Enron," *Houston Chronicle*, July 13, 2001.

Page 241: Analyst Donato Eassey's comments are from his research report on Enron, "Raising the Bar—Again!" from April 18, 2001.

Pages 241–242: James Chanos' comments are from Chanos' prepared testimony delivered to the U.S. House Committee on Energy Commerce on February 6, 2002.

Page 242: Information on Bethany McLean's article is from Bethany McLean, "Is Enron Overpriced?," *Fortune*, March 5, 2001.

Page 242: Skilling's exchange with Grubman is from the transcript of an April 17, 2001, conference call with analysts.

Page 243: Skilling's relationship with Carter is from "Skilling Marries Fellow Enron Executive," Associated Press, March 5, 2002; Skilling's talks with Lay and the board about resigning are from a January 16, 2002, summary of interviews with Ken Lay for the Powers Report.

Page 244: The announcements of Skilling's resignation are from an e-mail from Ken Lay to Enron employees worldwide, dated August 14, 2001, and from Jonathan Friedland, "Enron Chief Executive Skilling Steps Down Citing Personal Reasons; Lay Takes Duties," *Wall Street Journal*, August 15, 2001.

Pages 244–245: Reactions to Skilling's exit are from author interviews with John Allario and several confidential sources, and from James Chanos' prepared testimony delivered to the U.S. House Committee on Energy and Commerce on February 6, 2002. The United Way anecdote is from a confidential source.

Page 245: Reaction of Moody's is from testimony of John Diaz, managing director of Moody's, to the U.S. Senate Committee on Governmental Affairs on March 20, 2002.

Page 245: Skilling's *Journal* comments are from John R. Emshwiller, "Enron's Skilling Cites Stock-Price Plunge as Main Reason for Leaving CEO Post," *Wall Street Journal*, August 16, 2001. Lay's reaction is from a January 16, 2002, summary of interviews with Lay for the Powers Report. Enron's stock prices are from BigCharts.com.

Page 245: Details of the August 16 employee meeting are from a videotape of the meeting, and from an author interview with Francisco Duque.

CHAPTER 12   Downward Spiral

Pages 247–248: Details of Watkins' letter are from her August 15, 2001, letter to Ken Lay.

Page 248: Background on Sherron Watkins and her decision to write the letter is from the summary of an interview of Watkins by Vinson & Elkins dated September 18, 2001; Jennifer Frey, "The Woman Who Saw Red," *Washington Post,* January 25, 2002; Watkins' August 15 letter; and Watkins' testimony to the U.S. House Energy and Commerce Committee on February 14, 2002.

Pages 250–251: Watkins' advice to Lay is from Watkins' August 15 letter.

Page 250: Lay's and Fastow's reactions are from Watkins' testimony to the U.S. House Energy and Commerce Committee on February 14, 2002. Fastow's comments to Vinson & Elkins are from an August 30, 2001, memo by Max Hendricks III of Vinson & Elkins summarizing an interview with Fastow.

Page 250: The Watkins-Hecker call is from a memo by James Hecker to "the files" at Andersen, dated August 21, 2001.

Page 251: Advice on the question of firing Watkins is from an e-mail from Carl Jordan of Vinson & Elkins to Sharon Butcher of Enron, from August 24, 2001.

Pages 251–252: Lay's promise of better disclosure and news of Fastow's divestment from LJM is from Rebecca Smith and John Emshwiller, "Enron Aims to Be Easier Read in Order to Refuel Enthusiasm," *Wall Street Journal,* August 28, 2001.

Page 252: Lay's comment on investor confidence is from an August 27, 2001, e-mail to all employees.

Page 252: Lay's comments on the "ethink" site are from a January 18, 2001, press release from the Gottesdiener law firm, which sued Enron over employees' retirement savings; and "Transcript: Lay Said Stock Was 'Bargain,'" Reuters, January 19, 2002.

Pages 252–253: Data on sales of Enron stock by Enron officers and directors is from a list, dated February 14, 2002, released by the U.S. House Energy and Commerce Committee. Lay's comments on stock sales are from the January 16, 2002, summary of Lay interviews for the Powers Report and from Jonathan Weil and Alexei Barrionuevo, "U.S. Finds Compiling Its Case Against Kenneth Lay Is Tough," *Wall Street Journal,* August 26, 2002. Pai's stock sales being linked to his divorce is from Alan Bernstein, "Luck of the Draw," *Houston Chronicle,* March 3, 2002.

Pages 253–255: Enron's tax strategies are from April Witt and Peter Behr, "Enron's Other Strategy: Taxes," *Washington Post,* May 22, 2002; Glenn Kessler, "Enron Appears to Have Paid Taxes," *Washington Post,* February 3, 2002; and Enron's 2000 annual report.

Pages 255–256: The use of prepaid swaps involving Credit Suisse and J.P. Morgan Chase is from the Answer and Counterclaim (Civ. 11523) of J.P. Morgan Chase Bank, plaintiff, against Liberty Mutual Insurance Co., et al., filed December 19, 2001, in U.S. District Court for the Southern District of New York; Daniel Altman, "Enron Had More Than One Way to Disguise Rapid Rise in

Debt," *New York Times*, February 17, 2002; Kurt Eichenwald, "Enron Hid Big Loans, Data Indicate," *New York Times*, February 27, 2002; and Walter Hamilton, "Pacts with Enron May Be Loans in Disguise, Judge Says," *Los Angeles Times*, March 6, 2002.

Page 257: Details on the Sequoia deals are from a letter from U.S. Representative Henry Waxman (D-California) to William Harrison, the CEO of J.P. Morgan Chase, dated April 12, 2002, and a letter from Ahuva Genack of J.P. Morgan Chase to Henry Waxman, dated May 8, 2002.

Pages 257–258: Lay retaining Vinson & Elkins to probe Watkins' claims is from the January 16, 2002, summary of Lay interviews for the Powers Report, and from the Powers Report.

Pages 258–259: The V&E investigation and its conclusions are from "Preliminary Investigation of Allegations of an Anonymous Employee," a report from Max Hendrick III of Vinson & Elkins, October 15, 2001; Rebecca Smith, "Ex-Enron CFO Backed Partnerships in an Internal Interview Last August," *Wall Street Journal*, February 20, 2002; and the Powers Report.

Page 259: Watkins' view of the V&E probe is from a transcript of a February 26, 2002, hearing by the U.S. Senate Committee on Science, Commerce and Transportation.

Page 260: The buyout of the Raptors is from the Powers Report.

Page 260: Kaminski's doubts about LJM and the Raptors are from the December 19, 2001, summary of interview with Vince Kaminski done for the Powers Report.

Page 261: The Portland General sale agreement is from an Enron press release of October 8, 2001.

Page 261: Third-quarter results are from an Enron press release of October 16, 2001.

Page 262: The reduction of shareholder equity and the reaction of Moody's are from Rebecca Smith and John R. Emshwiller, "Enron Says Its Links to a Partnership Led to $1.2 Billion Equity Reduction," *Wall Street Journal*, October 18, 2001.

Pages 262–263: Information about Fastow's LJM-related compensation is from the Powers Report; the January 16, 2002, summary of Lay interviews for the Powers Report; and Rebecca Smith and John R. Emshwiller, "Enron CFO's Ties to a Partnership Resulted in Big Profits for the Firm," *Wall Street Journal*, October 19, 2001.

Page 263: The initial SEC request for information is from an Enron press release of October 22, 2001; background on the SEC's reviews of Enron is from Michael Schroeder, "Enron Reports Weren't Reviewed Fully by SEC for Many Years before Collapse," *Wall Street Journal*, January 18, 2002.

Page 264: Results for Global Assets are from Enron's third-quarter earnings press release, October 16, 2001.

Pages 264–265: Details of the management meeting where Kaminski spoke out are from the December 19, 2001, summary of interview with Vince Kaminski done for the Powers Report, and from April Witt and Peter Behr, "Losses, Conflicts Threaten Survival," *Washington Post,* July 31, 2002.

Pages 265–266: Details from the conference call are from a transcript of the Enron conference call with analysts, October 23, 2001.

Page 266: McMahon's promotion to CFO is from an Enron press release of October 24, 2001.

CHAPTER 13   Racing the Clock

Page 267: Lay's comment about removing Fastow is from an Enron press release from October 24, 2001.

Pages 267–268: Some remarks are from an interview with a confidential source. Enron's trading results are from Enron's earnings press release of October 16, 2001. Trading-related assets are from Enron's 2000 annual report. Partnoy's comment is from Frank Partnoy's testimony to the U.S. Senate Committee on Governmental Affairs, January 24, 2002.

Page 268: The credit challenges of EnronOnline are from an author interview with John Sherriff.

Page 269: Gross' comments are from "Call Fails to Calm Fears," a report by Richard Gross of Lehman Brothers, October 24, 2001; Enron's analyst ratings and the comments from Curt Launer and Carol Coale are from Susanne Craig and Jonathan Weil, "Despite Losses, Complex Deals Analysts Remain High on Enron," *Wall Street Journal,* October 26, 2001; William Mann's comments are from his testimony to the U.S. Senate Committee on Commerce, Science and Transportation, December 18, 2001.

Pages 269–270: Enron's assurances regarding billions in notes due on affiliated entities are from Rebecca Smith and John R. Emshwiller, "Enron May Have to Issue Stock to Cover Possible Shortfalls in Investment Portfolio," *Wall Street Journal,* October 24, 2001. Enron's drawdown of $1 billion from credit lines and McMahon's quote are from an Enron press release of October 25, 2001.

Page 270: Details of the October 23 employee meeting are from "Latest on Enron Collapse," *NBC News Transcripts,* January 30, 2002.

Page 270: Description of employees buying Enron stock at $15 or below is from author interviews with Beau Ratliff, John Spitz, and a confidential source.

Pages 270–271: Duncan's views on the phrase "non-recurring" and Causey's response are from an e-mail (subject: "Enron Press Release Discussion") from

David Duncan to "the files" and copied to four other Andersen employees, dated October 15, 2001; Temple's recommendations are from an e-mail from Nancy Temple (subject: "Press Release Draft") to David Duncan, dated October 16, 2001.

Page 271: The October 23 Andersen conference call and Duncan's order to begin shredding are from an e-mail from Mina M. Trujillo of Andersen (subject: "Core Consultation Team Conference Call—10/23/01") to various Andersen employees, dated October 23, 2001, and from the testimony of C. E. Andrews, a global managing partner at Andersen, and Dorsey L. Baskin Jr., an Andersen managing director, to the U.S. House Committee on Energy and Commerce, January 24, 2002.

Page 271: Temple's reminder about retention policy is from an October 12, 2001, e-mail from Nancy Temple to Mike Odom. Andersen's retention policy is from the testimony of C. E. Andrews, a global managing partner at Andersen, and Dorsey L. Baskin Jr., an Andersen managing director, to the U.S. House Committee on Energy and Commerce, January 24, 2002. David Duncan's interpretation of the Temple e-mail is from Tim Fowler, "Boss' Order to Shred Defended," *Houston Chronicle*, March 7, 2002.

Pages 271–272: Details of the paper shredding and deleting of computer files are from the grand jury indictment of Andersen, "United States of America against Arthur Andersen LLP," filed in U.S. District Court, the Southern District of Texas, on March 14, 2002.

Page 272: The SEC upgrade to formal investigation is from an Enron press release of October 31, 2001.

Page 272: Andersen's order to stop shredding on November 9 is from the testimony of C. E. Andrews, a global managing partner at Andersen, and Dorsey L. Baskin Jr., an Andersen managing director, to the U.S. House Committee on Energy and Commerce, January 24, 2002, and from the grand jury indictment of Andersen, "United States of America against Arthur Andersen LLP," filed in U.S. District Court, the Southern District of Texas, on March 14, 2002.

Page 272: Lay's call to Greenspan is from Dana Milbank and Susan Schmidt, "Rubin Asked Treasury about Aid to Enron," *Washington Post*, January 12, 2002.

Page 272: Lay's call to O'Neill is from Elisabeth Bumiller, "Enron Contacted Two Cabinet Officers before Collapsing," *New York Times*, January 11, 2002.

Page 272: Lay mentioning LTCM to O'Neill is from a White House press briefing with Ari Fleischer on January 10, 2002.

Pages 272–273: Enron's contacts with Peter Fisher are from Richard W. Stevenson, "Enron Sought Aid of Treasury Dept. to Get Bank Loans," *New York Times*, January 12, 2002, and Jonathan Nicholson, "Enron Sought Federal Help before Collapse," Reuters News, January 11, 2002.

Page 273: Enron's contact of Rubin is from Richard W. Stevenson, "Enron Sought Aid of Treasury Dept. to Get Bank Loans," *New York Times,* January 12, 2002.

Page 273: Lay's call to Evans is from Elisabeth Bumiller, "Enron Contacted Two Cabinet Officers before Collapsing," *New York Times,* January 11, 2002.

Page 273: Moody's downgrade of Enron debt is from a Moody's Investors Service press release of October 29, 2001.

Page 274: Watkins' meeting with Lay and her advice are from an October 30, 2001, memo from Sherron Watkins (subject: "PR for Enron") to Elizabeth Tilney of Enron.

Page 274: Enron's creation of a special board committee to investigate the partnerships is from an Enron press release of October 31.

Pages 274–275: Details of Enron's $1 billion credit line are from Rebecca Smith, "Enron Gets $1 Billion New Credit Line, but Must Pledge Gas Pipeline Assets," *Wall Street Journal,* November 2, 2001.

Page 275: The decision to consolidate Chewco is from the Powers Report.

Pages 275–276: Enron's restatement and firing of Glisan and Mordaunt are from an Enron press release of November 8, 2001, and from John R. Emshwiller, Rebecca Smith, Robin Sidel, and Jonathan Weil, "Enron Slashes Profits since 1997 by 20%," *Wall Street Journal,* November 9, 2002.

Page 276: The rise in earnings restatements is from a letter from Baruch Lev, New York University accounting professor, to Congressman Billy Tauzin of the House Energy and Commerce Committee, March 4, 2002.

Page 277: Bala Dharan's comments are from his testimony to the U.S. House Committee on Energy and Commerce, February 6, 2001.

Page 277: Background on Chuck Watson is from Greg Hassell, "Purchase Elevates Watson's Low Profile," *Houston Chronicle,* November 10, 2001; Christopher Palmeri, "Power Base," *Forbes,* February 21, 2000; and an author interview with Raymond Plank.

Pages 277–278: Details of the talks that led up to the Dynegy-Enron merger are from Kurt Eichenwald with Diana B. Henriques, "The Company Unravels: Enron Buffed Image to a Shine Even as It Rotted from Within," *New York Times,* February 10, 2002.

Pages 278–279: Terms of the Dynegy-Enron merger are from a joint press release from Enron and Dynegy of November 9, 2001, and from Alex Berenson and Andrew Ross Sorkin, "Rival to Buy Energy Trader after Dizzying Financial Fall," *New York Times,* November 10, 2001.

Page 279: Lay's mass voice mail message is from SEC Form 425 filed November 19, 2001.

Pages 279–280: Moody's delaying a downgrade because of the merger is from the testimony of John Diaz, managing director of Moody's, to the U.S. Senate Committee on Governmental Affairs on March 20, 2002.

Page 280: Some background on credit rating agencies is from SEC Commissioner Isaac Hunt's testimony to U.S. Senate Committee on Governmental Affairs on March 20, 2002.

Pages 280–281: Moody's downgrade of Enron's long-term debt is from the testimony of John Diaz, managing director of Moody's, to the U.S. Senate Committee on Governmental Affairs on March 20, 2002.

Page 281: S&P's downgrade of Enron's credit rating is from the testimony of Ronald Barone, managing director of Standard & Poor's, to the U.S. Senate Committee on Governmental Affairs on March 20, 2002. The obligation triggered by the S&P downgrade is from Enron's 10-Q quarterly report filed November 19, 2001.

Page 281: Lay giving up a severance payment is from Peter Behr, "Enron CEO Says No to $60.6 Million," *Washington Post*, November 14, 2001; Intercontinental-Exchange's rise in volume is from an ICE press release of November 13, 2001.

Pages 281–282: Whalley's and Lay's comments are from the transcript of a November 14, 2001, analyst conference call hosted by Enron.

Pages 282–283: The outlook for its 2001 fourth quarter and other information that Enron gave in its SEC filing are from Enron's 10-Q quarterly report filed November 19, 2001.

Page 283: Watson's comments on Enron's burning through cash are from a transcript of a Dynegy conference call with analysts and investors on December 3, 2001.

Page 283: Dynegy's comments about sticking to the merger are from a Dynegy press release of November 21, 2001.

Pages 283–284: The lack of work inside Enron is from an interview with Beau Ratliff.

Page 284: Enron's admission of its financial weakness and the talks to rework the merger terms are from a transcript of a Dynegy conference call with analysts and investors on December 3, 2001, and from Kurt Eichenwald with Diana B. Henriques, "The Company Unravels: Enron Buffed Image to a Shine Even As It Rotted from Within," *New York Times*, February 10, 2002.

Page 284: The decisions by Moody's and S&P to downgrade Enron to junk grade are from the testimony of John Diaz, managing director of Moody's, to the U.S. Senate Committee on Governmental Affairs on March 20, 2002, and from the testimony of Ronald Barone, managing director of Standard & Poor's, to the U.S. Senate Committee on Governmental Affairs on March 20, 2002.

Page 284: Enron employees' reactions to the credit rating downgrade are from author interviews with Francisco Duque and a confidential source.

Page 285: Enron's announcement of Dynegy's merger termination and its decision to suspend payments is from an Enron press release of November 28, 2001. *Page 285:* The fact that Enron's collapse didn't wreck energy markets is from Patrick Wood, chairman of FERC, in his testimony to the U.S. Senate Committee on Energy and Natural Resources on January 29, 2002. Comments from Dynegy president Steve Bergstrom are from a Dynegy conference call for analysts and investors on November 28, 2001.

Page 285: Some details about Enron's filing for bankruptcy are from Kurt Eichenwald with Diana B. Henriques, "The Company Unravels: Enron Buffed Image to a Shine Even As It Rotted from Within," *New York Times*, February 10, 2002.

CHAPTER 14   Endgame

Page 286: Details about Enron's bankruptcy are from an Enron press release of December 2, 2001, and from Rebecca Smith and Mitchell Pacelle, "Enron Units Seek Bankruptcy Protection; Firm Sues Dynegy over Aborted Merger," *Wall Street Journal*, December 3, 2001. The partial list of SPEs is from a motion filed February 7, 2002, in U.S. Bankruptcy Court, Document 1352. Enron's relatively large number of offshore units is from the U.S. Senate Committee on Commerce, Science & Transportation.

Page 287: The fact that 68 of 3,500 subsidiaries filed for bankruptcy is from Motion of Enron for an Order Authorizing and Approving Consent by Enron Corp. to the Sale by Enron International Korea LLC of the Securities of SK-Enron Co. (Docket entry 4534), filed with U.S. Bankruptcy Court on June 18, 2002.

Page 287: Enron's DIP financing is from Mitchell Pacelle, Jathon Sapsford, and Ann Davis, "Enron Secures $1.5 Billion in Financing, Lays Off about 4,000 Workers in the U.S.," *Wall Street Journal*, December 4, 2001, and from the DIP Credit Agreement, filed with the bankruptcy court December 4, 2001.

Page 287: Information on Enron's suit against Dynegy is from Enron's complaint in *Enron Corp., et al., v. Dynegy Inc. and Dynegy Holdings Inc.*, filed in U.S. Bankruptcy Court in the Southern District of New York on December 2, 2001.

Pages 287–288: Dynegy's statement about Enron's lawsuit is from a Dynegy press release of December 2, 2001.

Page 288: The number of corporate bankruptcies in 2001 and the fact that it was a record are from "Failures of Public Firms Set Record," Reuters, February 1, 2002.

Pages 288–289: Enron's layoffs are from author interviews with Diana Peters, Allan Sommers, John Spitz, and John Allario; from Mitchell Pacelle, Jathon Sapsford, and Ann Davis, "Enron Secures $1.5 Billion in Financing, Lays Off about 4,000 Workers in the U.S.," *Wall Street Journal*, December 4, 2001, and from Memorandum of AFL-CIO and the National Rainbow/PUSH Coalition as Amici Curiae in Support of Motion Pursuant to 11 U.S.C. Section 105(a) for Order Requiring Payment of Obligations to Employees, Filed in U.S. Bankruptcy Court; and David Barboza, "Enron Agrees to Increase Severance by $30 Million," *New York Times*, June 12, 2002.

Page 289: The problems with Enron's 401(k) plan and the employee lawsuits filed over it are from Theo Francis and Elle Schulz, "Enron Faces Suits by 401(k) Plan Participants," *Wall Street Journal*, November 23, 2001.

Page 290: The comments of Charles Prestwood and Robert Vigil are from their testimony before the U.S. Senate Committee on Commerce, Science, and Transportation on December 18, 2001.

Page 290: Comments from John Spitz and Diana Peters are from author interviews.

Page 290: The December 7 layoff of 200 power trading staffers is from "Enron Lays Off 200 More Workers," Reuters, December 7, 2001. The $55 million in retention bonuses is from Richard A. Oppel Jr. and Kurt Eichenwald, "Enron Paid Out 'Retention' Bonuses before Bankruptcy Filing," *New York Times*, December 6, 2001, and Rebecca Smith and Richard B. Schmitt, "Enron Pays $55 Million to 500 Staffers Whom It Considers Critical to Survival," *Wall Street Journal*, December 6, 2001.

Page 291: Lay's plan for reorganization is from "Enron Corp. Organizational Meeting," a PowerPoint presentation for Enron on December 12, 2001, and from Mitchell Pacelle, Michael Schroeder, and John Emshwiller, "Enron Unveils Restructuring Plan Centered on Pipeline, Power Assets," *Wall Street Journal*, December 12, 2001.

Page 291: The appointment of a 15-member creditors committee is from Kathy Chu, "U.S. Trustee Appoints 15-Member Enron Creditor Group," Dow Jones Newswires, December 12, 2001. The Justice Department starting an inquiry into Enron is from Richard A. Oppel Jr. and Riva D. Atlas, "Hobbled Enron Tries to Stay on Its Feet," *New York Times*, December 4, 2001.

Pages 291–292: Information on the credit woes and restructuring efforts of Dynegy and other energy traders is from "Dynegy Says Reviewing Capital, Confident of Liquidity," Reuters, December 14, 2001; Alexei Barrionuevo, "In Wake of Enron Collapse, El Paso Plans Moves Designed to Create More Liquidity," *Wall Street Journal*, December 13, 2001; "Mirant Announces Plan to Bolster Its Finances Following Downgrade," Wall Street Journal Online, December 20, 2001; Rebecca Smith, "Dynegy Hatches Restructuring Plan As Credit Problems Chill Investment," *Wall Street Journal*, December 18, 2001; Alex Berenson and Richard A. Oppel Jr., "Energy Industry Shudders Again after Downgrade of Dynegy Debt," *New York Times*, December 18, 2001.

Page 292: The Enron-Dynegy settlement on the Northern Natural Gas pipeline is from an Enron press release of January 3, 2002, and Jonathan D. Glater, "Enron Agrees to Transfer Prized Pipeline to Dynegy," *New York Times,* January 5, 2002.

Page 293: The Justice Department forming an Enron Task Force is from Kurt Eichenwald with Jonathan D. Glater, "Justice Dept. to Form Task Force to Investigate Collapse of Enron," *New York Times,* January 10, 2002.

Page 293: Bush's reference to accounting in the State of the Union address is from the State of the Union transcript, from the White House web site.

Page 293: O'Neill's comment and Lieberman's criticism of it is from H. Josef Hebert, "Bush Wasn't Informed of Enron Calls," Associated Press, January 13, 2002.

Pages 293–294: Enron donations to Lieberman and McCain, McCain's quote, and the fact that some lawmakers vowed to return Enron money are from Jim Puzzanghera, "Enron Gave Money to Many in Congress," *San Jose Mercury News,* January 15, 2002.

Page 294: Instances of "Enron" entering the lexicon are from William Safire, "Enroned," *New York Times Magazine,* February 10, 2002. Bush's joke about Iraq and Andersen is from Barbara Martinez, "On the Menu: Patriotism and Pretzels," *Washington Post,* January 28, 2002.

Pages 294–295: Enron's sale of its trading business to UBS is from an Enron press release of January 15, 2002, and Alan Clendenning, "UBS Won't Pay in Enron Deal," Associated Press, January 15, 2002.

Page 295: Enron not selling its trading book is from the Weil, Gotshal & Manges web site. The debate over the value of the trading book is from a motion filed in U.S. Bankruptcy Court on February 1, 2002, Document 1251.

Page 296: Trading companies' objections to UBS hiring Enron traders are from a motion filed in Bankruptcy Court on February 1, 2002, Document 1251.

Page 296: Enron's April estimate of the overestimated value of its trading and assets is from Enron's Monthly Operating Report, filed as a Form 8-K with the SEC on April 22, 2002.

Page 296: Enron's firing of Andersen is from "Enron Axes Andersen Accounting Firm," Associated Press, January 17, 2002. Andersen's firing of David Duncan is from Ken Brown, Greg Hitt, Steve Liesman, and Jonathan Weil, "Andersen Fires Partner It Says Led Shredding of Documents," *Wall Street Journal,* January 16, 2002.

Pages 296–297: Lay's resignation is from an Enron press release of January 23, 2002.

Page 297: The account of Linda Lay's TV appearance is from Bruce Nichols, "Ex-Enron Chair's Wife Defends Husband, Says Fortune Lost," *Dallas Morning News,* January 29, 2002.

Page 297: The appointment of Stephen Cooper is from an Enron press release of January 29, 2002, and Tom Fowler, "Bankruptcy Expert Named Enron CEO," *Houston Chronicle*, January 30, 2002. Cooper's comments are from a January 30, 2002, conference call hosted by Enron.

Pages 297–298: Cliff Baxter's suicide and his suicide note are from Jim Yardley, "Critic Who Quit Top Enron Post Is Found Dead," *New York Times*, January 26, 2002, and Eric Hanson and Armando Villafranca, "Baxter's Suicide Note Cites Emotional Burden," *Houston Chronicle*, April 12, 2002. Skilling's comments on Baxter are from Skilling's testimony to the U.S. House Committee on Energy and Commerce, February 7, 2002.

Pages 298–299: Fees charged by law firms for Enron's bankruptcy are from the Monthly Fee Statement of Weil, Gotshal & Manges, filed with Bankruptcy Court on February 20, 2002, Document 1592; Andrews & Kurth's Monthly Fee Statement, filed with the Bankruptcy Court February 20, 2002, Document 1593; Leboeuf, Lamb's Statement of Fees and Disbursements, filed with Bankruptcy Court on February 20, 2002, Document 1584; Cadwalader's Monthly Statement of Professional Services, filed with Bankruptcy Court February 20, 2002, Document 1573; and Correction Regarding Monthly Fee Statement of Wilmer, Cutler & Pickering, filed with Bankruptcy Court on April 3, 2002, Document 2654. The fact that Enron might set a record for legal fees is from Kathy Chu, "Enron Creditors, Workers Oppose Two Law Firms Added in Case," Dow Jones Newswires, March 6, 2002.

Page 299: The Astros deal is from a motion filed in Bankruptcy Court on February 5, 2002, Document 1289.

Page 299: The naming of the lead law firm and lead plaintiff in the class action shareholder lawsuit is from Michael Brick, "Lawyer Known for Class Actions Will Lead the Enron Plaintiffs," *New York Times*, February 16, 2002, and from *Mark Newby vs. Enron Corp., et al.*, Civil Action No. H-01-3624, filed in U.S. District Court, the Southern District of Texas, February 15, 2002.

Pages 300–301: The Powers Report findings, and Powers' quotes, are from Kurt Eichenwald, "Enron Panel Finds Inflated Profits and Few Controls," *New York Times*, February 3, 2002; the Powers Report; and the testimony of William C. Powers Jr. to the U.S. Senate Committee on Commerce, Science and Transportation, February 12, 2002.

Page 301: Enron's firing of Causey and Buy is from an Enron press release of February 14, 2002.

Pages 301–302: Accounts of congressional hearings are from testimony before the U.S. House Committee on Energy and Commerce on February 7, 2002; Stephen Labaton and Richard A. Oppel Jr., "Testimony from Enron Executives Is Contradictory," *New York Times*, February 8, 2002; and Richard A. Oppel Jr.

and Richard W. Stevenson, "An Enron Ex-Chief Uses Defiant Tone at Senate Hearing," *New York Times*, February 27, 2002.

Pages 302–303: The indictment of Andersen is from "Grand Jury Indicts Andersen in Connection with Enron Case," Wall Street Journal Online, March 14, 2002.

Pages 303–304: The guilty verdict and its repercussions on Andersen are from Kurt Eichenwald, "Andersen Guilty in Effort to Block Inquiry on Enron," *New York Times*, June 16, 2002, and an SEC statement of June 15, 2002.

Page 304: Enron's settlement with Dynegy is from an Enron press release of August 15, 2002.

Page 304: Information on Kopper's guilty plea is from an August 22, 2002, press release from the U.S. Department of Justice; the Cooperation Agreement between the United States and Michael Kopper, filed in U.S. District Court; and Kurt Eichenwald, "Ex-Enron Official Admits Payments to Finance Chief," *New York Times*, August 22, 2002.

Page 305: The SEC's order requiring CEOs to certify quarterly reports is from an SEC press release of June 28, 2002.

Page 306: Details of Cooper's reorganization plan are from a May 3, 2002, conference call hosted by Enron, and an Enron press release of May 3, 2002.

Epilogue

Page 309: Background on Enron's board of directors is from Enron's proxy (Form Def-14A) filed March 27, 2001.

Page 309: Information on new legislation adding to the duties of audit committees is from Shailagh Murray and Michael Schroeder, "Overhaul of Corporate Oversight Has Far-Reaching Consequences," *Wall Street Journal*, July 26, 2002.

Page 310: The SEC's inquiry into analysts is from an SEC news release of April 25, 2002.

Page 311: The SEC's understaffing is from Stephen Labaton, "SEC Is Suffering from Nonbenign Neglect," *New York Times*, July 20, 2002.

Page 311: Pennsylvania's savings from power deregulation is from the testimony of FERC Chairman James Hoecker to the U.S. House Committee on Energy and Commerce, September 11, 2000.

Page 312: Congress' criticism of FERC is from "Concerted Actions Needed by FERC to Confront Challenges That Impede Effective Oversight," a report from the U.S. General Accounting Office, June 2002.

Pages 312–313: Details of new legislation's rules on accounting are from Shailagh Murray and Michael Schroeder, "Overhaul of Corporate Oversight Has Far-Reaching Consequences," *Wall Street Journal*, July 26, 2002.

INDEX